Jane Taylor's classic guidebook to Istanbul is acknowledg[e]
the ultimate introduction to the city, and has been exten[s]
revised for this paperback edition. It leads travellers from
great monuments of Byzantium and early Constantinop
the mosques and palaces built for Suleyman the Magnificen[t]
the other Sultans while providing both practical information
a rich historical context. It also covers more recent sites: ra[n]
from the mundane (the Galatasaray fishmarket) to the
magnificent pavilions and villas of late Ottoman times. In addition to Istanbul, the cities of Iznik, Bursa and Edirne are covered
in extensive detail.

Filled with maps, itineraries, plans and detailed descriptions of
all the sites that any visitor could hope to see, this is the only
guidebook that a traveller to Istanbul will ever need.

Jane Taylor *is a writer, photographer and former TV producer. Her*
books include, 'High Above Jordan' *(1989) and* 'Petra' *(1993).*

"Splendid erudition . . . the secret of Taylor's book is a delightfully lucid style." – David Barchard of *The Financial Times*

"An invaluable guide" – *The Times*

"Among the best guidebooks" – *The Sunday Telegraph*

"A thorough and elegantly written guidebook to one of the
world's most fascinating cities." – *The Oxford Times*

In memory of
DMITRI NESTEROFF
who knew these cities

IMPERIAL ISTANBUL

A Traveller's Guide

INCLUDES IZNIK, BURSA AND EDIRNE

JANE TAYLOR

I.B. Tauris *Publishers*
LONDON ● NEW YORK

Revised edition published in 1998 by I.B.Tauris & Co Ltd
Victoria House, Bloomsbury Square, London WC1B 4DZ
175 Fifth Avenue, New York NY 10010

In the United States and Canada distributed by St. Martin's Press
175 Fifth Avenue, New York NY 10010

ISBN 1 86064 249 7

A full CIP record for this book is available from the British Library
A full CIP record for this book is available from the Library of Congress

Library of Congress catalog card: available

Printed and bound in Great Britain by WBC Ltd, Bridgend

CONTENTS

v

CONTENTS

CONTENTS

MAPS AND PLANS

INTRODUCTION

The very words Byzantine and Ottoman conjure up images of art and architecture, politics, intrigue and religion, each a pot-pourri of limitless colour and variety, a blend of east and west, Europe and Asia. Living in Istanbul in 1971–2, I was both fascinated by the multiplicity of characters in the double-bill drama of the Byzantine and Ottoman Empires and dizzied by the chronology of it all. This book is an attempt to provide the written guide I wished I had had then, when little was available, looking at the greatest monuments of each period in sequence, and in the context of the people and events that surrounded them, gradually building up a picture of two of the greatest empires the world has known, in four cities that were central to their stories. It is designed for people who enjoy their monuments spiced with the drama of the history that gave rise to them, the idiosyncracies of the powerful men and women who built them, and the comments – frequently witty and revealing – of early travellers to Turkey.

A chapter each is devoted to Iznik, Bursa and Edirne, all within 4 hours by bus or car from Istanbul, and the first two close enough to be combined in a single two or three day trip. Iznik, originally a Hellenistic city and set on a beautiful lake, was capital of the offshoot Byzantine Empire of Nicaea in 1204–61; but most of its monuments are Islamic and here many early Ottoman architectural ideas were tried out, later to be more fully expressed in the buildings of Bursa, Edirne and Istanbul. Bursa, overlooked by the towering snow-clad Mount Olympus, was the first capital of the nascent Ottoman state, and contains some of the most spectacular mosques, tombs and other buildings in the early Ottoman style – a style that was developed

1

further in their next capital, Edirne in Thrace, their first European seat of government, and their launching pad to Istanbul.

Iznik can be seen comfortably in a day, less comfortably in a ½ day. Bursa needs at least two days, but can be tantalizingly glimpsed in one. Edirne can be done in a day trip from Istanbul if you can tolerate a 4 hr drive each way; an overnight stay is better. Istanbul – the lion's share of the book – requires a lifetime. For those with less time I have arranged it in 15 sections, of which the first ten are either divided into one or two geographically homogeneous routes, or are devoted to a single building; each route or individual building can be seen in a half a day or less, though places like St Saviour in Chora and Topkapı Palace may tempt you to linger, or to return. Ideally one should work through the Byzantine Chapters (1–7), then visit Iznik, Bursa and Edirne (in that order), before returning to Ottoman Istanbul, progressing as the early sultans did themselves.

Chapters 11–12 are organized differently, taking a subject rather than a period – later Ottoman mosques, and late Ottoman palaces and pavilions – with only incidental geographical coherence; individual buildings may be seen en route elsewhere or in groups of two or three. Many of the palaces and pavilions, delightful in their late Ottoman exaggeration, have only recently been opened to the public and are not included in other guide books. The last three Istanbul chapters cover areas not included in the chronological sequence of the earlier chapters – in particular the Bosphorus, *bonne bouche* of any visit to Istanbul.

The Archaeological Museum, the Museum of the Ancient Orient, and the Princes' Islands are included in appendices. There is a list of Byzantine Emperors and Ottoman Sultans to help peg the chronology; and a note on Turkish language to help with the pronunciation of words commonly needed in the course of a stay. Those who wish to learn more of the language should acquire *Teach yourself Turkish* by Geoffrey Lewis, or *A Turkish Phrase Book* by Yusuf Mardin. There is no information on hotels as this changes constantly, and the best advisers are either travel agents, or the Turkish Ministry of Tourism which produces annual lists with indications of category and price.

I have received much help and generosity from Turkish friends in the preparation of this book. In particular in Istanbul from Neclâ and Selman Yaşar who smoothed more paths and provided more perceptive help and hospitality than I can adequately acknowledge or thank; Gülbikem Ronay of Unitur travel agency has been tireless in answering long lists of practical questions; she and her colleagues, Şeniz Terem and Sıdıkı Okar, have taken me on several exploratory trips in and around Istanbul, and have made all kinds of travel arrangements for me with calm efficiency; Ara Güler, one of the finest of Turkish photographers, has over many years provided me with information and introductions that have been of great value. His superb photograph adorns the cover. To all of them my warmest thanks.

The Turkish Ministry of Tourism has been most generous in its help – especially supportive in the early stages was Gülsen Kahraman, recently Deputy Director in the London office; then Ercihan Düzgünoğlu, Culture and Information Counsellor in London, provided much information and encouragement; and without Osman Cağaloğlu, most tireless, intelligent and humorous of guides, my recent travels in Turkey would have been less valuable.

Godfrey Goodwin, doyen of architectural historians of the Byzantine and Ottoman periods, was subjected to questions, to the reading of the typescript, and to yet more questions. His knowledge, patience and humour are equally appreciated and thanked. So too is his introduction to the talented architect Razmik Hadidian, who drew all the superb building plans and maps.

My greatest debt is to the late Dmitri Nesteroff, who lived in Istanbul and who tramped its streets with me in the 1970s to introduce me to 'his' city. He was a fund of arcane information and anecdote, and the most generous of friends. He should have written this book.

Postscript

I owe yet more gratitude to friends whose generosity and help while I up-dated this book were beyond the call of duty – Mary Berkmen whose humour, home, sea view and music I delighted in for 3 weeks; Neclâ Yaşar who wafted me along the Bosphorus; Gülbikem Ronay and Şeniz Terem who took me for a joyous trip to Iznik, and sent me to Bursa; Ara and Suna Güler; Fatma and Richard Reid; Lyn Waters; Giselle Odhner; Ian Sherwood ; Paddy Baker. And Güzin Berkmen who in the early 70s taught me Turkish so memorably that some of it miraculously survived the long years of neglect.

The 'Queen of Cities' continues to exercise her fascination. Despite changes (not all beautiful), this extraordinary city, with the garland of the seas that surround her and the Istanbullus who inhabit her, still makes any return to her a delightful renewal of discovery.

Amman, 1998

1

BIRD'S EYE VIEW OF BYZANTIUM

On a hilltop in Eyüp, in the north of Istanbul, stands a small vine-shaded café named after the 19th C. French writer Pierre Loti. Here, they say, he used to come and drink coffee and contemplate this most magnificent panorama of the city. In fine weather it is still a good place to come on your first evening in Istanbul for here, in the glow of the evening sun about an hour before sunset, the Golden Horn stretches out below in a shining curve, and crowning it are the ancient walls, the domes and minarets that form the skyline of this most eulogised of cities.

Byzantium, Constantinople, Istanbul – its three names span more than 2600 years, nearly 1600 of them as the capital of two of the greatest empires the world has known, Byzantine and Ottoman. It has been called, besides, 'the Queen of Cities', 'the Ruling City', 'the God-guarded City', or simply 'The City'. Procopius, one of the greatest writers of the Byzantine Empire, wrote in the 6th C. that 'the sea forms a garland about the city,' and it is still true that much of its character and delight spring from its position at the meeting of three waters; to the south the Sea of Marmara, the ancient Propontis; to the north the incomparable Bosphorus; while into the very heart of the city stretches the Golden Horn, one of the finest natural harbours in the world, able to conceal a whole fighting fleet. Whoever controlled this site controlled all shipping from the Pontus (Black Sea) on one side, and the Aegean on the other; and because of this it has been at the heart of the story of the city.

Around 657 BC a Greek from Megara called Byzas consulted the oracle of Apollo at Delphi about his colonial aspirations. He was no innovator – the eastern coast of the Aegean had long been dotted with

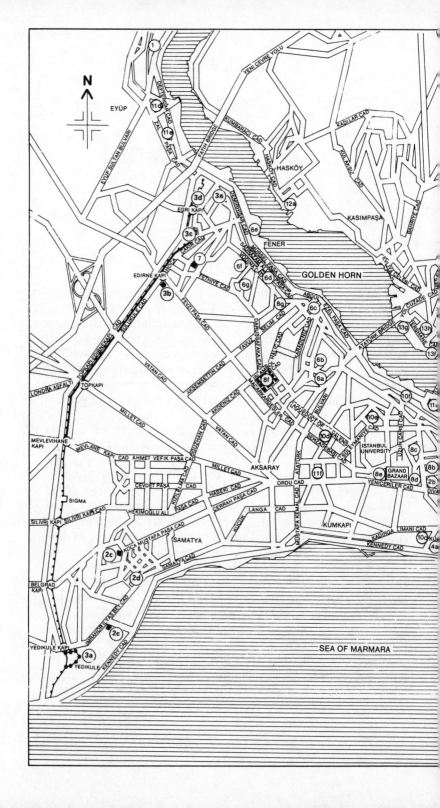

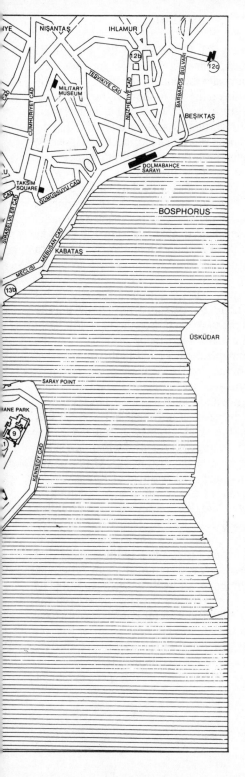

ISTANBUL MONUMENTS

(Numbers refer to chapters;
A = Appendix

1	Pierre Loti Café
2a	Binbirdirek Cistern
2b	Column of Constantine
2c	St John of Studius/Imrahor Camii
2d	Martyrium of SS Karpos & Paphylos
2e	St Andrews in Krisei
3a	Yedikule
3b	Mihrimah Camii
3c	Tekfur Sarayı
3d	Blachernae Palace
3e	Blachernae Ayazma
3f	Bucoleon Palace
4a	SS Sergius and Bacchus/Küçük Aya Sofya Camii
4b	Haghia Eirene
4c	Yerebatan Saray
5	Haghia Sophia
6a	St Saviour Pantocrator/Molla Zeyrek Camii
6b	St Saviour Pantepoptes/Eski Imaret Camii
6c	St Theodosia/Gül Camii
6d	Greek Orthodox Patriarchate
6e	St Stephen of the Bulgars
6f	St Mary of the Mongols
6g	Theotokos Pammakaristos/Fethiye Camii
7	St Saviour in Chora/Kariye Camii
8a	Çinili Köşk
8b	Mahmut Paşa Camii
8c	Mahmut Paşa Hamamı
8d	Nuruosmaniye Camii
8e	Beyazit II Camii
8f	Fatih Camii
8g	Sultan Selim I Camii
9	Topkapı Sarayı
10a	Aya Sofya Hamamı
10b	Ibrahim Paşa Sarayı
10c	Sokollu Mehmet Paşa Camii
10d	Şehzade Camii
10e	Süleymaniye Camii
10f	Rüstem Paşa Camii
11a	Sultan Ahmet Camii/Blue Mosque
11b	Arasta Çarşısı/Mosaics Museum
11c	Yeni Cami
11d	Eyüp Sultan Camii
11e	Zal Mahmut Paşa Camii
11f	Laleli Cami
12a	Aynalıkavak Kasrı
12b	Ihlamur Kasrı
12c	Yıldız Sarayı
13a	Tophane
13b	Nusretiye Camii
13c	Kılıç Ali Paşa Camii
13d	Yeraltı Camii
13e	Rüstem Paşa Hanı
13f	Galata Bedesten
13g	Azap Kapı Camii
13h	Arap Camii
13i	Galata Tower
13j	Crimean Memorial Church
13k	Swedish Consulate
13l	Russian Consulate
13m	Dutch Consulate
13n	British Consulate
A1	Archaeological Museum
A2	Museum of the Ancient Orient

Greek colonies, and in the early 7th C. BC a start had been made around the Propontis. The oracle's characteristically cryptic advice to Byzas to build his new city 'opposite the land of the blind' he clearly understood to refer to Chalcedon on the Asian shore of the Bosphorus where it meets the Propontis. It had been established just a few years before with what was widely regarded as a blind disregard for the vastly superior site on the European shore – already occupied it seems, but not yet fortified. Byzas acted promptly: Byzantium, named after himself, was established at the tip of the promontory, now crowned with Topkapı Palace and the church of Haghia Sophia. Its position was not only strategic for defence; the Greeks were developing profitable trade links with the people of the fertile Black Sea coasts, and Byzantium quickly became a vital staging post. For 150 years its life was busy, untroubled and prosperous, with merchant ships from all over the known world putting into the harbour *en route* to east or west.

Such prosperity attracted envy: Darius captured the city in his westward expansion around 512 BC, but Persian control lasted only 30 years or so, before the Spartans took over. For the next 150 years Byzantium was tossed between Sparta and Athens until 356 when the people rebelled and became independent. In 340 Philip of Macedon besieged the city in his bid to master the Greek world before leading a Greek army into Persian-dominated Asia. But the Byzantines clung ferociously to their independence and Philip was forced to withdraw. Six years later his son Alexander crossed into Asia and won his first victory over the Persians at the river Granicus. Impressed, the Byzantines sent overtures of friendship; but Alexander marched south and never set foot in Byzantium. After he died in 323, Greek power gradually declined, while the rising power was that of Rome.

Around 150 BC Byzantium made a treaty with Rome, retaining its freedom in return for tribute, and life continued in untroubled prosperity until the end of the 2nd C. AD and the death of the Emperor Commodus. Two men were then proclaimed Emperor – Pescennius Niger, governor of Syria, and Septimius Severus. In the ensuing civil war the Byzantines backed the loser, and to punish them Septimius Severus besieged the city for three years. Finally in 196 he captured it, tore down the walls of Byzas, sacked the city and massacred his opponents. It looked like the end of Byzantium; but a few years later the Emperor, recognising that the site was too strategic to be lost, set about rebuilding it. His new walls, beginning near Galata Bridge, enclosed more than twice the area of the city he had destroyed.

The Emperor Diocletian is best known for his persecution of

Christians, but also for his division of the Roman Empire, with one Emperor for both West and East, each with a Caesar as second-in-command. This division paved the way for the first Christian Emperor, and for the conversion of the Empire from paganism to Christianity. At first it looked as though Mithraism – a form of sun worship adopted from Persia – would be the dominant religion, for the army had taken to it almost to a man. But it was Christianity, with its superior intellectual base, its stunningly advanced inclusion of women, and its revolutionary view of the equality of all human beings before God, that won the day.

When Diocletian abdicated in 305, to spend his retirement tending his garden in Split, his high-minded division of the Empire almost immediately came unstuck. Instead of two Emperors and two Caesars there were, by 311, four Emperors. In the West Constantine quickly defeated his rival Maxentius, and it was on the eve of his final victory at Milvian Bridge outside Rome that he had his much disputed vision of the Cross of Christ with its legend, 'In hoc vinces' – In this shall you conquer. It was a powerful revelation; the Christians, despite persecution, had become the strongest and best organised group in the Empire – with their support what might he not achieve? Opportunist he may have been; he did, however, live out his choice with an almost equal degree of steadfastness, though he never saw the need for exclusivity. Nor did it change his behaviour to any noticeable extent – he disposed of his wife and one of his sons in an indisputably un-Christian manner, and it was not until he was on his deathbed that he made his final commitment and was baptised.

For 12 years Constantine kept up an appearance of harmony with Licinius, Emperor of the East who, though a pagan, was ready to adopt the Christian cause to maintain his rule. In 313 the two Emperors met at Milan where they issued a joint document by which, for the first time, Christians were given official recognition and security. Such harmony could not last; in 323 the Christian Constantine marched against the pagan Licinius and crushed him, their final and decisive battle being fought on 17 September 324 at Chrysopolis on the Asian shore of the Bosphorus, present-day Üsküdar. Byzantium, which had supported Licinius, surrendered to Constantine on the following day. The Roman Empire once again had only one master.

Soon afterwards Constantine decided to transfer his capital from Rome to Byzantium. The emphasis of the Empire had already shifted eastwards; all the new provinces, with the wealth they brought, lay east of the Mediterranean, and many old ones had been lost to the

Goths. All roads no longer led to Rome; people were more concerned with trade routes to the east, most of which passed through Byzantium. And Byzantium had the Golden Horn.

Over the next century great walls were built, and rebuilt, along the Sea of Marmara, up the southern side of the Golden Horn, and striding in a great arc across the land between the two seas. For extra safety a chain was placed across the entrance to the Golden Horn. Thus protected, the city withstood a succession of formidable attacks over the following centuries – from Goths, Huns, Lombards, Slavs, Avars, Persians, Arabs and Bulgars.

There were, however, two occasions when the city fell to its attackers, and in both cases the key to success was control of the Golden Horn. In 1203 the ships of the Fourth Crusade diverted to Constantinople en route to the Holy Land, captured the chain, sailed into the harbour and lined up in battle order. The siege lasted 10 months; on 12 April 1204 the Crusaders breached the walls of the Golden Horn and captured the city.

249 years later, the ships of the young Ottoman Sultan, Mehmet II, prevented by the Byzantine defenders from coming near the chain, were instead transported overland from the Bosphorus – according to the contemporary chronicler Kritovoulos, with sails flapping in the breeze and oars cutting the empty air to the accompaniment of the whistling and shoutings of the commanders. It was a miraculous and sinister image of a war fleet on the move. The ships were launched on the northern shore of the Golden Horn where a gap in the hills leads down to the water's edge. This tour de force enabled Mehmet to extend his assault to the walls of the Golden Horn, and to construct a pontoon across the top of the harbour, on which his army and cannons passed unmolested to the land-walls near the Byzantine Emperor's palace, where they finally broke through on Tuesday 29 May 1453. Anyone who ventures near the Golden Horn these days is assailed – even from some distance away – by an odour that is far from golden. This is nothing new. Lady Craven, visiting the city in the 1780s, wrote that 'all the filth and rubbish . . . are constantly flung into it – custom-houses, barracks, storehouses, dockyard, all are placed on the borders of it. Whole dunghills are swept into it.' Even in her day it was a long-established habit, and it continued unabated for the next 200 years; and the water had reached such a saturation of filth as would have made possible an acid bath murder without the need for an acid bath.

Until the 1980s there was not only the smell to contend with; on both sides of the Golden Horn were extended slums, teetering on the brink of collapse. For all their filth, and the accompanying potential for contagion, these were picturesque areas of the city. In 1984, to the accompaniment of howls of protest from preservationists, under-standably anxious to save the handful of lovely buildings, bulldozers moved into the decaying rabbit warrens by the water, the residents having been moved to less crumbling accommodation nearby; and a new system for the collection, treatment and disposal of sewage has been installed. Green parks have been laid out in the cleared areas by the water's edge, in spring aflame with tulips, a gift of the Dutch government in celebration of the first tulip bulbs that were taken to Holland from Constantinople in the 16th C.

Sewage works and slum clearance have made some improvement, but the Golden Horn is still far from being the fragrant place that the planners predicted. It seems an unmerited degradation for a waterway that has played so central a role in the grand imperial story of the city that surrounds it.

2

EARLY CONSTANTINOPLE

On 4 November 326 the Emperor Constantine initiated a massive building programme to transform Byzantium into a magnificent new capital, the centre of Greek art and learning, of Roman administration and law, and of Christian worship. It was to be called New Rome, but the name never stuck; from the beginning it was called what it truly was, Constantinople – Constantine's city.

On that November day the Emperor himself, spear in hand, marked out the course that the new defensive walls were to take. Here, too, it seems he had the benefit of a divine vision, for when asked how far he would go, he replied, 'Until He stops who now goes before me,' Of these divinely inspired walls not a trace remains. Constantine's New Rome did not have the same number of hills as the Old for parts of the fifth and seventh, and all of the sixth, lay outside the walls. It was left for Theodosius II a century later to equalise with the old capital.

The speed with which the new city was built is astonishing – it took under four years. As Christ's Vice-Regent on earth the Emperor ransacked the cities of pagan Greece and the Greco-Roman east for statues and other art treasures with which to beautify his Christian capital, so much so that St Jerome a few years later grumbled that Constantinople was 'clothed in the nudity of almost every other city.' Constantine also despatched his mother, the equally converted St Helena, to Jerusalem. With evidently miraculous archaeological perception, every time she ordered a spade into the earth of the Holy City she discovered a new site, or yet another relic, associated with Christ's Passion. Most spectacular of her finds was the site of Calvary and a portion of the True Cross; but there were also the crosses of the two thieves, the lance, the sponge and the crown of thorns, and several lesser artefacts. With these relics, Constantinople's status was assured. On 11 May 330 Constantine dedicated his city to the Holy Trinity and the Mother of God. The Byzantine Empire was born. It was to last 1123 years and 18 days.

In 325 Constantine had assumed the mantle of patron of the Christian church and summoned the bishops to the First Ecumenical Council at Nicaea (now Iznik) to discuss a dispute between Arius, an elder of the Alexandrian church, and his bishop over whether or not Christ was 'of one substance with the Father.' The dispute was not merely local and Alexandrian; it had spread widely, and protagonists of both sides were locked in bitter controversy. Although the Council condemned Arius' views as heretical, the Arian controversy continued to bedevil church and Empire for several generations, followed with dizzying frequency by a succession of other heresies.

Constantine the Great died seven years after the inauguration of his new capital, and was succeeded in mutual animosity by his sons, Constantine and Constans in the West, and Constantius in the East. It was, as always, a recipe for dissension and it was not until the first two were dead, that Constantius ruled the whole Empire alone. He embraced Arianism, and the bitter disputes that divided the church during his reign spilled over into the city, and assassination became commonplace, whether in the name of Arianism or orthodoxy. His immediate heirs were Julian the Apostate, who reverted to paganism, Jovian who was orthodox, and Valens, an Arian – a mixture that ensured the continuation of religious controversy, though without the earlier bloodshed.

Theological dispute was never considered the preserve of bishops and clergy; every level of society knew and cared about these things, and there were passionate partisans of both sides. According to the contemporary (and orthodox) St Gregory of Nyssa, 'the city is full of mechanics and slaves who are all of them profound theologians, and preach in the shops and in the streets. If you desire a man to change a piece of money for you he informs you wherein the Son differs from the Father; if you ask the price of a loaf of bread you are told by way of reply that the Son is inferior to the Father; and if you enquire whether the bath is ready, the answer is that the Son was made out of nothing.'

Fortunately for the Empire the next imperial appointment was more successful. Theodosius I, a Spaniard, won instant popularity by dealing firmly with the troublesome Goths, and making a satisfactory treaty with the power of Persia, a goal that had eluded his predecessors. As a Christian he was deeply orthodox, and he lost no time in appointing an equally orthodox Patriarch of Constantinople, the saintly theologian Gregory of Nazianzus. In 381, two years after becoming Emperor, Theodosius summoned the Second Ecumenical Council at Constantinople which reaffirmed the statement issued by the Council of Nicaea in 325, henceforth known as the Nicene Creed, proscribed pagans and Arians alike, and imposed a universal orthodoxy on the Christian world.

With peace a home, and with his borders secured, Theodosius turned his attention to extending and beautifying his capital. So successful was he that the orator Themistius outdid himself in his encomium: 'The beauty of the city is not as heretofore scattered over it in patches, but covers the whole area like a robe woven to the very fringe. The city gleams with gold and porphyry. It has a new Forum, named after the Emperor; it has baths, porticoes, gymnasia; and its former extremity is now its centre. Were Constantine to see the capital he founded, he would behold a glorious and splendid scene, not a bare and empty void. He would find it fair, not with apparent but with real beauty.'

In 395 Theodosius the Great was succeeded by his son Honorius in the West and Arcadius in the East. In less than a century the West was overrun by barbarians and the title of Emperor was extinct. That the East survived and prospered owed nothing to Arcadius, though somewhat more to his son and heir, Theodosius II. The main interest of Arcadius' reign is in the life of one of those remarkable churchmen that the age produced, St John Chrysostom, the golden-mouthed. Arcadius appointed him Patriarch of Constantinople in 397, and he and the Empress Eudoxia gave him their enthusiastic support, until he turned his reforming eyes and blistering tongue to the imperial court itself. He had plenty of scope for his strictures; wealth and luxury had led to licentious living and intrigues, and the Empress was seen to be at the centre of much of it. John Chrysostom inveighed against them all, and the people loved him for it. Not so Eudoxia. He had already likened her to Jezebel and been temporarily banished for his outspokenness; when he was reported to have compared her with Herodias, demanding the head of John on a charger, his fate was sealed. He was arrested, and in June 404 was sent into exile in Anatolia for the rest of his life. So enraged were the people of Constantinople that they ran riot and set fire to the first church of Haghia Sophia, just 44 years after its dedication.

The reign of Theodosius II, aged 7 when he became Emperor, presents a startling contrast. His sister Pulcheria, only two years his senior, was made Regent when she was 15 years old, and under her energetic and virtuous influence learning and true religion – in practice as well as in precept – became established at the imperial court. Theodosius himself was less interested statecraft than in astronomy, natural science, calligraphy and theology, but he was fortunate in his Praetorian Prefect of the East, the wise and loyal Anthemius, who had been revered even by that most exacting critic, St John Chrysostom. It was Anthemius who, recognising the threat posed by the Huns on the borders of the Empire, built great new walls to enlarge and protect the city. They were completed by one of his successors, the Prefect Constantine, and they still stand today. They are usually known, somewhat unfairly, as the walls of Theodosius.

Theodosius II's long reign (408–50) was mainly peaceful, and in it the University of Constantinople was established with ten Chairs of Greek grammar and ten of Latin, five Chairs of Greek rhetoric but only three of Latin, one Chair of Philosophy and two of Law. By now Latin was clearly declining in favour of Greek, the language of the majority of the people. Also Byzantine imperial law was codified for the first time, and issued in 438 as the *Codex Theodosianus*. Another innovation, quite different but equally useful in its own way, was the introduction of lighting in the streets of Constantinople at night.

Two new heresies matured during his reign. Nestorianism distinguished between Christ's humanity and divinity, and in stressing His human birth, stripped the Virgin Mary of her title 'Theotokos' –Mother of God. It was condemned by the Third Ecumenical Council at Ephesus in 431. The swing of the pendulum produced the next heresy, Monophysitism, which maintained that Christ had a single, wholly divine, nature; it was condemned in its turn by the Fourth Ecumenical Council at Chalcedon, but it was not eradicated. For the first time a ruling of an Ecumenical Council was rejected by large sections of the Christian church, and the divisions thus created were never healed.

Route 1

THE HIPPODROME

The hippodrome, at the heart of Constantine's city, is now a long narrow rectangle in front of Sultan Ahmet mosque with only its distinctive shape and three ancient columns to be seen; but the columns are remarkable, and they mark the place where almost everything of vital importance to the people of Constantinople occurred – chariot races and religious disputes. Septimius Severus built the first hippodrome here in 203 to placate the Byzantines whose city he had destroyed a few years before. It was never finished. Just over a century later Constantine wanted something bigger and grander for his new capital, and his immense hippodrome, about 480 m long by 117½ m wide, and with a seating capacity of 100,000, was completed in time for the inaugural ceremony on 11 May 330.

The spina, which ran down the centre of the hippodrome, was adorned with numerous obelisks and columns. Only three remain – the acquisitive Latins of the Fourth Crusade, who captured the city in 1204, carried off its finest treasures to Europe. The four magnificent bronze-gilt horses of Lysippus, brought here from Chios by Theodosius II, were among the tons of booty taken to Venice by the Doge Henry Dandolo. For centuries they adorned San Marco, now replaced by replicas. Nothing at all remains of the 30 or 40 rows of seats along the two sides. They survived the Ottoman Conquest by about a century, gradually falling into greater ruin until, in the mid-16th C., Süleyman the Magnificent appropriated most of them to build his mosque complex. And the last of its tumbled stones were taken in the early 17th C. as building material for Sultan Ahmet I's new mosque.

Half way along the east side of the hippodrome, probably near the courtyard of Sultan Ahmet's mosque, was the kathisma, a splendid imperial apartment carried on 24 marble columns and giving direct access to the Great Palace, a safety device that was doubtless a source of comfort to some Emperors at times when the audience in the hippodrome threatened to get out of hand.

Chariot racing was the most popular sporting event that occupied the hippodrome, with dancers, tumblers, musicians and performing animals filling the gaps between races. The semi-political factions of the Blues and Greens not only supported different chariot teams, but also opposite sides in theological disputes; and when the combined passions of sport, local politics and theology became too inflamed, arguments flared into violence.

Over the question of whether Christ had one nature or two feelings ran high for many years, deeply dividing the city. The spectacular culmination of this came in Justinian's reign when the Greens, Monophysite to a man, came to blows with the orthodox Blues who believed in the Dual Nature. Rioting broke out during a chariot race in January 532; but antagonism to the Emperor, and to his hated ministers with their crippling taxes, proved even stronger than theological debate, and the rioting soon turned to anarchy with both sides sinking their differences and joining together in arson and looting, shouting 'Nika' – Victory – at the tops of their voices. After five days, in which large areas of the city were reduced to smouldering ruins, Justinian ordered out the 4000-strong Imperial Guard under his general Belisarius. About 30,000 people were trapped in the hippodrome and massacred.

The first monument we see is one of ostentatious early 20th C. ugliness – a **fountain** presented by Kaiser Wilhelm II to Sultan Abdül Hamit II. It marks roughly the position of the straight end of the hippodrome where races began and finished.

Next, some distance further on, is the granite **Egyptian obelisk**, originally cut for the Pharaoh Thutmose III in the mid-15th C. BC, with hieroglyphs celebrating his victories. On it is written, 'Thutmose, who crossed the great river of Naharin [Euphrates] as a mighty conqueror at the head of his army.' For centuries it stood at Karnak in Upper Egypt, then was brought to Constantinople at an unspecified date in the 4th C. AD and abandoned for many years until Theodosius the Great had it set up here in 390. It used to have a bronze ball on top, long since disappeared, and it rests on four bronze blocks on a marble base. This base is fascinating for it has carved reliefs on all four sides, commissioned by Theodosius and portraying the Emperor and his family attending events in this very hippodrome: watching a chariot race, giving prizes, erecting the obelisk, and receiving homage from suitably obeisant captives. Inscriptions in both Greek and Latin eulogise the Emperor for having the obelisk erected; but there seems to have been a difference of opinion, or perhaps just a slip of the chisel, over how long it took to do the job. According to the Latin scribes it took 30 days, while the Greeks maintain 32. The obelisk stands in a large hole about 4½ m deep, as does the serpent column nearby, the bottom of which indicates the original level of the hippodrome.

A length of coiled green bronze is all that remains of the **serpent column**, three intertwined serpents with a remarkable history. Made as a thank-offering to Apollo by the 31 cities who had defeated the Persians at Plataea in 479 BC, and formed from the shields and other bronze booty taken at the battle, it had stood for 800 years in the temple of Apollo at Delphi. In the days of its full glory the three serpents' heads supported a golden tripod, on which was a golden vase. All the gold was gone even before Constantine the Great, in his quest for suitable adornments for his new capital, removed the column from Delphi; today it also lacks the heads of the serpents, though the upper jaw of one of them can be seen in the Archaeological Museum.

How and when the heads came off is undocumented, but Lady Mary Wortley Montagu, in a letter from Constantinople in 1718, writes of a 'brazen column, of three serpents twisted together, with their mouths gaping,' so presumably they were still there then, for Lady Mary prided herself on writing only of what she had seen. She also declared that there was 'no sign of its having ever had any inscription'; in her day the names of the Greek cities, visible near the bottom of the coils, lay buried by the accumulation of earth above the original ground level. Tales of the miraculous powers of the column have varied. One, not surprisingly, claimed that touching it was a cure for snake-bite; while Pero Tafur, a Spaniard who visited the city a few years before the Ottoman conquest, and who thought there were only two snakes, was told that wine used to pour from the mouth of one and milk from the other. 'It seems to me,' he continues sagely, 'that too much credit must not be attached to the story.'

The third remaining monument on the spina is a roughly built stone obelisk commonly, though misleadingly, called the **column of Constantine Porphyrogenitus**. In fact it is much older than this implies, possibly dating to the time of Constantine the Great or Theodosius the Great; but Constantine VII Porphyrogenitus (912–59) had it encased in bronze-gilt and inscribed in celebration of the deeds of his grandfather, Basil I the Macedonian. This casing was part of the loot taken by the men of the Fourth Crusade, leaving only the plain obelisk beneath.

Facing the end of the hippodrome, we take the road to the left, Nakılbent Sok., which sweeps downhill and then right. Look up, and you will see the remains of the massive supporting walls of the **sphendone**, the semi-circular end of the hippodrome, which had to be borne up on great arches as the hillside falls away at this point. Outlines of the arches are still clearly visible, though now filled in, and the walls give some idea of the vast scale of the hippodrome, and the impressiveness of Roman architecture.

THE MARTYRIUM OF ST EUPHEMIA OF CHALCEDON/PALACE OF ANTIOCHUS

Returning to the northern end of the hippodrome, shortly before the main road some steps go up to the left. They lead to an open space in which are the remains of some ancient walls. Excavations in the 1950s uncovered the foundations of an hexagonal building with five semi-circular apses, the remains of an early 5th C. palace were built for a nobleman called Antiochus. 200 years later it was turned into a martyrium for St Euphemia of Chalcedon, a victim of one of Diocletian's persecutions in the early 4th C., for in the early 7th C. her body was transferred from Chalcedon to Constantinople and needed a suitable home. This was not to be St Euphemia's last resting place, however, for after the Conquest, when the site was requisitioned, her relics were rescued and kept by the Patriarchate. They are now in the Patriarchal church in the Fener.

THE MESE

The road north of Antiochus' palace is Divan Yolu, now a tram and bus route, but once the main artery of Constantine's city, the Mese, or Middle Way. It must have looked magnificent then, most of it lined with columned porticoes interspersed with marble statues of lions. It started from near the northern end of the hippodrome, marked by a monument called the Miliarium Aureum, the Golden Milestone, or Milion for short, from which all distances to Constantinople were measured. It is thought to have consisted of four triumphal arches surmounted by a cupola on which statues of Constantine and his mother St Helena held the cross of Christ. The Mese followed the line of the street orignally laid out by Septimius Severus, but Constantine and his successors enlarged and adorned it out of all recognition.

THE BINBIRDIREK CISTERN

A short distance beyond the Palace of Antiochus we turn first left off Divan Yolu up Işık Sok., which leads to a large open space, on the other side of which there is a small building. The name plate by the door announces that this is the entrance to 'Philoxenes' cistern', or 'Binbirdirek', the cistern of 1001 columns. It has recently been restored – much needed for it is a spectacular structure, with a towering forest of columns which had been partially clogged with the accumulated silt of centuries. It is also probably the oldest of the underground water cisterns in the city, having been constructed about 200 years earlier than the Yerebatan cistern which we will see on a later visit (see pages 47–8).

The cistern was built in the time of Constantine the Great, possibly by a Roman senator called Philoxenus who came with the Emperor to Constantinople. It appears to have been restored in the 6th C. 1001 columns is, needless to say, an exaggeration, the classic Turkish and Arab shorthand for an uncountable number; those who have counted make a total of 224 columns in 16 rows of 14, but 12 of them were walled off almost from the beginning. The columns stand 17 m high, though they are not all of a single piece – the available columns (presumably remains of pre-Constantine structures that were re-used to build the cistern) were clearly not tall enough, so an extra piece was added at the bottom to give the required height. On top are plain impost capitals (some with the stonemasons' monograms on them) which support the herring-bone design brick vaults that cover the whole area of the cistern, the second largest in the city after Yerebatan Sarayı.

THE COLUMN OF CONSTANTINE

Returning to Divan Yolu and turning left, after about 400m we reach the Column of Constantine, on the right hand side of the road. It is known to the Turks as Çemberlitaş, the hooped stone, a literal description of the means of holding together the six drums of damaged porphyry of which the column now consists. In English it is often called the Burnt Column, an equally literal indication of how it came to be in the blackened condition it is. Once it stood at the centre of the great colonnaded Forum of Constantine which was adorned with statues and other monuments of both Christian and pagan origin, and surrounded by fine public buildings and churches.

The column presents a sad appearance today. Originally it consisted of seven drums on a base and plinth, all of polished porphyry, and resting on a square stepped pedestal. It towered majestically above the great Forum, crowned by a larger-than-life statue in bronze-gilt representing Constantine as Apollo. It was an astonishing example of diplomatic syncretism: the Christian Emperor, in his hand an orb containing a fragment of St Helena's True Cross, yet shown in the guise of the pagan sun god who in turn incorporated the Mithraic concept of the Unconquered Sun. Some of the nails that were believed to have crucified Christ even formed part of the rays around Apollo's head. Whatever a person's beliefs, he was presumably meant to feel at one with his Emperor on high.

Buried at the foot of the column was an equally syncretic horde of relics, including more of St Helena's archaeological treasure trove – the crosses of the two thieves, the alabaster jar of St Mary Magdalene, and the baskets complete with remnants of loaves gathered up after Christ had fed the multitude. There were Old Testament relics too, such as Noah's hatchet and the stone which Moses struck to make water flow; and for the pagan side the palladium of ancient Rome and the wooden statue of Athena taken from Troy by Aeneas. With so much sanctity from every camp, the Forum and its statue must have seemed, at least to Constantine and his mother, the beating heart of the city.

Constantine's statue, and probably its capital too, fell from the top of the column in an exceptional gale in 1106; but in the middle of the same century the Emperor Manuel I Commenus tried to make good the loss by adding the masonry which we see at the top today and, rising from this, a large golden cross which did not survive the Ottoman Conquest. Frequent fires swept through the wooden buildings of the area and all have left their mark on this blackened, battered relic of Constantine's brave new capital.

THE FORUM OF THEODOSIUS

Divan Yolu has by now changed its name to Yeniçeriler Cad., the street of the Janissaries, and a further 500 m on we see the great mosque built by Beyazit II, son and heir of Mehmet the Conqueror. On the other side of it is Beyazit Square, site of the ancient Forum of Theodosius, also called the Forum Tauri from the bronze statue of a bull at its centre. The forum was made for Theodosius the Great in 393, and was even bigger than that of Constantine. It too was surrounded by handsome porticoes and filled with statues and other monuments, not least a huge triumphal arch.

To make the people of Constantinople even more mindful of Theodosius' triumphs, a great column was erected at the centre of the Forum in the year after he died, with reliefs depicting his various military victories carved in a spiral from bottom to top. It was plainly emulating Trajan's Column in Rome. On top was a silver statue of Theodosius, but it fell in an earthquake in 480.

The column was still standing in 1204 when it provided the unsqueamish leaders of the Fourth Crusade with a convenient execution block for the Emperor Alexius V Murzuphlus, who was taken to the top and thrown off. A few carvings from the column are built into the base of the disused Beyazit hamam on Ordu Cad., some upside down. Several pieces from the triumphal arch, which fell in an earthquake in the 8th C., still lie on the other side of the street, including some huge columns, carved all over with peacock-eyes.

THE AQUEDUCT OF VALENS

Going to the north side of Beyazit Square, we climb the steps and turn

21

left into Darülfünun Cad., passing an 18th C. baroque medrese which now houses the Institute of Turkology. The street changes its name to Vezneciler Cad. and then, at Şehzade Camii, to Şehzadebaşi Cad., at which point we see on our right the arched outline of the aqueduct of Valens. High-flown words like 'noble' and 'majestic' are usually used to convey an impression of Valens' monument, but to me it remains just an efficient and unsubtle means of transporting water into the city, a good example of Roman engineering. No more.

The aqueduct was built by the Emperor Valens around 375, and it was his only real success. The stones, it is said, came from the walls of Chalcedon which Valens had ordered to be torn down because the citizens had rebelled against him. Just over half its original length of about 1 km remains, bestriding the valley between the third and fourth hills of the city, and also the modern Atatürk Bul. It was repaired and restored by succeeding generations of Byzantine Emperors and Ottoman Sultans, and for 15 centuries it channelled water, brought in underground pipes from outside the city, to a vast central cistern near Beyazit Square.

THE CHURCH OF ST POLYEUCTOS

In the west corner of the Şehzadebaşı/Atatürk Bul. intersection are the remains of what was once the very large and richly endowed church of St Polyeuctos. Its existence was discovered during excavations for the underpass in the mid-1960s, and over the following years it was thoroughly investigated by a team from the Centre for Byzantine Studies of the University of Harvard. A long and finely carved inscription revealed the name of the church which was built by the Princess Anicia Juliana in 524–27, and it survived the Nika riots. Parts of its masonry were taken to Venice by the Fourth Crusade, and are still exhibited in the Piazzetta beside San Marco. Today the church consists only of a bare outline of the walls and a few fragments of once magnificent columns and carvings. The finest pieces, with their jewel-like decoration, can be seen in the Archaeological Museum.

Route 2

THE CHURCH OF ST JOHN OF STUDIUS/IMRAHOR
CAMII (currently closed; the bekçi may allow a view from his yard)

The oldest church in Istanbul, the only one to survive from the period between Constantine the Great and Justinian the Great, is the church of St John the Baptist of Studius, now known as Imrahor Camii. One of the most attractive of ruins, roofless and romantically overgrown around its edges, it stands on a side street off Imrahor Ilyas Bey Cad. about 500 m inside the great walls of Theodosius, making it an easy stop en route to a tour of the walls. The side street is on the south of the main road, opposite Uşşakı Camii.

The church was founded in 463, 16 years after the Theodosian walls were completed, by a Roman patrician called Studius. Every year on the feast of the beheading of St John the Baptist (29 August) the Emperor would come by sea to visit the church whose most sacred relic was the head of the Baptist. In the 13th C., it apparently acquired the gift of bilocation for after the loot of the Fourth Crusade had been distributed around Europe both Soissons and Amiens boasted the head of John the Baptist.

We approach the church today through what was originally the atrium, 1000 or so years later to become the mosque courtyard, from which the ablution fountain remains. The narthex still has much of its fine entrance portal with magnificently carved capitals, architrave and cornice. Inside, the church is an empty shell, apart from six lovely columns, each formed of a single block of verd-antique. The entablature on top of this colonnade is still in place, propped up by scaffolding, but its once rich carving is now badly weathered. Above it was originally another row of columns supporting the wooden roof. Parts of the fine opus sectile floor remain, the gift of Michael VIII Palaeologus after the restoration of the Byzantine Empire in 1261, to replace the one destroyed by the Fourth Crusade. The shell of the semi-circular apse still contains some of the structure of the mihrab with its askew orientation. But to re-dress the walls with the rich marble revetments and mosaics of the days of the church's glory, we have to rely on our imagination.

Besides being the oldest church, it is also the only example in Istanbul of a pure basilica, the first type of building used for Christian worship. Until the early 4th C. there had been no such thing as church architecture; then, suddenly released from the need for secrecy in its worship, the church had to find a suitable building in a hurry. The style of the ancient temples was too identified with paganism, so they chose instead the secular basilica, long used for public assemblies of various kinds from legal to social or imperial.

The church of St John of Studius was originally attached to a monastery whose monks were known as 'Akoimetai', the sleepless ones, from their round-the-clock celebration of the liturgy, with intercessions for the sins of the world, organised on a relay basis. Under the Iconoclast Emperors of the 8th C., the monastery clung tenaciously to the use of images in art and worship; but it was not until 799 that it rose to its full prominence, when the great Theodore became Abbot. Under his guidance the monastery became not merely a centre of resistance to Iconoclasm, with the inevitable persecutions that this entailed, it became a world-famous centre for scholarship, painting of icons, illuminating of manuscripts and composition of sacred music.

The Studite monastery produced several Patriarchs; and in the 11th C. two Emperors, Isaac I Commenus and Michael VII Ducas, spent their enforced retirement here as monks; Isaac I had also studied here in his youth. Another Emperor, the hated Michael V Calaphates, was dragged screaming from his sanctuary here in April 1042, to be deposed and blinded. And a son of the Ottoman Sultan Beyazit I, a covert Christian, was buried here in 1417.

After the Conquest the church and monastery remained Christian until about 1500 when Ilyas Bey, Beyazit II's Master of Horse (imrahor), evicted the few remaining monks and converted the church into a mosque – Imrahor Ilyas Bey Camii. Of the monastery hardly a stone remains; both it and the mosque were badly damaged in a fire in 1782, and its last traces were destroyed in an earthquake of 1894 which turned the mosque into a roofless ruin.

THE MARTYRIUM OF SS KARPOS AND PAPYLOS

The remains of a 4th or 5th C. martyrium, dedicated to SS Karpos and Papylos who were put to death in the persecutions of the Emperor Decius (249–51), stand on A. Nafiz Gürman Cad. about ½ km back towards the centre of Istanbul. The tower of the modern Greek church of St Menas, high above the road, acts a landmark for immediately underneath it, opening off the street, is the martyrium, or rather its crypt. It is easy to miss because it looks like what it is today – a workshop for making doors, door-frames and cabinets. However, if you venture into any unlikely-looking workshop muttering 'Eski kilise' (old church) in an interrogative tone of voice, you will be shown the right place with characteristic Turkish goodwill.

From the street you enter the erstwhile apse; but the most extraordinary sight is the huge circular chamber of the main body of the crypt, reached under a low arch. The great shallow dome, superbly constructed of narrow courses of brick, today covers bits of old timber and discarded metal. Through a door (usually locked) in the apse opposite the entrance, the proprietor may be persuaded to show you the beginning of a narrow vaulted ambulatory, also built of brick, which runs all round the central circular chamber. It is now blocked with junk. Sadly degraded today, the martyrium must, around 1500 to 1600 years ago, have been a large and very impressive structure.

Detour The church of St Andrew in Krisei/Koca Mustafa Paşa Camii

An interesting detour of about 400 m takes us somewhat out of our historical period to a lovely Byzantine church, now Koca Mustafa Paşa Camii, one of the most popular Islamic shrines in Istanbul.

Turning left out of the Martyrium of SS Karpos and Papylos onto A. Nafiz Gürman Cad., take first left uphill. It is a delightful area of the city, full of the vivid life and old houses of a community that has been established for centuries. On Saturdays all the streets are taken over by the local market with colourful displays of fruit and vegetables, fish on bright red wooden platters, and an abundance of cheap jewellery, perfumes, fabrics, clothes and household goods. Taking the right fork at the T-junction and continuing uphill, the road winds round to the right before coming into a corner of Koca Mustafa Paşa Cad. Turn left and the mosque is on the left.

The origins of the building probably go back to the 6th C., with a church dedicated to St Andrew the Apostle. Then in the 740s Andrew, Archbishop of Crete and a famous hymn writer, came to Constantinople to rebuke the Emperor Constantine V Copronymus for his over-enthusiastic Iconoclasm. As a result, he joined the host of Iconodule martyrs. His body was rescued by his followers and buried in the church of St Andrew the Apostle. It was almost completely rebuilt around 1284 by the Princess Theodora Raoulina and re-dedicated to St Andrew of Crete. In 1486 it was turned into a mosque by Koca Mustafa Paşa, a renegade Greek who was Grand Vezir to Beyazit II, and betrayed his Sultan to his son, Selim the Grim, who soon after rewarded him with execution.

The pretty courtyard contains four türbes, two of which account for the mosque's popularity. In one is buried a 16th C. holy man and mystic, Sümbül Efendi, first şeyh of the dervish tekke here; in another is his daughter, Rahime, gifted in helping women looking for husbands. In the middle of the courtyard is a very dead cypress tree whose powers are so important that it is propped up with concrete and protected by a wooden house so that it can carry on with its miraculous works – which do not, it seems, include keeping itself upright without help.

There are two entrances, and it is best to go to the one at the far end which leads into the exo-narthex. At the centre is a little dome supported on columns with lovely 6th C. capitals, and a door leads into the inner narthex, divided from the main body of the building by two verd-antique columns, crowned by capitals with a finely carved lace-like pattern of acanthus leaves.

Passing between the columns, we see the clear, simple space of the interior, with its deep barrel-vaulted apse, which conversion into a mosque has done unusually little to alter, largely because the reorientation was of a full 90°. The mihrab bay in the south wall, and the bay opposite, with their semidomes, were part of the conversion, as was the central dome which replaced a little Byzantine cupola. The recent restoration was done with much architectural tact, and even the decoration is restrained, making the overall effect exceptionally pleasing.

THE WALLS OF THEODOSIUS

The great triple fortifications on the landward side of Constantinople, ruined in parts as they are, form one of the most impressive monuments of the city, extending in a great arc, 7 km long, from the Sea of Marmara to the Golden Horn. The first wall was built in 413 when Theodosius II was 13 years old. Three years earlier Rome had fallen to Alaric and his Goths, while the Huns – even more barbarous than the Goths – were causing widespread terror further east. Anthemius, Prefect of the East, concerned for the safety of the city which had long since outgrown the walls of Constantine, built a massive wall 5 m thick and 12 m high, fortified with 96 towers. In 447 a violent earthquake toppled great stretches of it, and 57 of its towers.

The disaster could not have happened at a worse moment, for Attila the Hun and his Golden Horde were poised to descend on Constantinople. The repair of the walls was put in hand at once by Constantine, the new Prefect of the East, and so great and so imminent was the threat that for once even the Blues and Greens dropped their antagonisms of the hippodrome and worked together in full co-operation, their only rivalry to outdo each other. Within two months not only had Anthemius' wall been rebuilt, but another smaller wall, 2 m thick and 8½ m high, also flanked with 96 towers, had been built in front of it; and in front of this they had dug a great moat, 20 m wide by 10 m deep.

This triple line of defence, completed in such a stunningly short space of time, was immediately successful for Attila evacuated his forces and devastated the Empire of the West instead. The walls were perfectly designed to withstand the armaments of the day, and they remained unbreached for over 1000 years. As attackers tried to cross the moat, defenders launched missiles at them from the tops of their towers – arrows, great stones hurled from engines such as the ballista or onager, and later the terrifying Greek fire. It was gunpowder and cannons in the 15th C. that finally proved too much for the old walls.

Most of Anthemius' great wall still stands, though shaken and tumbled by earthquakes, assaults and sheer age. Some of the towers still stand to their full height. The outer walls have fared less well, with only about half the towers still visible; while large sections of the moat support flourishing market gardens. But the restorers have moved in, and have started a rather heavy-handed rebuilding of several of the towers and adjacent walls.

A tour of the walls
Yedikule, the Seven Towers, the starting point for our tour of the walls, stands not far from the Sea of Marmara at the far end of Imrahor Ilyas Bey Cad. It includes four towers from the Theodosian wall, and an add-on by Mehmet the Conqueror of three very large towers, and 12 m high curtain walls connecting them. It seems an odd thing for Mehmet to build; he was under no external threat and Yedikule was never used as a fortress. Indeed its strength proved more useful for keeping people in than out, for it was used as a prison – not least for foreign ambassadors who displeased later Sultans, or who had carelessly failed to return home before their country was at war with Turkey. Their sad graffiti abound, elegantly carved, around the entrance of the east tower, the Tower of the Ambassadors.

It was also a place for executions, not always performed in a strictly conventional manner, and from which even Sultans were not exempt. On 22 May 1622 the 17 year old Osman II, after four years of rule, was dragged here by the Janissaries whom he had displeased. Fighting for his life, the powerfully built Osman killed six of his attackers before being run through with a sabre. In the next century an Italian called Bocaretto, on a visit to the city, wrote: 'At the Seven Towers a number of prisoners, among them several Christians, were thrown the other day over the parapet . . . You can see from the road naked and still living men, caught on long spikes, where they will have to remain until death delivers them.'

The entrance into Yedikule is near the east tower. In the centre of the courtyard are the crumbling remains of a little brick-built mosque, while some large stone cannon balls form a guard of honour on either side of the path to it. Part of the courtyard has been converted into an open-air theatre, used for some performances of the annual Istanbul Festival in June/July. Steps lead up inside the towers, and on the outside of the curtain walls, and it is very agreeable to walk along the top of the parapet and through the towers, like the Ottoman gaolers of old. From the southern corner you can look down to the Sea of Marmara where the walls end at the Marble Tower.

The **Golden Gate**, between the two central towers of the Theodosian wall, was built by Theodosius I in 390 to celebrate his victory over a usurper of the Empire of the West. As was customary with such monuments, it consisted of a large central arch and a smaller one on either side. In those days it was well outside the city, bestriding the Via Egnatia along which all Byzantine conquerors returned to the city. Its gates were sheathed in gold, and decorating the façade were statues of Theodosius and the winged Victory and, most spectacular of all, a group of four bronze elephants.

On the propylaeon of the Golden Gate were relief carvings of the labours of Hercules, the tortures of Prometheus and other classical subjects. In 1625 Sir Thomas Roe, English ambassador to Constantinople, tried to acquire these by fair means or foul for the Earl of Arundel and the Duke of Buckingham. He thought he had succeeded when he handed over a substantial sum of money for their covert removal, but such was the feeling of the people, who thought that the success and safety of the city depended on the carvings remaining *in situ*, that the shady deal fell through.

Under Theodosius II the Golden Gate was incorporated into the new walls of Anthemius. Conquering Emperors still passed through it as they returned to Constantinople, and they could still be moved by the inscriptions on either side, picked out in letters of gold. On the west, as they entered the city, they could read, 'Theodosius adorns this place after the doom of the usurper'; and looking back after passing through the gates they could see the words, 'He who constructed the Golden Gate brings in the Golden Age.' It was the heady stuff of which their history was made. Today we can only see the holes in which the letters were fixed.

The best view of the Golden Gate is from near the crowded little cemetery outside the walls, on the left outside Yedikule Gate. But from whatever angle, it is a sad relic of a once magnificent triumphal arch and the state entrance into the city.

From Yedikule we set off on our circuit of the walls, which go first north and then veer north-east. This can be done by car or taxi, either in a non-stop drive along the road which follows the wall closely, or stopping off at various points for detours into different historical periods. Walkers can take the footpath between the main road and the market gardens that flourish inside and outside the moat in front of the walls. Between Yedikule and Silivri Kapısı the walls are in fairly good condition.

The first gate we come to, about 600 m from Yedikule, is known as **Belgrad Kapısı**, the Belgrade Gate. Originally called the Second Military Gate (the first is between the Marble Tower and Yedikule), its present name comes from 1521 when Süleyman the Magnificent settled here a group of artisans whom he brought back after his capture of Belgrade. Both it and the walls have been heavily restored.

Another good stretch of wall, again of about 600 m, brings us to **Silivri Kapısı**, an impressive double gate piercing both the outer and inner walls. Its most glorious moment was the entry of Michael VIII Palaeologus' general, with a small Byzantine force, on 25 July 1261. It was the prelude to the eviction of the Latin usurpers, masters of Constantinople since the Fourth Crusade in 1204, and the restoration of the Byzantine Empire. It, too, has been heavily restored.

Detour: **Balıklı Kilise**

Opposite Silivri Kapısı, across the main road, is a narrow road; taking the first turning to the right, it leads after ½ km to a small village. On the left, a doorway in a high wall opens into the spacious outer courtyard of the Balıklı Kilise, the Fishy Church, with its monastery.

From early Byzantine times this church was dedicated to the Virgin, and was associated with the monastery and shrine of the Zoodochus Pege, the Life-giving Spring; indeed, so famous was it that it gave its name to what is now the Silivri Gate, throughout the Byzantine period called the Gate of the Pege. In the 6th C. Procopius described an idyllic setting: 'In that place is a dense grove of cypresses and a meadow abounding in flowers in the midst of a soft glebe, a park abounding in beautiful shrubs, and a spring bubbling silently with a gentle stream of sweet water.' Every year on Ascension Day the Emperor and members of his court would come here to worship; several Emperors even built churches. Today it is an all but forgotten backwater and the little chapel that contains the sacred spring dates only from 1833.

The present name of the church relates to the fish that swim in the sacred spring, who featured in a miraculous incident on 29 May 1453. On that day a monk was frying fish when a messenger brought news that the city had fallen to the Turks. The sceptical monk said that he could more easily believe that the fish would jump out of his pan into the spring; whereupon they did precisely that, and their descendants were said to have remained brown on one side and red on the other thereafter. After more than 500 years it appears they have recovered.

The outer courtyard has unusual paving stones: re-employed tombstones with inscriptions in the old Karamanlı script in which Turkish, then written in the Arabic script, was instead written in Greek letters. The vocation of some of the interred is also indicated with little drawings incised in the stone. The inner courtyard contains some highly decorated tombs of Greek Orthodox patriarchs and bishops; and the chapel with the sacred spring is reached down a flight of steps between the two courtyards, to the right of the office. The spring, with its handful of goldfish, is at the west end of the chapel, protected by glass.

After Silivri Kapısı the walls are rather more dilapidated than the first two sections, in particular the towers. About 200 m further on is the Third Military Gate, now blocked up, and just beyond it the walls perform a double jog, called the **Sigma** because its shape resembles the Greek letter sigma written as a capital C.

After another 500 m we come to the **Mevlevihane Kapısı**, named after the convent of Mevlevi dervishes that once stood here. In Byzantine times it was the Rhegium Gate as the road through it led to the town of Rhegium. It was here that the Greens, who had built northwards from the Sea of Marmara, met the Blues, who had started from the Golden Horn. To celebrate, inscriptions were carved on the gate in the outer wall. The Greek shows modest restraint: 'In 60 days, at the command of the sceptre-loving Emperor, Constantine the Eparch built wall to wall.' But the Latin scribes indulged their pardonable pride: 'By the command of Theodosius, Constantine erected these strong fortifications in less than two months. Scarcely could Pallas herself have built so strong a citadel in so short a time.' Another inscription records that the tower was restored in the reign of Justin II and Sophia, 'our most pious sovereigns', by the great general Narses, the conqueror of Totila and his Goths.

It is about 1 km to **Topkapı**, the Cannon Gate. Two-thirds of the way along is the walled-up Fourth Military Gate, and shortly after this a great modern breach in the walls makes way for Millet Cad., one of the two main roads in and out of the city.

In Byzantine times Topkapı was called the Gate of St Romanus after a nearby church dedicated to that saint. Its present name dates from the Conquest for it was here that Mehmet II positioned his most formidable cannon, given the name of Orban, some of whose cannon balls are displayed inside the gate.

Between Topkapı and Edirne Kapı the walls – known here as the

Mesoteichion, the middle wall – drop down into a valley; but where once the river Lycus flowed, is now the Adnan Menderes Bulvarı, largest and newest of the roads in and out of t he city. This section of wall was always the most vulnerable, for the land rises immediately outside it making it the one point where any attacker would have the advantage of height over the defenders. It was here that the fatal breach in the walls was made by the Turks in the early hours of 29 May 1453.

Knowing that all hope was lost, the last Byzantine Emperor, Constantine XI Dragases, stripped off his imperial insignia and launched himself into the advancing Ottoman forces. What became of him no one ever knew for certain, though rumour and legend more than filled the gap. A head, said to be Constantine's, was sent to Mehmet the Conqueror who exhibited it on a column before stuffing it and sending it with macabre vainglory on a tour of the leading cities of the Islamic world. When they searched for the body, it is said that one was found with the imperial eagles embroidered on the buskins.

Edirne Kapı stands at the top of the sixth hill, known to the Byzantines as the Gate of Charisius, but also as the Adrianople Gate for through it the Mese passed on its way to that city. Through it Mehmet the Conqueror rode in triumph into Constantinople that afternoon of 29 May, followed by thousands of cheering Turks, wild with the elation of their conquest.

Detour **Mihrimah Camii**

One of the finest mosques of Süleyman the Magnificent's great architect, Sinan, stands just inside Edirne Kapı, built in 1562–5 for Mihrimah Sultan, Süleyman's favourite daughter and wife of his longest serving Grand Vezir, the deplorable Rüstem Paşa, who had died in 1561. It was a large complex, built on the site of the Byzantine monastery of St George, and attached to it was a medrese, mektep, imaret, hamam, türbe (though not for Mihrimah herself) and shops. Earthquakes have caused much damage and only the mosque and medrese have been consistently restored.

A gateway off the main road gives access to a staircase up to the platform on which the mosque stands. On the right a passage leads to the **courtyard**, a long rectangle with a pretty şadırvan at the centre, bordered on three sides by the **medrese** cells. The irregular shape is caused by the awkwardness of the site (on a hilltop and cheek by jowl with the Theodosian walls), compounded by earthquake damage and subsequent restoration. The 8-columned portico once had a second one in front of it, its sloping roof resting on 12 columns, but there is now no trace of them.

From here we go into the **mosque**, one of the lightest and most feminine of Sinan's interiors. The soaring dome rises from a square base on each side of which is a tympanum pierced by 19 windows, making an almost continuous area of light under the dome. On either side two ancient granite columns, and the piers on the front and back walls, support a lofty triple arcade, through which is a side aisle and gallery under the three domes. Windows, some with stained glass, fill every available space, giving the sense that the mosque is walled with light. The **mihrab** is a simple affair of grey marble, with a stalactite canopy; less simple is the **mimber** which is large and handsomely carved. The stencillers have covered every inch of wall with their designs, but nothing can detract from the miracle of space and light that Sinan create here.

The last section of Theodosian walls runs for another 600 m or so, ending at Tekfur Sarayı. On our way we see the remains of a postern gate, **Porta Xylokerkou** (the gate of the wooden circus, named from an ancient hippodrome in the area), which played an ominous part in the Ottoman attack on 29 May 1453. Inadvertently the gate was left open by the hard-pressed Byzantines, and it was here that the first group of Janissaries entered the city. In the tower beside it the Turkish flag was first raised.

TEKFUR SARAYI (usually closed, but the bekçi may agree to open)

Tekfur Sarayı, the Palace of the Emperor, also known as the Palace of the Porphyrogenitus (born in the purple), is tucked between the inner and outer walls of the Theodosian defences. The word Tekfur is derived from the Armenian 'tagavor', or king, which had for centuries been applied by Muslim writers to the Byzantine Emperor and other Christian rulers. The origins of the palace are uncertain, but it was probably built in the late 13th or early 14th C. as an extension of the Blachernae Palace next door. Today, only a mournful shell survives of what must have been an exceedingly handsome hall. It was a rectangular building of three storeys, built in a mixture of brick and stone to make a striking polychrome design. On the ground floor two double arches open onto a courtyard. Above the arches are five windows with marble frames on the first floor, and seven on the towering second floor. The other façades have similar arched windows, one of the east with the remains of the balcony on the top floor.

After the Conquest the palace was deserted for some time. John Sanderson, visiting Constantinople just over a century later, described it as 'a fragment, standing memory of the ould Emperiall pallas, with certayne galleries, waist romes, and pillors within itself, [and it] doth well shewe the great power of time the distroyer and overthrower of all, that a prince of the wourld his pallas is now become a lodge for oliphants, panthars, and other beasts.' One of its most popular inmates was a giraffe, a *cosa mirabile* for Europeans who had never seen one before. De Busbecq, Imperial ambassador some 40 years before Sanderson, was so mortified that the giraffe of the day had died shortly before his arrival that he had it dug up to satisfy himself about the outlandish rumours of its size and shape.

Towards the end of the 17th C. the palace was converted from a zoo into a brothel; then, in the early 18th C., into the workshop of the famous but short-lived Tekfur Sarayı potteries whose products, while pretty, never matched the quality of the earlier Iznik potteries. Then, at the beginning of the 19th C. it became a home for impoverished Jews. Today it provides an apparently ideal training ground for youthful wall-scalers who are constantly, but ineffectually, shooed away by the bekçi's family.

THE LATER WALLS

Between Tekfur Sarayı and the Golden Horn the walls have been rebuilt several times. The first section, the **walls of Manuel Comnenus**, were built by that Emperor in the 12th C. to allow space for the new Comnene Palace of the Blachernae that was growing ever larger. It is a single wall without a moat, very strongly constructed, with nine towers and a gate, then called the Gate of the Caligaria. Today it is **Eğri Kapı**, crooked gate, from the wiggle in the road as it avoids an 18th C. türbe standing in front of it. The türbe is said to contain the grave of Hazret Hafız, Companion of the Prophet, killed according to pious legend on this very spot during the first Arab siege of Constantinople. Beyond the third tower after Eğri Kapı the wall is of later and inferior construction, with four square towers.

North of these walls are two towers, the **Tower of Isaac Angelus** and the **Prison of Anemas**, both part of the Blachernae Palace. The Emperor Isaac Angelus, who built the tower named after him, was deposed and blinded in 1195 after ten years' rule, and was immured in

34

the Prison of Anemas, a place much favoured for the incarceration and mutilation of unpopular Emperors.

The final stretch of walls, visible from the terrace to the east of the two towers, is again double – the **walls of Leo and Heraclius** – and form a kind of citadel at the northern extremity of the land walls. The inner one is the older and stronger, built by the energetic Emperor Heraclius in 627 in a bid to keep out the Persians and Avars, both of whom were attacking the city. On it is built three magnificent hexagonal towers. In 813 Leo V, under attack from King Krum of the Bulgars, built the outer wall, a much slighter affair with four small towers.

THE PALACE OF THE BLACHERNAE

The terrace to the east of the Tower of Angelus and the Prison of Anemas is the site of the Palace of the Blachernae. It is best approached from Dervişzade Sok., through the entrance to Ivaz Efendi Camii. Although the Palace is rightly associated with the Comnene Emperors of the 12th C., it was Anastasius, in about 500, who first built a palace here, near the immensely sacred shrine associated with the ayazma of the Blachernae.

The Comnenes in the 12th C. turned an occasional residence into a permanent palace, rebuilding, enlarging and embellishing it so that it became the wonder and envy of visitors. When the Jewish Rabbi Benjamin of Tudela visited Constantinople in 1161, during the reign of Manuel Comnenus, he was stunned by its magnificence – 'The pillars and walls are covered with pure gold, and all the wars of the ancients, as well as his [Manuel's] own wars, are represented in pictures. The throne in this palace is of gold, and ornamented with precious stones; a gold crown hangs over it, suspended on a chain of the same material, the length of which exactly admits the emperor to sit under it. This crown is ornamented with precious stones of inestimable value. Such is the lustre of these diamonds, that, without any other light, they illumine the room in which they are kept.'

Small wonder that the rapacious Latins of the Fourth Crusade coveted the city in 1204. It was mainly here that the Latin Emperors lived, stripped of its treasures and deteriorating rapidly from poverty and neglect. After 1261 it was restored for the Palaeologi, the last dynasty of the Byzantine Empire. In 1437, when the Spaniard Pero Tafur visited the city, the Palace of the Blachernae was again suffering from neglect. 'The Emperor's Palace must have been very magnificent,' he writes, 'but now it is in such a state that both it and the city show well the evils which the people have suffered and still endure.' If there was little magnificence then, today there is none.

The most interesting building on the empty site is the pretty **Ivaz Efendi Camii**, just inside the walls on the terrace. It was built in the early 1580s by Kadiasker Ivaz Efendi. The notice above the entrance announces it as a mosque of Sinan; however, it does not appear in the official list of his buildings, though it may have come under his general control. Despite its smallness, inside all is space and light, its chief glory the superb Iznik tiles around the mihrab.

The **ayazma of Blachernae** still exists, about 200 m from Ivaz Efendi Camii, and is still a Christian shrine, though the spring is now housed in a 1960s chapel. Turning left onto the road outside the mosque, follow Dervişzade Sok., the road of the dervish's son, downhill as it curves to the right. At the junction turn left and the road again curves to the right; the shrine is on the right in the middle of a garden. In 451 a church was built over the spring which was believed to have miraculous powers of healing. In it were lodged the robe and mantle of the Virgin, brought from Jerusalem by Pulcheria, the saintly sister of Theodosius II. It was the most important and beloved shrine in a city of shrines, and was regularly visited by the Emperor and his family. It remains a popular place of pilgrimage for the Greeks of the city.

Coda

THE SEA WALLS

Some 26 years after Anthemius built his single land wall, Cyrus, his successor as Prefect of the East, extended Constantine's sea walls along the Golden Horn and the Sea of Marmara to meet the new wall and close the circuit. Along a 5 km stretch of the Golden Horn, the walls, about 10 m high, were reinforced with 110 square defence towers, and there were at least 14 gates into the city; the 8 km Marmara walls, varying from 12 to 15 m in height, had 188 towers and 13 gates. In the 9th C. these walls were rebuilt by the Emperor Theophilus to strengthen the city against Arab attack.

Parts of the surviving Golden Horn walls we will see as we visit the Byzantine churches in that area (Chap. 4). Much of the Marmara walls are in ruins, or have disappeared completely thanks to the building of the railway for the Orient Express in the 1880s, and most of what is left can just as well be seen while driving past to or from the airport. Just under 1 km beyond the modern lighthouse is the only place marginally worth stopping at – the remains of the **sea-palace of the Bucoleon**, so named from a sculpture of a lion attacking a bull that once adorned it. It is identifiable by three great marble-framed windows in a recess in the walls. Once they looked out onto the Porta Leonis, the private harbour of the Great Palace of the Byzantine Emperors, guarded by the statues of two lions (now in the Archaeological Museum). Even in the mid-1950s fishing boats were moored at the foot of the walls; but today a little park with trees and benches fills the space between the walls and the modern coast road. Under the windows once ran a balcony, of which only the marble corbels remain. At ground level is a row of 32 square marble blocks some of which have had their surrounding stones chipped away a little, revealing that they are in fact Doric capitals set on their sides, relics of some 5th C. BC pagan temple from Byzantium, pressed into renewed service in a somewhat unimaginative manner by a later builder.

Originally built by Constantine the Great and rebuilt by Justinian and several of his successors, the Bucoleon was just one of a whole complex of buildings that formed the Great Palace. Now hardly one stone stands on another; but then, within a rough triangle bounded by the church of Haghia Sophia, the hippodrome and the Sea of Marmara, stood the palaces of Magnaura, Mangana, Daphne, Chalke, Bucoleon and the Sacred Palace, and a multitude of churches and pavilions, set in lovely gardens and courtyards, all filled with rare treasures, fountains, lakes and trees. Emperor after Emperor outdid his forebears with new adornments of gold, silver, mosaic and marble. Most spectacular of all, the Emperor Theophilus in the 9th C. introduced fantastic mechanical toys that were the wonder of all who saw them. An iconoclast, he learned from the Caliphs of Baghdad how to indulge in splendid ornaments without infringing the law against images. In a gold enamelled tree perched gilded birds, each singing its own song; near it the Emperor's throne was guarded by golden lions who roared and beat their tails on the ground as a prelude to the whole throne being wafted heavenwards before the astonished gaze of those who had the privilege of an audience with the Emperor.

Even when the 12 C. Comnene Emperors moved to the Palace of the Blachernae, the Great Palace remained a place of breathtaking splendour. Needless to say, it was the Fourth Crusade that put an end to its glory. With all its treasures looted, and the economy in a parlous state, the last Latin Emperor, Baldwin II, was so poor that he used the lead from the palace roofs to mint coins. By the time the Byzantines were restored in 1261, not only was the Great Palace denuded of all adornments, it was too decayed to live in, and the imperial residence was permanently transferred to the better preserved Blachernae Palace. 200 years later, as Mehmet the Conqueror contemplated the desolation of the once fabled palaces of Constantinople, he was moved to quote the Persian poet Saadi:

> The spider is the curtain-holder in the palace of the Caesars,
> The owl hoots its night call on the Towers of Aphrasiab.

The first site in the next chapter is an easy walk from here.

4

JUSTINIAN AND THEODORA

The brilliance of the parvenu Emperor Justinian dominates the 6th C. Inspired by a vision of himself as heir to both Old and New Rome, he set out to restore the full extent of the Empire and to establish within it a unified legal system and a unified church. Only in the law did his massive achievements endure; but there are also his buildings – in particular his miraculous church of Haghia Sophia – which still stand as memorials to the vision of one of the most remarkable and improbable characters of the age.

His uncle Justin, an illiterate peasant from Illyria, had served in the imperial army where, despite the drawbacks of low birth and no education, he had risen to become a commander of the guards. When the Emperor Anastasius I died in 518 Justin, aided by his own low cunning, was the surprising choice as his heir, and when it all proved too much for him, he turned to his clever nephew whom he had brought to Constantinople and given a good education and a job in the civil service.. So influential had he become that when Justin died in 527, Justinian's elevation to the purple merely gave him the title to the role he already held.

For Justinian the grand design – of a universal Empire with himself at its apex – held an irresistible attraction; and he had generals, lawyers, administrators and master-builders of astonishing talent and loyalty through whom he sought to translate the grand design into reality. He also had Procopius, an historian of exceptional literary gifts who wrote two books heroising Justinian's achievements; but he also wrote *The Secret History*, a deliciously scurrilous work as unreliable in its antipathy to the Emperor as his other books are in their eulogy.

From Procopius' less pamphleteering passages we learn that

Justinian was not an impressive-looking man. He was of medium height, lean but not thin despite habitually eating a bare minimum of food; he was 'not uncomely', and 'his complexion remained ruddy even after two days of fasting.' We also learn that he was always accessible to his subjects, and that he was a workaholic – working through the night by the light of a poor lamp, or walking restlessly about the palace – all to no good purpose, according to Procopius, for 'Nature seemed to have removed all baseness from the rest of mankind and to have concentrated it in the soul of this man.' On a more balanced view, Justinian had a brilliant intellect and driving ambition; he was arrogant, but also at times irresolute and vacillating and lacking in physical courage; but he believed he had been chosen by God to restore the power and prestige of the Roman Empire.

Justinian's wife Theodora is an equally complex and fascinating character, and her courage, energy and shrewd cool-headedness provided just the stiffening that the Emperor often needed. Her origins were even shadier than her husband's for her father had been Master of the Bears at the hippodrome, and after his death Theodora had taken up a career on what Procopius euphemistically refers to as 'the stage', where she was a talented comedienne and mimic in performances of a startling lewdness. Moonlighting from this career, Theodora was also a courtesan of apparently infinite variety and resourcefulness, and with an insatiable appetite. Later she plied both trades in Alexandria and other cities of the near East for a couple of years, and it was when she returned to Constantinople that Justinian first saw her, was dazzled by her beauty and fell irretrievably in love with her. He had to raise her to the rank of Patrician and change the law which prohibited senators from marrying courtesans before he could regularise their relationship – a risky thing to do for he was still the upstart nephew of an unrespected Emperor, and his own popularity was already on a knife-edge. But in 527 when Justinian became Emperor, the courtesan Theodora became Empress.

From a very early stage Justinian's autocratic government and the heavy taxes he collected to pay for his grandiose schemes caused bitter resentment. The Blues and Greens, whose aspirations were political as well as sporting and religious, both had a grudge against the new Emperor, the Greens because he was not a Monophysite as they were, the Blues because instead of favouring them as he had before becoming Emperor, he was now making himself independent of their support. Both factions were in the habit of taking to the streets in a manner that the 20th C. might have taken as a model. Gang warfare in 6th C. Constantinople was made more colourful by the hairstyle affected by gang members, disparagingly referred to by more conservative citizens as the 'Hun style'. Procopius says that this involved letting the moustache and beard flow long, 'but the hair of their heads they cut off in front back to the temples, leaving the part behind to hang down to a very great length in a senseless fashion.'

Opposition to the Emperor and his two most hated ministers – Tribonian the lawyer, and John of Cappadocia the praetorian prefect – came to a head in the terrible Nika riots of 532. The Blues and Greens, having for once made common cause and reduced most of the city to smouldering ruins, adopted two nephews of Anastasius I, Hypatius and Pompey, and acclaimed Hypatius as Emperor. Justinian, who had already given in to the extent of replacing Tribonian and John, now appears to have gone into a nervous decline, his hopes of glory crumbling. He was on the point of flight when the redoubtable Theodora stiffened his shattered resolve by indicating that as far as she was concerned, she would rather be a dead Empress than a live nobody, and that the imperial purple would make a fine shroud. There is no doubt that in so doing she changed the course of history. Justinian, shamed into action, ordered out the Imperial Guard under his general Belisarius and, after 30,000 of his opponents had been massacred in the hippodrome, enthusiasm for resistance waned. Hypatius and Pompey were executed along with 18 accomplices, and all their property was confiscated to the imperial coffers. So secure did Justinian feel in his victory that even Tribonian and John were reinstated.

The destruction of so much of Constantinople would strike most people as a disaster. Justinian, in his new mood of firmness and optimism, regarded it as a challenge. His reconstruction of the city was prompt, glorious and cripplingly costly. It also marked a break with the past and its Orpheus-like looking back to the style of ancient Rome; Justinian's new city set the pattern for what came to be known as the Byzantine style. In the churches he had built up to this time, Justinian had already abandoned the simple basilica and adopted a domed plan. Now he gave free rein to this innovative preference, made possible by advances in the science of mathematics, and the new church of Haghia Sophia, completed within six years, demonstrated the final and spectacular triumph of the dome.

As if rebuilding the city were not enough, Justinian also pushed forward his plan of restoring the full extent of the Roman Empire – an even more costly undertaking, and vastly more time-consuming. It appeared to start well, for in 533 Belisarius set sail for North Africa and by the next year had won the territory from the Vandals. Two years later he moved against the Ostrogoths in Italy, and captured Sicily, Naples and Rome with deceptive ease. Then, having taken the Ostrogoth capital of Ravenna in 540, the tide turned and, under their new and energetic leader Totila, the Ostrogoths won back everything that the Byzantines had captured. It was Belisarius' successor Narses who finally, after a long and debilitating war, defeated Totila and restored a devastated Italy to the Byzantine fold in 554. In the meantime Justinian had sent a force against the Visigoths in southern Spain and within a few years that too had been won, almost completing the circuit of Byzantine occupation of the Mediterranean shores.

In the same year as the Nika riots Justinian had concluded an 'everlasting' peace treaty with the mighty Persian King of Kings, Chosroes I Anushirvan, in return for a punitive tribute. If he thought he had bought a secure peace in the east which would leave him untroubled to pursue war in the west, Justinian was soon sadly disillusioned, for in 540 Chosroes attacked the eastern borders of the Byzantine Empire and sacked Antioch. Only by increasing the tribute, with further increases every five years or so, was a fragile peace with Persia maintained.

Justinian's aim of creating a unified church within the unified Empire meant that an accommodation had to be reached not only with the orthodox Papacy in Rome which claimed supreme authority in the Christian church, but also with the Monophysite Patriarchates of Antioch and Alexandria who showed a disturbing enthusiasm for independence. He himself was orthodox, but his own wife, the powerful Theodora, was a Monophysite. Justinian spent much of his life trying to devise compromise formulae that would satisfy everyone. Hardly surprisingly he failed.

Apart from his buildings, Justinian's most enduring achievement was the great codification of Roman law, the work of the brilliant but hated Tribonian, which drew from, though far surpassed, the *Codex Theodosianus* of 100 years before. Working with incredible speed, Tribonian produced the first edition of the *Codex Justinianus* in 529 and the final version five years later. This was followed by three other compilations, and from now on these four works, whose content had been suitably adjusted to the requirements of a Christian society, constituted the *Corpus of Civil Law*, and regulated all matters of public, private and business law both for the individual and for the state.

The execution of Justinian's grand design was at the price of the total economic exhaustion of the Empire. Onerous taxes were extorted and many people became desperately impoverished. It was not unusual for whole villages to be deserted to avoid the tax collectors. Land fell into disuse, leading to even greater hardship. Still Justinian urged his subjects to 'pay the taxes willingly and in full.' Attempts to stimulate trade were short-lived for the profits were too quickly mopped up by the tax collectors. In any case, by the middle of the 6th C. the concept of a universal Empire was an anachronism, for its component parts were so diverse that only the exercise of permanent and overwhelming force could keep it together. For this there were neither the men nor the money. Within a few years of Justinian's death in 565 most of Italy had been lost to the Lombards, and by the early 7th C. southern Spain had been regained by the Visigoths. Justinian's Empire survived only in the East.

THE CHURCH OF SS SERGIUS AND BACCHUS

The earliest of the three surviving Justinianic churches of Constantinople was built inside the sea walls of the Marmara just west of the Great Palace. It is an easy 250 m walk from the south end of the hippodrome, dropping downhill from the SE corner. As the sphendone curves sharply to the right, we turn left, and then right at the main road, Küçük Aya Sofya Cad. After about 100 m we come to a 5-point junction. The first road on the left goes under a rail bridge but we continue straight; a few yards further on we reach, on our left, the gate into the courtyard of the church of SS Sergius and Bacchus, now known as Küçük Aya Sofya Camii, little Aya Sofya mosque.

From the sea walls and the Bucoleon Palace, turn right after about 400 m to go under the rail bridge, then left at the 5-point junction.

The courtyard, with the şadırvan at its centre, has been restored and the surrounding cells now have a library and workshops as well as a café and restaurant. If the mosque is shut, one of the ubiquitous children will probably be able to find the man with the key.

The church owes its origin to two obscure 3rd C. Christian soldiers, martyred in one of the persecutions of Maximian, Diocletian's co-Emperor. As a warrior-Emperor Justinian might be expected to have been particularly devoted to St Sergius and St Bacchus as they were the patron saints of the army; but in addition they had saved his life at a time when he was under sentence of death, accused of plotting against the Emperor Anastasius; the two saints appeared to Anastasius in a dream and interceded on his behalf. When he became Emperor himself in 527 Justinian lost no time in repaying the debt by building this church in the same year. It was one of a pair of adjoining churches, built at an angle to each other. Of this other church, dedicated to SS Peter and Paul, nothing remains. Interestingly it was a basilica, so the old style stood linked with the new domed style that from now on dominated Byzantine architecture.

If the outside of Küçük Aya Sofya disappoints, with its add-on Ottoman portico, the interior is almost guaranteed to delight, not least because of its charming irregularity. It is as though the builders relied on unconfined inspiration rather than bothering with the tiresome restrictions of a plan. What they were aiming at was similar to its near contemporary in Ravenna, the church of San Vitale – an octagon inscribed in a square, with a projecting apse and a large central dome; but here all is delightfully crooked, off-centre and out of alignment. The askew orientation of the mihrab and the mimber compounds the effect which can best be seen from the gallery.

Eight polygonal piers, joined by arches, support the dome which is formed of 16 sections alternately flat and concave. Between the piers – excluding those in front of the apse – are two pairs of columns, the lower ones supporting the gallery and the upper ones a triple arcade within the great arch beneath the dome. These columns are arranged alternately straight along the sides and curved into the exedras at the four corners. The colour of the columns also alternates, with pairs of deep green verd-antique followed by pairs of red Synnada marble. All are crowned with wonderfully carved capitals, as though lace had been made out of marble; the lower ones are of an elegant undulating shape, the so-called 'melon' type; while those above are rather heavy, and square at the top, of a type known as pseudo-Ionic.

All around the church, just above the level of the lower capitals, runs the superbly carved architrave and cornice, in the midst of which is a frieze with a long inscription in honour of the founders of the church – 'our sceptred Justinian, fostering piety,' and the erstwhile courtesan, 'the God-crowned Theodora whose mind is bright with piety.'

Of the rich mosaics and marble revetments that decorated the interior, nothing remains, but Procopius described the church as 'outshining the sun by the gleam of its stones, and adorned throughout with an abundance of gold.' In this glittering environment later in the 6th C. we may imagine the future Pope Gregory the Great saying Mass. He was for several years Papal Nuncio to the Byzantine court and this church had been set aside for the use of those who followed the Latin rite. For its 6th C. decoration we have only the glorious interiors of Ravenna to go by, where no Iconoclasm stripped them of their figurative works, as certainly happened here. The church was redecorated after 867, but was vandalised in 1204 by the Latin Crusaders. Although it remained Christian for about 50 years after the Conquest, it was converted to Islam around 1500 by Hüseyin Ağa, Chief of the White Eunuchs of Sultan Beyazit II.

THE CHURCH OF HAGHIA EIRENE

Returning to the hippodrome and resolutely resisting the temptation to visit Haghia Sophia, keeping it as the *bonne bouche* of our Justinianic exploration, we should turn right before we reach it, and then left at its eastern end. This brings us to the **fountain of Sultan Ahmet III**. For a fountain it is an extraordinarily large and imposing structure, and a charming example of Turkish rococo. Built in 1728, it is square, with a deeply overhanging roof crowned with five little domes, and is decorated with carved marble, tiles, long decorative inscriptions and ornate bronze grilles. The çeşmes on each of the four sides and the sebils atthe four corners are now, alas, entirely dry.

Behind the fountain is the Imperial Gate which leads into the first courtyard of Topkapı Sarayı (see Chap. 9). A short distance inside we see on the left the rose-coloured apse of Haghia Eirene, set in a deep cutting, an indication of the extent to which the surrounding earth has risen. Neither this church, nor its great neighbour Haghia Sophia, is named after a saint but after attributes of God Himself – hence this is the church of the Divine Peace; Haghia Sophia the church of the Divine Wisdom.

Tradition has it that in pre-Christian days there may have been a pagan temple of Peace on the site of Haghia Eirene; and that on its site was built the first Christian church of Byzantium. More certainly, Constantine the Great or Constantius rebuilt the church on a grander scale, and it was used as the cathedral of Constantinople until the first church of Haghia Sophia was dedicated in 360. At that time the two churches stood in the same precinct – it was only after the Ottoman Conquest, when Mehmet the Conqueror built Topkapı Sarayı, that they were divided by the great wall designed to surround and protect the palace. As the acting cathedral Haghia Eirene was at the centre of the bitter controversy between Arianism and orthodoxy that rocked the 4th C. church. So inflamed did the matter become that in 346 a riot broke out in the courtyard here, and over 3000 people died. Less riotous, but equally impassioned, were the deliberations of the Second Ecumenical Council, held here in 381. From Haghia Eirene the doctrine formulated at the earlier Council of Nicaea was issued in what we know as the Nicene Creed.

When Haghia Sophia was burnt down for the first time in 404, Haghia Eirene was again used as the cathedral church until the new Haghia Sophia was dedicated 11 years later. Then, in 532, both churches were destroyed in the Nika riots, and Justinian rebuilt them side by side, Haghia Sophia with its dazzling new style, Haghia Eirene a more tentative combination of the old basilica and the new Greek-cross plan with a dome over the crossing. A year before Justinian's death it was badly damaged by a fire, but it was promptly restored. It was almost destroyed by a severe earthquake in 740, and again it was restored in its original style – permanently this time.

Unlike most churches, it was never converted into a mosque after the Conquest; instead Mehmet the Conqueror gave it to the Janissaries who used it as an arsenal for the defence of the Saray for nearly 400 years. When Mahmut II abolished the Janissaries in 1826, the building was used as a store for antiquities, later taken to the Archaeological Museum, and at the turn of the century it was opened as a military museum – also removed to new premises. It has recently been restored, and was re-opened in September 1987 as an exhibition hall. It is also used for concerts, in particular during the international Istanbul Festival.

A stone ramp takes us down into the church from the entrance on the north side. It brings us to the back of the **nave** under a lovely elliptical dome, with the narthex on our right at the west end. A wooden staircase (a Turkish addition) leads up to the galleries which run down both sides of the nave. A first glance down the wide, empty nave gives the impression of a domed basilica, with great piers and arches supporting the main dome, and between the piers on the north and south an arcade springing from four columns. But as we walk up the nave, and stand under the great dome, the cruciform shape becomes clear for the arms and head of the cross are indicated by deep barrel vaults behind the arcades and in front of the apse.

The **apse** is semi-circular, with a synthronon, rows of seats for the clergy, rising within its curve. Unusually, this has an enclosed ambulatory running underneath it. It probably dates to the 8th C. restoration; and from the same period, when Iconoclasm was the order of the day, is the mosaic in the semi-dome of the apse – a simple cross outlined in black on a gold ground. The semi-dome is bordered with a geometric design within which is a quotation from Psalm 65, vv 4–5; 'Blessed is the man whom thou dost choose and bring near, to dwell in thy courts! We shall be satisfied with the goodness of thy house, thy holy temple! By dread deeds thou dost answer us with deliverance, O God of our salvation, who art the hope of all the ends of the earth, and of the farthest seas.' This mosaic is all we have of the early decoration of the interior of the church.

At the west end of the nave five doors lead into the **narthex**, where the mosaic remains are almost certainly from Justinian's time. From there we can go into the **atrium**. The regular rectangle of the inner courtyard is deceptive, partly because it is a Turkish addition, but also because it masks the irregularity of the outer walls, for the western end is built at a deviant angle making the north portico longer than the south. In it are two enormous porphyry sarcophagi, one without a lid. The atrium has been closed to the public for many years, and various schemes have been rumoured for its future use – so far unrealised.

Detour **Soğuk Çeşme Sokağı**

This is not a geographical detour, for it is on the way to our next Justinianic site, but it is a considerable detour in time.

Returning through the Imperial Gate to the fountain of Ahmet III, we should turn right and walk along the little cobbled street that runs between the Topkapı wall and Haghia Sophia. Soğuk Çeşme Sok., cold fountain road, is bordered by charming wooden houses built against the Topkapı wall. In the early 80s they showed all the signs of crumbling into oblivion, but then they were bought by the Turkish Touring and Automobile Club which has restored and furnished them in their original 19th C. style, and opened them in the autumn of 1986 as a series of tourist guest-houses – the Aya Sofya Pansiyonları.

Towards the lower end of the street one of the buildings has been turned into a library, the special brain-child of the Touring Club's then Director, Dr Çelik Gülersoy, who started if off with his own collection of books on Istanbul. The library is on the first floor and is a pleasant airy room, its walls lined with bookcases, or hung with 19th C. engravings of Istanbul. Çelik Gülersoy's dream is that it will become a research centre, housing all published works on the city.

YEREBATAN SARAYI/THE BASILICA CISTERN
Open daily

Where Soğuk Çeşme Sok. divides, we take the left fork along the west side of Haghia Sophia. At the main road we cross over, and a few metres along Yerebatan Cad. on the left is Yerebatan Sarayı, the sunk-into-the-ground palace. In Byzantine times it was known as the

Basilica Cistern because it lay beneath the Stoa Basilica, one of the two great public squares on the first hill.

The Basilica Cistern was built by Justinian after the Nika riots to extend the water supply because, as Procopius tells us, 'in the summer season the imperial city used to suffer from scarcity of water as a general thing, though at the other season it enjoyed a sufficiency.' The water stored here supplied the Great Palace and other buildings in the area; after the Conquest it was diverted to keep the gardens of Topkapı Sarayı green and blooming. It seems that the source of the water was forgotten, for when the inquisitive Frenchman Pierre Gilles visited the city in the mid-16th C. he found people lowering buckets through holes in their floors and bringing up water, but with not the least suspicion of where the water came from. By chance he went into a house with steps that led down into the cistern and was astonished at the magnificent sight that met his eyes.

Today we pay our money at the ticket office and descend a stairway to the well restored cistern, one of the most remarkable monuments in the city. It is worth remembering that it is merely one of many that stored water for Constantinople, though it is the largest and, in its restored state, unquestionably the most beautiful. 336 vast columns, some with Corinthian capitals or carved bases, and in 12 rows of 28, support the fine brick vaulting, covering an overall area of 140 by 70 m. In the course of restoration, when the cistern was drained of its water, it was found that two of the columns were resting on huge and magnificent carvings of Medusa heads, one on its side, the other upside down, both very similar to one in the Archaeological Museum. There is also a very handsome column with a peacock-eye design carved all over it, like the remnants beside the erstwhile forum of Theodosius. Now the water has been restored, and the receding lines of columns stretch with their reflections into the distance, rather disconcertingly lit by coloured and flickering lights, and accompanied by Beethoven's 5th Symphony piped over the echoing loudspeaker system.

5

HAGHIA SOPHIA

Open daily except Monday

The first church of Haghia Sophia was probably planned by Constantine the Great, but it was built by his son and heir Constantius II, and dedicated by him on 15 February 360. It lasted barely 44 years for on 20 June 404 it was burned down by a riotous mob in protest at the exile of their beloved Patriarch, John Chrysostom. The ruins lay untouched until Theodosius II became Emperor some four years later, and the second church of Haghia Sophia was dedicated on 10 October 415. Its lifespan showed some improvement on that of its predecessor, but in January 532 it too was destroyed by another mob in the conflagration caused by the Nika riots.

Showing a fine disregard for mere money, Justinian put compulsory purchase orders on all the buildings on the site that had survived the fire, for the express purpose of pulling them down; he ordered the finest marbles from the quarries of Greece, Egypt, Africa and Asia Minor; and he brought the most skilled workmen from all over the Empire to Constantinople. They began work just one month after the disaster; 7000 stone-masons, bricklayers, plasterers, carpenters, painters, sculptors, mosaicists, sweepers and polishers worked over-time to complete the work in record time – it took only 5 years and 10 months.

As master-builders Justinian chose two Greek mathematicians from Asia Minor who were not primarily builders at all, though both had translated works by Archimedes on structure and pulleys. The chief was Anthemius of Tralles, celebrated in the field of solid geometry and the construction of burning mirrors; while his assistant, Isidorus of Miletus, an expert on Plato and Pythagoras, had recently been made

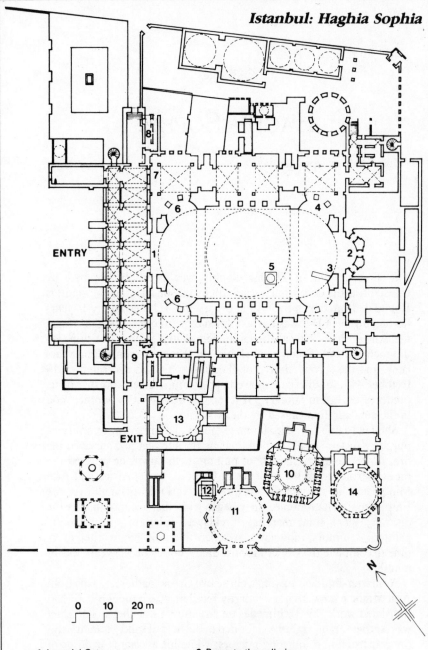

Istanbul: Haghia Sophia

ENTRY

EXIT

0   10   20 m

N

1 Imperial Gate
2 Apse and mihrab
3 Mimber
4 Imperial loge
5 Muezzins' Tribune
6 Alabaster lustration urns
7 Perspiring column

8 Ramp to the galleries
9 Vestibule of the Warriors
10 Türbe of Selim II
11 Türbe of Murat III
12 Türbe of the Princes
13 Baptistery/Türbe of Mustafa I and Ibrahim
14 Türbe of Mehmet III

redundant when Justinian had seen it as his Christian duty to close the highly renowned, but pagan, Academy of Athens in 529.

It was precisely the enormous advances in mathematics, together with the brilliant application of those mathematical principles to architecture that Anthemius and Isidorus achieved, that made Justinian's choice of master-builders such an inspired one. First the complex theory was worked out on paper, then it was put to the test in marble, stone and brick. None the less, it must have been an acutely experimental process, even allowing for Procopius' hyperbole in recounting occasions when things went dangerously wrong and Anthemius and Isidorus, terrified at the possibility of disaster, took the problem to Justinian who, 'impelled by I know not what, but I suppose by God (for he is not himself a master-builder)', gave them the solution. By such miracles was Haghia Sophia built. Never again did the Byzantines attempt anything so risky or so magnificent.

On 26 December 537, St Stephen's Day, the new church of the Divine Wisdom was dedicated. The Patriarch Menas received the Emperor at the great west door, the Orea Porta, or Beautiful Gate; and as Justinian entered the completed church he proclaimed with imperial modesty, 'Glory to God who has deemed me worthy of accomplishing such a work! Oh Solomon, I have surpassed thee!'

Yet even within Justinian's lifetime disaster struck, for in 558 an earthquake brought down the eastern arch and semi-dome and the eastern half of the dome itself. By rights, the earthquake should not have caused so much damage, but it showed up the fact that Anthemius' design had been too daring in one respect – the spectacular shallowness of the dome had created such an outward thrust as to distort the great piers and arches on which it rested. The work of rebuilding was given to another Isidorus, nephew of Isidorus of Miletus, and he solved the problem by adding a low drum with buttresses all round the outside, and by increasing the height of the dome which he supported by 40 ribs and pierced by 40 windows. He also wisely strengthened the side walls. However, part of the dome collapsed again in 989; the two enormous buttresses we see on both sides were added in 1317, but despite this another part of the dome collapsed in 1346. The damage was once again successfully repaired, and the dome we see today is still basically the work of Isidorus the Younger.

Many churches in the Empire had to indulge in trade in order to make ends meet; and to make their income more secure, rights of monopoly and exemption from taxation were frequently acquired. On the assumption that mortality was likely to remain at 100%, Haghia

Sophia had providently cornered the market in funerals for the whole of Constantinople. The considerable income that this generated was much needed, for the staff of the church consisted of 60 priests, 100 deacons, 40 deaconesses, 90 sub-deacons, 110 readers, 25 singers and 100 door-keepers.

On 13 April 1204 the Byzantine capital fell to the mixed Venetian, French and Flemish forces of the Fourth Crusade. For three days these Christians of the West pillaged, raped and massacred their co-religionaries of the east. In Haghia Sophia drunken looters tore apart the altar and iconostasis, dividing the silver and gold between them; sacred vessels, also of silver and gold, were used to increase the general drunkenness and then pocketed; sacred books and icons which could not be melted down were trampled underfoot; mules brought into the church to carry off the loot skidded and fell on the polished marble floors; and a prostitute climbed onto the Patriarchal throne, sang a lewd French song and kicked up her heels in a dance.

Nearly 250 years later Haghia Sophia witnessed a similar nightmare. On the evening of 28 May 1453 the people of Constantinople made their way to the Great Church. In the flickering light of a thousand candles and lamps, they held their last desperate service of intercession for God's help against the Turks at their walls. Later that night the Emperor Constantine XI Dragases rode from his post on the walls to join them, then returned to await the final assault. The following morning hordes of Turkish soldiers, wild with elation from their victory, forced their way into the church where many men, women, children, nuns and monks had taken refuge. Some were killed on the spot; most were tied together in pairs, and many of the young girls and boys were assaulted and almost torn to pieces as their captors fought to possess them. Gold and silver vessels, jewelled reliquaries, and all the treasures of the church were snatched; altars were used as tables, and then thrown over for the horses to feed from.

That afternoon Mehmet the Conqueror rode into the city and went first to Haghia Sophia. In marked contrast to his soldiers earlier in the day, he stooped at the door to gather a handful of earth which he sprinkled over his turban as a symbol of humility before God. Then, when he had entered the church, he ordered one of his men into the pulpit to proclaim, 'There is no God but God, and Mohammed is the Prophet of God.' For the first time the Muslim ritual was performed in this Christian church which from now on was known as the mosque of Aya Sofya. No change of name was necessary since Holy Wisdom belongs also to Allah; but the building had fallen into disrepair in the last decades of the Byzantine Empire, and Mehmet put in hand extensive repairs.

Aya Sofya, its specifically Christian mosaics gradually painted and plastered into oblivion, and with the addition of a mihrab and mimber and all the trappings of an imperial mosque, kept its supreme place in the worship of the Ottoman capital for nearly 500 years. Mehmet the Conqueror had the first minaret built at the SE corner; his son, Beyazit II balanced it with another on the NE; and the two on the western corners were built in the 1570s for Murat III by the great Sinan. In the mid-19th C. Sultan Abdül Mecit I commissioned two Swiss architects, the Fossati brothers, to survey and repair the mosque.

The final stage of its history began in 1935, when Atatürk turned Aya Sofya into a museum, to the consternation of many Muslims. If its atmosphere of worship has gone, so too have the layers of paint and plaster that covered the mosaics which now stand revealed in something of their former brilliance.

The interior

Like Justinian the Great on that St Stephen's Day 537, we enter Haghia Sophia through the not noticeably beautiful Orea Porta, recently reopened after centuries of closure. The atrium in front of the original gate no longer exists. Our first step inside is into the long narrow exo-narthex from which five doors lead into the **narthex**, a splendid vestibule of nine vaulted bays, each with a door leading into the church. The ceiling of the narthex still retains some of its original mosaic, none of it figurative so it survived both the demolition of the Iconoclasts and the less destructive plaster and paint of the Ottomans. The great central door, the **Imperial Gate**, said to have been made from the wood of Noah's Ark, was reserved for the Emperor and his procession.

In the lunette above the Imperial Gate we see the first of the great mosaics of Haghia Sophia, the **mosaic of Leo VI**. It was re-discovered in 1933 when the building was still a mosque, and it shows Christ enthroned, his left hand holding a Gospel with the Greek legend – 'Peace be with you. I am the light of the world' – and his right hand raised to bless the prostrated figure of the Emperor Leo VI (886–912). He was known as Leo the Wise, though more for his intellect than for his marital habits. He was an enthusiastic preacher, and the images of his patrons, the Virgin and the Archangel Gabriel, in roundels on either side of Christ, may recall his famous early sermon on the Annunciation. However, later in life his interest in theology and church law began to look merely academic for on the death of his second wife who had proved as unfruitful as his first, Leo married for a third time, a state of affairs not sanctioned by the eastern church. When even this wife died childless, Leo resigned himself to the inevitable – until his mistress Zoë Carbonospina (coal-black eyes) bore him a son. In his haste to legitimize the child, Leo scandalized everyone by marrying for the fourth time, and was promptly excommunicated by the enraged Patriarch, Nicholas Mysticus. At Christmas 906, and again 12 days later at Epiphany, Leo VI was turned away from Haghia Sophia within sight of the door over which he now prostrates himself. Whether this mosaic was in situ at the time is unknown; but his expression would seem to indicate an awareness of a need for forgiveness.

Now, as we enter the Great Church, we can see for ourselves something of what Anthemius and Isidorus achieved. Gone is the wealth of light-reflecting mosaics and the high polish on the marble surfaces which caused Procopius to wonder at the 'radiance' and 'abundance of light.' To us the light seems dim, though far from religious after several decades of deconsecration. Its atmosphere now is of a building that has outlived its purpose, like a very grand railway station where trains no longer run and only the empty shell remains, old and grey, though still with much of its ancient finery. Repainting has certainly brightened this magnificent building, but it can never restore the atmosphere of worship. Yet there is still a magic here, some whiff of past glory which we draw willy-nilly from what is left of the mosaics with their shining gold and colour; from the astonishing delicacy of the carving of the capitals; from the harmonious proportions which enclose that spectacular space; and, suspended over all, that miraculous dome which dominates every view of the interior.

The vital statistics of the church are as follows: the dome, rising to a height of 56 m, covers an area roughly 31 m square, and rests on four huge and irregular piers. Four great arches join the piers, and the four pendentives translate the square into the circle of the base of the dome. To east and west two smaller piers support the semi-domes which extend the central space, with semi-circular exedras on either side of the Imperial Gate on the west and the recessed apse on the east. The north and south sides of the central square each have four huge monolithic columns of verd-antique which support the galleries, in which six smaller verd-antique columns support the tympanum walls within the semi-circle of the great arch, each pierced by 12 windows. In the exedras, two monolithic porphyry columns support the gallery, with six of verd-antique supporting the semi-dome. Through the arches to north and south are the vaulted side aisles, in which further columns and piers support the gallery.

Walls and piers are covered with magnificent **revetments of polychrome marble**, the blocks sliced in two or four and opened out like the leaves of a book to create lovely 'mirror-image' patterns in the veining. So brilliant was the effect that Procopius declared that 'one might imagine that he had come upon a meadow with its flowers in full bloom. For he would surely marvel at the purple of some, the green tint of others and at those on which the crimson glows and those from which white flashes, and again at those which Nature, like some painter, varies with the most contrasting colours.' In counterpoint with the revetments are the superbly carved **capitals**, lace-like in the delicacy of their acanthus leaf designs; inset on medallions are the joint monograms of Justinian and Theodora.

Some of the original Justinianic mosaic decoration survives in the side aisles, none of it figurative, and also in those 13 ribs of the dome which have remained in place since Isidorus the Younger built it. The rest of the dome is painted to match. The design once included a great cross. On the two eastern pendentives, the **seraphim** or cherubim probably date to the restoration after the partial collapse of the dome in 1346; the two western ones are 19th C. painted copies done by the Fossatis.

In the conch of the apse is the lovely **mosaic of the Virgin Mary with the infant Christ**. Against a gold background, the Virgin in a deep blue robe sits on a jewelled and cushioned throne. Her hands rest gently on Christ's right shoulder and left knee; while He holds a Gospel in His left hand and raises His right hand in blessing. This was the first figural mosaic to be executed in Haghia Sophia after the restoration of icons in 843; it was dedicated on Easter Day 867 by the Patriarch Photius. It was considerably restored in the 14th C.

On the south side of the vault in front of the apse are the remains of a **mosaic of the Archangel Gabriel** whose face is of exceptional beauty. In his right hand is a staff, and in his left an orb – clearly of transparent crystal since his thumb can be seen through it on the other side. A cloak falls in graceful folds over an embroidered undergarment at ankle level, and his magnificent multi-coloured wings sweep down to the ground. On the opposite wall the Archangel Michael has fared worse than Gabriel; all that is left of him are a few desultory feathers.

Looking up to the base of the tympanum on the north side of the nave, above the gallery arcade, we can see mosaics in three of the seven niches. From left to right they represent St Ignatius the Younger, St John Chrysostom and St Ignatius Theophorus, all three canonised patriarchs of the early church.

In the extreme NW corner of the church is the curious **perspiring column**, which has legendary powers attributed to St Gregory Thaumaturgus, the miracle-worker. For centuries the pious and credulous – especially those with ophthalmic or fertility problems – have dipped a finger into the cavity in the column and have withdrawn it wet with the moisture drawn up, they say, within the column itself – a sign of the efficacy of St Gregory. For me it has always been quite dry.

Turkish additions to the interior
Mehmet the Conqueror ordered the first acts needed to convert the church into a mosque – the setting of a mihrab into the apse and the erection of a mimber. According to Evliya Celebi, Murat III in the late 16th C. commissioned several new additions to the interior: near the piers are 'four raised stone platforms for the readers of the Koran, and a lofty pulpit on slender columns for the muezzins.' He also installed the two splendid **alabaster lustration urns**, one in each of the western exedras, 'for all the congregation to perform their ablutions and quench their thirst.' Evliya says they were brought from the island of Marmara, and they are believed to be of Hellenistic workmanship from Pergamum.

In the 17th C. Murat IV built a marble **preacher's throne** between the columns of the north arcade; and the grand imperial loge in the NE exedra was built by the Fossatis for Abdül Mecit I in the mid-19th C. The Fossatis also had to put up the eight huge round green **medallions**, inscribed in gold with the names of Allah, the Prophet Mohammed and the first Caliphs and Imams. As calligraphy they are superb, the work of Mustafa Izzet Efendi; as ornaments in this building they are hopelessly out of place, breaking the harmonious lines of the great piers and arches.

The galleries and gallery mosaics
Access to the galleries is through a door at the northern end of the narthex which leads to a ramp – better than steps when those of exalted rank had to be carried, or for those who rode up on horseback. Having ourselves climbed up on foot in a rectangular spiral, we emerge at the corner of the west and north arms of the gallery, all of which used to be reserved for the use of women.

In the **north gallery**, on the east face of the first pier, is the **mosaic of the Emperor Alexander**, the brother and nominal co-Emperor of the

56

much married Leo VI whom we saw prostrating before Christ above the Imperial Gate in the narthex. Alexander had been a devout hedonist all his life, with not the least interest in government, and when Leo died in 912, with his son Constantine VII only 6 years old, Alexander's assumption of power did nothing to change his habits. Fortunately, he only survived a year in the job, and it was during that time that he had this mosaic portrait made. A nod to God is given in the four inscribed medallions which read, 'Lord help thy servant, the orthodox and faithful Emperor Alexander.' The mosaic was found in 1958.

On the other side of this pier is a splendid graffito of a galleon with billowing sails. There are several other graphic **graffiti** in the galleries, but most are written, indicating the names, places and dates of people who attended, and seem to have been bored by, long services here in the distant Byzantine past.

In the middle of the **west gallery** a circle of green marble is let into the floor in front of the balustrade, with columns on either side. This was the site of the **Empress's throne**, from which she observed the colourful pageant of the services below, and enjoyed a spectacular view of the interior of the church.

Turning left into the **south gallery**, we pass through the so-called **Gates of Heaven and Hell**, an elaborate marble screen of whose origins nothing is known, though it is thought that synods of the church used to be held on the far side of it.

The latest in date of the mosaics in Haghia Sophia, and one of the finest works of art of the whole Byzantine era, is a short distance beyond the Gate on our right, on the eastern face of the first bay – the **mosaic of the Deesis** (intercession). Although large portions are missing, the faces of the three figures are virtually unmarred. Christ stands between the Virgin and John the Baptist who intercede for the sins of the world. There has been much difference of opinion over when the Deesis was executed, varying between the early 12th and the late 14th C.; but the astonishing refinement and delicacy of the modelling of the faces, almost in the manner of painting, have led most scholars to identify it with the Palaeologue Revival that followed the restoration of the Byzantine Empire in 1261, and to date it to the early 14th C.

In the floor opposite the Deesis is the **tombstone of Henry Dandolo**, Doge of Venice, the man who, more than any other, was responsible for the destruction of Constantinople in 1204. In the division of power that followed the Latin victory, the Venetians were allotted nearly half the city, including Haghia Sophia. For 14 months

Henry Dandolo ruled over his new domain, and on his death on 16 June 1205 his memorial stone was placed here in the gallery.

At the eastern end of the south gallery are the last two mosaic panels that remain inside the church. The first one we see is the later of the two, the **mosaic of the Emperor John II Comnenus and the Empress Eirene**. In the centre stands the Virgin holding in her arms the infant Christ who holds a scroll in his left hand while his right is extended in blessing. The Emperor John offers a bag of money, while the Empress Eirene presents a scroll. Above them are inscriptions identifying their names, titles and piety. So great was Eirene's piety that she was later canonised – a habit in her family, it seems, for her father was St Ladislas, King of Hungary. John was the son of the great Emperor Alexius Comnenus, and his moneybag represents the 1000 gold pieces he gave for the embellishment of the church. On the adjoining pier an extension of the mosaic portrays John and Eirene's son Alexius. While the main panel is believed to date to 1118, the year that John came to the throne, the extension was added in 1122 when Alexius was proclaimed co-Emperor at the age of 17. Within a few months he was dead.

To the left of this panel is the **mosaic of the Empress Zoë and Constantine IX Monomachus**, executed almost 100 years earlier and considerably less fluent in style. Between the royal couple Christ sits enthroned, a jewelled Gospel in his left hand, and his right hand raised to bless. Here, too, the Emperor holds a moneybag and the Empress a scroll, while above their heads their names, exalted stations and piety are duly attested.

Piety is not the first word one thinks of with Zoë. When her father Constantine VIII died in 1028 his heirs were his middle-aged, unmarried daughters, Eudocia, Zoë and Theodora. Eudocia was ruled out since she was a nun and also deeply pock-marked from smallpox; and the 50 year old Zoë elbowed Theodora out of the way and launched herself into a spectacular series of marriages and affairs, apparently making up for lost time. When her first husband and co-Emperor, Romanus III Argyrus, was murdered in his bath in 1034 (with Zoë's approval), she married her young lover, a peasant's son from Paphlagonia, who became Michael IV. When he died in 1041, he was succeeded as co-Emperor by his odious nephew Michael V Calaphates whom Zoë had been persuaded to adopt. It was an unwise move, for he soon had her banished to a nunnery on the island of Prinkipo in the Sea of Marmara; but the evergreen and surprisingly popular Zoë had him deposed and blinded and, at the age of 64, married Constantine IX Monomachus who survived her. Zoë died in 1050 aged 72.

It is worth noticing that Constantine's head and the inscription above it have been altered – probably the original was of Zoë's first husband, and the unfortunate mosaicist then had to keep up with her matrimonial progress. But the heads of Zoë, and of Christ himself, have also been changed. It is easy enough to suppose that Michael V had his difficult adoptive mother's head erased, and that she herself had it restored, along with that of her new husband, to this image of sugar-sweet youth. But why Christ's head had to be restored is a puzzle.

Descending to the ground floor by the same ramp, we walk the length of the narthex to the door at the far end which leads into the **Vestibule of the Warriors**, at the far end of which a great gate leads outside. For centuries this was the main entrance after the original gate on the west had been closed, and the name – Orea Porta – seems to have moved with it. The name of the vestibule comes from its function as a waiting room for the Emperor's bodyguard while their master was inside the church.

On the ceiling are some lovely geometric design mosaics which have survived from Justinian's time. But of supreme interest is the magnificent **mosaic of Constantine and Justinian with the Virgin and Child** in the lunette above the door we have just come through. Like the mosaic of Leo VI in the narthex, this was found in 1933 and has been restored to its former brilliance. In the centre the Virgin sits enthroned holding in her arms the infant Christ who holds a Gospel in his left hand and blesses with his right. To their left stands Constantine the Great, identified by an inscription, 'Constantine the great Emperor among the Saints', offering to the Virgin and Child a model of his walled city of Constantinople. On the other side 'Justinian the illustrious Emperor' offers a model of his church, Haghia Sophia. It is believed to be a work of the late 10th or early 11th C., executed during the reign of Basil II, the Bulgar Slayer.

The splendid **bronze doors** through which we leave Haghia Sophia are Hellenistic work of the 2nd C. BC from a temple in the ancient city of Holmi (present-day Taşucu). They were not part of Justinian's church, but were added in the 10th C.

Detour   Ottoman türbes of Aya Sofya

Turning left soon after leaving Aya Sofya, we find a pretty paved garden filled with 16th C. türbes. Here five Ottoman Sultans, several wives and an inordinate number of princes and princesses lie buried. Not all the türbes tend to be open all the time.

Türbe of Selim II

The first türbe to be built here is the second of the two that face us as we enter the garden. This square domed building was built by the great Sinan for Selim II, commonly known as Selim the Sot, the short, fat, alcoholic and unappealing son and heir of Süleyman the Magnificent. He became Sultan in 1566 and died eight years later in a manner that fitted with his life: drunk with Cyprus wine, he tottered to take a bath, slipped on the shiny marble floor of the hamam and broke his skull.

This magnificent türbe was completed three years after his death, adorned around the doorway and throughout the interior with the finest Iznik tiles. Beside Selim's outsize sarcophagus is that of his scheming favourite wife, the Venetian-born Nur Bânu Sultan, who died in 1583; and around them are those of various of Selim's children and grandchildren – a total of 42. Selim's sons were strangled within hours of his death, on the orders of their eldest brother Murat who, we are told, gave the order reluctantly and with tears, persuaded by his ministers, and probably by his mother, that his own safety depended on it.

Türbe of Murat III

Retracing our footsteps a little, we come to the türbe of Selim II's son and heir, Murat III, who died in 1595. Murat had been addicted to money and women, though it is unclear in which order, but also to intellectual pursuits and building. It was he who built the last two minarets of the mosque of Aya Sofya, and we have already seen his benefactions to the interior of the mosque.

His türbe was built by Davut Ağa, Sinan's successor as chief architect. It was completed four years after Murat's death and, like that of his father, is decorated with superb Iznik tiles. Inside, apart from Murat himself, a large crowd is buried: his favourite wife Sâfiye Sultan; 19 of his sons, strangled – apparently also with regret – by order of their eldest brother, Mehmet III; 21 daughters, 17 of whom died of plague; and 12 others including a handful of his concubines – 54 people in all. Small wonder that 32 of Murat's children had to be buried in his father's türbe. It was said that Murat fathered 103 children altogether and became epileptic as a result of so much activity.

Türbe of the Princes

This little türbe stands just to the right of Murat III's, and in it lie five sons of Murat IV (1623–40). The strangling of younger brothers of the new Sultan had by this time become outmoded; they were instead incarcerated in part of the Topkapı harem that came to be known as

Kafes, the Cage. There they were protected from all outside influences, and prevented from any independent action. They were not, however, immune from the periodic bouts of plague that swept the city – hence these five princes.

The Baptistery/Türbe of Mustafa I and Ibrahim
On the other side of the path from the main türbes stands the former baptistery of Haghia Sophia, part of Justinian's original structure. It was converted to its new role in 1623 on the death of Mustafa I, the first Sultan to come to the throne after many debilitating years in the Cage. So vacant and demented was he that he was deposed and sent back to the Cage after only three months. Four years later, when his considerably less insane nephew, Osman II, had displeased the Janissaries sufficiently for them to arrange for his deposition and murder (the first, but certainly not the last, case of regicide in Ottoman history), Mustafa was dragged back to the throne. His second term lasted 16 months before he was deposed and quietly strangled.

25 years later Mustafa was joined by his equally demented nephew, known as Mad Ibrahim, younger brother of Osman II and Murat IV, Sultan for eight brutish years after 22 years in the Cage. Having drained his physical strength in the harem, his military strength on a long and costly siege of Candia in Crete, and what was left in the exchequer on his insatiable passion for furs, the Janissaries moved in and deposed him in favour of his 7 year old son Mehmet IV. Ibrahim was returned to the Cage where he became yet madder and caused so much disturbance that he too was strangled – the third regicide in four reigns.

Türbe of Mehmet III
Passing again the türbe of Selim II, we come to the last, and latest in date, of the türbes in this imperial graveyard, that of Mehmet III, son and heir of Murat III, an octagonal building, also adorned with superb Iznik tiles. It just misses the 16th C. since Mehmet III died in 1603, after eight years of being ruled by his mother, the redoubtable Sâfiye Sultan. Mehmet was the first Sultan since Süleyman the Magnificent to lead his army into battle, but this sounds more dashing than it was since he remained in imperial inactivity on the edge of the battlefield, surrounded by his bodyguard.

6

LATER BYZANTINE CHURCHES

Justinian's successors were unable to keep the newly recovered territories of the Empire. Chronically short of funds, and consequently of popularity and manpower, succeeding Emperors could do nothing to hold on to the west because they were already overstretched in the north by the Avars and Slavs and, most debilitating of all, in the east by the Persians. Then there were the Arabs, newly welded into a powerful force by the Prophet Mohammed. Soon after his death in 632 Arab armies under the banner of Islam attacked and captured large and wealthy areas of the Byzantine Empire, and penetrated deep into Asia Minor. For the next two centuries the Arabs posed the most persistent and powerful threat to the reduced and impoverished Empire. They also took to the sea, and by 655 had occupied Cyprus, Rhodes and Cos and defeated the once supreme Byzantine fleet. It was patently clear that their goal was Constantinople itself.

In 674 the Arabs began their first siege of the city by land and sea, and the chances for Constantinople would have been slim had it not been for the genius of an architect and mathematician called Callinicus, a refugee from Baalbec, who invented Greek fire which decimated the Arab fleet. After four years of terrible losses, the Arabs called off the siege, only to renew it in 717. Once again Greek fire and the mighty walls of the city forced them to give up, this time after only one year. By now the Byzantines had one of their most competent Emperors, Leo III, who in 726 defeated the Arabs so convincingly that the effects were to last for many years. However, it was not until 863 that a decisive victory over the Arabs in northern Asia Minor finally altered the balance of power in favour of the Byzantines.

Religious controversy, that peculiarly Byzantine obsession, took yet another turn at this period, closely linked with the low ebb in Byzantine fortunes. Threatened by Bulgars and Arabs, and unable to remedy the parlous state into which the Empire had declined, Leo III concluded that God must be allowing such ills to touch his chosen people because of some error they had fallen into. Increasingly he came to believe that the cult of icons, which had been growing since the 6th C., was the cause of God's disfavour. Was not the representation of God and his saints a form of idolatry? In 726 Leo preached a sermon in Haghia Sophia, condemning the use of icons, and then he ordered the destruction of all images of Christ and the saints. Opposition was immediate and widespread; but when Leo won such a resounding victory over the Arabs soon after, it seemed – to him at least – like a restoration of God's favour and a vindication of Iconoclasm.

Constantine V was the most fervent Iconoclast of all, and in his reign persecution of Iconodules reached its barbaric peak, creating a terrible split in Byzantine society. It was not until 843 that icons were finally restored, and when Michael III won his great victories over the Arabs and the Bulgars some 20 years later, it seemed that God smiled on the Iconodules after all.

The Macedonian dynasty

After 300 years of struggle for survival, the Byzantine Empire now entered two centuries of territorial expansion and artistic revival under the Macedonian dynasty. For the first time there was an imperial family that lasted more than a few generations, and the resulting stability provided a stimulus for creativity.

Artists and craftsmen, free of the constraints of Iconoclasm, launched themselves with enthusiasm into a revival of religious art. Mosaics, illuminated manuscripts, ivory carvings, gold, silver and enamel work – all showed new vitality and freedom. Literature blossomed too: historians, biographers, poets and encyclopaedists poured out work, and copyists transcribed ancient manuscripts, both religious and secular, onto new vellum in the new style of writing. This renewal was especially alive under the erudite Leo VI and his son Constantine VII, who was not only a prolific writer of distinction, but no mean artist and craftsman.

The two Basils contributed little to this; soldiers first and last, they concentrated on territorial conquest. It was the Bulgars who caused the most trouble, twice reaching the walls of Constantinople. Their final stand was under the energetic King Samuel, and Basil II spent most of his reign bringing the Bulgars to heel. In 1014, having crushed their main army, Basil had all 15,000 prisoners blinded, except for every hundredth man whom he left with one eye to guide the rest home. When King Samuel saw this terrible, mutilated throng returning to his capital, he died of shock. The overjoyed Byzantines thought nothing of the atrocity and gave Basil the honorific 'Bulgaroctonus', Bulgar Slayer. Bulgar Blinder would not have had the same cachet.

The last 30 years of the Macedonian dynasty saw a decline in stability, though not in territory. The imperial stage was dominated by the life and loves of the Empress Zoë (see pages 58–9); and the death of her surviving sister, the Empress Theodora, in 1056 brought the Macedonian dynasty to an inglorious end.

The Comnene dynasty

In the chaos and civil war that followed, when Emperor followed Emperor with unsettling rapidity, the Empire's enemies on all sides took their chances. In 1064 the Hungarians took Belgrade; the next year the Selçuk Turks took Armenia and later Caesarea in Cappadocia; and in 1071 the Normans took the last Byzantine lands in Italy. Under Romanus IV Diogenes (1068–71) the Byzantines initially rallied and pushed the Selçuks back a little; but in August 1071 the army was annihilated at Manzikert in eastern Anatolia, and Romanus himself was captured. It was a shattering blow. In the confusion that followed, the Selçuks advanced almost without opposition through the Byzantine heartland and even captured Nicaea, within striking distance of Constantinople, which became the capital of their Sultanate of Rum – the Roman Sultanate. The name declared their ultimate goal of taking over the whole of the Eastern Roman Empire and its capital.

In 1081 Alexius Comnenus ousted the current incompetent usurper in Constantinople with scarcely a blow being struck, and was proclaimed Emperor, initiating a century of hope and glory under the Comnene dynasty. He faced a powerful enemy in the Selçuks who already occupied most of Asia Minor; the expansionist Normans were turning to the Balkans; his subjects and army were demoralised, and the exchequer was empty. Such was his genius that he succeeded not only in holding the Selçuks at bay, but also in keeping the Normans out of the Balkans, and the barbarian Pechenegs out of Constantinople itself.

Meanwhile, in 1077 the Selçuks had taken Palestine, and Jerusalem itself. In 1096 Pope Urban II called on the Christians of Europe to take up arms to liberate the Holy Places. Alexius promised provisions, transport across the Bosphorus, and guides through Asia Minor in return for an oath of allegiance to him as the Byzantine Emperor, and the restoration to him of all cities and lands that they might win back from the Selçuks. From all over Europe thousands of people, from great feudal lords to poor peasants, set off on the First Crusade – first to Constantinople, and thence through Asia Minor to Jerusalem and glory.

It did not turn out quite as Alexius had hoped. Although the Crusaders restored several cities to the Byzantines, including Nicaea, they pillaged and looted as they went and seeemed more like an enemy than an allied army. Also, such was their hunger for land that several could not wait to reach the Holy Land, but set up their own illegitimate states within the Empire.

All this military effort cost the Empire dear: Alexius had to pawn the church treasure more than once; he bought naval help from Venice in return for trading concessions, and warehouses and anchorage on the Golden Horn; a similar agreement was later made with Pisa, and later still with Genoa, taking profitable long-distance trade away from Byzantine merchants to the commercial impoverishment of the Empire. To add to the financial loss, the Byzantine coinage was debased; and increasing taxes, collected by corrupt officials, put an unbearable burden on the people. Whatever the successes during the century of brilliant rule by Alexius and his at least equally gifted son, John II (1118–43), and grandson, Manuel I (1143–80), in the long-term the seeds of economic destruction which they sowed were bound to bear fruit.

The Fourth Crusade

In 1203 the leaders of the Fourth Crusade were persuaded by the Doge of Venice, Henry Dandolo, to divert their ships to Constantinople. The ostensible reason was to replace the current Emperor Alexius III with their own candidate Alexius IV and his father, the blinded and imprisoned Isaac II. This they did; but Alexius IV was in an impossible position, on the one hand hated by the people of Constantinople as a Latin stooge, on the other faced with a bankrupt state and pressed by the Crusaders to pay them the vast sums of money he had rashly promised them. Early in 1204 there was a rebellion in the city. Alexius IV was killed and for a short time Alexius V Murzuphlus, a son-in-law of Alexius III, became Emperor. Immediately the Crusaders attacked, and on 13 April captured the city. There followed three days of unparalleled massacre, rape, looting and destruction. According to the French chronicler of the Crusade, the booty 'included gold and silver, table-services and precious stones, satin and silk, mantles of squirrel fur, ermine and miniver, and every choicest thing to be found on this earth. Geoffroy de Villehardouin here declares that, to his knowledge, so much booty had never been gained in any city since the creation of the world.'

For the Byzantines it seemed the end of everything. Nicetas Choniates, who saw it with his own eyes, lamented: 'Oh City, City, eye of all cities, universal boast, supramundane wonder, wet nurse of churches, leader of the faith, guide of Orthodoxy, beloved topic of orations, the abode of every good thing! Oh City, that hast drunk at the hand of the Lord the cup of his fury!'

In 16 May 1204 Count Baldwin of Flanders was crowned in Haghia Sophia as the first Latin Emperor – 'of Romania' as they called their new Empire, now consisting only of Thrace, the NW tip of Asia Minor, some islands in the Aegean and Constantinople itself. Baldwin was little more suited to rule than his immediate Byzantine predecessors had been, and he alienated the conquered Greeks by forcing on them the hated and long fought-against Latin rite. When he died in the following year he was succeeded by his brother Henry, the only competent Latin Emperor. After his death eleven years later the decline was permanent. The last of the Latin Emperors, Baldwin II (1228–61), spent most of his time seeking help from Europe for his desperate plight.

As year succeeded year the people of Constantinople became poorer and fewer. The Nicaean Empire gradually won more and more territory from the Latins until they were left with only a small area around Constantinople itself, extending to the Black Sea on both sides of the Bosphorus. In 1261 the troops of Michael VIII Palaeologus, Emperor of Nicaea, forced their way through the Gate of the Pege (Silivri Kapısı) and captured the city.

The Palaeologus dynasty

The Nicaean Empire had flourished economically and, with careful housekeeping, had been able to live within its means. Now, reentering a ruined and depopulated Constantinople, with Thrace devastated by war, Michael Palaeologus was faced with expenses and problems that were beyond his capacity to deal with. At Nicaea there had been a brilliant flowering of the arts, and this increased after the return to Constantinople, producing some of the greatest works of art of the Byzantine era. As the condition of the Empire deteriorated, the city's cultural preoccupations began to look like a desperate attempt to turn the collective Byzantine face from the inevitable disaster that awaited it.

In the late 13th C. several new bands of Turks entered Asia Minor and settled in the lands of the disintegrating Selçuk Sultanate. One of these bands, under Osman Gazi, established itself on the frontier of the Byzantine Empire. These Osmanlı Turks, known to the west as the Ottomans, expanded their borders westwards under a succession of able leaders. In 1326 they captured Bursa and made it their main capital. Three years later they took Nicaea, and in 1337 Nicomedia. In 1356 they began to settle in Thrace and five years later captured Adrianople, the most important city after Constantinople, which they made their new capital. By 1390 they had taken Bulgaria and Serbia and were in control of all territory as far as the Danube.

It was only a matter of time before the Ottomans turned their full attention on their ultimate goal – Constantinople, now in full decline. When the Spanish merchant Pero Tafur visited the city in 1437, he found a scene of desolation – threatened by the Turks and neglected by the Latin west, its buildings decayed and its administration corrupt. 'The city is sparsely populated,' he wrote, adding with a mixture of compassion and Latin superiority, 'the inhabitants are not well clad, but sad and poor, showing the hardship of their lot which is, however, not so bad as they deserve, for they are a vicious people, steeped in sin . . . They go continually about the city howling as if in lamentation.' Still Catholic Europe turned a blind eye to the beleaguered Christians in the east. During Tafur's stay the Turks made a pretence of attacking the city, and had to be bought off with gifts. But the time of gifts was over; when Sultan Murat II died in 1451 and was succeeded by the brilliant and ambitious Mehmet II, the death knell sounded. On 29 May 1453, after a terrible siege, Constantinople fell to the Ottomans and the last Byzantine Emperor was killed in battle. The Byzantine Empire had died.

THE CHURCH OF ST SAVIOUR PANTOCRATOR/ MOLLA ZEYREK CAMII (only accessible after prayer times)

About half-way between the aqueduct of Valens and the Golden Horn, set in a charmingly dilapidated square behind Atatürk Bul., stands the monastery church of the Pantocrator, today a mosque known as Molla Zeyrek Camii. The houses that surround it are mainly wooden, some at worrying angles to the street, and the whole area is still relatively untouched, a picturesque if rather grubby backwater of the city.

From the outside it is a pretty rose-pink rambling structure, built and added to between about 1120 and 1136 by John II Comnenus and his wife the Empress Eirene, whose mosaic portraits we saw in Haghia Sophia. The monastery was one of the largest and richest foundations in Constantinople, with 700 monks. It included a 50-bed hospital for the poor, an asylum for the insane and an alms-house for 24 old men. All were provided with a generous allowance of bread, beans, onions, olive oil and wine. All of this, and the first of the churches (the one at the south end), were built by the Empress Eirene and dedicated to St Saviour Pantocrator – the omnipotent Saviour. When Eirene died in 1124 her husband built a second church cheek by jowl with the first, dedicated to the Virgin Eleousa, the Compassionate. Soon after, John decided to convert the two churches into one by building a chapel between them and pulling down large sections of the walls so that all three parts opened into each other. As the two original churches were not the same size, the connecting chapel had to be built with very odd angles. It was intended as a funerary chapel for the Empress Eirene, for John himself and for their heirs. In the 15th C. two Palaeologus Emperors, Manuel II and John VIII, were also buried here.

When John II died in a hunting accident in the south of Asia Minor in 1143, his body was shipped back to Constantinople to be buried beside that of his wife. He had unconventionally chosen his younger son, Manuel I, to succeed him and the new Emperor, unsure of his elder brother Isaac's loyalty, had him shut up in the monastery of the Pantocrator for some time. Later they were reconciled and Isaac was freed from his monastic prison, even commanding armies on Manuel's behalf. The monastery was again used as a residence for the imperial family during the Latin occupation – the last Latin Emperor, Baldwin II, moved in when both the Great Palace by the Marmara and the Blachernae Palace became uninhabitable. From here he fled when the troops of Michael VIII Palaeologus captured the city. The monastery was burned down in the conflict, but was quickly rebuilt. Under the last Palaeologan Emperors the great Gennadius was a monk at the Pantocrator, and was such an outspoken opponent of unity with the Roman church, which Constantine XI was trying to promote, that the Emperor had him confined to his monastery.

After the Conquest, when Gennadius was appointed Patriarch of the Greeks by Mehmet the Conqueror, his monastery church was converted into a mosque by Molla Zeyrek Mehmet Efendi, a learned but fanatical divine whose name, Zeyrek, means intelligent. He left Istanbul in a huff soon after, having been worsted in a theological debate, and spent the rest of his life in Bursa.

The outside does not prepare us for the extraordinary scale of the interior. The entrance on the west takes us through the lofty exo-narthex (one of John's additions, oddly only half the width of the whole building), then through the south narthex and into the towering south church, the oldest and largest of the three sections, which houses the mosque. The original marble revetment of the apse is still in place, and some marble from the side aisles has found its way onto the mimber. As the once fine opus sectile floor is now covered with boards and carpets, only patches can still be seen at the sides, with rich greens and reds in sweeping circular patterns. The great red marble door frames from the narthex are also original, but the four piers which support the central dome are clumsy Ottoman replacements of the original. They still create the shape of a cross set inside a square, surmounted by a little dome – the classic design of the later Byzantine church, the symbol of the earthly and the heavenly united through the cross of Christ. This is most clearly seen in the smaller north church. When Pero Tafur visited Constantinople in 1437, he described this church as 'very richly adorned with gold mosaics.' They were still there in the early 18th C. when Richard Pococke visited the church, but the faces had been disfigured. A small patch can be seen in a window arch in the north wall, giving a hint of the ancient glories of this remarkable building. But the lovely carved stone cornices, which run round the church on two levels, are still almost complete.

Several years ago the American Byzantine Institute did some valuable investigation in this church, and later the vakf removed some of the unsightly wooden partitions which unnaturally divided the three sections of the church. Restoration has been rumoured for decades, but in 1997 it was actually just beginning.

THE CHURCH OF ST SAVIOUR PANTEPOPTES/ESKI IMARET CAMII (only accessible after prayer times)

Taking the road that runs west from Pantocrator, bears left and winds between old houses, we turn right down Hacı Hasan Sok. and left after about 100 m in front of a little mosque. This is **Hacı Hasan Mescidi**, once known as Eğri Minare (crooked minaret); but it has been straightened, and the main interest is the rope-design carving on the base, and also the brick and stone cross-hatching on the shaft are unusual; but the şerefe, for all its fine stalactite carving on the corbel, seems disproportionately large. The mosque was founded around 1500 by Kazasker Hacı Hasanzade Mehmet Efendi.

Turning right on the other side of the mosque into Küçük Mektep

Sok., we see, standing immediately ahead of us, a little Byzantine church, a few decades older than the Pantocrator. It is the church of St Saviour Pantepoptes, the all-seeing Saviour, today used as a mosque and Koran school under the name of Eski Imaret Camii.

The church, and a convent that was attached to it, was built between 1085 and 1090 by Anna Dalassena, the erudite and shrewd mother of Alexius I Comnenus. She acted as Alexius' regent during his frequent and protracted absences from Constantinople fighting his many enemies, and was described by her formidable granddaughter, the historian Anna Comnena, as 'an ornament of human nature.' In 1100 this remarkable woman retired, to spend the last five years of her life, and to be buried, in the convent she had founded. In 1204 the short-lived Emperor Alexius V Murzuphlus pitched his scarlet tents around the Pantepoptes and made it his headquarters during the last siege of the city. He fled so fast when he saw the Latins breaking through the seawalls of the Golden Horn below him, that his tents were left standing, and Count Baldwin of Flanders, soon to be made Emperor, moved into them instead. Shortly after the Ottoman Conquest the Pantepoptes was converted into an imaret, supplying food for the medreses attached to the new mosque of the Conqueror nearby. As soon as the medreses' own imaret was finished, the building became a mosque – Eski Imaret Camii, the old imaret mosque.

On the outside the church is largely obscured by houses – until recently wooden, but now mainly concrete boxes – which crowd its walls. But we can see some pretty decorative brickwork, including a cross set in a roundel, the 12-sided dome, and two small crosses carved on stones beneath the south windows. The door leads through the double narthex and into the church itself which has a somewhat down-at-heel charm. The splendid red marble door-frames from the narthex are original, and the cornice on which the little dome rests is still complete, with its lovely trailing design of flowers and palmettes intact. Small stretches remain of the similar cornice which once ran all around the inside of the church. As at the Pantocrator, the original four columns which supported the dome were replaced with less aesthetic piers after the building's conversion to Islam; but the cross-in-square design, with its theological symbolism, remains.

THE CHURCH OF ST THEODOSIA/GÜL CAMII

(only accessible after prayer times).

Continuing downhill from Pantepoptes, we turn left at the T-junction, then right down steps. Thereafter we negotiate a labyrinth of often charming streets to the Golden Horn (Haliç). At Abdül Ezel Paşa Cad., the coast road, we turn left, and left again into Karasarıklı Sok. where we see the much restored church of St Theodosia, now Gül Camii, rose mosque. Built on a slope, it towers dauntingly above the streets, more like a prison than a church, but a prison with three apses and some beautiful Byzantine brickwork on the exterior, especially on the corbels of the two side apses. It also has a handsome early 17th C. minaret, built when it was converted into a mosque.

The church was probably built in the 9th C. by Basil I the Macedonian, when figurative decorations were once again being lavished on church interiors. The original dedication was to St Euphemia of the Petrion, but it seems that the name was changed soon after to commemorate the more fashionable popularity of the recently canonised St Theodosia whose miracle-working relics were in the church. Theodosia was a Constantinopolitan nun with the talents of a gang-leader. She had the misfortune to be an Iconodule just at the time when Leo III became convinced that the use of icons was the cause of all the ills of the Empire. When Leo ordered the destruction of the great icon of Christ above the gate to the Great Palace, Theodosia led a gang of women to the Augusteum and shook the ladder on which a soldier was standing to reach the icon, and knocked him off. The fall killed him. Revenge was immediate, Theodosia was dragged off to the Forum Bovis and executed, thus becoming the first Iconodule martyr.

The church was plundered of all its relics and treasures in 1204, but it remained a popular shrine throughout the Palaeologan era. During the night before the 29 May 1453, the Emperor Constantine XI Dragases stopped here on his way back to the walls from Haghia Sophia and joined the throng that had gathered to pray to St Theodosia for deliverance the following day, her feast-day. The church was filled with roses in honour of the saint – and so it was still when the Turkish forces broke into it the next morning. Hence, it is said, the name of the mosque. If so, the memory lasted long, for the church was not immediately converted; until the early 17th C. it was used as a naval depot, being within easy reach of the harbour.

Inside, the daunting impression disappears for the interior is light and attractive. There has been a considerable amount of Turkish reconstruction, but the basic shape remains that of the original Byzantine church, with a central dome supported by four irregular piers, and side aisles whose apses connect with the main apse through the thickness of the eastern piers. Above the side aisles are

galleries. The Turkish reconstructions are the dome and its supporting arches, and most of the windows.

In the SE pier, to the right of the main apse, is a door with a Turkish
inscription above it which asserts rather oddly that this is 'The tomb of
the Apostle of Christ – peace to him' (or her). It opens onto a spiral
staircase at the top of which is a small funerary chamber with a window
overlooking the nave – the site of the mysterious tomb which turns out
to be a sarcophagus covered with a green embroidered cloth. But the
identity of the 'Apostle of Christ', to whom the Turkish calligrapher so
teasingly referred, is a mystery, though some say it was Constantine
XI Dragases, the last Byzantine Emperor.

THE SEA-WALLS OF THE GOLDEN HORN

Dropping downhill from Gül Camii, we come to Abdül Ezel Paşa Cad.
which follows the shore of the Golden Horn. The whole waterfront has
been transformed in the past few years, with bulldozers clearing the
confusion of filthy (but occasionally beautiful) old buildings to create a
park along the water's edge. The Dutch government has helped
relieve its nakedness, at least in spring, by the gift of thousands of tulip
bulbs – a token of appreciation for the first bulbs that were shipped
from Istanbul to Holland, to its fame and fortune, in the 16th C.

Beside the road can be seen fragments of the old sea-walls that were
battered first by the Crusaders in 1203–4, and then by the Ottomans in
1453. For anyone with an unquenchable appetite for dilapidated
arches, about 100 m along the road to the right is **Cibali Kapı**, the
Byzantine Porta Puteae. From there, NE up the Golden Horn, the
Venetians lined up their battle fleet for their final assault on the walls.
Less voracious arcophiles should turn left and, after 50 m or so, just
beyond the little 18th C. Greek **church of St Nicholas**, is a small
Byzantine gate, **Aya Kapı**, the holy gate, known to the Byzantines as
the Gate of St Theodosia since it led to that church. A short distance
further on is a larger gate, **Yeni Aya Kapı**, the new holy gate, so called
because it is later than the original one, having been built in 1582 by
the great architect Sinan to enable the residents inside the walls to take
a short cut to the new hamam that had recently been built just outside.

About 100 m beyond Yeni Aya Kapı is the site of the most famous of
all the gates of the Golden Horn, the **Gate of the Petrion**. Today there
is nothing to be seen, but it was at just about the point where Sadrazam
Ali Paşa Cad. turns left off the main road. Here the dreadful but
indomitable Doge, Henry Dandolo, 90 years old and blind, insisted

on being among the first ashore in the first siege of the city. Nine months later it was at the Petrion that the first breach of the walls was made that led to the capture of the city. In the Ottoman attack in 1453 the men of the Petrion surrendered once they heard that the land walls had been breached and all hope was lost. As was the law, Mehmet the Conqueror excluded the Petrion area from sack and pillage by his over-exuberant soldiers.

THE GREEK ORTHODOX PATRIARCHATE

Following Sadrazam Ali Paşa Cad., we come after about 100 m to the main gate of the Greek Orthodox Patriarchate. It is worth noticing the gate before going into the Patriarchal church, not for any aesthetic value, but for its story and symbolism. Here, on 22 April 1821 the Greek Patriarch of Constantinople, Gregory V, in all his Patriarchal vestments, was hanged, accused of treason against the Ottoman Empire. It was at the beginning of the Greek War of Independence, the war so hopelessly romanticised by Byron; and from that day **Orta Kapı**, the middle gate, has stood welded shut and painted black, never to open again.

The **Patriarchal church of St George** is on the left of the gate. When Mehmet the Conqueror appointed Gennadius as Patriarch in 1454, he gave him the church of the Holy Apostles as his seat, since Haghia Sophia had been transformed into a mosque. Two years later he was transferred to the church of the Pammakaristos. In 1586 the Patriarchate was moved again, to the Fener area, and for some years had no permanent home until given this site in 1601.

The present church, built in 1720, is a basilica – sombre apart from the much gilded iconostasis. After the Conquest Christians were not permitted to build domes on their churches, or any kind of masonry roofs, so they reverted to the earliest type of Byzantine basilica with a wooden roof. The great ivory inlaid Patriarchal throne, set on the right of the aisle, has optimistically been said by some to be that of St John Chrysostom, the early 5th C. Patriarch; a more realistic judgment opts for late Byzantine, while other scholars believe it to be 16th C. Ottoman work from its similarity to other inlaid furniture of that period. Another treasure of the church, a framed mosaic icon of the Virgin from the Pammakaristos church, now hangs in the south aisle. It probably dates to the 11th C. Most precious of all are the relics of three saints – Omonia, Theophano, and Euphemia of Chalcedon whom the Greeks had rescued when her martyrium by the hippodrome was requisitioned by the Ottomans.

Immediately behind Orta Kapı towers the newly rebuilt Patriarchal residence and offices. The Orthodox Patriarch is still officially the spiritual head of the entire Orthodox Church; but in reality he is now little more than the leader of the Greeks resident in Istanbul and a few Aegean islands.

FENER

Continuing along Sadrazam Ali Paşa Cad., the first turning on the right brings us back to the main Golden Horn road at the site of another famous but non-existent gate, **Fener Kapısı**, known to the Byzantines as Porta Phanari, the lighthouse gate. After the Conquest the surrounding area of Fener became virtually a Greek state, subservient to the Ottomans but controlled by its own members under the jurisdiction of the Patriarch. The restrictions were religious ones – no new churches, no repairs to old ones, no church bells – but they could trade, indeed they were encouraged to do so, and many served the Ottoman Empire both at home and in Europe in positions of high authority. Feneriotes were in charge of Ottoman financial administration in the conquered Balkan states, ruling the Rumanian principalities of Moldavia and Wallachia. The enormous wealth they acquired mostly made its way back home to the Golden Horn, beside whose waters stood their palaces and mansions of frequently ostentatious magnificence. Most have disappeared without trace; the rest are crumbling.

The wealthy old Greeks would not recognise the area now, especially since the bulldozers moved in and left behind them an unnaturally level swathe of open ground where once waterside mansions overlooked the Golden Horn. One good thing the bulldozers have done is to make visible the **church of St Stephen of the Bulgars** about 200 m beyond Fener Kapısı. It is an extraordinary structure, built in 1871 in a bold neo-Gothic style as a statement of Bulgarian independence from the Greek Patriarchate, and constructed entirely of cast iron. It was made in Vienna – in pieces, like a giant jig-saw puzzle – then shipped down the Danube, into the Black Sea and along the Bosphorus, and put together here beside the Golden Horn. Painted battleship-grey, it rides its green park setting like a great ecclesiastical ship at anchor.

Parallel with the main Golden Horn road just beyond Fener Kapısı is Vodina Cad. on which is a large walled enclosure with two churches inside, one early 19th C., the other in ruins. Climbing up the hill behind is the heart of Fener, still largely Greek, and buzzing with life, but in sadly reduced circumstances. Once-lovely wooden houses now totter precariously beside precipitous cobbled streets, garlanded with multi-coloured laundry hung out across the street from window to opposite window. Crowning the skyline is an egregiously ugly building of violent red brick which, until all non-Turkish institutions of higher education were closed in 1971, housed the immensely distinguished **Greek Lycée of the Fener**. Since before the Conquest the Greek Patriarchate ran a school on this site where both theology and secular subjects were taught. In 1840 the school was secularised. The present melancholy monstrosity dates from 1881.

THE CHURCH OF ST MARY OF THE MONGOLS/ PANAGHIA MOUCHLIOTISSA (open on Sundays)

If we turn left just before the walled enclosure on Vodina Cad., and head up the hill, taking the first right up a winding street of steps, we will see on the left an oddly shaped Byzantine church, painted bright red, dedicated to the Theotokos Panaghiotissa, the all-holy Mother of God. It is known to local Christians as Panaghia Mouchliotissa, and to us as St Mary of the Mongols. It is surrounded by a wall in which is a locked door, and it is nowadays unlikely that it will be unlocked except for Sunday services.

St Mary of the Mongols has the unique distinction of being the only unconverted Byzantine church in Istanbul, and it still owns what may be a copy of the original firman, or imperial decree, of Mehmet II confirming the Greeks in their possession of it. Christians have worshipped here without interruption for over 700 years, since the first church was founded by Isaac Ducas, uncle of Michael VIII Palaeologus. He must have built it soon after the restoration of the Byzantine Empire in 1261; but it was added to or rebuilt around 1282 by Princess Maria Palaeologina, an illegitimate daughter of Michael VIII. Maria had had all too exciting a life up to this point; in 1265 she was sent to marry Hulagu, Khan of the Mongols of Persia, but as he was dead when she arrived, she married his son and heir Abaga instead. This branch of the Mongols were Shamanists and enemies of Islam which made them useful allies of the Byzantines. Maria did a sterling missionary job during the 15 years she was in Persia, converting not only the Khan but many of his entourage as well. But the Khan's brother Ahmet was a Muslim, and in 1281 he murdered

Abaga and sent Maria home to Constantinople. Here she chose to become a nun rather than be married off to the Khan of another branch of the Mongols, and she retired to her convent and church of St Mary, dedicated to the patron saint of the Mongol Christians.

Inside, the church is dark and dingy and, after the open interiors of mosques, seems overcrowded. Everything is at odd angles, largely due to some recent and insensitive alterations. The original part of the church is covered with a little dome on a high drum, beneath which are three semi-domes, one of them almost completely hidden behind the screen in front of the altar. On the south side, where the fourth semi-dome was, the church has been extended, and an unsightly narthex added, distorting the original plan. Like the Patriarchal church, the church owns a fine 11th C. portative mosaic icon – of the Theotokos Pammakaristos, the all-blessed Mother of God – also locked away.

THE CHURCH OF THE THEOTOKOS PAMMAKARISTOS/FETHIYE CAMII

Currently closed except by special (and costly) permission – check in case this has changed. In any case the exterior is worth seeing.

It is possible to walk on up the very steep hill from St Mary of the Mongols and turn right into Manyasizade Cad. At the point where this road turns left and changes its name to Fethiye Cad. a cul-de-sac on the right called Fethiyekapısı Sok. leads into an open space with a lovely Byzantine church set in it.

It is, however, most easily visited en route to the church of St Saviour in Chora, Kariye Camii, about 700 m to the west. From the centre of town it can be reached along the extension of Şehzadebaşı, then into Daruşşafaka Cad. which is renamed twice, to Manyasızade Cad. and then to Fethiye Cad. at the turning where the cul-de-sac strikes off to Fethiye Camii. No one, including taxi drivers, has heard of Fethiye Camii until you reach Fethiye Cad., but perseverence and the frequent repetition of names of streets en route will get you to the right place, and you will be rewarded by one of the loveliest of Byzantine churches, with beautiful brickwork outside and some glowing mosaics inside. If you are fortunate enough to get in you will be rewarded with a rare treat.

The position of the Pammakaristos is magnificent, set on a terrace on the brow of the fifth hill, overlooking Fener and the Golden Horn. From the open ground in front of it we can enjoy the agreeable cluster

Istanbul: Church of the Pammakaristos

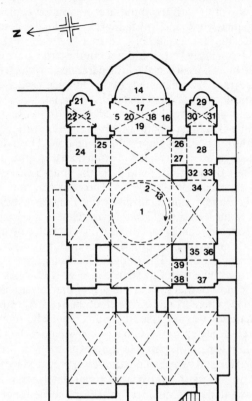

1 Christ Pantocrator
2 Moses
3 Jeremiah
4 Zephaniah
5 Micah
6 Joel
7 Zechariah
8 Obadiah
9 Habakkuk
10 Jonah
11 Malachi
12 Ezekiel
13 Isaiah
14 Christ Hyperagathos
15 Virgin Mary
16 St John the Baptist
17 Archangel Michael
18 Archangel Raphael
19 Archangel Gabriel
20 Archangel Uriel

21 St James, the brother of Christ
22 St Clement
23 St Metrophanes of Constantinople
24 St Ignatius of Antioch
25 St Philip
26 St Gregory Thaumaturgus
27 St Gregory of Agrigentum
28 St Gregory the Illuminator
29 St Gregory the Theologian (of Nazianzus)
30 St Cyril
31 St Athanasius
32 St Antipas
33 St Blasius
34 Baptism of Christ
35 St Sabas
36 St John Climacus
37 St Euthemius
38 St Chariton
39 St Arsenius

of its domes and the fine decorative brickwork of the exterior, the most elaborate in the city, with its round-arched windows, niches, blind arcades, chequer-work and medallions – wickedly described by Osbert Lancaster as 'an unholy alliance between Fabergé and Butterfield.' It is a fairly large building, but the part we are concerned with, because of its mosaics, is the little parecclesion which faces us as we enter the terrace. The main body of the church is used as a mosque, its plan drastically altered from that of the original.

The church was built in the early 12th C. by John Comnenus and his wife Anna Ducaena, both otherwise unknown, but clearly members of the inter-related imperial Comnene and Ducas families. It was dedicated to the Theotokos Pammakaristos, the all-blessed Mother of God. Between 1292 and 1295 the church was extensively restored by Michael Ducas Glabas Tarchaniotes, the Prostrator (Master of the Horse), and a cousin of the Emperor Andronicus II Palaeologus. Some time after 1310 the parecclesion was built onto the church as a funerary chapel for Michael Tarchaniotes by his widow, whose names grandiloquently proclaim her multiple imperial origins – Maria Ducaena Comnena Palaeologina Blachena.

The building remained Christian for over 130 years after the Conquest, for most of that time as the seat of the Patriarchate. When Gennadius moved here from the church of the Holy Apostles in 1456 the Pammakaristos was occupied by nuns whom he moved to the smaller church of St John in Trullo nearby. Mehmet the Conqueror used to visit him here in the parecclesion, to question him on points of Christian doctrine and belief. Gennadius even prepared for the Sultan a statement of his faith which was immediately translated into Turkish. It was all part of Mehmet's thirst for knowledge of all kinds, but it gave rise in the west to an excited and wholly misplaced belief that the Ottoman Sultan was on the point of becoming a Christian.

The site of the Pammakaristos was too splendid not to be coveted, and in 1586 the Patriarchate was moved down the hill to Fener. In 1591 Murat III had the church converted into a mosque and gave it the name of Fethiye, conquest, in celebration of the recent successful conclusion of his 12-year war with Persia. In the process of conversion the main body of the building was altered out of all recognition, and the parecclesion had its north wall and two of its columns pulled down to integrate it with the mosque. In the 1960s the Byzantine Institute of America undertook an investigation and restoration of the building. Following this the parecclesion, once more in its original shape and beautifully restored, was closed off from the mosque and opened as a museum to display the superb 14th C. mosaics that had been uncovered in it.

The interior
The parecclesion is a perfect example of the 4-column, cross-in-square plan, surmounted by a cupola, that had become the classic design for Byzantine churches. The very shape of the building, representing as it did the union of heaven and earth through the cross, together with the profusion of sacred images with which it was decorated, transformed the church into an image of the cosmos symbolising heaven, the Holy Land with scenes from Christ's life, and the world of the Christian saints and martyrs, culminating – as in the apex of the cupola here – with Christ Pantocrator, the omnipotent, the image of God Himself. Surrounding Him are 12 Old Testament prophets. Curiously these mosaics in the cupola were never covered over, though all the others were.

In the conch of the apse Christ is portrayed in another mode – Hyperagathos, the greatly loving – and, with the Virgin on the left wall of the apse and John the Baptist on the right wall, it thus becomes a Deesis, overlooked by the four archangels in the vault above. All the other mosaics are of saints and patriarchs. The one exception is the only surviving mosaic from the cycle of Christ's life on earth, the Baptism of Christ on the east face of the south vault beside the dome.

On the south wall Maria Blachena placed a long and moving inscription which can still be seen, a poem by the contemporary Manuel Philes, a testament to her love for the husband she had buried here:

> Therefore I will construct for thee this tomb as a pearl oyster shell,
> Or shell of the purple dye, rose of another clime,
> Even though being plucked thou art pressed by the stones
> So as to cause me shedding of tears. . . .

7

THE CHURCH OF ST SAVIOUR IN CHORA/KARIYE CAMII

Open daily except Tuesday

From the centre of town take the main road to Edirne Kapısı, where there is a bus terminal, turn right into Hoca Çakır Cad. just inside the walls, and third right into Nester Sok. Kariye Camii is about 200 m on the left. From Fethiye Camii it is roughly a 700 m walk – turn right onto Fethiye Cad. which changes its name first to Draman Cad. and then to Nester Sok. The first turning on the right after the junction with Tomruk Cad. leads to Kariye Camii. Alternatively, it is one of the small handful of sites in Istanbul known to virtually all taxi drivers.

Nothing is known for sure about the origins of the church of St Saviour in Chora, though its name – St Saviour in the country – indicates that the first church here was outside the built-up areas of the city. It may even have been established before the Theodosian walls were built in 413. But the word 'chora' is used in a different, metaphorical, way in several mosaics inside the church where Christ is referred to as 'the dwelling-place (chora) of the living', and the Virgin as 'the dwelling-place of the uncontainable' – perhaps an ecclesiastical pun to justify keeping the name long after the church had ceased to be 'in chora'.

This early church, almost certainly a basilica, was restored by Justinian but was again in ruins in the latter part of the 11th C. The rebuilding then was commissioned by Maria Ducaena, mother-in-law of Alexius I Comnenus. The main structure of the centre of the present church dates to this time when it appears to have been a classic 4-column, cross-in-square plan. But early in the 12th C. severe damage to the east end led to an extensive restoration by Maria Ducaena's grandson Isaac Comnenus, youngest son of Alexius I, whose patron-

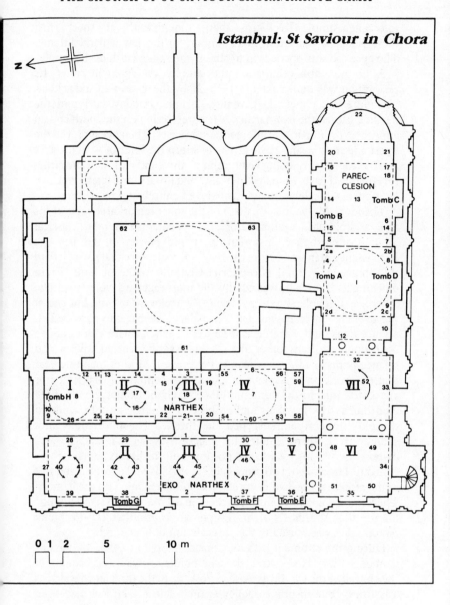

Istanbul: St Saviour in Chora

age is commemorated in a portrait of him in one of the principal mosaics. It was at this time that the present form of the church was established, with piers replacing the columns and filling in the corners

81

to create a simple Greek-cross shape, though with very short arms; these piers also made a stronger support for the new, enlarged dome. The apse too was opened up to almost the same width as the dome.

After the Latin occupation the church was again in ruins. Its restoration was undertaken in 1315–21 by the statesman and scholar Theodore Metochites who gave it the form it has today. He rebuilt the narthex, added the exo-narthex, the parecclesion on the south and an annexe on the north, and altered the side apses. Then he employed the finest and most avant-garde artists to adorn the interior with mosaics and frescoes of surpassing beauty and vitality, and with superb marble revetments. He also donated his renowned library, and later wrote two long poems in celebration of his beloved church and monastery.

Theodore Metochites was one of the most remarkable men of his age, a diplomat, administrator, theologian, astronomer, classical scholar, philosopher, historian, poet and patron of the arts – a Renaissance man well before the Italian Renaissance that gave birth to the phrase. His pupil Nicephorus Gregoras wrote of him: 'From morning to evening he was wholly and most eagerly devoted to public affairs, as if scholarship were absolutely irrelevant to him; but late in the evening, after having left the palace, he became absorbed in science to as high a degree as if he were a scholar with absolutely no connection with any other affairs.' He was the trusted adviser and finance minister of Andronicus II Palaeologus, and in the same year that the work on St Saviour in Chora was completed, the Emperor appointed him to the supreme office of Grand Logothete. In 1328 Andronicus II's frivolous and ambitious favourite grandson ousted the old Emperor and usurped the throne. Theodore Metochites shared his Emperor's fate, his palace was sacked, and he was dispossessed of his wealth, his position and his liberty. Soon he was exiled to Thrace, but two years later he was allowed to return and live in the monastery he had restored, becoming a monk with the name of Theoleptos – taken by God. He died on 13 March 1332, exactly one month after the death of his Emperor, Andronicus II, the monk Antony. He was buried in the parecclesion of his church.

During the Ottoman siege of Constantinople in 1453, the famous icon of St Mary Hodegetria (she who points the way) was brought to the church of the Chora, as close as possible to the threatened walls, as a last desperate insurance policy against defeat. The icon had been brought to the city from Jerusalem in the 5th C. in the conviction that it had been painted by St Luke. Its powers were thought to be exceptional; but it needed more than that to keep out the Turks. Early in the morning of 29 May, St Saviour in Chora was the first church to be pillaged, the icon apparently hacked to pieces in the process. The church remained in Christian hands for some time after the Conquest, but in 1510 it was taken over by Beyazit II's Grand Vezir, Hadım (eunuch) Atık Ali Paşa, who installed an unusually discreet mihrab in the apse, in a matching grey marble, and built the minaret. Most of the mosaics and frescoes were given a coat of whitewash; and in the 18th C. a new dome was built on the original drum.

From 1948 to 1958 the Byzantine Institute of America restored the church to the superb state in which we see it today, the vital mosaics and frescoes that adorn the interior making a visit here an overwhelming aesthetic experience.

THE MOSAICS

Since Byzantine church decoration followed clearly defined iconographical rules, and since Paul Underwood of the Byzantine Institute has elucidated these so clearly in relation to St Saviour in Chora, we should look at the mosaics in the prescribed order as a flowing narrative of the divine hand in human life.

A DEDICATORY OR DEVOTIONAL PANELS

These six large panels are situated in lunettes in the narthex and exonarthex.

1. Christ Pantocrator

Exo-narthex; lunette above door to narthex
Facing us as we enter the exo-narthex is this great mosaic showing Christ holding a jewelled Gospel in his left hand, while his right hand is raised in blessing. The right side of Christ's face and body are larger than the left, to give the impression of a slight turning to the left. The inscription describes Christ as 'chora ton zonton' – the dwelling-place, or land, of the living – a reference to Psalm 116,9: 'I walk before the Lord in the land of the living'; and also to the name of the church.

2. The Virgin Blachernitissa and angels

Exo-narthex; lunette above main entrance (opposite Pantocrator)
The Virgin has her hands outstretched in prayer, an attitude associated with an icon at the church of the Blachernae nearby. On either side of her are two angels in mid-flight. The inscription describes the Virgin as 'chora tou achoretou' – a double play on words meaning the dwelling-place (or container) of the uncontainable. This

reference to the Incarnation is visually demonstrated here by the 'uncontainable' divinity of Christ being contained within the figure of the Virgin, surrounded by a mandorla to emphasise His divinity. The position of this mosaic of the Virgin, opposite the Christ Pantocrator, suggests that the church was probably dedicated to her as well as to Christ.

3. Christ enthroned, with the donor

Narthex; lunette above door to nave
Theodore Metochites, on his knees before Christ, humbly presents a simplified model of his church. He is clothed in the rich silk robe and enormous striped turban-like hat (called skiadeion = sunshade!) that betoken his official status which is identified in the inscription: 'The Founder, Logothete of the Genikon [Treasury], Theodore Metochites.' The inscription on either side of Christ again describes Him as the 'chora' of the living.

4. St Peter – the keys of the kingdom of heaven in his left hand, and in his right the scroll of his epistles.
5. St Paul – his epistles in his left hand, the right raised as if teaching.
Narthex; either side of door to nave

6. The Deesis

Narthex; E wall, to right of 3–5 above
A Deesis (Intercession) normally portrays the Virgin and John the Baptist on either side of Christ, but here the Baptist has been omitted. The mosaic is sadly damaged, but miraculously most of the figures, including faces and hands, are intact. Unusually, two further intercessors are included, suitably small to show their inferior status. Beside the Virgin is a figure whose inscription identifies him as 'the son of the most high Emperor Alexius Comnenus, Isaac Porphyrogenitus' – the Isaac Comnenus who had the church redesigned in the early 12th C. On the other side of Christ are the face, nun's headdress and hands of another benefactor of the Chora; sadly an area of damage has obliterated the first part of her inscription which now reads: '. . . of Andronicus Palaeologus, the Lady of the Mongols, Melane the nun.' The loss is tantalising as there were two Palaeologue princesses who married Mongol Khans and who became nuns in later life. One was the illegitimate half-sister of Andronicus II who founded St Mary of the Mongols; the other was the illegitimate daughter of the same Emperor.

B THE GENEALOGY OF CHRIST

7. Christ Pantocrator

At the apex of the south dome, surrounded by two rows of figures; in the upper row, 24 ancestors from Adam to Jacob, a selection from Luke 3, 23–38; in the lower row, the 12 sons of Jacob, with 2 grandsons and a great-grandson.

8. The Theotokos, or Mother of God, with the infant Christ

At the apex of the north dome, surrounded by two rows of figures: in the upper row, 16 Kings of the House of David, from Matthew 1, 6–12; in the lower row, 11 other ancestors, or prefigurers, not listed in either of the gospel genealogies.

C THE LIFE OF THE VIRGIN

This cycle, based on the Protoevangelium, or Apocryphal Gospel of St James, and other apocryphal sources, starts in Bay I of the narthex, and proceeds into Bays II and III. Of the original 20 scenes, 19 remain.

9. Joachim's offerings rejected

Bay I, NW pendentive (left half of scene missing)
The High Priest Zacharias, father of John the Baptist, stands before the altar, his hands raised in rejection. The scene on the adjoining pendentive to the right is lost, but it must have portrayed Joachim and his wife Anne who brought to the temple offerings which were refused because the couple was childless.

10. Unidentified fragment

Bay I, N lunette
A maidservant looks out of a doorway, with two partridges on the flat roofs above. The rest of the scene is lost, but may have shown Joachim and Anne returning home.

11. Joachim in the wilderness

Bay I, SE pendentive
The Protoevangelium says Joachim went to the wilderness to fast and pray for a child. On the right two shepherds look anxious.

12. The annunciation to St Anne

Bay I, E lunette (left half of scene missing)
An angel announces to Anne that the Lord has heard her prayer and

that she will bear a child. She stands in a leafy garden outside a fanciful domed house; in one tree is a nest with fledgelings in it, and the mother bird flies towards them – the fecundity of the birds of the air had been a cause of Anne's earlier lament.

13. The meeting of Joachim and Anne

E soffit of arch between Bays I and II
On Joachim's return from the wilderness, Anne meets him at the gate of the town and tells him of the angel's visit. Anne's maidservant Judith peeps over a wall.

14. The birth of the Virgin

Bay II, E lunette
A rich composition, full of movement and detail. Anne sits up in bed, as Joachim looks on from a doorway at a discreet distance. Below him the midwife prepares to bathe the infant Mary, while in front of Anne's bed a diminutive figure prepares the cot.

15. The first seven steps of the Virgin

E soffit of arch between Bays II and III
One of the most expressively human scenes. 'And day by day the child waxed strong, and when she was six months old her mother stood her upon the ground to try if she would stand; and she walked seven steps and returned unto her bosom.' (Prot. 6, 1)

16. The Virgin blessed by the priests

Bay II, W half of domical vault
Joachim strides with enthusiasm, the infant Mary in his arms, towards three high priests, 'and they blessed her, saying: O God of the high places, look upon this child, and bless her with the last blessing which hath no successor.' (Prot. 6, 2)

17. The Virgin caressed by her parents

Bay II, E half of domical vault
A beautiful, tender scene with no specific reference in the Proto-evangelium. In each pendentive stands a handsome peacock, symbol of immortality.

18. The presentation of the Virgin in the temple

Bay III, domical vault
A single scene in a circular composition showing 'the daughters of the Hebrews' with torches processing to the temple with Joachim and Anne and the 3-year old Mary. 'And the priest received her and kissed

her and blessed her and said: The Lord hath magnified thy name among all generations: in thee in the latter days shall the Lord make manifest his redemption unto the children of Israel. And he made her to sit upon the third step of the altar. And the Lord put grace upon her and she danced with her feet and all the house of Israel loved her.' (Prot. 7, 6) In the E pendentives are two pheasants. A second figure of Mary, in the Holy of Holies, points to the subject of the next mosaic.

19. The Virgin receives bread from an angel
E soffit of arch between Bays III and IV
'And Mary was in the temple of the Lord as a dove that is nurtured: and she received food from the hand of an angel.' (Prot. 8, 1) She remained in the temple until the age of 12.

20. The instruction of the Virgin in the temple
W soffit of same arch
Most is damaged and only the architectural setting remains.

21. The Virgin receives the skein of purple wool
Bay III, lunette above door to exo-narthex
'Now there was a council of the priests, and they said: Let us make a veil for the temple of the Lord. And the priest said: Call unto me pure virgins of the tribe of David . . . and the priest said: Cast me lots, which of you shall weave the gold and the undefiled [white] and the fine linen and the silk and the hyacinthine, and the scarlet and the true purple [the royal colours]. And the lot of the true purple and the scarlet fell unto Mary.' (Prot. 10) This recalls the prophecy that the Messiah would be from the royal house of David.

22. Zacharias prays before the rods of the suitors
W soffit of arch between Bays II and III
When the time came for Mary to be married, 'an angel of the Lord appeared unto [the High Priest]: Zacharias, Zacharias, go forth and assemble them that are widowers of the people, and let them bring every man a rod, and to whomsoever the Lord shall show a sign, his wife shall she be.' (Prot. 8, 3) Mary sits before the 12 rods in the Holy of Holies and Zacharias prays. The rod fourth from the right sprouts green leaves.

23. The Virgin entrusted to Joseph
Bay II, W lunette
Joseph steps forward to receive his sprouting rod from Zacharias whose other hand rests on Mary's head. The rejected suitors stand disgruntled behind Joseph.

24. Joseph takes the Virgin to his house

W soffit of arch between Bays I and II

Joseph, together with one of his sons by his first wife, leads Mary from the temple as they set out for home.

25. The annunciation to the Virgin at the well

Bay I, SW pendentive

Mary 'took the pitcher and went forth to fill it with water: and lo a voice saying: Hail, thou that art highly favoured: the Lord is with thee: blessed art thou among women. And she looked about her . . . to see whence this voice should be.' (Prot. 11, 1)

26. Joseph takes leave of the Virgin/Joseph reproaches the Virgin

Bay I, W lunette

Two scenes in one: *left*: 'And Joseph said unto Mary: Lo, I have received thee out of the temple of the Lord: and now do I leave thee in my house, and I go away to build my buildings and I will come again unto thee' (Prot. 9, 2); *right*: Joseph returns after 6 months to find Mary 'great with child. And he smote his face, and cast himself down upon the ground on sackcloth and wept bitterly.' Rising from the ground again, he asks her accusingly, 'What is this that thou hast done?'

D THE INFANCY OF CHRIST

This cycle of mosaics occupies the lunettes of the exo-narthex, starting in Bay I and continuing clockwise through the seven bays (except for Bay III where the lunettes are occupied by the two great dedicatory mosaics), returning to Bay I at the end of the circuit. With two exceptions, each scene is based on a verse from the canonical Gospels, all or part of which is inscribed on it.

27. Joseph dreaming/The Virgin and two companions/The journey to Bethlehem

Bay I, N lunette, three scenes in one

i) 'Behold, an angel of the Lord appeared to him in a dream, saying, 'Joseph, son of David, do not fear to take Mary your wife, for that which is conceived in her is of the Holy Spirit.' (Matt. 1, 20)

ii) No inscription apart from the abbreviated 'Mother of God' above Mary's halo. The third woman is only visible as a shadow between Mary and her companion on the left.

iii) 'And Joseph also went up from Galilee, from the city of Nazareth, to Judea, to the city of David, which is called Bethlehem.' (Luke 2, 4) Joseph's son strides ahead of the donkey on which Mary sits, while Joseph follows. The figures appear to float over the ground as they go off to the enrolment.

28. The enrolment for taxation
Bay I, E lunette
'. . . because he was of the house and lineage of David, to be enrolled with Mary, his betrothed, who was with child.' (Luke 2, 4–5) Quirinius, governor of Syria, sits on a gold throne with a guard behind him. A scribe and guard interrogate Mary, while Joseph leans forward to help, his four sons behind him.

29. The Nativity
Bay II, E lunette
A composite scene, set on a rocky mountain, which the central inscription entitles 'The birth of Christ'; in front of the angel and above the astonished shepherds are the words: 'Be not afraid; for behold, I bring you good news of a great joy which will come to all people.' (Luke 2, 10) Four more angels on the left rejoice over the new-born Christ, watched over by an ox and an ass, while two women wash the child, and Joseph sits alone contemplating.

30. The journey of the Magi/The Magi before Herod
Bay IV, E lunette, two scenes in one panel
'Behold, wise men from the East came to Jerusalem, saying, "Where is he who has been born king of the Jews?" ' (Matt. 2, 1–2)

31. Herod inquiring of the priests and scribes
Bay V, E lunette
Much is destroyed. The full inscription was: 'And assembling all the chief priests and scribes of the people, he inquired of them where the Christ was to be born.' (Matt. 2, 4)
  The scene of the adoration of the Magi is missing.

32. The return of the Magi to the East (fragment)
Bay VII, E lunette above entrance to pareclesion
Only the youngest of the three Magi survives.

33. The flight into Egypt
Bay VII, S lunette
Much is missing, including the main characters, of whom we see only one pair of legs and the front legs of the donkey. The inscription is

simply the title. On the right are the walls and towers of an Egyptian town from which idols fall at the passage of the Holy Family (from an apocryphal source).

34. Herod orders the massacre of the innocents/The soldiers go out to kill

Bay VI, S lunette, two scenes in one
'Then Herod, when he saw that he had been tricked by the wise men, was in a furious rage, and he sent and killed all the male children in Bethlehem and in all the region who were two years old or under.' (Matt. 2, 16)

35. The soldiers kill the children

Bay VI, W lunette
The centre and the inscription are missing.

36. The mothers mourn their children (fragment)

Bay V, W lunette
'A voice was heard in Ramah, wailing and loud lamentation.' (Matt. 2, 18 quoting Jer. 31, 15) On the right sits a group of heart-broken women, some holding their dead babies.

37. The flight of Elizabeth

Bay IV, W lunette
The inscription is the title. 'But Elizabeth, when she heard that . . . [the executioners] sought for John [the Baptist, her infant son], took him and went up into the hill-country and looked about her where she could hide him: and there was no hiding place. And Elizabeth groaned and said in a loud voice: O mountain of God, receive thou a mother with a child. For Elizabeth was not able to go up. And immediately the mountain clave asunder and took her in.' (Prot. 22, 3)

38. The return of the Holy Family from Egypt

Bay II, W lunette
'Being warned in a dream he [Joseph] withdrew to the district of Galilee. And he went and dwelt in a city called Nazareth.' (Matt. 2, 22–3) A composite scene, showing Joseph dreaming and the angel warning him; Joseph carrying Jesus on his shoulders followed by an anxious Mary, and Joseph's son leading the laden donkey; a charming representation of the walled city of Nazareth.

39. Christ is taken to Jerusalem for the Passover

Bay I, W lunette
'Now his parents went to Jerusalem every year at the feast of the

Passover.' (Luke 2, 41) Joseph, followed by Jesus, now aged 12, and two of Joseph's older sons with Mary, make their way towards the walled and turretted city of Jerusalem.

E CHRIST'S MINISTRY

This cycle occupies the domical vaults of the exo-narthex, first in Bay I, continuing through to Bay VII, then in to Bay IV of the narthex. Almost all scenes in the exo-narthex are badly damaged.

40. **Christ among the teachers** (fragment)

Exo-narthex; Bay I, N side of vault
Based on Luke 2, 46–7: 'After three days they [Joseph and Mary] found him in the temple, sitting among the teachers, listening to them and asking him questions; and all who heard him were amazed at his understanding and his answers.'

41. **John the Baptist bears witness of Christ A** (fragment)

Exo-narthex; Bay I, S side of vault
Based on John 1, 26–7: 'I baptize you with water; but among you stands one whom you do not know, even he who comes after me, the thong of whose sandal I am not worthy to untie.'

42. **John the Baptist bears witness of Christ B**

Exo-narthex; Bay II, N side of vault
'This is he of whom I said, "He who comes after me ranks before me, for he was before me." ' (John 1, 15 & 30) John by the Jordan talks to a group of priests and Levites and points to Christ.

43. **The temptation of Christ in the wilderness**

Exo-narthex; Bay II, S side of vault
A composite scene with four portrayals of Christ confronting Satan, and seven inscriptions from Matt. 4 – Satan's temptations and Christ's responses, the final one to the left of centre. From left to right: a) *below* 'If you are the son of God, command these stones to become loaves of bread (v. 3); *above* 'It is written, "Man shall not live by bread alone, but by every word that proceeds from the mouth of God".' (v. 4). b) *below* 'All these things will I give you, if you will fall down and worship me.' (v. 9); *above* 'Begone, Satan!' (v. 10). c) *above* 'Then the devil took him to the holy city.' (v. 5). d) *below* 'If you are the Son of God, throw yourself down.' (v. 6); *above* 'It is written, "You shall not tempt the Lord your God".' (v. 7)

44. The miracle at Cana

Exo-narthex; Bay III, N side of vault
Based on John 2, 1–11. The centre is lost; the NW pendentive shows a bullock being slaughtered for the wedding feast. In the NE pendentive Christ and the Virgin, with Peter and John behind, walk towards six earthenware jars being filled with water by two servants; a third man offers Christ a glass (water or wine?).

45. The multiplication of the loaves

Exo-narthex; Bay III, S side of vault
Based on Matt. 14, 15–21 (and in the other gospels): the feeding of the 5000. The centre is lost. Christ blesses the loaves; in the SE pendentive he gives the multiplied bread to two disciples beneath whom a group of children eat; on the other side of the disciples sit some of the 5000; in the SW pendentive Christ and three disciples with 12 baskets of fragments.

46. Christ heals a leper (fragment)

Exo-narthex; Bay IV, E side of vault
Based on Matt. 8, 1–4. It is badly damaged, with only the lower parts of the figures extant – Christ and a disciple move towards the leper (with spotty legs) who has three men behind him.

47. Unidentified scene (small fragment)

Exo-narthex; Bay IV, W side of vault
All that remains is a narrow strip of mosaic showing the waves of the sea. It was probably of Christ walking on the water.

All mosaics in Bay V are missing.

48. Christ heals the paralytic at the Pool of Bethesda

Exo-narthex; Bay VI, NE pendentive
Based on John 5, 2–15. The inscription summarises: 'Christ at the sheep pool raises the paralytic from his bed by his word.' Above, the paralytic sits up, and below he carries his bed.

49. Christ heals the dropsical man (fragment)

Exo-narthex; Bay VI, SE corner (above)
Based on Luke 14, 2–5. The inscription is the title. Most is lost. In the pendentive we see Christ in an unidentified scene, probably healing the man born blind.

50. Christ heals the paralytic at Capernaum

Exo-narthex; SW corner
Based on Matt. 9, 1–8: '. . . they brought to him a paralytic, lying on

his bed; and when Jesus saw their faith he said to the paralytic, 'Take heart, my son; your sins are forgiven.' And behold, some of the scribes said to themselves, 'This man is blaspheming.' But Jesus, knowing their thoughts, said, 'Why do you think evil in your hearts? . . . But that you may know that the Son of man has authority on earth to forgive sins' – he then said to the paralytic – 'Rise, take up your bed and go home.' And he rose and went home.'

51. Christ and the Samaritan woman at the well

Exo-narthex; Bay VI, NW pendentive
Based on John 4, 4–27. The inscription summarises: 'Christ conversing with the Samaritan woman.'

52. Christ calls Zacchaeus (fragment)

Exo-narthex; Bay VII, S side of vault
Part of the inscription remains; '. . . saying, "Zacchaeus, make haste and come down." ' (Luke 19, 5) The feet of Christ are identifiable from His blue garment; part of Zacchaeus is in the tree. To the right is an unidentified scene with two disciples.

53. Christ heals the blind and dumb man

Narthex; Bay IV, SW pendentive
Based on Matt. 12, 22; 'Then a blind and dumb demoniac was brought to him, and he healed him, so that the dumb man spoke and saw.'

54. Christ heals two blind men

Narthex; Bay IV, NW pendentive
Based on Matt. 20, 30–24: 'And behold, two blind men sitting by the roadside, when they heard that Jesus was passing by, cried out, "Have mercy on us, Son of David" . . . And Jesus in pity touched their eyes, and immediately they received their sight and followed him.'

55. Jesus heals Peter's mother-in-law

Narthex; Bay IV, NE pendentive
Based on Matt. 8, 14–15: 'And when Jesus entered Peter's house, he saw his mother-in-law lying sick with a fever; he touched her hand, and the fever left her, and she rose and served him.' The inscription simply gives the title. Christ in the centre, John and Andrew in conversation behind him, pulls Peter's mother-in-law to a sitting position on her bed. Peter stands behind her.

56. Christ heals the woman with an issue of blood

Narthex; Bay IV, SE pendentive
Based on Matt. 9, 20–2; 'And behold, a woman who had suffered from a haemorrhage for twelve years came up behind him and touched the fringe of his garment . . . Jesus turned, and seeing her he said, "Take heart, daughter; your faith has made you well." And instantly the woman was made well.' The inscription is the title.

57. Christ heals the man with the withered hand

Narthex; Bay IV, E side of soffit of S arch
Based on Matt. 12, 9–13: 'And behold, there was a man with a withered hand . . . Then he said to the man, 'Stretch out your hand.' And the man stretched it out, and it was restored, whole like the other.'

58. Christ heals the leper

Narthex; Bay IV, W side of soffit of S arch
Based on Matt. 8, 1–4: '. . . And behold, a leper came to him and knelt before him, saying, 'Lord, if you will, you can make me clean.' And he stretched out his hand and touched him, saying, "I will; be clean." And immediately his leprosy was cleansed . . .'

59. Unidentified healing miracle (fragment)

Narthex; Bay IV, S lunette
Much damaged, including Christ's head and part of the inscription which now reads: 'Christ healing . . .'

60. Christ heals those afflicted with various diseases

Narthex; Bay IV, W lunette
This wonderfully integrated composition completes the cycle of Christ's ministry, showing Him healing 'the lame, the maimed, the blind, the dumb and many others.' (Matt. 15, 30) The inscription is from Mark 1, 34.

F THE NAVE MOSAICS

61. The Dormition of the Virgin

Above door from narthex
A superb scene, throbbing with life, the only survivor of a cycle on the great feasts of the church. The source is the apocryphal *Discourse of St John the Divine concerning the Koimesis [Dormition] of the Holy Mother of God.* Christ, in a double mandorla, stands behind the deathbed of

the Virgin to receive her soul, shown as a new-born baby. In the outer mandorla are two angels; above hovers a 6-winged seraph. Around are apostles, evangelists and bishops of the early church, and some women.

62. Christ

E wall of nave, left of apse
The inscription describes Christ as 'the dwelling-place (chora) of the living.' His face is sadly damaged. The open Gospel bears the words, 'Come to me, all who labour and are heavy laden, and I will give you rest.' (Matt. 11, 28)

63. The Virgin Hodegetria

E wall of nave, right of apse
The inscription describes the Virgin as 'the container of the un-containable' – again a double play on the word 'chora'. The Virgin is of the type known as Hodegetria (she who points the way) after the famous icon attributed to St Luke. Above is a sculptured tympanum with Christ Pantocrator in fresco, added later in the 14th C.

G PORTRAITS OF SAINTS AND MARTYRS

i) Martyr-saints of the eastern church, mostly little known, are on the soffits of the arches in the exo-narthex. 29 are busts in medallions, the names of most still legible. 8 are full-length figures; only 2 still with names.

ii) 6 wall panels contain remains of mosaics of precursors of the Incarnation, on the pilasters at the base of the transverse arches between the bays of the exo-narthex. Originally 12 panels faced each other on the 6 pairs of pilasters.

Between Bays I and II; St Anne holding the infant Mary opposite St Joachim.

Between Bays II and III; The Virgin and Child (St Joseph, on the opposite pilaster, is lost)

Between Bays III and IV; St John the Baptist – small fragment

Between Bays IV and V; unidentified military saint

Between Bays VI and VII; St Euthymius, one of the Palestinian Desert Fathers.

(Notice the very beautiful and unusual angel carvings on the capitals of the columns between Bays VI and VII).

THE FRESCOES IN THE PARECCLESION

The parecclesion, added by Theodore Metochites as a funerary chapel, was decorated in fresco rather than mosaic. It may well be the work of the same artist, and was almost certainly executed immediately after the completion of the mosaics. The chapel consists of two square bays, the western one domed, the eastern vaulted and with an apse at the E end. The culminating theme – suited to a funerary chapel – is of redemption and resurrection. The frescoes are in two horizontal layers: the lower a frieze of saints, martyrs and church fathers; the upper the great narrative scenes of prefiguration, judgment and resurrection.

A THE VIRGIN MARY AND HER PREFIGURATIONS

The western bay, dominated by the Virgin, is a prelude to the main themes of the eastern bay and the apse, for here she is seen as the bridge between heaven and hades, life and death, her Old Testament prefigurations one after another underlining this role.

1. The Virgin and Child surrounded by angels
In the dome
At the apex the Virgin and Child; around them, 12 of the heavenly host. Each is inscribed, 'Angel of the Lord'; the 4 archangels hold an orb in the left hand.

2. Four hymn-writers
In the pendentives of the dome
a) St John Damascene (NE)
b) St Cosmas (SE)
c) St Joseph (SW)
d) St Theophanes (NW)
Clad as monks, and in the act of composing, they link the Virgin in the dome with the scenes below, for all wrote hymns and poems in praise of the Virgin, and referred to her Old Testament prefigurations.

3. Jacob's ladder/Jacob wrestles with an angel
N lunette, left side
Joseph lies below the ladder; Genesis 28, 11–12 inscribed on either side: 'And Jacob, taking one of the stones of the place, put it under his head and lay down in the place to sleep. And he dreamed . . .'; continuing above: '. . . there was a ladder set up on the earth, and the top of it reached to heaven; and behold the angels of God were

ascending and descending on it! And behold the Lord stood above it.'
At the top is the Virgin and Child, a graphic underlining of her role as
bridge between earth and heaven. Beneath the ladder Jacob wrestles
with an angel.

4. Moses and the burning bush

N lunette, right side
An angel and the Virgin and Child are portrayed in the bush which,
burning yet unconsumed, is a type of the Virgin. Above is written:
'Now Moses came to Horeb, the mountain of God. And the angel of
the Lord appeared to him in a flame of fire in the midst of the bush.'
(Exod. 3, 4) Below is another figure of Moses and the words: 'Put off
your shoes from your feet, for the place on which you are standing is
holy ground.' (Exod. 3, 5)

5. Moses hides his face

N soffit of adjoining arch, between E and W bays
'Moses hid his face for he was afraid to look at God.' (Exod. 3, 6)

6. The bearing of the ark of the covenant

Just in E bay, right side of S lunette
'Thus all the work that the King [Solomon] did on the house of the
Lord was finished . . . Then [he] assembled the elders of Israel . . . to
bring up the ark of the covenant of the Lord out of the city of David,
which is Zion . . . and the priests took up the ark. And they brought
up the ark of the Lord, the tent of meeting . . .' (1 Kings 7, 51–8, 4)
The ark of the covenant, the container of the uncontainable, is a
prefiguration of the Virgin.

7. The bearing of the sacred vessels

S soffit of arch between E and W bays
Much damaged and the inscription lost, but it doubtless read:
'. . . and all the holy vessels that were in the tent.' (1 Kings 8, 4) The
vessels are here the prefigurations of the Virgin.

8. Solomon and all Israel

S lunette, left side
'And the King and all the congregation of Israel . . . [were with him]
before the ark.' (1 Kings 8, 5)

9. The installation of the ark in the Holy of Holies

S lunette, right side
'Then the priests brought the ark of the covenant of the Lord to its

place, in the inner sanctuary of the house, in the most holy place, underneath the wings of the cherubin.' (1 Kings 8, 6)

10. Isaiah prophesies/The angel smites the Assyrians before Jerusalem

S soffit of W arch

Based on Isaiah 37, 21 & 33 & 36: 'Then Isaiah the son of Amoz sent to Hezekiah, saying, 'Thus says the Lord, the God of Israel: 'Because you have prayed to me concerning Sennacherib king of Assyria . . . He shall not come near this city' . . . And the angel of the Lord went forth, and slew 185,000 in the camp of the Assyrians.' The Virgin's image on the gate of the inviolate city of Jerusalem marks it as her prefiguration.

11. Aaron and his sons before the altar

N soffit of W arch

The inscription is damaged, but may be Lev. 9, 7: 'Then Moses said to Aaron, draw near to the altar, and offer your sin offering and your burnt offering and make atonement for yourself and for the people.' The altar itself is the Virgin's prefiguration.

12. The souls of the righteous in the hand of God (fragment)

Crown of W arch

God's hand holds souls shown as babes in swaddling clothes.

B THE LAST JUDGMENT

EASTERN BAY

13. The second coming of Christ

Domical vault

This composite scene, of great power and complexity, occupies the whole vault. At the centre the **scroll of heaven**, containing the sun, moon and stars, is unrolled by an angel in flight. **Christ in judgment** sits enthroned on a rainbow and in a mandorla between the Virgin and John the Baptist; behind Him a host of angels, and on either side a row of apostles, with an astonishing diversity of expression, posture and drapery. Below and above, clouds bear up **choirs of the elect** (anticlockwise from SW); bishops (in cross-pattern robes), holy men, holy women (damaged), martyrs, apostles and prophets (above NE pendentive). Beneath Christ, the Etimasia, or **preparing of the throne**, before which Adam and Eve prostrate themselves; below is the **weighing of souls**, with scales suspended from the throne. From the left come two angels, laden with the records of souls to be weighed. Under the scales a soul awaits judgment; to the left condemned souls huddle together, and others are led in chains to the **fiery stream and the lake of fire** in the SE corner. The lake is in poor condition, but figures in the fire can still be seen, as well as a group half out of the lake at the top. At the bottom is the outline of a monster.

14. The land and sea give up their dead

SW pendentive

Based on Revelation 20, 13: 'And the sea gave up the dead in it, Death and Hades gave up the dead in them.' Although damaged, we can still see two angels with trumpets above figures of the dead standing up. Below, the beasts of the sea disgorge their dead.

15. An angel and a soul

NW pendentive

An appealing theory is that this represents the archangel Michael interceding for the soul of Theodore Metochites; but it may show the soul of the beggar Lazarus being presented for judgment.

16. The beggar Lazarus in Abraham's bosom

NE pendentive

Abraham sits in Paradise surrounded by souls of the just, with the soul of Lazarus in his lap, dressed in the finest clothes.

17. The rich man Dives in hell

SE pendentive

Dives in the fires of hell, an arm across his well-fed stomach, his gold and moneybags falling into the flames, turns to Abraham in the adjacent pendentive, begging him to 'send Lazarus to dip the end of his finger in water and cool my tongue; for I am in anguish in this flame.' (Luke 16, 24)

18. The torments of the damned

S lunette, right side

Quartered in red and black. Bottom left (black): white squiggles, superimposed on human figures, represent 'the worm that sleepeth not'; bottom right: 'the unquenchable fire'; top right: 'the outer darkness'; top left (damaged): 'the gnashing of teeth'.

19. The entry of the elect into Paradise

N lunette

St Peter leads the elect to the gate of Paradise, guarded by a cherub with drawn sword. On the other side the good thief points to the enthroned Virgin, the Queen of Heaven.

C THE RESURRECTION

On the apsidal arch, two miracles of Christ raising from the dead are a prelude to the great Anastasis that fills the semi-dome.

20. **Christ raises the widow's son**
N side of apsidal arch
Based on Luke 7, 11–15: '[Jesus] went to a city called Nain . . . as he drew near to the gate of the city, behold, a man who had died was being carried out, the only son of his mother, and she was a widow . . . And when the Lord saw her, he had compassion on her . . . And he said, 'Young man, I say to you, arise.' And the dead man sat up and began to speak.'

21. **Christ raises Jairus' daughter**
S side of apsidal arch
Based on Matt. 9, 18–19 & 23–25: 'Behold, a ruler came in and knelt before him, saying, "My daughter has just died; but come and lay your hands on her and she will live" . . . And when Jesus came to the ruler's house . . . he went in and took her by the hand, and the girl rose.'

22. **The Anastasis**
Semi-dome of apse
One of the finest works of Byzantine art of any period, and the focal point of the parecclesion, portrays Christ's descent into Hades to raise and redeem the righteous of the pre-Christian era. Its source is the 4th or 5th C. Apocryphal Gospel of Nicodemus.

Radiant in the centre is the resurrected Christ, a figure of exceptional strength and vigour, robed in shining white within a triple mandorla. With irresistible force He drags Adam and Eve from their graves, and they respond with urgency to His strong, vivifying grasp. Beneath Christ's feet lies Satan, bound hand and foot and neck, around him the toppled gates of hell and all the shattered paraphernalia of captivity – locks, keys, bolts, hooks, augers, hinges etc. Above Adam, John the Baptist points to Christ and looks towards a group of the righteous of the old order. *Left*: King Solomon and King David, between them another king, followed by six anonymous figures – all hold out hands in supplication. *Right*: Adam and Eve's son Abel, with his shepherd's crook, stands on Eve's sarcophagus, behind him six more of the righteous. The serenity of the groups at either side contrasts powerfully with the dynamic intensity at the centre of the fresco which celebrates Christ's triumph over death.

D PORTRAITS ON THE WALLS

23. Church Fathers
Apse
Left to right: a) unidentified; b) St Athanasius; c) St John Chrysostom; d) St Basil; e) St Gregory the Theologian (of Nazianzus); f) St Cyril of Alexandria.

24. The Virgin Eleousa (the Compassionate)
S apse wall
On the opposite wall was a figure of Christ, now destroyed.

25. Saints
On walls of eastern and western bays
20 saints and martyrs of the Byzantine Empire.

26. Medallion portraits in the arches
a) Melchizedek (much damaged) and b) Christ face each other at the top of the transverse arches on either side of the dome. c) A second medallion of Christ is on the soffit of the arch immediately below the first. d) At the centre of the apsidal arch is the archangel Michael.

THE TOMBS

A *Parecclesion, N wall of western bay*
The inscription is lost, but this is believed to be the tomb of Theodore Metochites. Outside the arch is an elaborately carved design of acanthus leaves and palmettes, with a bust of Christ at the centre flanked by the archangels Michael and Gabriel.

B *Parecclesion, N wall of eastern bay*
Unknown who was buried here, and no original decoration remains.

C *Parecclesion, S wall of eastern bay*
The original decoration remains: a group of 4 figures, the central 2 in princely garb, but with no identification.

D *Parecclesion, S wall of western bay*
The tomb of Michael Tornikes, Grand Constable of Andronicus II, a friend of Theodore Metochites, and also a poor monk at his death. Remains of a mosaic Virgin at the centre is flanked by frescoes of Tornikes and his wife who reappear in mosaic on the soffits in

monastic habits, their names in religion above them – Makarios and Eugenia. A long inscription also survives.

E *Exo-narthex, Bay V, W wall*
The tomb of Irene Raoulaina Palaeologina, related by marriage to Metochites. The soffit has frescoes of the Virgin and Child, with st Cosmas of Maiuma (left) and St John Damascene (right).

F *Exo-narthex, Bay IV, W wall*
For an unidentifiable member of the Palaeologus family; a fresco of the lower parts of a man, woman and child in rich garments.

G *Exo-narthex, Bay II, W wall*
Built only a few years before the Ottoman Conquest, it was decorated in fresco, of which only the lower part remains, with a figure standing before a seated Virgin and Child. It shows considerable influence of the early Italian Renaissance.

H *Narthex, Bay I, N wall*
The tomb of Demetrius Ducas Angelus Palaeologus, youngest son of Andronicus II. It was decorated in mosaic, but only a figure of the Virgin, some decorative border and part of an inscription survive. It reads: 'You are the fount of life, the Mother of God, the Word. And I am Demetrius, your slave in devotion.'

8

MEHMET THE CONQUEROR
AND HIS HEIRS

When the 21 year old Mehmet II rode into Constantinople as its conqueror on 29 May 1453, he saw his victory as the first step not merely in re-establishing the eastern Roman Empire, but in creating a new worldwide dominion. Brought up on tales of the heroes of the ancient world, he saw himself as a new Alexander the Great combined with Julius Caesar. And had not the 9th C. Arab philosopher al-Kindi prophesied that there would arise a Mahdi, a man guided by Allah, who would 'renew Islam and cause justice to triumph. He will conquer the Spanish peninsula and reach Rome and conquer it. He will travel to the East and conquer it. He will conquer Constantinople, and dominion over the whole earth will be his.' Assuming the role of this Mahdi, though altering his order of conquest, Mehmet saw Constantinople as the first, and Rome as the final key that would unlock the world.

His record up to the time of his accession in 1451 was hardly promising. Born on 30 March 1432, he was the third, and much the youngest, of Sultan Murat II's sons. In 1437 his eldest brother Ahmet died suddenly and Mehmet, aged five, was appointed governor of Amasya in his stead, two years later swapping posts with his other older brother, Alaêttin Ali, in Manisa. In 1443 Alaêttin Ali was murdered, and the 11 year old Mehmet, for whom his father had little affection, became heir to the Ottoman throne.

It seems he deserved his unpopularity with his father for he was uncontrollable, rude and arrogant, and rejected any attempts at education or correction. As a last resort Murat appointed a scholarly and awe-inspiring, Mullah, Ahmet Gürani, as the boy's tutor, giving him a cane the better to enforce his instruction. When Mehmet laughed in his face at their first meeting, Gürani gave him such a thrashing as to inspire his enduring respect.

At the end of 1444 the 40 year old Murat II, still filled with grieving melancholy for the loss of his favourite son the year before, and longing for a life of intellectual and mystical withdrawal, abdicated in favour of the nearly 13 year old Mehmet. Earlier that year Murat had subdued the troublesome Karamanids in Anatolia, and seen off a formidable European crusading army bent on driving the Ottomans out of the Balkans; everything seemed stable for the youthful new Sultan under the competent guidance of Murat's Grand Vezir, Çandarlı Halil Paşa. But relationships with Europe remained tense and the Janissaries did not like Mehmet, so in late spring 1446 Halil Paşa sent a secret message to Murat, in idyllic retirement in Manisa, begging him to return. Reluctantly Murat made his way in slow stages to Edirne, and the humiliated Mehmet was sent to Manisa to nurse his wounded pride. He never forgave Çandarlı Halil Paşa, but he bided his time until he was secure enough to move against him.

It was hardly surprising that when Murat II died suddenly of a fit of apoplexy in February 1451, the nearly 19 year old Mehmet was regarded by Turks and Europeans alike as an inexperienced and ineffectual youth. All were soon to realise their mistake.

While Murat's widow had an audience with her stepson, the new Sultan, Mehmet sent orders that her baby son, Küçük Ahmet, his only remaining half-brother, should be drowned in his bath. It was not the first time that a brother had been murdered to ensure the peaceful accession of a new Ottoman Sultan; what was new was Mehmet's subsequent elevation of the deed into law – 'Whichever of my sons inherits the Sultan's throne, it is fitting for him to kill his brothers to ensure the repose of the state.'

Having first secured his borders in Anatolia and mastered the rebellious Janissaries, Mehmet then concentrated on the capture of Constantinople. In the spring and summer of 1452 he built Rumeli Hisarı, a fortress on the European shore of the Bosphorus opposite Anadolu Hisarı, on the Asian shore, built some 60 years earlier by Beyazit I. With his love of classical allusion, the site he had chosen was not only strategically the best to control the Bosphorus, but also the place where Darius of Persia built a bridge of boats in the 6th C. BC before capturing Byzantium.

For all the richness of its remaining treasures, the Constantinople that Mehmet captured was a sadly ruined, impoverished and depopulated city, with little more than 60,000 inhabitants. Mehmet's first act was to take over Haghia Sophia and convert it into the supreme mosque of the Ottoman Empire. Two days later he dismissed his Grand Vezir, Halil Paşa, who had consistently opposed his assault on Constantinople, accused him of complicity with the Byzantines and imprisoned him. Six weeks later he ordered his execution, thus settling his old score with the man who had humiliated him seven years before.

Mehmet garrisoned the city with 1500 Janissaries and appointed Turkish officials to supervise the new administration. Over the years that followed he built up the population of this Greek and Christian capital, which soon assumed the character of an oriental and Islamic one. Eight churches were converted into mosques, the rest being left to the Greeks, and several new mosques were built. He brought in both Muslims and Christians from other conquered cities, and he encouraged Jews from Europe, sorely persecuted in the countries where they were, to settle here. At his death in 1481 he had roughly doubled the population of Istanbul; only about half were Muslims.

Istanbul did not immediately become the new Ottoman capital. Three weeks after the Conquest Mehmet returned to Edirne, and for several years preferred his old capital and palace. But he also set in hand the building of a new palace in Istanbul in 1454, on a magnificent site where today the University of Istanbul stands. Most of this palace, later known as Eski Saray, the old palace, went up in flames in 1714, and the rest was pulled down in 1870 when the new Dolmabahçe Palace had made it redundant. He also built his own great mosque complex, Fatih Camii, the mosque of the Conqueror, and a covered market, thus establishing the essential ingredients of an imperial Ottoman city. Five years after the first palace, Mehmet ordered another to be built on the ancient citadel of Byzantium. Topkapı Sarayı was not originally designed as a residence, but to house the administration of the growing Empire, and it was not until this was completed in 1472 that Istanbul truly became the capital of the Ottoman Empire.

Mehmet filled his court, by now transferred to Istanbul, with European scholars and artists, welcoming there Gentile Bellini who painted his likeness. Italians were especially in evidence, perhaps to enable him to learn more of the territory that he wished to conquer – in particular Rome – as well as to discover the locations associated with the ancient heroes with whom he identified. The Venetian Giacomo de' Languschi, who visited Mehmet's court, wrote that the Sultan was 'at great pains to learn the geography of Italy and to inform himself of the places where Anchises and Aeneas and Antenor landed, where the seat of the Pope is and that of the Emperor, and how many kingdoms there are in Europe.' He added that Mehmet had declared that he would 'advance from East to West as in former times the Westerners advanced into the Orient. There must, he says, be only one emperor, one faith, and one sovereignty in the world . . . It is with such a man that we Christians have to deal.'

Though Mehmet never reached his goal of Rome, he did take Otranto in 1480, striking such terror into Italian hearts that even the Pope was said to be on the point of flight from Rome. But the threat came to nothing and Mehmet died in the following year, aged only 49, his dreams of world domination unfulfilled. He had, however, brilliantly extended Ottoman rule not only in Europe, but also in Anatolia.

Mehmet was succeeded by his eldest son, Beyazit II, a man of occasional stern asceticism, less enamoured of conquest for its own sake than his father. Left on his own , Beyazit might have gone for political, economic and social consolidation, living a life of devout and cultivated simplicity. As it was he was faced with civil war, challenged for the throne by his younger brother, Cem Sultan, a prince who combined the poetic gift with a ruthless martial tendency. Until his death in 1495, some 14 years later, Cem was adopted in turn by various European powers who tried to use him to destabilise the rising Ottoman power.

By 1502 Beyazit was ready to withdraw from active life, leaving the field open for more martial elements to take power into their own hands. These centred on Beyazit's second son, Selim, who in April 1512 deposed his father and became Sultan for eight years of ruthless rule and brilliant military conquests, extending further than ever before both the boundaries of Ottoman dominion, and the wealth of its coffers.

Route 1

ÇINILI KÖŞK/CERAMICS MUSEUM

Open Tuesday only, though this can change – check first. This is part of the compound of the Istanbul Archaeological Museums; the sections open on any given day are posted at the main entrance.

Çinili Köşk, the tiled pavilion, is one of the few of Mehmet the Conqueror's known works where elegance outweighs size. It is also one of the very few non-religious buildings of the period to have survived. Mehmet built it just as Topkapı Sarayı was being completed in 1472 – clearly he already felt the need for a place of retreat when the business of government weighed too heavily, and here he could indulge his personal architectural taste and fantasies. Its appearance is hardly Ottoman; both in its overall design and in the style of its tile decoration, it seems more like a palace magically wafted here from Persia or central Asia.

From the first floor terrace the Conqueror, his sons and members of his household, could watch a stirring game of cirit – a cross between polo and a full-scale cavalry charge – on the flat ground now largely occupied by the Archaeological Museum. When Topkapı Sarayı was abandoned in the mid-19th C., Çinili Köşk remained empty for about 20 years. From 1874 it became a storehouse for antiquities (now in the Archaeological Museum), and in the 1950s it was restored and opened as a tile museum.

The main façade consists of a lofty portico of 13 arches at first floor level, supported by 14 slender columns, rebuilt in stone in an 18th C. restoration, to replace the wooden originals. Steps lead up to the terrace which is decorated with mosaic tile panels in geometric designs of turquoise, dark blue and white. They may have been made in the Iznik kilns, then in the very earliest period of their production. The deep recess around the main doorway includes not only mosaic work, but also inscriptions and a vine motif executed in the *cuerda seca* technique, and extending the colour range to include yellow, green and purple.

A small vestibule leads into the central room in the form of a Latin cross crowned by a high dome. Here, according to Mehmet's architectural cosmology, was the symbolic centre of his universe, with a room in each angle of the cross representing the four corners of the earth which he wished to rule. Every room is gloriously vaulted. To left and right the court leads into open eyvans (now glazed for comfort), while straight ahead is a bow-fronted room which projects beyond the main line of the outer wall. This inner sanctum of the royal apartments looked out onto gardens described in paradisical terms by Mehmet's enthusiastic Greek biographer, Kritovoulos – today's Gülhane Parkı.

The tiles which adorn the walls inside Çinili Köşk are almost museum enough in themselves, with designs formed in a mosaic of hexagonal and triangular tiles in turquoise, dark blue and white, some of them over-painted in gold in delicate patterns of leaves and flowers. But the rooms also contain both individual tiles and whole compositions from the 12th C. onwards, all superbly displayed. The earliest exhibits are some lovely Selçuk tiles from the 12th to 14th C.;

then some transitional work, including Bursa-type tiles of the 14th to 15th C.; but the chief glory is the Iznik work of the best periods of their production from the early 16th to the early 17th C. Particularly striking is the 16th C. mihrab from Ibrahim Bey Camii in Karaman in southern Turkey. Later work, from the 18th to 19th C., is also displayed, including some pretty plates from the Çanakkale potteries.

For those wishing to visit the Archaeological Museum or the Museum of the Ancient Orient, please see Appendices A and B.

Leaving the museums' compound, we turn right and go down the hill which brings us just inside the gate in the palace walls that is now the entrance to Gülhane Parkı. Detours 1 and 3 that follow are detours in history only; they are directly on our route to Mahmut Paşa Camii. Detour 2 is for those who would like a gentle stroll in the park.

Detour 1 **Alay Köşkü** (Open daily)

Just inside the park gates a ramp leads up to a small pavilion built into an angle of the outer walls of Topkapı Sarayı. Alay Köşkü, the parade pavilion, is so named because from it the Sultan would watch the various official and military parades, the most spectaculiar being the Procession of the Guilds. According to Evliya Çelebi, who watched a procession in 1638, there were 1001 guilds (in other words, an uncountable number), divided into 57 sections. All wore costumes associated with their guild and, like some glorified carnival, with tumblers, mime actors and every kind of entertainer doing their best to delight the Sultan, and fill his ears with a merry din. According to Evliya, 'these guilds pass before the Alay Kiosk with a thousand tricks and fits which it is impossible to describe'.

The original pavilion was built here in the mid-16th C., but the present one dates from a rebuilding in 1819 by Sultan Mahmut II. Until recently it housed a collection of embroidery and rugs; today it stands empty.

Detour 2 **Gülhane Parkı**

Gülhane Parkı, rose-house park, is named after the now defunct building in which rose-flavoured sweetmeats were made for the royal court. If today's park has little relationship with Mehmet's gardens of paradise here, it is still a very pleasant place for a stroll beneath the trees, especially in blossom time. The sad little zoo, however, is not worth a detour. We should take the path directly beneath the Museums, noticing in particular the tiles of the lofty rear façade of

Çinili Kösk. Another kiosk, which projects from the walls of Topkapı Sarayı, is that of Osman III, built in the baroque style in 1754–7. The path curves to the right and uphill, leading to an open space below the Fourth Court of Topkapı, on which stands a great monolithic granite column – probably the oldest monument in the city. It is known as the **Goths' Column** from the dedicatory inscription on its base; FORTUNAE REDUCI OB DEVICTOS GOTHOS – to Fortune who has returned because of the defeat of the Goths. Nothing is known for sure of its origins – the Goths troubled Byzantium, and later Constantinople, over many centuries. One theory favours the 3rd C. AD Claudius II Gothicus as its originator; another, Constantine the Great.

Detour 3 **The Sublime Porte**

Returning to Alay Köşkü, we go out of the park gates and turn right down the hill. At the next corner, on the other side of the road opposite Alay Köşkü, we see a once imposing rococo gateway with a widely overhanging roof. This is Bab-ı Ali, the Sublime Porte, the famous gateway to the great offices of government in the Ottoman Empire from the latter part of the 16th C. on. It was Sokollu Mehmet Paşa, Süleyman the Magnificent's last Grand Vezir, who moved his office from Topkapı to a palace that he built on this site. By the late 18th C. all the main administrative and executive offices had moved here. Foreign ambassadors would present their credentials here and were known as 'Ambassadors to the Sublime Porte'. This particular gateway was known only to ambassadors from the mid-19th C. on, for it was built by Abdül Mecit I in 1840. Today's ambassadors reside in Ankara.

MAHMUT PAŞA CAMII

We take Alay Köşkü Cad. to the left of the Sublime Porte, and turn right after about 200 m into Hilali Ahmer Cad. 100 m further on we turn left into Nuruosmaniye Cad. and, after another 200 m or so, right into Vezirhanı Cad. The first turning on the right, Kılıççılar Sok., the street of the sword-makers, brings us to Mahmut Paşa Camii, set in a charming if dilapidated square. We first see Mahmut Paşa's elegant octagonal **türbe**, built in 1473. It is covered in stunning turquoise, deep blue and green mosaic tiles, similar in type (though different in design) to those of Çinili Köşk which had been built only the year before. These too may come from the earliest Iznik kilns.

Mahmut Paşa is one of the most remarkable figures of Ottoman history, descended on his father's side from the Byzantine royal dynasties of the Angeli and Comneni. When his mother, a Serbian, was captured and taken to the Ottoman capital at Edirne, her son was taken into the Pages' School at the Sultan's court where he became a Muslim, quickly distinguished himself for his brilliance and struck up a close friendship with Prince Mehmet. In 1453 Mehmet, now Sultan, appointed his favourite beylerbeyi of Rumeli. In the following year he made him Grand Vezir, a year after the execution of Çandarlı Halil Paşa.

Mahmut Paşa was a man of immense learning, and an able administrator and general to whom Mehmet owed many of his notable conquests. He was a generous patron of poets, artists and scholars, and was no mean poet himself, writing in both Persian and Turkish under the name of Adni (of Eden). He was beloved of every level of society, and widely regarded as a saint; but his honesty and outspokenness, which had won him the friendship of the Sultan, may also have played a part in his downfall. He was summarily dismissed from office in 1467, thanks to the evil scheming of another converted Greek, the Second Vezir Rum Mehmet Paşa, who stepped into his shoes. At the end of 1472, however, Mehmet recalled him, dismissing him for the second time a year later, for no specific reason other than the Sultan's suspicious and unpredictable nature. He was executed on 18 July 1474, his türbe having been providently completed some months before.

Mahmut Paşa's mosque was built in 1462–3 when his career was at its zenith. It was part of an extensive complex which included a medrese, a law court, an imaret, a mektep and a han – the first such complex to be built in Istanbul after that of the Sultan himself. Mahmut Paşa made no startling innovations here; rather he looked back to, and adapted, the style associated with Bursa, of which there are few examples in Istanbul.

With no courtyard preceding it (the hideous şadırvan is a later addition), the mosque is entered through a 5-bayed portico whose original columns were encased by the ungainly octagonal stone piers we see today, in the second of two restorations (1755 and 1828) to which the mosque has been subjected. Inside is a narthex, unusual in an Istanbul mosque, the central vault with a fine stalactite design. Steps lead up to the main prayer hall – a double square divided by a great arch, each part covered by a dome. The pendentives of both domes are curiously plain compared with the elaboration of the stalactite or ribbed work around most of the other domes – probably the result of restoration. The undistinguished mihrab and mimber are

18th C. incongruities; and the 19th C. Sultan's gallery would not seem so bad were it not painted green. On either side of the prayer hall openings admit to narrow, barrel-vaulted passages, each opening into three further domed rooms intended (as in Bursa mosques) as tabhanes.

MAHMUT PAŞA HAMAMI

A handsome hamam was added to Mahmut Paşa's complex in 1466, three years after the completion of the mosque and only a year before his first fall from favour. Its revenues, like those of the han, went to the upkeep of the mosque and its various pious foundations. To find it we should return to Vezirhanı Cad. and turn right, which brings us to Mahmut Paşa Yokuşu. Mahmut Paşa Hamamı, with its cluster of domes, stands back from the street on the left, the oldest Ottoman hamam in Istanbul. Only half the original building remains, for the women's section was pulled down to accommodate a new han. It is well worth a look inside for its domes and semi-dome are handsomely ribbed or whorled, and there is some fine stalactite work on some of the squinches.

Negotiating the Kapalı Çarşı, or Covered Bazaar, can be an ordeal, with endless opportunities for getting lost. Those with a developed sense of self-preservation should return past Mahmut Paşa Camii to Nuruosmaniye Cad. and turn right through a gateway into the precinct of Nuruosmaniye Camii. This leads into a street of the Covered Bazaar which goes without deviation to Beyazit.

Detour **Nuruosmaniye Camii**

While passing, we may cast a glance at this handsome baroque structure which was begun by Mahmut I in 1748, and finished seven years later by the brother who succeeded him, Osman III. Since he had the last word, Osman named the mosque after himself – Light of Osman. It is said that Mahmut wanted a mosque built in the European baroque style that was gaining a considerable vogue in secular buildings. But the religious authorities maintained that this would be unsuitable for a mosque, so the result was a compromise, which still succeeded in shocking the more conservative Islamic opinion. It is thought that the architect was a Greek called Simeon who had studied in Europe.

Inside, it consists of a vast square covered by a lofty dome, its monumental symmetry mercifully broken by the large mihrab apse which projects in what could be called a 5-sided semi-circle. A deep frieze, containing a handsome inscription in relief, runs all around the interior of the mosque at the level of the springing of the tympanum arches, also taking in the apse around the base of its semi-dome. Light floods in through the multiple windows in the soaring arches of the tympana, while 32 windows (four of them blind) are let into the base of the dome. The courtyard is most unusual, being horse-shoe shaped, with nine domed bays running round in an elongated semi-circle to join the ends of the 5-domed portico.

KAPALI ÇARŞI/THE COVERED BAZAAR

Say Istanbul and the Grand Bazaar comes to mind:
Beethoven's Ninth hand in hand with the Algerian March.
Bedri Rahmi Eyuboğlu

Today there is little left of the Algerian March, and Beethoven's Ninth has encroached even into the heart of the Grand Bazaar, for it has been restored and painted, and many shops look more European than oriental with their trim matching façades. But the painted designs have a delightful touch of the Ottoman; and the clearing of wires and garish plastic and neon signs has revealed the grand sweep of arched and intersecting passages of this vast labyrinthine city within a city. It is not really as confusing as it appears at first sight, for much of it is designed on a grid system – but a compass would occasionally be welcome.

Since no Ottoman town was complete without its bedesten, Mehmet the Conqueror at once set about creating one. Kritovoulos, in characteristically superlative terms, tells us that Mehmet 'commanded them to construct a very large and very fine market place in the centre of the City, somewhere near the palace, protected by very strong walls on the outside, and divided on the inside into very beautiful and spacious colonnades. It was to have a roof of fired tile and to be ornamented with dressed stone.' Thus began the İç Bedesten, the Inner Bedesten at the heart of the market which grew and multiplied around it. No other Ottoman city had had so large a bedesten. No other city had more than one; but such was the prestige of Istanbul, and the volume of trade that passed through it, that it was not long before a second – Sandal Bedesteni – was built, either by Mehmet himself or by his son and heir Beyazit II.

Members of the same trade guild tended to set up their shops in the same area, a practice still reflected in the names of the streets – cobblers, purse-makers, belt-makers, skullcap-makers, tassel-makers, and so on. Today these divisions are less clear, but they still

Istanbul: The Covered Bazaar

remain in principle. At first the Bazaar was an agglomeration of flimsy structures, and in 1546 it was devastated by a terrible fire – the first in its history, and probably the worst; though another in 1660 was almost as bad, described by an Istanbullu of the day as 'turning the nights into days with brilliant flames, and days into nights with smoke.' The most recent fire was in 1954. Earthquakes too have taken their toll, the worst in 1894 when many domes and vaults collapsed. After each disaster the Bazaar was rebuilt more stoutly than before.

Entering the Bazaar from the courtyard of Nuruosmaniye Camii, we come into Kalpakçılar Cad., the street of the fur cap sellers. This runs straight along the side of the Bazaar, emerging just below the precinct of Beyazit II Camii. If we always return to the street of the fur cap sellers after any historical or commercial detours, the danger of getting lost is much reduced.

Almost immediately on our right as we enter the Bazaar, an entrance leads into the **Sandal Bedesteni**, the later of the two bedestens, named after a type of rich silk cloth. It is a magnificent old hall, with 20 brick domes supported on 12 great stone piers – the commercial twin of the Bursa Ulu Cami. Until recently auctions of rugs and jewellery were held in the Sandal Bedesteni, but this has been discontinued.

Taking the second turning on the right after the Sandal Bedesteni – Terzi Başı Sok., head tailor road – we come after two blocks to Kuyumcular, the goldsmiths' area. On our left is the **İç Bedesten**, the Conqueror's original foundation. Set into the wall above Kuyumcular Kapısı, the eastern gate of the bedesten, is a curious Byzantine relief carving of a single-headed eagle – the emblem of the 12th C. Comnene Emperors. Some scholars have inferred from this that the bedesten was of Byzantine origin; but its credentials seem unequivocally Ottoman, and from the time of the Conqueror, and it was common practice to incorporate good building material and decoration from earlier structures. Inside, it is difficult to see the basic shape of the bedesten, so crowded is this most secure part of the Covered Bazaar, its shops bursting with every kind of ancient and precious article – often of very fine craftsmanship but also, it should be noted, of varying authenticity. But behind and above it all are 15 domed bays supported on 8 massive piers.

Leaving the bedesten in a southerly direction inevitably leads back to Kalpakçılar Cad. where we turn right and continue to Beyazit, emerging at a corner of Beyazit II Camii, on a terrace immediately above. Turning right into Çadırcılar Cad., there is a gateway a short distance down on the left – Hakkaklar Kapısı, the gate of the metal engravers – through which steps lead up to Sahaflar Çarşısı and Beyazit II Camii.

Detour **Sahaflar Çarşısı**

Sahaflar Çarşısı, the second-hand booksellers market, is a fascinating corner in the outer courtyard of the Beyazidiye where stalls for second-hand and antiquarian books rub shoulders with university textbooks under the gentle shade of rambling vines. The booksellers took over this area in the 18th C., and it quickly became one of the most flourishing centres of the book trade – 'the Paternoster Row of Constantinople,' according to Charles White who spent three years in the city in the mid-19th C. He added that the booksellers' 'reputation for avarice and merciless extortion is so notorious among their countrymen, that it is common, when speaking of a close-fisted dealer, to exclaim, "he is worse than a sahhaf".' Once the hub of the book trade, this market is now a quiet backwater where scholars seek rare books in secluded interiors, while others browse among dog-eared paperbacks in almost every known language.

BEYAZIT II CAMII

The mosque of Beyazit II stands in solitary imperial state in a wide and open square on the third hill, its two minarets set grandly apart at the ends of projecting wings. Beyazit Square is on the site of the Byzantine Forum of Theodosius, and beside that of the first Ottoman palace, Eski Saray. It is the oldest surviving imperial mosque in Istanbul, for the original Fatih Camii, built by Beyazit's father, Mehmet the Conqueror, was destroyed in an earthquake in 1766. Building began here in 1501 and the complex was completed in 1506, just six years before Beyazit's deposition and death.

Beyazit II, 'the Pious', was something of a puritan; it is said that he destroyed some Italianate frescoes in his father's palaces which offended his religious sense, and sold other portable works of which he disapproved. But he was a great builder; and it was in architecture that the greatest advances were made during his reign, establishing the beginnings of a distinctively Ottoman style that was to be developed over the next two centuries. In this mosque, the masterpiece of Beyazit's reign, his architect was Yakup Şah ibn Sultan Şah who had built two hans for the Sultan in Bursa a few years before, whose revenues were designated to help build and maintain this mosque.

The square **courtyard** is filled with harmonious and subtle contrasts – of richly coloured marbles offsetting the plain stone of the main structure; of glorious carved stalactite decoration highlighting the basic simplicity of the design; the whole bound together with perfect symmetry. The 20 ancient columns, of verd-antique, porphyry and red granite, are especially handsome, and the voussoirs of the arches between them are in alternate bands of red and white marble. In the arch above the main portal white marble alternates strikingly with verd-antique. All the capitals have fine stalactite carving, and a deeply incised frieze runs all round above the arches. At the centre is a pretty şadırvan whose less elegant canopy was added by Murat IV in the 17th C. Very impressive is the great portal into the mosque, with its rich stalactite carving.

Just inside the **mosque**, we stand beneath the first of the two semi-domes that flank the central dome – recalling Haghia Sophia with its long rectangular central space. Here the dome springs from four massive piers, and between each pair on either side is an ancient monolithic granite column. Down both sides run side aisles which extend the interior of the mosque into a perfect square of exactly the same dimensions as the courtyard. The **sultan's loge** – unusually on the right hand side instead of the left – is supported on very fine columns of different coloured marble and has a beautifully carved balustrade; and both the **mihrab** and **mimber** are richly carved.

Looking to left and right from just inside the main entrance we have the impression of a narthex, for the two projecting wings of the building that we saw from the outside are incorporated into the main body of the mosque. Originally, it seems that these were separate and were the traditional tabhane, but here treated in a manner quite different from previous mosques.

Beyazit's **türbe** – a domed octagon of limestone trimmed with verd-antique – stands in a little tree-filled garden behind the mosque. Beside it are two other türbes, one of his daughter Selçuk Sultan and the other, incongruously, of a 19th C. Grand Vezir, Koca Reşit Paşa. Below the türbes is an arcade of shops (a reconstruction of Sinan's original of 1580), and beside it is a building with two domes which was the **mektep** of the Beyazit complex. The **imaret** stands near the eastern minaret, a large and handsome building with a very grand portal. Originally it doubled as both charity kitchen and caravansaray; now it caters to the press as a research library. The large **medrese**, on the NW edge of the square, now houses the Vakf Museum of Calligraphy. Further on down the main street stands the very large **hamam**, once a building of exceptional splendour but now much in need of restoration. It was constructed partly with material from the tumbled column and triumphal arch of Theodosius the Great, including some carvings from the column showing soldiers with shields and helmets and spears. Some stones are set upside down, including one depicting two soldiers in a boat on a wavy sea.

Detour   **The University of Istanbul**

The main campus of the University of Istanbul stands immediately to the north of the Beyazidiye, behind a monumental gateway, on the site of Mehmet the Conqueror's first palace. It was Mehmet who founded the first Islamic institution of higher education in his new capital in the medreses of his great Fatih complex, the ancestor of today's University. Subsequent Sultans added further medreses, notably Süleyman the Magnificent at his own mosque complex. In the 19th C. both Abdül Mecit I and Abdül Aziz tried to establish the Ottoman Imperial University for secular higher education; but it was not until 1900, in the reign of Abdül Hamit II, that it was definitively established. In 1933, under the Republic, it was reorganised as the University of Istanbul and transferred to the main building here – an example of mid-19th C. ostentation built for the Ministry of War which, along with all other ministries, had moved to the new capital of Ankara.

Standing inside the University grounds is the Beyazit Tower which takes its place, along with the minarets and domes, in the classic skyline of the city. It is a 50 m high marble tower, built in 1828 by Mahmut II as a fire tower. The architect was Senekerim Balyan, one of the renowned architectural dynasty, and he replaced an earlier wooden tower built by his brother Kirkor. For many years its main function was to indicate at night, by means of coloured lights, what the weather was expected to be the following day – green for rain, blue for clear, red for snow. It did not always get it right. By day there are magnificent panoramic views from the top of the tower – but it is not usually open to the public.

Route 2

FATIH CAMII

The great mosque complex of the Conqueror stands on a high terrace on the fourth hill beside Fevzi Paşa Cad., the highway that leads to Edirne Kapısı. The main entrance is from Islambol Cad. The mosque we see today is not the one built by Mehmet the Conqueror, for that was destroyed in an earthquake in 1766 and completely rebuilt by Mustafa III on the old foundations, but with a different design; but other parts of the complex were less damaged and remain as they were in the 15th C.

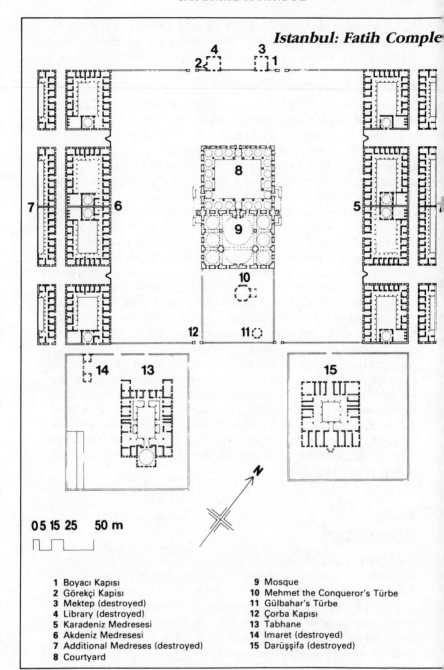

Istanbul: Fatih Comple

1 Boyacı Kapısı
2 Görekçi Kapısı
3 Mektep (destroyed)
4 Library (destroyed)
5 Karadeniz Medresesi
6 Akdeniz Medresesi
7 Additional Medreses (destroyed)
8 Courtyard
9 Mosque
10 Mehmet the Conqueror's Türbe
11 Gülbahar's Türbe
12 Çorba Kapısı
13 Tabhane
14 Imaret (destroyed)
15 Darüşşifa (destroyed)

According to Kritovoulos, 'the Sultan himself selected the best site in the middle of the City, and commanded them to erect there a mosque which in height, beauty and size should vie with the largest and finest of the temples already existing there [i.e. Haghia Sophia]. He bade them select and prepare materials for this, the very best marbles and other costly polished stones as well as an abundance of columns of suitable size and beauty.'

Much of this splendid building material came from the church of the Holy Apostles, built here by Justinian in the 6th C., and by 1453 sadly ruined. After Haghia Sophia it had been the grandest church in Constantinople, and most of the earlier Byzantine Emperors had been buried here. Initially Mehmet gave it to the Greeks as their patriarchal church, but in 1456 the Patriarch Gennadius was moved to the less ruinous church of the Pammakaristos. Then, or soon after, the Conqueror decided to use the site to build his own imperial mosque complex, which was begun in February 1463 and completed in December 1470.

Mehmet's architect is named in an inscription as Atık Sinan, old or manumitted Sinan, of whom very little is known; but his epithet may imply that he was of non-Muslim origin, perhaps Greek slave who had been granted his freedom. He died on 12 September 1471 – executed by his Sultan, apparently for failing to make the dome as big and high as that of Haghia Sophia. Evliya Çelebi recounts a variant of this story, saying that Mehmet cut off both the architect's hands. The judge to whom the injured man appealed bravely summoned the Sultan and, when he arrived, even more bravely (and improbably) ordered him not to sit but to stand on equal terms with his accuser. Having heard the case he ordered Mehmet to pay the man out of his own purse a substantial pension as compensation. The judge 'then apologised for having treated him as an ordinary suitor . . . "Efendi," said the Sultan, somewhat irritated . . . "if thou hadst shown favour to me . . . and wronged the architect, I would have broken thee in pieces with this mace".' Atık Sinan was executed on Mehmet's orders soon after, doubtless in one of the Sultan's not uncommon fits of rage.

Had Mehmet the Conqueror not been so obsessed with Haghia Sophia, he could have drawn comfort from the fact that nowhere in the Ottoman Empire had so vast a complex been built; and at 26 m diameter the dome was larger even than that of his father's Üç Şerefeli Cami in Edirne. But it was 5 m less than that of Haghia Sophia. The complex embraced every need in the life of the time – a mosque, 8 medreses, a mektep, library, imaret, hamam, leather market, hospital, tabhane and caravansaray.

The north side of the complex is still partly bounded by a wall, but the central portion is now demolished. Here were the original little mektep and library, twin buildings set just outside the wall between the two main gates – the **Boyacı Kapısı** (painter's gate) and the **Çörekçi Kapısı** (bun seller's gate).

The vast terrace on which the mosque stands is almost square, and is flanked in perfect symmetry on the east and west by 8 **medreses**, all of them part of the original complex. The four on the east are known as Karadeniz Medreseleri, the Black Sea Medreses; those on the west as Akdeniz (White Sea, or Mediterranean) Medreseleri. In both groups, each of the four courtyards is surrounded by 19 cells and a dershane, all domed. Behind them were further buildings (now destroyed) which provided accommodation for additional students. In these medreses about 1000 young men studied grammar, syntax, logic, rhetoric, geometry and astronomy, as well as the four legal-theological subjects: dogmatics, jurisprudence, the 'traditions' of Muhammed, and Koranic exegesis. It was the first Islamic university in Istanbul, but its pre-eminence was superseded when the Süleymaniye medreses were built in the next century.

A fine **entrance portal** in the north wall, with stalactite carving over the gate, leads into the mosque courtyard – not destroyed in the earthquake and remaining as it was originally. Before entering the courtyard it is worth noticing the unusual, and unusually beautiful, inscriptions in the lunettes above the lower outside windows – of white marble inlaid into verd-antique, the work of the 15th C. master-calligrapher Pir Yahya as-Sufi. The words are those of the first *Sura* of the Koran.

It is a lovely **courtyard**, shaded by cypress trees which tower around the şadırvan with its conical 18th C. roof with a wide overhang. Many of the columns are of ancient verd-antique or porphyry; the rest are marble. The lunettes above the windows at either end of the mosque portico contain their original tile inscriptions, also extremely fine, and probably early Iznik *cuerda seca* work in yellow, blue, green and white.

The entrance portal is the only part in this wall of the courtyard that is from the original construction, and it includes inscriptions – attributed to Ali as-Sufi, the son of Yahya who did the inlaid inscriptions outside – in gold letters on a green background, giving the dates and dedication of the mosque, and the name of the unfortunate architect. The plaque on the right bears the words of the suspect traditional saying of the Prophet that Mehmet the Conqueror took as his own: 'They will conquer Constantinople. Hail to the prince and the army to whom this is given.' Above is a handsome stalactite canopy.

120

Inside the 18th C. **mosque**, Mustafa III's architect adopted a well-tried centralised plan with a dome flanked by four semi-domes, first introduced by the greater Sinan in his Şehzade Camii (which he dismissed as his 'apprentice' work) and copied by others in several later mosques, notably that of Sultan Ahmet. Four huge piers support the central dome, and most of the available surfaces have been tediously stencilled. The mihrab is from the original mosque, apart from the lower marble panels which are picked out in gold around the edges. The mimber, an imposing edifice of multi-coloured marble, is pure 18th C. baroque, as is the sultan's loge. In the NW corner stands a wonderful old drinking fountain, in sore need of restoration. The bronze pump is painted grey, the silver cups have been replaced with ugly modern equivalents, with taps and other appendages to match, and it is held together with nylon string.

In a pretty garden behind the mosque are the **türbes** of Mehmet the Conqueror and one of his wives – Gülbahar, the Slav slave girl who bore his first son, and eventual heir. Both türbes were rebuilt after the earthquake. Mehmet's is an elaborate baroque affair, with a wide canopy over the entrance, and the interior is richly appointed. Gülbahar's türbe, by contrast, is classical in its design, and is believed to be much like the original. A curious story, current in the 17th C. and told by Evliya Çelebi, maintained that Gülbahar was no ordinary slave, but the daughter of the King of France, and that she died in her Christian faith; but it is sheer fancy. Nor was she buried here because Mehmet loved her above his other wives: she died some years after him, and was buried by her son, Beyazit II. The stone and brick building in the corner is a library built in 1742 by Mahmut I.

While I was there, enjoying the türbes and the crowded little graveyard with its elaborate tombstones, and watching people coming and going, two small boys in their black school uniforms ran up to one of the windows and stood there for a moment, their hands held open, whispering prayers for who knows what at the Conqueror's tomb. It is curious how this Sultan, regarded even in his own time and by his own people as a monster of cruelty, has with the passage of time been endowed with the qualities of a holy man, in death able to intercede with Allah on behalf of the common people for whom in life he showed no signs of caring.

Leaving the graveyard by the south gate and turning left, we go through a pretty gateway – known as **Çorba Kapısı**, the soup gate, because nearby stood the imaret, long since disappeared. The gate is part of the original precinct and is elaborately decorated in the crown above its arch with arabesques of porphyry and verd-antique inlaid into the base stone. Just outside the gate is the **tabhane**, a superb building whose central courtyard is surrounded on all four sides with a domed portico carried on 16 columns of verd-antique, white and red marble, probably salvaged from the church of the Holy Apostles. The surrounding cells provided accommodation for travelling dervishes, while in the domed room at the SE end they held their meetings and ceremonies.

The caravansaray stood just to the south of the tabhane – a very large building, said by Evliya Çelebi (doubtless with some hyperbole) to have been able to accommodate 3000 horses and mules. Beside it on the west was the imaret, which must also have been a large building if it had to supply food for all the institutions associated with the mosque, and also the poor of the neighbourhood, amounting to perhaps 2000 people twice a day. NE of the tabhane, and also in its own little precinct, stood the darüşşifa. It was totally destroyed in the earthquake, and not a trace of it remains under extensive building. It seems to have been a mixed hospital for both physical and mental ailments,and in the treatment of the latter music therapy was used. There was also a very large and handsome hamam just SE of the hospital, but it was destroyed in a fire in 1916.

Detour **Nakşidil Sultan Türbesi**

Opposite the tabhane stands the imposing marble türbe of Nakşidil Valide Sultan, mother of the reforming Sultan Mahmut II. A fanciful tale identifies Nakşidil with Aimée Dubec de Rivéry, a cousin of the Empress Joséphine, who was captured by Algerian pirates and, it was said, presented to Sultan Abdül Hamit I by the Bey of Algiers. Alas, there is no truth in it, and Mahmut II's francophile tendencies grew from some other source.

Nakşidil built her türbe in 1818, full of baroque verve and Empire grandeur, with 14 curved faces separated by delicate columns crowned by capitals that are a cross between acanthus leaves and flames. Nakşidil also endowed a mektep in the opposite corner, and a sebil.

SULTAN SELIM CAMII

Leaving the Fatih complex at the NW corner, we follow Daruşşafaka Cad. for 400 m before coming to an intersection with Yavuz Selim Cad. (Selim the Grim street), and then on for a further 200 m where a turning to the right – Sultan Selim Cad. – takes us to the entrance of the mosque of Selim I.

Selim I, like his grandfather Mehmet the Conqueror before him, cherished the ambition to be a second Alexander the Great. A man of ruthless determination, for whom the sword always seemed a preferable alternative to either pen or ploughshare, he forced the abdication of his peace-loving father, Beyazit II, and then may have arranged for him to be poisoned as he journeyed to his chosen place of exile. Next Selim systematically eliminated his surviving brothers and nephews; and in the course of the eight years of his reign he executed as many Grand Vezirs. Small wonder that his contemporaries called him Yavuz Selim, Selim the Grim.

In his brief reign he conquered the whole of eastern Anatolia as far as Lake Van and beyond, Syria, Palestine, the Hejaz and finally Egypt, seat of the Mamluk Caliphs, assuming the title 'Servant and Protector of the Holy Places.' Now the richest trading centres of the world belonged to the Ottomans, and revenue cascaded into the imperial coffers.

Selim's mosque complex stands on the fifth hill, on a terrace overlooking the Golden Horn. It is hardly surprising, in view of his war-mongering life, that Selim did not finish his mosque himself. It is not even certain if he began it; but it was completed in 1522 in the reign of his son Süleyman the Magnificent – not by Sinan as has been sometimes optimistically claimed, for it was several years before he became imperial architect; but by an unknown builder who seems to have looked back unashamedly to the style of the mosque that Beyazit II had built in Edirne.

The rectangular **courtyard** is surrounded by a domed portico on all four sides, with polychrome voussoirs to the arches. In the centre, surrounded by four cypress trees, is a large domed şadırvan, with a broadly overhanging roof which was added by Murat IV just over 100 years later. In the lunettes above the windows in the outer walls, framed by the arches in front of them, are panels of lovely early Iznik *cuerda seca* tiles. Sadly some have been patched with tiles of quite different design. Notice the attractive flower design in the paving of the portico; and also the tall entrance portal with its stalactite canopy.

The plan of the **mosque**, as in the Edirne Beyazidiye, is a simple square crowned with a wide but shallow dome which is carried on four soaring arches. These spring from low in the corners, with plain pendentives between them. The painted decoration is unusually restrained, and its white background admirably offsets the soft honey colour of the stone walls inside the great arches, pierced by several windows. The lower windows have tiled lunettes above, similar to those in the courtyard. The plain green carpet enhances the simplicity of the overall design, and provides a perfect background for the more elaborate features. The handsome marble **mihrab** has a stalactite niche, and inset in the sides are two miniature columns of verd-antique. The **mimber** is also a grand structure of carved marble, as is the **müezzins' tribune** by the west wall which stands in front of a deep recess, crowned by an elaborate arch. In the SE corner the **sultan's loge** is borne on six columns of varied and rare marbles, with a carved marble border above; beneath it is a superb painted ceiling in a variety of classical floral and foliate motifs, some probably added in the 18th C., but the multiple border, with its rich colours and gilded decoration, is certainly earlier.

On either side of the mosque, built into the corners formed with the outside of the courtyard, are two identical **tabhanes**, each under its cluster of nine domes, modeled on those of the Beyazidiye at Edirne. The **türbes** in the garden of tombs behind the mosque include not only the very large octagonal one of Selim himself (with some unusual and beautiful tile panels in the porch); but another, also octagonal, and also with lovely tiles in the porch, which contains four of his grandchildren, part of the large family of Süleyman the Magnificent. It was built in 1556, and may be the work of Sinan. Another is that of Selim's daughter, Şah Sultan, who married one of her brother Süleyman's Grand Vezir's, Lutfi Paşa, whom she disliked sufficiently to intrigue for his downfall. Yet another is that of Abdül Mecit I who died in 1861 and chose to be buried beside his inexorable and provident ancestor, whose qualities he did not share. Both the medrese and the imaret have disappeared; but the **mektep** survives, rebuilt in its original form and still in use as a primary school, in the SW corner of the untidy outer courtyard. It is an attractive domed building, fronted by a pretty portico.

Beside Selimiye Camii are the remains of an early Byzantine reservoir, the **Cistern of Aspar** named after the powerful leader of the Caucasian Alans whom Leo I executed in 471. Its Turkish name of Çukur Bostan, the sunken garden, was apt until a few years ago, for at the bottom of the huge hole, was a garden of fruit trees and vegetables in abundant growth, interspersed with houses. Today this has gone, and the vast cleared space now hosts informal matches of Turkey's favourite game – football.

9

TOPKAPI SARAYI

Open daily except Tuesday.
The ticket office is in the right-hand wall of the First Court,
just before Orta Kapı

According to Mehmet the Conqueror's panegyrist, the Greek Kritovoulos, the Sultan's second palace in Istanbul was built 'with a view to variety, beauty, size and magnificence, shining and scintillating with an abundance of gold and silver, within and without and with precious stones and marbles, with various ornaments and colours, all applied with a brilliance and smoothness and lightness most attractive and worked out with the finest and most complete skill, most ambitiously.'

Not only this, but all around the palace, on the slopes of the first hill and along the Marmara shore, 'were constructed very large and lovely gardens abounding in various sorts of plants and trees, producing beautiful fruit. And there were abundant supplies of water [from Justinian's great cistern – Yerebatan Sarayı] flowing everywhere, cold and clear and drinkable, and beautiful groves and meadows. Besides that there were flocks of birds, both domesticated fowls and songbirds, twittering and chattering all around, and many sorts of animals, tame and wild, feeding there. Also there were many other fine ornaments and embellishments . . . such as he thought would bring beauty and pleasure and happiness and enjoyment.'

This paradise on earth was originally known as the Sarayı Cedid-i Amire, the Sultan's new palace. Its present name, the cannon gate palace, was adopted in the 19th C. from one of the gates in that part of the old sea walls that embraced the new palace. As was usual with Ottoman, and indeed Byzantine palaces, Topkapı Sarayı was never a single building but an apparently rambling, though in fact carefully planned, collection of pavilions and halls, set in a series of courtyards, each filled with gardens and opening into the next through an

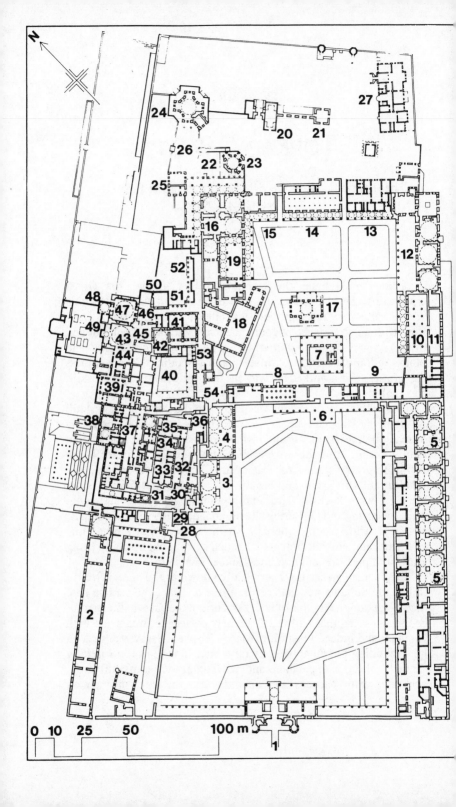

Istanbul: Topkapı Sarayı

1 Gate of Salutations
2 Stables
3 Divan
4 Inner Treasury
5 Kitchens
6 Gate of Felicity
7 Arz Odası
8 Küçük Oda
9 Büyük Oda
10 Seferli Oda
11 Hamam
12 Imperial Treasury
13 Kiler Odası
14 Hall of the Treasury
15 Silâhdar Treasury
16 Pavilion of the Sacred Mantle
17 Library of Ahmet III
18 Ağalar Camii
19 Has Oda
20 Sofa Köşkü
21 Hekimbaşı Odası
22 Pool
23 Revan Köşkü
24 Bağdat Köşkü
25 Sünnet Odası
26 İftariye Köşkü
27 Mecidiye Köşkü

HAREM
28 Carriage Gate
29 Dolaplı Kubbe
30 Guardroom
31 Black Eunuchs' Mosque
32 Black Eunuchs' Courtyard
33 Black Eunuchs' Barracks
34 Princes' School (upstairs)
35 Chief Black Eunuch's Apartment (upstairs)
36 Cümle Kapısı
37 Courtyard of the Cariyeler
38 Rooms of the 3 senior women
39 Apartments of the Valide Sultan
40 Courtyard of the Valide Sultan
41 Apartments of the 1st and 2nd Hasekis
42 Ocaklı Oda
43 Hünkâr Sofası
44 Sultan's Hamam
45 Çeşmeli Oda
46 Anteroom of Murat III
47 Salon of Murat III
48 Library of Ahmet I
49 Dining room of Ahmet III
50 Çifte Kasırlar
51 Consultation Hall of the Djinns
52 Courtyard of the Favourites
53 Golden Road
54 Kuşhane Kapısı

imposing gateway. Around this great complex was built a high wall, an innovation in Mehmet's first Istanbul palace and repeated here. Before this, Ottoman palaces had been open to their surroundings, with an ease of access to the Sultan that recalled the days when he had been simply the first amongst equals. From now on the Byzantine habit of Olympian seclusion remained the norm.

Paradise as it was, Mehmet never intended Topkapı to be a home – he already had the palace on the third hill for that. It was the seat of government, housing the offices of the Divan, or Council of State; the Palace School for the education and training of boys intended for the upper echelons of government and the civil service; the treasury; an arsenal; and also a hospital, a bakery, kitchens, stables and store-houses, as well as accommodation for courtiers, guards and servants. It was Mehmet's great-grandson, Süleyman the Magnificent, who first turned the palace into a royal residence as well as the hub of government; so it remained until the mid-19th C.

Later Sultans made their own additions to accommodate the ever increasing entourage of the imperial court. Each built to his own taste, and according to the style of the period, so that Topkapı today is a pattern book of architectural and decorative history. Two fires – in 1574 and 1665 – devastated large areas, giving Murat III and Mehmet IV broad scope to exercise their powers of restoration; a challenge also taken up by Osman III in the mid-18th C. without any such incendiary excuse. A third fire in 1856 also caused extensive damage.

The First Court
The main entrance to Topkapı Sarayı stands behind Aya Sofya and beside the fountain of Ahmet III. Solid and imposing, the Bab-ı Hümayun, or **Imperial Gate**, was originally built by Mehmet the Conqueror and it remained throughout the Ottoman period the ceremonial gate through which the colourful imperial processions would pass into and out of the palace on state occasions. The gate was opened every day after the first prayers of the morning, and closed at the last call to prayer in the evening.

Above the gate is the tuğra of Mehmet II and an inscription which dates the original construction to 1478. Another inscription records its reconstruction in 1867 by Sultan Abdül Aziz who added all the marble that now encases it. In doing so he demolished a wooden pavilion on the upper level of the gate, from which, it is said, the women of the imperial harem could watch the processions. Opening off the inside of the gateway are rooms for the imperial guard – 50-strong in the Conqueror's day.

The First Court, immediately on the other side of the Bab-ı Hümayun, was severely damaged by fire in the mid-19th C., and is today a much more vacant space than it was in earlier times. It covers a huge area, and was never part of the palace proper, but housed various offices and buildings associated with the wider imperial household, including pavilions from which the palace judges dispensed justice. It was also a gathering point for those seeking access to the Divan in the Second Court, and an assembly area for Janissaries on palace duty – hence its second name, the Court of the Janissaries.

Just to the right inside the gate once stood the palace infirmary, and beside it the offices of the treasury officials. Behind the wall along the right hand side of the court was the bakery, a large complex where all the bread for the palace residents and staff was baked, the finest and whitest flour, we are told, being reserved for the Sultan's household. There was also accommodation and a mosque for the bakery staff.

On the other side of the court stands the 6th C. church of Haghia Eirene (see pages 45–7). North of it, through a marble gate, is a large group of 19th C. buildings which, until 1967, housed the **Imperial Mint**. Mehmet II's original mint in Istanbul was near his first palace, Eski Saray, and it is thought to have moved to Topkapı in the 18th C. Only gold and silver coins were struck here; the commoner copper ones being made elsewhere. In 1992 work began on a long-term project to establish a major Istanbul Museum here by 2001. Basic preservation work on the buildings and machinery has allowed this fascinating complex to open as a mint museum and exhibition halls.

Thronging with people as the First Court invariably was, one of the things that struck European visitors was the prevailing silence. Joseph Pitton de Tournefort, who visited Constantinople around 1700 described now 'everything is so still, the Motion of a Fly might be heard in a manner; and if anyone should presume to raise his voice ever so little, or shew the least want of Respect to the Mansion-place of their Emperor he would instantly have the Bastinado by the Officers that go the rounds; nay, the very Horses seem to know where they are, and no doubt they are taught to tread softer than in the streets.'

Near the ticket office in the far right hand corner of the First Court is a fountain with what looks like an abbreviated column near it. They have a sinister past. The Cellât Çeşmesi, or **executioner's fountain**, was used by the Chief Executioner, who was also the Head Gardener, for washing his hands and sword after executions. The detached heads were displayed on the pillars (there used to be more than one), aptly known in Turkish as İbret Taşları, example stones, as an awful warning to anyone tempted to indulge in crime or disloyalty.

A more cheerful note is struck by the magnificent stone gate in the centre of the far wall – Bab-üs Selam, the **Gate of Salutations**, commonly known by its more prosaic name of Orta Kapı, the middle gate. This was, and is, the true entrance to the palace, though it is unclear how much of it Mehmet the Conqueror would recognise as his original structure for it was rebuilt by Murat III. Between the towers runs a crenellated parapet on which soldiers and cannons kept watch. Inscribed on the outside of the gate is the central tenet of Islamic faith – 'There is no God but God, and Mohammed is his prophet.' The splendid hand-beaten iron doors which close the gateway are inscribed with the name of the blacksmith who made them, Giyas bin Mehmet, and dated 1524, in the reign of Süleyman the Magnificent. Only the Sultan could pass through these doors on horseback; anyone else who was permitted to enter the Second Court had to dismount and bow before proceeding on foot.

The Second Court

From the Gate of Salutations we emerge into a spacious garden, surrounded by porticoes and punctuated with ancient cypress and plane trees, and bright with roses. Imagine it at the height of its imperial past, on one of the bayrams (Islamic feast days), or on the accession of a new Sultan, filled with processions of princes, courtiers and statesmen, all dressed in rich Bursa brocades, their turbans of differing designs rising high on their heads, all attention focused on the Sultan, most gorgeously attired of all, seated on a golden throne studded with emeralds under the wide canopy of the Gate of Felicity at the far end. To the European imagination the scene is hardly comprehensible without the accompaniment of music, or at least the murmuring and movement of men. But it was not so – if the silence of the First Court was striking, that of the second was unearthly; and doubtless the penalty for breaking it was worse than a mere bastinado, for here one was in the very presence of Majesty.

Even on less special days, perhaps one of the four days a week that the Divan met, the assembly – and the silence – in the court was impressive. But on days when there were no such colourful goings-on, the garden reverted to a more earthly stillness – gazelles cropping the grass beneath the trees, and numerous fountains filling the court with the gentle sound of flowing water. Gazelles and fountains are gone, their place taken by flowers and footpaths.

Five paths radiate from the Gate of Salutations: that furthest right leads diagonally to the palace kitchens, crowned with domes and distinctive conical chimneys, which house one of the richest collections of Chinese porcelain in the world; the next leads to the Gate of Felicity; the third to the Divan; the fourth to the entrance to the Harem; and that on the far left towards the stables which are not yet open to the public. I would suggest visiting the Divan first, followed by the kitchens, then through the Gate of Felicity into the Third Court, reserving the Harem as the final *bonne bouche* of our visit.

The **Divan**, the true heart of the palace, is a group of three connected domed rooms, fronted by a wide eaved portico, and with the Divan Tower rising immediately behind it. An early 19th C. engraving shows the previous tower to have been a much squatter affair with a pyramidal roof, but in 1820 it was replaced by the present structure with its Corinthian columns. The whole complex was originally built by Mehmet the Conqueror, but it has been substantially altered. The fire of 1574 caused much damage and the rooms were restored by Murat III, very likely under the direction of the great architect Sinan, who was engaged in rebuilding the kitchens on the other side of the court. In the 18th C. Ahmet III, the Tulip Sultan, redecorated the rooms with rococo gaiety – this survives in two rooms, but the first room on the corner was re-restored in 1945 to an approximation of its 16th C. appearance.

This first room was the actual Divan, or Imperial Council Chamber, also known as Kubbe Altı, beneath the dome. Here deliberations of state took place, the vezirs seated on low divans along the walls which are adorned with some very fine 16th C. Iznik tiles. The positions in which the vezirs sat were strictly ordained according to rank, the chief place opposite the door being that of the Grand Vezir. In the early days the Sultan attended meetings with his Imperial Council; as early as Mehmet the Conqueror's time that practice ceased, but the metal grille let into the wall above the Grand Vezir's place enabled the Sultan to listen in to meetings when he chose, from a small room in the tower. The grille was called the Eye of the Sultan. A wide arch leads into the second room, the Public Records Office, which retains its Ahmet III rococo decor. Here were kept all documents relating to Divan meetings. Beyond it is the Grand Vezir's office.

As the administration of the Ottoman Empire grew, so various departments of government moved out of the palace and into other buildings. By the late 18th C. all the main executive and administrative departments of government were concentrated in the nearby Bab-ı Ali, the famous Sublime Porte, and these rooms in the palace lost their original function.

Beyond the Grand Vezir's office, and entered from the court, is the İç Hazine, or **inner treasury**, a large 8-domed room supported in the centre by three great piers, built – appropriately – much in the manner of a small bedesten. Revenue from the provinces was brought here and kept until the quarterly pay-days for Janissaries and palace staff, as well as being used for government business. Any surplus was then transferred to the Imperial Treasury in the Third Court. The treasury now houses a fine collection of arms and armour, mostly Turkish, but there are also some captured European pieces.

Just south of the Divan is the **hall of the Halberdiers of the Tresses**, newly restored and well worth a visit to see its elegant proportions, its rich painted wood decoration, and Iznik tiles.

In the far south corner of the Second Court, between the Gate of Salutations and the palace kitchens, are two enormous 5th or 6th C. **Byzantine capitals**, dug up in this very courtyard some years ago. How they came here is a puzzle; it is thought the larger one may have supported the famous equestrian statue of Constantine the Great.

The fire in the spring of 1574 started in the sooty chimneys of the **palace kitchens**. Murat III took the opportunity to have them rebuilt on a larger scale, slicing a swathe off the Second Court in the process. The work was done by the ageing but still supreme architect, Sinan, who kept the basic plan of the original kitchens with 10 halls, each with a lofty dome and chimney; his addition of 10 conical chimneys on the court side created the largest kitchen in the Empire.

The increased size was only to be expected; Topkapı Sarayı contained the greatest concentration of people in any one place, with about 6000 mouths to be fed on a regular basis. Different sections of the kitchens cooked meals for different sections of the household – one for the Sultan himself, another for the Valide Sultan, others for the Divan, the concubines, eunuchs etc. A record from the early 17th C. mentions a daily consumption of 200 sheep, 100 lambs or kids, 40 calves, 60–100 geese and 100–200 chickens. Besides this there were prodigious quantities of rice, fruit, vegetables, cheese, sugar, oil, vinegar and honey, as well as ice and snow brought by mule from Mt Olympus near Bursa.

The magnificent display in the kitchens represents less than half the total **Topkapı porcelain collection** which was started by Beyazit II in the 15th C. and added to by successive Sultans, notably by Süleyman the Magnificent. The Chinese celadon is outstanding not just for the astonishing number of items, but for their flawless perfection, ranging from 13th C. Sung pieces, through Yuan (1280–1368), to Ming (1368–1644). There is also Chinese blue and white porcelain from the 14th C. onwards; Ming polychrome (16th–17th C.); imperial yellow (15th–17th C.); K'ang-hsi famille vert and powder blue (17th–18th C.); and 18th C. famille rose with its European influence. By comparison the European items are less exciting.

The two halls at the NE end of the kitchens are still paved with their old flagstones and are done up as old Ottoman kitchens, complete with cauldrons of suitably impressive size, sweetmeat trays about 1½ m in diameter, as well as a fascinating variety of old kitchen utensils.

Between the kitchens and the Second Court, on the other side of a narrow open passage, is a long, low, narrow building which contained storerooms. Today they house a breath-takingly vulgar **collection of silverware**, including some pieces of bizarre 19th C. ostentation, presented to Sultan Abdül Hamit II on the 25th anniversary of his accession.

At the NE end of the Second Court stands the spectacular Bab-üs Saadet, the **Gate of Felicity**, which leads into the seclusion of the Third Court and the private apartments of the palace. It was also called the Gate of the White Eunuchs for it was they who stood guard here. This gate would certainly be unrecognisable to Mehmet the Conqueror, for it was rebuilt in the 16th C., restored after the second great fire of 1665, and rebuilt again in its present rococo style in the late 18th C. under Selim III.

The Third Court

On the other side of the Gate of Felicity stands the Arz Odası, or **Throne Room**, surrounded on all four sides by a widely overhanging roof supported by antique marble columns, some of verd-antique, the rest of red or white marble. Here the Sultan received the Grand Vezir and other ministers at the end of their sessions in the Divan. Mehmet the Conqueror's original building has disappeared, rebuilt by Selim I in the early 16th C., and further restored in the early 18th and early 19th C., as well as after yet another fire in 1856. It is worth noticing the lovely early 16th C. Iznik tiles in the entrance, in striking greens and yellows, executed in the *cuerda seca* technique. A small and empty ante-chamber opens off the throne room which contains a throne, overhung by a splendid canopy, made for Mehmet III in 1596. It is now wisely encased in plate glass. An engraving on one of the walls portrays Sultan Abdül Hamit I (1774–89) seated on this throne in this room, receiving an ambassador, and shows how richly decorated and carpeted the room was in its heyday.

The whole SW side of the Third Court, on either side of the Throne Room, was occupied by the Küçük Oda (Little Hall) and Büyük Oda (Great Hall) of the famous **Palace School**, as well as two large rooms for the White Eunuchs who ran it. Indeed, most of the Third Court was devoted to the school, apart from the Throne Room and the Pavilion of the Holy Mantle. The Little and Great Halls provided the preliminary training for the new recruits, who then passed on to one of the three Chambers in the Sultan's service – the Hazine (treasury), Kiler (larder) or Seferli (campaign). The 40 most senior and gifted pages would go on to service in the Has Oda, the Privy Chamber.

The Palace School was the creation of Mehmet the Conqueror, devised as a means of educating future administrators of the Empire. It was an astonishing and unique institution, for the pupils were from Christian families, taken in the devşirme, the periodic levy of boys aged 10 or more, imposed on Christian communities within the Empire. All were forcibly converted to Islam and those who showed the most promise were sent to the palace school where they received an unusually comprehensive education. From it emerged some of the most brilliant servants of the crown, including several Grand Vezirs.

In the Küçük Oda, to the right as you look back to the Gate of Felicity, is an interesting **collection of Turkish embroidery**; while the Büyük Oda to the left houses offices of the Topkapı Museum. Passing this we see facing us on the SE side of the court a building fronted by a handsome domed portico with Byzantine verd-antique columns, known as the Seferli Oda, the Hall of the Campaign Force. The pages here were responsible for the royal laundry, hamams, barbering and, curiously, musicians. It is a fine room, supported in the centre by two rows of seven piers. Opening off the back is a long narrow room which Selim II, the Sot, converted into a hamam for the use of himself as well as the students. It was here that he met his untimely end, for in one of his habitual drunken stupors he slipped on the polished marble floor and broke his skull. Today the whole building houses a fascinating collection of Sultans' robes.

The **Imperial Costume Collection**, like most of the displays in Topkapı, exhibits only a fraction of the total. What we see are some of the most magnificent and perfectly preserved costumes, worn by succeeding Sultans from Mehmet the Conqueror to Mehmet V Reşat, the penultimate Sultan, who died in 1918. The dazzling silk, satin and velvet brocades from the Bursa looms seem as bright in their colours and as fresh in their texture as the day they were made. Winter kaftans were either quilted or snugly lined with fur, an enormously popular commodity acquired by trade with Russia. Indeed Sultan Ibrahim (1640–8), deservedly known as Mad Ibrahim, had such an insatiable appetite for sable that he almost bankrupted the exchequer. Particularly enchanting are the children's clothes.

Beyond the Seferli Oda is the **Imperial Treasury**, housed in a suite of four rooms known as the Pavilion of the Conqueror. These were used by Mehmet II and several of his successors as reception rooms, or selamlık, a purpose for which they seem admirably suited with their noble proportions – especially the first two rooms which are domed – and the lovely open loggia in the far corner which gives a wide view over the Marmara to Asia. Originally the imperial treasure was kept in the vaults below, but in the 17th C. more storage space was needed so these rooms were made over for that purpose. Now they house some of the most spectacular items of the fabled Topkapı treasure, including the famous Topkapı dagger, several richly ornamented thrones, one of the world's largest cut diamonds (the Spoonmaker's Diamond), and emeralds of prodigious size and quality – and quantity.

Immediately beside the Treasury, on the NE side of the court, is the Kiler Odası, or Hall of the Pantry, for the 30 or so pages who prepared and served the Sultan's meals. It was completely rebuilt after the fire of 1856 and is now used as the offices of the Museum Director. Beside it, and similarly fronted by a domed portico, is the Hall of the Treasury which housed the 60 pages who acted as treasury guards. It too was badly damaged in 1856.

The Hall of the Treasury now houses the **Collection of Miniatures and Portraits**. The miniatures, a mixture of Turkish and Persian work, form probably the finest of all the Topkapı collections, both in quality and quantity, numbering some 13,405 manuscripts. The exhibition varies from time to time but normally includes miniatures from the misleadingly named *Fatih [Conqueror] Albums* (in fact brought to Istanbul by the Conqueror's grandson Selim the Grim in 1514). They contain a series of powerful primitive paintings, some including vivid demons, all attributed to Mehmet Siyah Kalem, Mehmet of the Black Pen. Little is known of their origin, but it is believed that they may come from Turkestan and Transoxania in central Asia; that they possibly date to the 14th and 15th C.; that they probably relate to a people of shamanistic beliefs; and that they are certainly the work of more than one artist. There is also a fine 16th C. *Şahname of Firdawsi* from Persia, and other Safavid works.

Ottoman works include the famous miniature of Mehmet the Conqueror by Sinan Bey; splendid works by Süleyman the Magnificent's court painter, Matrakçı Nasuh, in particular his *Süleymanname*; the *Hünername* (Book of Accomplishments), *Şahanşahname* (Book of the King of Kings) and *Surname* (Book of Festivals), all commissioned by Süleyman the Magnificent's cultivated grandson, Murat III, and illustrated by his court painter Nakkaş Osman; some

135

early 18th C. works by the artist Levni, including his *Silsilename* (an album of royal portraits), and the *Surname-i Vehbi* commissioned by the tulipophile Ahmet III. The two *Surname* manuscripts celebrate the circumcision festivities held for the sons of the respective Sultans, and provide a fascinating contrast in styles between the late 16th and early 18th C.

The last room on this side of the court, the Silahdar Treasury, houses the **Collection of Clocks and Watches**, about half of which are on display. Many of them were gifts to the Sultan of the day from foreign rulers, and they speak volumes for the taste, self-image and ambitions of the various donors, as well as for the perceived value of the recipient. There are pocket and fob watches, carriage, table, mantel, long-case and pedestal clocks, some chiming and some musical, from England, Germany, Austria, Switzerland, France and Russia; and from Turkey itself.

In the same corner of the court, in the adjacent wall, is the entrance to the **Pavilion of the Sacred Mantle** (Hırka-i Saadet Dairesi), which consists of four connecting domed rooms arranged in a square, with a fifth room opening off to the left at the back, recently opened to the public. In essentials the pavilion dates to the time of Mehmet the Conqueror when it was part of his selamlık. But it was made over to its present function when Selim I brought the holy relics to Istanbul after his conquest of Egypt in 1517. Later in the century Murat III restored the rooms, and added the tiles, and Mahmut II contributed some incongruous 19th C. features. Throughout the Ottoman period the relics were guarded here, passages from the Koran being chanted over them day in, day out, and on the 15th day of Ramazan every year the Sultan would make a ceremonial visit to open the casket containing the Prophet's mantle, the holiest of all the relics.

The first room has an attractive fountain in the middle, in which the guards of the pavilion performed their ablutions before praying. Straight ahead, through a wide arch, the second room contains the Prophet's bow, one of his swords, the swords of the first four Caliphs who succeeded him, silver-gilt water-spouts from Mecca suspended overhead, and a door from the Great Mosque at Mecca. The third room, to the right of the fountain as we enter, is the Arzhane, or petition chamber, where pilgrims would gather before proceeding to the room with the sacred mantle. It contains several relics of its own – gold, jewel-encrusted caskets, one holding earth from the Prophet's grave, another, one of his teeth; hairs from the Prophet's beard; a blackened letter from the Prophet to the leader of the Copts urging him to become a Muslim; his agate seal; his footprint; etc. The fourth room we may not enter; instead we look through a doorway into a room almost entirely revetted with the finest 16th C. Iznik tiles. All attention here is focused on a great heavily worked golden box, commissioned by Abdül Aziz in the 19th C., under a splendid gold baldachino. In it are the remains of the Prophet's mantle; another box contains the Prophet's standard. The fifth room contains more relics.

Before continuing into the Fourth Court, it is worth looking at the exterior of other buildings in the Third Court, though most are not open to the public. The court itself is charming, with neat lawns shaded by great trees, and blooming with roses. It is particularly lovely when the magnolias are in flower.

Almost at the centre of the court stands a grey marble building, the **Library of Ahmet III**, built for that Sultan in 1719. Unusually for Ahmet III, whom we associate with rococo abundance, the library shows classical restraint, the main external elaboration being an ornate fountain on the outside of the portico. If it is open, you will find a central domed area flanked on three sides by bays of unequal size, each behind a pair of columns. The vaults of the bays and the inside of the dome are all painted, and the book cupboards around the walls of the bays are of fine wood inlay.

Immediately north of the library stands **Ağalar Camii**, the mosque of the Palace School, now a library and not open to the public. Between this and the Pavilion of the Holy Mantle, is the Has Oda, the **Hall of the Privy Chamber**, which was reserved for the 40 best and most senior students who were drafted into the Sultan's personal service.

The Fourth Court

A passage between the rooms displaying clocks and miniatures leads down into the Fourth Court, which is not so much a court as an abundant garden on varying levels, with pavilions like overgrown summer-houses scattered about it. We come first into the **Tulip Garden of Ahmet III** (1703–30), a Sultan who combined a distaste for government with an equal love for peace, the arts, learning and women, together with a wild extravagance and a positive passion for tulips. For the love of tulips he created a new post of Master of the Flowers, and anyone who brought him a new strain of tulip was almost guaranteed high office.

In April at the full moon, when the gardens were ablaze with every variety of Turkish and Dutch tulips, Ahmet would hold his tulip festivals, with dancers, poets and musicians, as well as caged singing birds and parrots, providing the entertainment. Miles of specially-constructed shelves all around the gardens were adorned with vases of tulips, glasses of coloured water and coloured glass lamps. Then, as the sun set and the full moon rose, the gardens were illuminated by the flickering glow of a thousand moving candles, fixed onto the backs of tortoises.

The charming little pavilion on the edge of this garden would doubtless have provided the Sultan with the perfect place from which to enjoy his festival for the windows are unusually large. Known as the **Sofa Köşkü**, or alternatively the Kara Mustafa Paşa Köşkü, it was built in the late 17th or early 18th C. and redecorated by Ahmet's successor Mahmut I in full rococo glory. To the right is a solid, squat tower called either **Hekimbaşı Odası**, the chamber of the head doctor, or Başlala Kulesi, the tower of the head tutor, identifying two of the officials who occupied it at some time during its long history, dating at least as far back as Mehmet the Conqueror.

Turning to the left, we come to a flight of steps at the end of the garden which takes us up onto a spacious marble terrace on which stand three pavilions and a gilded canopy. In the centre is a large, shallow pool with a carved marble fountain, behind which is a minor forest of columns forming an L-shaped portico.

The earliest in date of the pavilions is the **Revan Köşkü**, a small building with a central dome and three projecting bays, overlooking the tulip garden. But the days of tulips were still to come when Murat IV, a strong but deeply unlovable Sultan, built this pavilion to celebrate his capture of Erivan from the Persians in 1634. The interior is almost completely covered with Iznik tiles, though this stage of the 17th C. was not the best period, and the window shutters and cupboard doors are inlaid with tortoise-shell and mother-of-pearl.

Similar in style, though larger and altogether more lovely, is the same Sultan's **Bağdat Köşkü**, built not long after the Revan to celebrate an even greater victory – his reconquest of Baghdad on 25 December 1638. Set on the high northern corner of the terrace, it is surrounded by a widely overhanging roof supported on slender columns. Inside, it is a charming room, its central domed area flanked by four symmetrical bays containing richly covered divans, and with window shutters and cupboard doors inlaid with tortoise-shell and mother-of-pearl. The tiles are lovely, in blue and turquoise on white, and earlier in date than the pavilion itself. The inside of the dome, painted on leather, has been restored to its vivid early colours; but a small patch of the original has been left for us to mark the contrast.

The remaining monuments on the terrace are the work of Murat IV's demented younger brother and heir, Mad Ibrahim, who emerged from 22 years in the total seclusion of the Harem 'Cage' to be Sultan for eight brutish years. The Sünnet Odası, or **circumcision room**, was built in 1641 and covered with tiles both inside and out, apparently with more concern to cover the walls than to create an integrated whole. The tiles are of different dates, designs and colours, but all from the best Iznik periods between the early 16th and early 17th C. – as though Ibrahim was drawing on the unused imperial tile store to create a haphazard but glorious posthumous pattern book of the finest Iznik work. Until the move to Dolmabahçe Palace 200 years later, all Ottoman princes were circumcised in this room.

The **pool** too, though not made by Ibrahim, was used by him as the scene of some of his wilder and more debauched revels with the women of his extensive harem. But his almost redeeming act was the making, in 1640, of the charming little bronze-gilt canopy over a balcony at the edge of the terrace. He called it **Iftariye Köşkü** from the first meal after sunset during the sacred month of Ramazan. Perhaps his madness was not so complete if, as we are told, he loved to eat his *iftar* here, enjoying one of the finest views that Istanbul affords, with Golden Horn stretching into the distance and that magical skyline of domes and minarets silhouetted against the afterglow of the setting sun.

At the far eastern corner of the Fourth Court is the **Mecidiye Köşkü**, the last building to be erected at Topkapı, wonderfully sited to overlook the meeting of the three waters – the Sea of Marmara, the Bosphorus and the Golden Horn. It was built in 1840 for Sultan Abdül Mecit I, who named it after himself, by Sarkis Balyan, one of a remarkable family of Armenian architects (see page 190), at a time when distinctively Ottoman principles of architecture were being abandoned for the European grand manner. 13 years later Topkapı Sarayı was itself abandoned for the opulence of Dolmabahçe.

Here in the Mecidiye Köşkü we can take a well-earned break in the very pleasant restaurant on the lower floor and terrace, with its splendid view, before launching with renewed vigour into the glories of the Harem.

THE HAREM

More than any other part of Topkapı, the harem gives an over-powering sense of the claustrophobic, inward-looking atmosphere of the Ottoman royal household, full of distrust and intrigue. This maze of corridors and staircases, paved courts and richly decorated apartments housed the Sultan and his wives and concubines, the Valide Sultan, the princes and princesses, their servants and slaves, and the Black Eunuchs who were in charge of the day to day organisation of the harem. All had their own apartments, all were insulated from the outside world, and the lives of all depended on the whim of the Sultan.

It was not Mehmet the Conqueror's intention to house his family at Topkapı – the Eski Saray fulfilled that purpose, while Topkapı was reserved for the administration of his expanding Empire. It was not until the reign of his great-grandson, Süleyman the Magnificent, that this arrangement began to change, a result of the machinations of Süleyman's wife, the formidable Roxelana, who wished to live in close touch with the reins of power. It seems that accommodation at that time was in a number of wooden pavilions, and so it remained until Süleyman's grandson, Murat III, replaced them with more durable structures. From then on, succeeding Sultans added rooms and pavilions and courtyards, each putting their own stamp on the labyrinthine but logical arrangement of this palace within a palace.

The public entrance to the harem is through the Carriage Gate under the Divan Tower, and tickets are on sale beside it. Unlike the rest of Topkapı, guided tours in groups are the order of the day here, with a choice of English, French, German or Turkish-speaking guides. The tour takes about half hour. Not all the 300 or so rooms are open to the public – or the tour would take several days. We see about 20, including the most important and spectacular: some in the haremlik area reserved for the Sultan's mother, his wives and concubines; and some in the selamlık, the grand reception rooms of the Sultan. The route varies as some apartments are opened after restoration, and others are closed for the restorers to move in; so some of what follows will be irrelevant to any particular tour of the harem.

The **Carriage Gate** through which we enter was built in 1588 by Murat III. Here the heavily draped carriages would draw up, perhaps bringing a new woman to the Sultan's harem, or to take some of the inhabitants on an outing. Immediately inside is a small dark hall literally named **Dolaplı Kubbe**, the dome with cupboards, which leads to a group of rooms that were occupied by the Black Eunuchs, the only men besides the Sultan and a few close relatives allowed into the harem, their physical condition being their passport. They came mostly from Egypt and the Sudan and were castrated during the caravan journey to Istanbul. The operation was preformed by Christian traders since the Koran prohibited the practice to Muslims – though apparently not the employment of the eunuchs and the creation of a market for them. Once in the capital they had to be educated and rigorously trained before being taken into service inside the harem.

The Quarters of the Black Eunuchs

From the Dolaplı Kubbe we enter a rectangular **guardroom**, with an arch across the centre, its walls covered with floral tiles, while stone slabs run all round for the use of guards on duty. Two doors stand on the left, the first opening into a long, narrow passage which leads to the gardens, the second into a vestibule which gives onto the **Black Eunuchs' mosque**. This is a lovely little room, covered with tiles, including idealised views of Mecca. It leads out into the Black Eunuchs courtyard, divided down the middle by a handsome colonnade on which hangs a row of wrought-iron lamps to light the way from the harem to the entrance in those pre-electric days. The courtyard, and also the living rooms in the 3-storey **barracks** behind, are all tiled.

All these rooms were built in 1668–9 by Mehmet IV as part of his restoration after the devastating fire of 1665 (started, it is said, by a discontented servant) which virtually gutted the Harem. The tiles are pretty, but date from well after the best period. The barracks give a fascinating view of the conditions in which the Black Eunuchs lived, the 30 or so small rooms stacked one above the other on either side of a central court, with one fireplace to warm them. Winters can be very cold and wet in Istanbul. The numbers of Black Eunuchs employed seems to have varied. Menavino, a reliable 16th C. source, says there were 40 in 1517; they certainly increased later, but estimates of up to 800 seem wildly exaggerated – what would they have had to do?

After 1909, when the imperial harem was abolished, the only inhabitants of the palace were a handful of Black Eunuchs. It is said that when Kaiser Wilhelm II, came to Istanbul on one of his state visits, he and his wife were taken on a tour of Topkapı; introduced to an aged Black Eunuch, the Empress politely inquired if he had inherited his position from his father.

At the far end of the barracks a staircase on the left leads up to the **Princes' School**, an 18th C. addition at a time when the princes no longer had to fear the bowstring. The rooms are decorated with charming European tiles portraying parrots, doubtless apt for the rooms where the Sultan's sons received their primary education, and there is a wonderfully elaborate rococo fireplace. Beside the school rooms is the **private apartment of the Chief Black Eunuch**, surprisingly small for someone who by the end of the 16th C. had become one of the most powerful officers in the palace – and, indeed, the Empire. But he did have his own little alcove for making coffee.

The Quarters of the Harem Women

At the far end of the courtyard of the Black Eunuchs is the **Cümle Kapısı**, the main gate into the harem itself, which opens into another guardroom whose walls are covered with mirrors. Ahead is the so-called Golden Road which we shall come back to later, while on the left a long narrow passage leads to the **courtyard of the Cariyeler**, or female slaves. It is a pretty court, with a colonnade on three sides, and around it are the living quarters of most of the women of the harem, as well as baths, a kitchen, offices and store rooms. Immediately ahead as we enter the courtyard from the passage are three suites of very pleasant domed and tiled rooms for the three senior women officials of the harem – the kahya kadın who superintended the training of the young slaves, the treasurer and the head laundress.

Most of the women here were originally foreign slaves, bought as young girls by the Chief Black Eunuch and chosen for their beauty and grace. After training in the principles of Islam, embroidery, dancing, music etc., they would progress to waiting on the chief women of the harem, while the best waited on the Sultan himself. Those whom the Sultan chose for his bed were known as gözde (lit. in the eye), and those who became regular favourites were promoted to the rank of ikbal (fortunate). Should an ikbal give birth to a child, she rose further to be a haseki – Haseki Sultan for a son, Haseki Kadın for a daughter. The four senior hasekis were the élite, for each had her own apartment in another part of the harem, her own income and her own servants. The mother of the Sultan's eldest son was known as Baş (head) Haseki Sultan, progressing, if her son became Sultan, to Valide Sultan, the most powerful woman in the Ottoman Empire.

Those who did not succeed in gaining the attention of the Sultan might, if infertile or past child-bearing age, be made over to the princes, for whom procreation was prohibited; or the lucky ones might be married off to pages from the Palace School when they graduated to postings outside the palace.

The Apartments of the Valide Sultan

North of the courtyard of the female slaves, an entrance leads into the Valide Sultan's apartment, strategically sited between the harem and the Sultan's apartments. Particularly lovely is the **dining room**, with 17th C. tiles from Kütahya on the lower half of the walls, and early 19th C. painted scenes from the time of Mahmut II above, tortoise-shell and mother-of-pearl inlay in the cupboard doors, and the whole crowned by a high painted dome. A gallery conceals the charming rococo apartments of Mihrişah Sultan, the mother of Selim III (1789–1807). The Valide's **bedroom** and her **prayer-chamber**, pretty 17th C. tiled apartments, open off the dining room, while in the other direction is her salon which overlooks the **courtyard of the Valide Sultan**. On the other side of the courtyard are the **apartments of the First and Second Hasekis**; and beside them, opening off the NW corner, is the **Ocaklı Oda**, the hall of the hearth, a large tiled room which takes its name from its handsome and very large bronze fireplace.

Had Süleyman the Magnificent's wife Roxelana not died before he did, she would certainly have been the first of the powerful Valide Sultans, controlling the activities of her unlovely son, Selim the Sot, whose succession she had done so much to ensure. Selim's greatest influence was instead his remarkable sister, Mihrimah Sultan, until her death two years before his own; and then the scheming Venetian-born Nur Bânu, mother of his first son. But it was not until after Selim's death in 1574 that Nur Bânu was able to exert real influence over the Sultan – her son, Murat III. From then until 1687 a succession of Valide Sultans dominated the palace – and not infrequently the government of the Empire – exercising, with the help of the Chief Black Eunuch, a frequently maleficent influence.

The Sultan's Apartments
A narrow passage along the western side of the Valide Sultan's apartment leads directly to the **Hünkâr Sofası** the imperial hall, a magnificent room, and the largest in the palace, where the Sultan gave entertainments and received guests. According to the 17th C. writer, Evliya Çelebi, there was a regular weekly rota of events – on Fridays the Sultan received divines, şeyhs, and readers of the Koran; on Saturdays singers of spiritual songs; Sundays were reserved for poets and reciters of romances; on Mondays he was entertained by dancing boys and Egyptian musicians; on Tuesdays he received the old experienced men of 70 or more; on Wednesdays there was an audience for the pious saints; and on Thursdays the dervishes.

The room was probably originally built for Murat III (perhaps by Sinan) at the end of the 16th C., but was restored in the baroque style by Osman III in the mid-18th C. The main part of the room is more or less square, covered by a great painted dome supported on four pointed arches. The upper part of the room was restored some years ago to a rough approximation of its 16th C. appearance, while the baroque flourishes remain below.

143

Just off the Hünkâr Sofası is the **Sultan's hamam**, three marble rooms which were restored in the mid-18th C. in the baroque style. They include a step-into marble bath, and a carved marble basin with wonderfully ornate taps, set behind a metal grille. The Sultan's hamam is, in fact, adjacent to that of the Valide Sultan so that both could be heated by the same furnace.

On the other side of the Hünkâr Sofası we go into the **Çeşmeli Oda**, the hall of the fountain, a beautiful tiled room with a charming wall fountain dated 1666, part of the restoration by Mehmet IV after the fire of the year before. This leads into an oddly-shaped room with lovely tiles and half a dome – the result of reconstruction, probably in the early 17th C., to create the enchanting pair of tiled rooms which we shall see later.

First we see the square, high-domed **salon of Murat III**, restored to its original glory, and surely the loveliest room in the palace. It was built in 1578 by Sinan. On the left as we enter is a splendid carved 3-tier marble fountain, the sound of whose cascade made a constant gentle music to soothe the Sultan's ears. In the wall opposite stands a superb bronze fireplace, on either side of which divans border the corners of the room under handsome canopies. The room is covered with some of the finest late 16th C. Iznik tiles, especially the panel of plum blossom around the fireplace, and also the inscription in white on blue that runs around the whole room, containing some of the Verses of the Throne from the Koran.

At the far end of Murat III's room we enter the **library of Ahmet I**, another domed room, much smaller than Murat's room, added in 1608–9 by his grandson. It is a lovely light room, with windows on two sides which look over the gardens to the Bosphorus and the Golden Horn. The walls are covered with marble revetments in the centre, while above and below are fine early 17th C. Iznik tiles in mainly blue and green on white; the window shutters and cupboard doors are inlaid with tortoise-shell and mother-of-pearl on one side and ivory on the other; the dome is painted with gold arabesques on a red background; and there is an elaborately carved little fountain just inside the door on the left.

Very nearly 100 years later Ahmet III, the extravagant tulip-loving Sultan, added an even tinier room, the Yemiş Odası, or fruit room, also known as the **dining room of Ahmet III**. An inscription dates it to 1705–6. It is an enchanting little room, entirely lined with wood panelling and painted from top to toe with abundant vases of flowers and bowls piled high with fruits.

Making our way back through Murat III's room and the truncated antechamber beyond it, we come on the left to the pair of rooms that caused the disfigurement of the antechamber. These **Çifte Kasırlar**, or twin pavilions, were once thought to be the notorious Kafes, or Cage, where the younger brothers of the Sultan were confined after the fratricide law had fallen into disuse in the 17th C. This is no longer accepted – different rooms were used for the Cage at various times, out of a number of considerably less attractive rooms on the floor above.

It seems that these delightful and intimate little rooms were made in the early 17th C., and that they may have been allocated for the use of the crown prince. The shallow dome of the first room is richly painted on canvas, in a mixture of geometric designs with gilded arabesques. The tiles are lovely, some of Iznik's best, mainly of floral design, but there are also inscriptions from the Koran and devotional verses. The inner room has a flat ceiling, also richly painted, and a handsome copper-gilt fireplace. During restoration a lower floor level was discovered (seen just beyond the fireplace) and also some 16th C. tiles – both from the time when this room was part of what is now the antechamber to Murat III's room.

Beyond the twin pavilions is an attractive colonnaded courtyard, whimsically known as the **consultation hall of the Djinns**, which leads to an open terrace on the left called Gözdeler Taşlığı, or the **courtyard of the favourites**, behind which stands a building where the Sultan's favourites lived, with a view over the selamlık gardens. Turning right here we are in the **Golden Road**, the corridor along which, it is said, new Sultans, just girded with the sword of Osman, scattered gold coins among the women of the harem. There are less happy memories here too; in 1808, as the 20 year old Prince Mahmut fled along the Golden Road from the Janissaries who had just murdered his cousin, Selim III, a formidable Georgian slave-girl, Cevri Khalfa, hurled a brazier of red-hot coals into the faces of his pursuers. The prince escaped, crept through a chimney onto the roofs and appeared, doubtless black and tattered, to be acclaimed as Sultan Mahmut II, known as the Reformer.

At **Kuşhane Kapısı**, birdcage gate, we leave the harem, emerging into a corner of the Third Court of the palace. At this gate on the night of 2–3 September 1651 one of the most powerful of all the Valide Sultans met her death. Kösem Sultan had exercised enormous influence on her husband, Ahmet I, and on her two sons who succeeded him. When her grandson, Mehmet IV, became Sultan, Kösem met a powerful rival in her daughter-in-law, Turhan Hatice Sultan, the new Valide; and when Kösem's plot to murder the young Sultan was discovered, Turhan arranged for her mother-in-law to be disposed of by Tall Süleyman, Chief of the Black Eunuchs. 'She was in a moment despoiled of her Garments,' wrote the contemporary diplomat and collector of hot gossip, Sir Paul Rycault. 'Her furs were torn off into small pieces; and being stript of her rings, Bracelets, Garters and other things, she was left naked without a Rag to cover her . . . The Queen, though she were by this time besides her Senses, and worn out with Age, being above 80 years old, and without Teeth; yet she with her Gums onely did bite the thumb of his left hand, which by chance came into her mouth, so hard that he could not deliver himself untill with the haft of his Poinard he struck her on the forehead near her right eye.' Then he strangled her. On which baleful and doubtless imaginative note we make our way out of Topkapı Sarayı.

10

SÜLEYMAN THE
MAGNIFICENT AND THE
ARCHITECT SINAN

'Say Istanbul and Sinan the Great Architect comes to mind
His ten fingers soaring like mighty plane trees
On the skyline.'

Bedri Rahmi Eyuboğlu

'Pope Leo, having made certain of the death of Selim, gave command
that prayers be sung throughout Rome, and men should go barefoot to
their prayers . . . All men agree that a gentle lamb has succeeded a
fierce lion . . . for Süleyman is young, without experience – altogether
given to quiet repose.' Within a year the Roman physician and
commentator, Paulo Giovio, was eating his words, and Pope Leo X,
instead of singing thanks to God, was offering urgent prayers for the
safety of Christendom. The gentle lamb, far from indulging in quiet
repose, had in the first campaign of his reign captured Belgrade. 'The
news is lamentable, and of importance to all Christianity,' commented
Henry VIII. Greater lamentations were to follow: by the end of the
following year Süleyman had driven the Knights of St John from
Rhodes; then Buda was taken, and later the Ottoman army reached
the walls of Vienna. In 1543 Titian included in his 'Ecce Homo' a
portrait of Süleyman as one of the enemies of Christ.

Süleyman I inherited the Ottoman Empire in September 1520, at an
extraordinary moment in history following the discovery of the New
World, when grandeur and the pursuit of new lands and wealth and
power were the norm. Henry VIII, his senior by four years, had been
King of England since 1509; his exact contemporary, François I of
France, had reigned for five years; the Hapsburg Emperor Charles V,

five years his junior, had succeeded in the previous year, uniting Germany, Austria and Spain. Süleyman was to outlive them all, dominating the history of Europe almost as much as he dominated the Ottoman Empire for nearly half a century. The Venetian Bernardino Contarini, who was in Istanbul at the time of Süleyman's accession, described the 25 year old Sultan as 'tall but wiry, with a rather long neck, a thin face and aquiline nose. He has only a slight moustache and beard; his expression is pleasant, but his complexion is somewhat pale. They say he is a wise Lord and fond of study, and men of all types hope for good from his reign.'

He came to the throne with enormous advantages: he was the only surviving son of Selim I, so had no rivals for the throne; his father, in the eight years of his reign, had vastly increased not only the size of the Ottoman Empire but also its revenues; and he inherited a strong and loyal Janissary force. He started with a golden reputation for good fortune, and everything that he did only served to enhance this. It was no great exaggeration when he described himself as 'Süleyman the Sultan, by the grace of God, King of Kings, sovereign of sovereigns, most high Emperor of Byzantium and Trebizond, all powerful King of Persia, Arabia, Syria and Egypt, Supreme Lord of Europe and Asia, Prince of Mecca and Aleppo, Master of Jerusalem, and Ruler of the Universal Sea.'

In Europe he was known as Süleyman the Magnificent, and the very mention of his name caused frissons of fear. To the Turks he was known as Kanûni, the law-giver, for he employed hundreds of scholars and jurists to revise the whole system of Ottoman and Islamic law and justice. It was a monumental achievement, doing for the Ottoman legal system what Justinian had done for the Byzantine; in it the rights and responsibilities of all levels of society were clearly defined.

There was one thing that his subjects were deeply disturbed about, and that was the degree of his devotion to his wife, Haseki Hürrem. They had reason for their anxiety. When he was Crown Prince and Governor of Manisa, the main woman in Süleyman's life had been Gülbahar, the rose of spring. As the mother of his eldest son, Mustafa, she automatically became the first woman in the harem after Süleyman's mother, Hafsa Sultan. But not long after Süleyman had become Sultan, a new girl was brought into the harem who was given the name Hürrem, cheerful or smiling, from the laughter that was never far from her. She is believed to have come from that area of Poland known as little Russia, the daughter of a priest, captured in one of the frequent Tatar raids in the area and sold as a slave in Istanbul. In

1521 Hürrem gave birth to a son, Mehmet, and when a quarrel broke out soon after between the two women, with Gülbahar calling Hürrem 'sold meat', the end of Gülbahar's supremacy was in sight. Under Hürrem's influence Süleyman sent her rival into virtual exile in Manisa.

When Süleyman made Hürrem his official wife soon after, it was not only the Turks who were astonished. 'This week took place an event without precendent in the annals of previous Sultans,' a Genoese wrote home. 'The Grand Signior took to himself as Empress a slave woman from Russia called Roxelana, and great feasting followed . . . at nights the streets are illuminated, with music played, and wreaths hung from the balconies. In the old Hippodrome a stand was set up with gilded latticework to screen the Empress and her ladies while they watched a tournament of riders, both Christian and Muslim, as well as jugglers and trained beasts, including giraffes with necks that reached to the sky.'

Roxelana bore Süleyman five more children: a daughter, Mihrimah, and four sons, of whom three – Selim, Beyazit and Cihangir – survived to manhood. As the years passed, so Roxelana acquired more and more influence over Süleyman. She engineered the downfall of the Grand Vezir, Ibrahim Paşa, Süleyman's boyhood favourite, and made sure that none of his successors could have the same degree of influence over the Sultan in future. A few years later, after a fire had ravaged the Eski Saray in 1541, Roxelana persuaded Süleyman to allow her and her entourage to move into Topkapı Sarayı, the hub of government, where no woman had lived before. When her son-in-law, Rüstem Paşa, became Grand Vezir in 1544, Roxelana found the instrument through whom to effect her policies – in particular the elimination of the Crown Prince Mustafa, Gülbahar's son, so that one of her own sons would succeed instead. The alternative, as she knew, was that all her sons would die when Mustafa became Sultan.

There were two problems in her scheme – one was that Süleyman loved his eldest son; the other that Mustafa was greatly beloved both by the army and the people at large for his brilliance and generosity. But Roxelana, with Rüstem Paşa's help, worked on Süleyman's suspicious nature to make him believe that Mustafa was disloyal and aimed to replace his father. Finally convinced of his son's treachery, Süleyman ordered the bowstring. Rüstem Paşa was removed from office, probably at his own request, until the rage of the Janissaries had died down. Two years later, in 1555, he was restored, remaining in office until his death in 1561.

For the rest of her life, Roxelana hardly let Süleyman out of her sight. Now the rivalry for the succession lay between their two surviving sons, Selim and Beyazit. For some reason Roxelana seems to have favoured the ugly and usually inebriated Selim – perhaps because everyone else saw in the attractive and open-hearted Beyazit a second Mustafa. When she died in 1558 the contest between the brothers quickly developed into civil war. Beyazit had the worst of it and fled to Shah Tahmasp of Persia, convincing Süleyman that he was a traitor, and he induced the Shah to deliver his son to his executioner, thus securing the succession for the unamiable Selim.

Süleyman's last years were sad, lonely and embittered. His health was poor, and his complexion, always pale, was now thought to stem from some hidden malady. According to de Busbecq, he had for years tried to remedy his bad colour 'by painting his face with a coating of red powder, when he wishes departing ambassadors to take with them a strong impression of his health.' But although he took little active part in affairs, something of his fire remained, and in 1566 he set off on another campaign into Hungary. He died there on 7 September, on the eve of the capture of the fortress of Szigetvar.

What endures from Süleyman's reign are not his conquests, but the work of one of the most creative, wide-ranging, productive and long-lived architects of the age – Sinan, for nearly 50 years 'Architect of the Abode of Felicity'. Precise information on his early life is scarce, but it seems he was the son of Christian parents from near Kayseri, probably taken in the first devşirme of Selim I's reign in 1512. The most widely accepted date for his birth is 1491 or 1492, making him rather on the old side for the levy, and around 97 when he died. A recent theory by a respected Turkish scholar suggests instead that he was born around the turn of the century, which would certainly make his age for the devşirme more normal.

Sinan was not part of the élite who were educated in the Palace School, but became a member of the crack Janissary force, seeing service at the capture of Rhodes, Belgrade and Baghdad, and at the siege of Vienna. Doubtless he was not only soldiering, but also building bridges and siege-works that impressed his commanders, and ultimately the Sultan, with the effectiveness and harmony of their design, and the strength and speed of their construction – how else explain why in 1539 he was suddenly appointed Architect of the Abode of Felicity? He remained in the post throughout the reign of Selim II, and for most of that of Murat III, creating mosques, schools, hospitals, hamams, palaces, bridges, and a wealth of other buildings that are the greatest monuments to Ottoman architecture.

Route 1

AYA SOFYA HAMAMI

The splendid double hamam that Sinan built for Süleyman the Magnificent's wife, Roxelana, stands under its cluster of domes behind the public gardens between Aya Sofya and Sultan Ahmet Camii. It was built in 1556, just two years before Roxelana died, as a pious foundation to serve Aya Sofya. It has been restored and is now an exhibition gallery for modern Turkish hand-woven carpets, all of which are for sale. This enlightened project, sponsored by the Ministry of Culture, is both an income-generating project for women, and also aims to revive this ancient Turkish craft, using traditional designs (look for the originals in the Ibrahim Paşa Sarayı!), vegetable dyes and pure wool, and keeping prices realistic.

The men's half on the Aya Sofya side, and the women's opposite Sultan Ahmet, set back to back with the hot rooms at the centre, are virtually identical apart from the entrances which are in different positions – the men's through a confident 6-columned porch across the front, the women's discreetly down steps on the garden side.

The camekân is a square hall, converted into an octagon by semi-domes at the corners and surmounted by a high dome. A narrow door admits to a long room with three domes – this is the soğukluk, with marble revetments on the lower walls. In the central bay, another narrow door in the leads to the hararet, also marble-clad, a splendid octagonal room with a patterned marble dais under the dome, and with four eyvans, between which narrow passages lead into four small 3-bayed rooms, each with a little dome over the centre. A doorway has been opened in the wall that separated men and women.

IBRAHIM PAŞA SARAYI/MUSEUM OF TURKISH AND ISLAMIC ARTS

Open daily except Monday

North of the hippodrome stands a handsome house, one of the few surviving examples of Ottoman domestic architecture of the 16th C. – the palace of Ibrahim Paşa. This Ibrahim Paşa, one of many Grand Vezirs of that name, was a Greek devşirme boy from Parga on the coast of Epirus who was educated in the Palace School and then attached to the service of Prince Süleyman, then governor of Manisa. During this time he became Süleyman's inseparable companion, reflected in his nickname Makbul (favourite), several years later to be changed to Maktul (executed) when he fell from favour and was strangled.

When Süleyman became Sultan in 1520, Ibrahim Paşa became Hasodabaşı, Head of the Privy Chamber, in which post he exercised an influence even greater than that of the various ranks of vezir. A year later he began the building of this great palace, an architectural statement not only of his influence but of his ambitions; it was in some respects grander than that of the Sultan himself. In 1523 Ibrahim was appointed Grand Vezir, and in the following year he married, with spectacular pomp, the Sultan's sister, Hatice Sultan, who was later alienated by her husband's obvious preference for another, non-royal, wife.

A curious incident occurred in 1532, a few years after Ibrahim had brought back with him from the capture of Buda three bronze statues of Hercules, Artemis and Apollo. Displayed in front of his palace, their un-Islamic poses caused much offence, expressed by a brilliant but wild poet called Fiğani in a Persian epigram – 'Two Ibrahims came into this world: one destroyed idols (the Prophet Abraham), and the other erected them.' It was his death warrant. The enraged Ibrahim had him paraded through the streets and then hanged for daring to criticise the Grand Vezir.

Ibrahim alienated many people not only by his irreligious attitude, but also by his arrogance and extravagance, and his arrogation of the Sultan's power – letters from Ibrahim were signed as if they came from the Sultan. Yet he was a brilliant administrator and general, and for nearly 13 years Süleyman confidently left the management of wars and affairs of state in his able hands. But he became too powerful for Roxelana – 'You ask me why I am angry with Ibrahim Paşa,' she wrote to Süleyman. 'When, God willing, we are together again, I shall explain and you will learn the cause.' Doubtless she did. In March 1536 Süleyman invited his Grand Vezir to dine and spend the night at Topkapı, as he had many times in the past. The following morning his body was found outside the gate, with the tell-tale signs of strangulation. On the Sultan's orders it was taken and buried in an unmarked grave in Galata on the other side of the Golden Horn, and his vast wealth and property reverted to the crown.

Later in the same century, according to Sanderson, the palace was occupied by another Ibrahim Paşa, son-in-law and Grand Vezir of Murat III; and it seems to have been used variously as an extension of the Palace School, the High Court of Justice, barracks for unmarried Janissaries, and a prison. Many of the original buildings of this extensive palace have crumbled out of existence, and the lovely gardens with which it was surrounded have been covered with unlovely buildings. In 1843 the part that we see now was rebuilt in stone, but to the same design.

Ibrahim Paşa Sarayı has recently been handsomely restored, and today houses the Museum of Turkish and Islamic Arts, one of the most superbly planned and displayed museums in Turkey, containing some of the finest artefacts, ranging from carvings to calligraphy, faience to carpets. A wide stairway, once guarded by a Janissary on every step, leads up to the main rooms on the first floor, set around a pretty garden, once filled with scented violets, now bright with roses, hydrangeas and shrubs, and shaded by a great plane tree. A vaulted corridor on the northern side opens into a succession of small rooms, each with a canopied fireplace, in which are displayed smaller objects from various periods and places – Selçuk, Mamluk, Timurid, early and classical Ottoman. There is also some Safavid and Kajar work from Iran.

On the west side are two much larger rooms which open onto the Great Hall of the palace, a magnificent room, far grander than any at Topkapı Sarayı. Here Ibrahim Paşa would hold his audiences, for all the world like a Sultan rather than a slave. 'Although I am the Sultan's slave,' he informed an Austrian ambassador, in this very room, 'whatsoever I want done is done . . . I can give kingdoms and provinces to anyone I like, and my master will say nothing to stop me. Even if he has ordered something, if I do not want it to happen, it is not done; and if I command that something should be done, and he happens to have commanded the contrary, my wishes and not his are obeyed' – except the Sultan's wish that he should be strangled.

Today the Great Hall and its two ante-rooms contain probably the finest collection of Turkish carpets in the world, some fragments dating to the 13th C. In the vaulted rooms below is a fascinating display of the crafts of the Yörük tribes, still semi-nomadic in parts of Anatolia, including a wool tent filled with the rugs and cushions and utensils of their daily lives. There are also, by contrast, interiors of a smart Bursa house of the 19th C., and an even smarter early 20th C. Istanbul mansion.

SOKOLLU MEHMET PAŞA CAMII

At the SW corner of the hippodrome is a narrow street called Şeyit Mehmet Paşa Yokusu which, after about 100 m, turns right downhill, bringing us after another 150 m (the last part very steep) to perhaps the most harmonious of all Sinan's smaller mosques in Istanbul. Sokollu Mehmet Paşa Camii was built for Süleyman the Magnificent's last Grand Vezir who remained in office throughout the reign of his heir, Selim II and for the first five years of Murat III's reign – a total of 14 years.

Sokollu Mehmet Paşa was born around 1505 in the castle of Sokol (falcon's nest) in Bosnia, the eldest son of a Christian priest. He was taken as a youth in the devşirme and educated at the Palace School, where his brilliance was quickly noticed, and he was given a series of important posts in the royal household. In 1546 he was appointed Grand Admiral, and three years later beylerbeyi of Rumeli, during which time he proved himself a gifted soldier. In 1562, such was the high regard in which he was held by Süleyman, he married Esmahan Sultan, daughter of Prince Selim, a girl of 17 and 40 years his junior. What his bride lacked in looks, which was evidently a great deal, she made up for in character and intelligence, and it was in her name that Sokollu Mehmet Paşa built this mosque in 1571. Rather unfairly it has always been known by the name of her more famous husband.

Throughout the reign of Selim II, Sokollu Mehmet Paşa was the real ruler of the Ottoman Empire, and it is almost entirely due to him that decline did not begin immediately after Süleyman's death. He was a man of brilliant intellect and deep faith, a tough but unfailingly courteous negotiator. He won the respect of all but, such was his reserve that he made few friends. His political enemies plotted against him for years; he was assassinated as he left the Divan in Topkapı Sarayı on 11 October 1579, by a man disguised as a beggar.

The awkwardness of the site of Esmaham Sultan's mosque posed the kind of problem that often brought out Sinan's most brilliant and original solutions. Here he built up massive vaults on the slope of the hill to create a platform, and he hit upon the idea of taking the main entrance through the vaults beneath the north end of the courtyard, and up a broad flight of steps.

Climbing these tunnel-like stairs, the vision of harmonising cupolas above changes like a kaleidoscope with every step, opening at the top to a full view of the **courtyard**, surrounded by two rows of domes, and with an elegant 12-sided şadırvan in the centre. The courtyard doubles as a medrese, the dershane in the middle of the north side suspended over the stairs of the main entrance. 16 cells flank three sides, and in front of them are porticoes with pretty ogee arches; the mosque portico has seven much taller arches. The lower windows of the mosque wall have above them handsome rectangular panels of faience inscriptions, in white on blue with a floral border, and the central portal is covered with a richly carved stalactite canopy.

The inside of the **mosque** is jewel-like in its perfection, with panels of Iznik tiles glowing in a plain setting of honey-coloured stone. Far from lavishing tiles over every surface as at Rüstem Paşa Camii, Sinan's restraint here enables us more fully to appreciate their beauty. Most brilliant of all is the wall of tiles which frames the mihrab, with its mixture of floral and foliate motifs in turquoise, green and red on white; into this are set panels of flowing calligraphy in white on blue. Above the mihrab, three lovely (later) stained glass windows are also surrounded by tiles; and tile inscriptions crown the windows in rectangular panels, and all but fill the pendentives of the dome in controlled medallions framed with floral designs.

The mosque is basically rectangular, with semi-domes in the four corners converting it into a hexagon crowned by a soaring dome. Here there are no detached piers at all to obstruct the view, for the arches of the semi-domes spring from exceptionally tall piers set into the walls, and rise through three tiers of windows, as well as a row of windows in the semi-domes, to emphasise the height of the dome. These semi-domes rest on honeycombed stalactite squinches, and beneath them galleries with beautiful lace-like balustrades run down both sides, carried on delicate columns, with arches whose voussoirs are of alternate white and green marble. Further galleries are above the deep recesses on either side of the entrance portal.

Every detail of this mosque repays attention. The **mimber** is richly carved and crowned with a conical cap of superb tiles. The **mihrab**, too, has a fine stalactite niche, and set into the sides are two miniature columns of grey marble which revolve – a device to indicate whether the building has been affected by an earthquake. The ceiling under the **muezzins' tribune** is worth noticing, covered in the faded, but still lovely, remains of painted decoration. Special treasures of the mosque are the four small pieces of the black Ka'aba stone from Mecca, given to Sokollu Mehmet Paşa after he had ordered restorations at the Holy City. One piece is set into the mihrab, two into the mimber, and the fourth above the door. When leaving the mosque, as you look up to the piece of Ka'aba stone, notice too the flowing arabesques that are all that remain of the original painted decoration of this enchanting mosque.

Route 2

ŞEHZADE CAMII

Şehzade Camii, the mosque of the Prince, stands on a spacious terrace between Şehzadebaşı Cad. and the southern end of the Aqueduct of Valens. It is surrounded by a considerable complex, including a medrese, tabhane, imaret, mektep and the magnificent türbe of Şehzade Mehmet.

In November 1543, when Süleyman the Magnificent had just returned to Istanbul in triumph after his fifth Hungarian campaign, word was brought to him that his favourite son, the 22 year old Mehmet, had died of smallpox in Manisa. At first the Sultan was inconsolable, sitting beside his son's body for three days and nights before allowing him to be buried; but as he emerged from the depths of his grief he conceived the idea of building a splendid mosque complex – the finest in the city – as a memorial, and he commissioned Sinan to build it. A few years before, Sinan had built a complex for Haseki Hürrem (Roxelana), Mehmet's mother, and it had clearly found favour. Now he was to build his first imperial complex, and although in later life he called it a work of his apprenticeship, at the time he was breaking new ground in his aspiration to enclose the maximum space with the minimum visible support to obstruct the view. It was completed in 1548.

The main portal at the northern end of the courtyard has some elaborate cresting on the top, and a handsome stalactite canopy over the entrance. The **courtyard** is a perfect square, the same size as the mosque itself, with surprisingly few columns for such a large courtyard, making the arches wide as well as tall. The voussoirs of the arches are picked out in alternating bands of pink and white marble. At the centre is a marble şadırvan whose overhanging roof was added by Murat IV (1623–40). For a Sultan who spent much of his reign on the battlefield, and showed a dramatic lack of concern for human life, it is astonishing how many of Istanbul's şadırvans he roofed, presumably for the altruistic purpose of sheltering the faithful at their ablutions. The **minarets** are especially worth noticing, set at the corners where the courtyard meets the mosque, for both are covered with charming relief decoration, as well as having stalactite carving and terracotta inlays under the two pairs of şerefes.

The interior of the **mosque** is a vast square, built in a pale honey-coloured stone, crowned with a central dome flanked by four semi-domes. Each semi-dome has two exedras let into it while the ends are flat, including that in which the mihrab is set. The exception is in the north wall which includes a further exedra to take in the main entrance. One thing that is noticeably missing is any trace of tilework; this seems to have been reserved for the prince's türbe. The **mimber** is superbly carved in a mixture of pierced geometric designs, and flowers in low relief. The window shutters too have some pretty geometric carving. The piers are huge, with no supporting columns between them, and in an attempt to reduce the impression of immensity the tops have been fluted and the inside corners cut out. This gives them a curious irregularity, not unattractive in a building of such manifest symmetry, though it does little to make the piers look less ponderous. Sinan certainly succeeded in creating an overall impression of uncluttered space, but the price is the excessive symmetry of such a centralised design. He never repeated it; but some later architects took it as a model for their major mosques, in particular Sultan Ahmet, Yeni Cami and the second Fatih Camii.

The outer courtyard of Şehzade Camii is spacious enough to accommodate the caravans of the merchants who encamped here, and it is surrounded by the other institutions of the complex. At the NE corner is the **medrese**, a large building with cells and a dershane around a handsome courtyard with a 12-sided şadırvan at its centre. It is now used as a residence for women students. Next to it stands the L-shaped **tabhane** which has found a modern function as science laboratories for the secondary school next door. The **imaret** is on the other side of Dede Efendi Cad. which flanks the SE side of the mosque, and its four domes covered three large kitchens and a refectory. The **mektep** is built into the western precinct wall beside one of the gates, and beyond it near the west entrance to the cemetery stands a curious tower, known as a suterazisi (lit., water balance), a later addition for the provision of water by hydrostatic pressure.

The chief glory of the complex is the garden of tombs, with the **türbe of Şehzade Mehmet** at its heart. It is not always open. If you are fortunate, Mehmet's türbe is a beautiful octagonal structure whose marble facing is inset with verd-antique and terracotta, while the arches of the upper windows are in alternate red and white marble. Around the top runs a frieze of carved crests inside which rises the little drum and dome with fluted ribs. The porch has a handsome *opus sectile* pavement, and on either side of the main door are panels of superb Iznik *cuerda seca* tiles in brilliant green, yellow, blue and white – a foretaste of the glories inside; so too is the inscription above the door which likens the interior to the garden of Paradise. These dazzling, spring-like tiles are rare examples of an early period of production. The stained glass windows are superb 16th C. work, as is the exuberant arabesque painting in the dome.

Mehmet's sarcophagus is covered with a finely carved canopy, the legs inlaid with ivory. On one side of it is the sarcophagus of his daughter, Humuşah Sultan; on the other, that of his brother, the hunch-backed Cihangir, youngest of Roxelana's sons and much beloved of Süleyman. He died in 1553 aged 23, overcome with grief, it is said, at the murder of his eldest half-brother, Mustafa, on the orders of his father and at the instigation of his mother. De Busbecq, the Imperial ambassador who arrived in the city the year after Cihangir's death, believed that the prince was frightened to death, the law of fratricide being what it was, at the prospect of his own inevitable murder when one of his two surviving brothers became the next Sultan.

Behind Mehmet's türbe to the left stands a later work of Sinan, the **türbe of Rüstem Paşa**, the longest-lasting and least appealing of Süleyman's Grand Vezirs, who conspired with Roxelana for the death of Prince Mustafa. He was married to Mihrimah Sultan, the daughter of Süleyman and Roxelana, and died in office in 1561. Rüstem Paşa seems to have had a passion for tiles, for his Istanbul mosque, as we shall see, is almost completely covered with them, and so is the interior of his türbe.

A third period of Iznik tiles can be seen in the **türbe of Ibrahim Paşa**, one of several Grand Vezirs of that name. This one was a brother-in-law of Murat III, and on his death in 1601 his türbe was built here by the then Chief Architect, Dalgıç Ahmet Ağa, and adorned with some fine early 17th C. tiles.

The three other türbes in the garden – those of Prince Mahmut, son of Mehmet III; Murat III's daughter Hatice Sultan; and Fatma Sultan, granddaughter of Şehzade Mehmet – are unadorned and unremarkable.

Detour 1 **Burmalı Mescit Camii**

In Saraçhane Park, at the NW end of the Şehzade complex, stands an unusual little mosque which need detain us only for a look at its exterior. It was built in 1550, two years after the completion of its imposing neighbour, for Emin Nurettin Efendi, Kadıasker of Egypt. Its main claim to fame is the spiral brick minaret from which it derives its name (burmalı = spiral), copied from a Selçuk design and the only one of its kind in Istanbul. The mosque is not domed, but has a pitched roof, and the porch rests on four columns whose capitals are recycled Byzantine Corinthian – not the originals, which were too damaged to be usable when the mosque was restored some years ago, but exactly matching substitutes found in the Archaeological Museum storerooms. Rather oddly, the entrance is off-centre behind a column.

Leaving the Şehzade complex, or Saraçhane Park, we turn left onto Şehzadebaşi Cad. which, after about 200 m brings us to a multiple junction, the left arm of which – Süleymaniye Cad. – leads direct to Süleymaniye Camii. On the left, just before an arch through one of the remaining sections of the Aqueduct of Valens, is a lovely rose-pink Byzantine church-turned-mosque. It is worth a detour if it is open, or if a hovering child will find the imam who holds the key.

Detour 2 **Kalenderhane Camii/Church of the Kyriotissa**

In the 1970s this building was closed for some years for a thorough archaeological investigation and restoration, resulting in some quite unexpected discoveries. Prior to this it had been believed that this church was either the Church of St Mary Diaconissa or that of St Saviour Akataleptos, and that it dated to around the 12th C. The investigators established that it was neither of these, but the 9th C. Church of the Kyriotissa. It had been added to later in the Byzantine period, and also after the Ottoman Conquest when it became a tekke for dervishes of the Kalender order. The most exciting find was the remains of a series of mid-13th C. frescoes of the life of St Francis of Assisi, including the scene of the saint preaching to the birds, painted only a few years after his death in 1226. This was the period of the Latin occupation of Constantinople, and it clearly reflects the Latin rather than the Orthodox hagiology of the time. The artist is believed to have been the court painter of Louis, Latin King of Jerusalem.

These remarkable frescoes are now beautifully displayed in the Archaeological Museum; but there are still remains of others above the door from the exo-narthex into the narthex. The main body of the church – now beautifully restored and functioning again as a mosque –is cruciform, with a dome of 16 sections over the crossing. It is as well to avert eyes from the lurid green mihrab and mimber, and concentrate on the rest of this lovely building – most of the original marble revetment remains, the predominant colour being pink, but there are also greens and greys, and all are of differing shades and textures; and there are some beautiful columns and carved capitals and relief panels. The ceilings must once have been covered with frescoes, but now only the underlying brickwork remains.

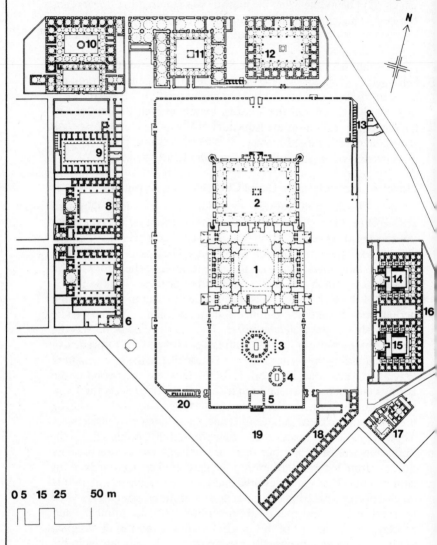

Istanbul: Süleymaniye Complex

N

0 5 15 25   50 m

1   Mosque
2   Courtyard
3   Süleyman's Türbe
4   Roxelana's Türbe
5   Dar-ül Kura
6   Mektep
7   Evvel Medrese
8   Sani Medrese
9   Tip Medrese (mostly destroyed)
10   Darüşşifa

11   Imaret
12   Tabhane
13   Sinan's Türbe
14   Salis Medrese
15   Rabi Medrese
16   Mulazimler Medresesi
17   Hamam
18   Dar-ül Hadis
19   Wrestling Ground
20   Latrines

THE SÜLEYMANIYE

This masterpiece of Sinan, the largest of all his mosques, is in architectural achievement outshone only by the Selimiye in Edirne. Construction began in 1550, two years after the completion of Şehzade Camii, and less than a century after the Conquest. In Rome the 75- year-old Michelangelo had already been working on the dome of St Peter's for four years; but such was his shortage of men and money that he was still at work long after Sinan, with the vast resources of the Ottoman Empire at his disposal, had finished the Süleymaniye in 1557.

By this time Süleyman and his wife Roxelana were living permanently in Topkapı Sarayı, the move having been precipitated by a fire at Eski Saray in 1541, after which the old palace housed only the widows of dead Sultans. What better solution could there be, when the Sultan was looking for a suitably magnificent site for his mosque, than the northern half of the old saray gardens, with its splendid view over the Golden Horn, situated on the crown of the Third Hill where its silhouette could dominate the skyline?

There was just one problem – the site was on such a slope that a year was taken up in levelling the ground and building up the foundations, to make a terrace flat and firm enough to carry not only a moque of heroic proportions, but also several medreses, a medical school, a school for teaching the traditions of the Prophet and another for the study of the Koran, a hospital and asylum, an imaret, tabhane, mektep and hamam, and a cemetery for the türbes of both Süleyman and Roxelana. Such was his success that John Sanderson, who visited Constantinople at the end of the century, called the mosque 'a buildinge wourthy of sutch a monarke, in the best and most frequented part of the citie, which passeth in greatnes, wourkemanshipp, marble pillors, and riches more than kinglie, all the other churches of the empirors his predecessors; a wourke which meriteth to be matched with the seven wounders of the wourld.' Other travellers throughout the centuries have written in similarly glowing terms.

Our first view of the mosque, rising with majestic assurance within its encircling wall, shows at once one of the major changes that Sinan made from the Şehzade Camii, replacing the two side semi-domes with a flat tympanum wall enclosed in a soaring arch. Below are two rows of arcades behind which are galleries – an attractive way of masking the heavy buttresses that support the walls and piers. The overhanging roof shelters the washing arrangements below. All the domes, starting at the lowest level of the courtyard, build up to the great crowning curve at the apex of the pyramid; and the two pairs of minarets, the shorter ones at the north end of the courtyard and the taller at the meeting of courtyard and mosque, accentuate this upward thrust.

The grandest of the three entrances to the courtyard, in the middle of the north façade, rises well above the level of the wall. It is highly decorated, crested at the top, and with a fine stalactite canopy. On either side of the gate are rooms that were used by porters and the mosque astronomer. The **courtyard** itself is rectangular, its 24 columns – of mixed porphyry, white marble and red granite – reputedly salvaged from the tumbled kathisma in the hippodrome. All have handsome stalactite capitals, not all original. It is worth noticing the accommodation that Sinan had to make in the capitals of the two columns that flank the main entrance in the north wall, making a transition between the two different heights of columns that support the gateway arches. In the centre of the court stands a fine rectangular şadırvan – of no great size since ablutions were catered for by a row of taps along the side of the mosque. The marble **portal** into the mosque is covered by a very elaborate stalactite canopy; and look too at the wooden doors with their geometric patterns, and mother-of-pearl, ebony and ivory inlay.

Inside the **mosque**, four massive, irregularly shaped piers support the lofty central dome. This – as we saw from outside – is flanked on the north and south with semi-domes, but on the east and west with great tympanum arches, each pierced by 23 windows and supported on a triple arcade which springs from two huge monolithic porphyry columns between the piers. The columns inside the mosques are said to have come from the early Byzantine church of St Euphemia in Chalcedon. This central area is very similar in plan to Haghia Sophia; though at 27.5 m diameter the dome is still smaller than that of its predecessor, which was by that time already over 1000 years old.

There are no galleries, and the side aisles are covered with five domes, alternately large and small. Both semi-domes have two exedras, whose semi-domes rest on stalactite squinches. The north semi-dome has a third narrow exedra to take in the portal between the two central buttresses which had rather awkwardly to be brought inside here to maintain the smooth flow of the courtyard. The mihrab wall, by contrast, is more or less flat, with only slight recessing, for at this end the buttresses have been placed outside the building. The **mihrab** itself, of grey Proconesian marble with a stalactite niche, is very restrained; so too is the **mimber**, which has some elegant geometric carving on the balustrade; also the **muezzins' tribune** and the **royal loge**.

The imposing severity of the interior is splendidly relieved in the mihrab wall not only by a subtle use of some very lovely Iznik tiles, but also by some stunning stained glass windows. Flowing inscriptions in the dome, semi-domes and pendentives, and on either side of the mihrab, are also fine work, originally executed by one of the most celebrated Ottoman calligraphers, Çerkes (Circassian) Hasan Çelebi, pupil of the even greater Ahmet Karahisarı. All have since been restored, and that in the dome completely reworked after the earthquake of 1766 brought it down.

Two gates, facing each other in the cemetery wall just beyond the end of the mosque, lead into the garden of the dead, filled with gravestones of all shapes and sizes, and designs of carving, from the simplest to the most elaborate. At its centre stands the great octagonal **türbe of Süleyman the Magnificent**, dated 1566, the year of his death. There is a touch of the macabre in the story of Süleyman's death. It occurred during the night of 7 September while he was on yet another Hungarian campaign, despite his age (he was over 70) and ill-health. The problem facing the Grand Vezir, Sokollu Mehmet Paşa, was that news of the Sultan's death would not only demoralise the army, but also cause riots amongst those who did not want Prince Selim to succeed to the Ottoman throne. At once, and in great secrecy, he sent word to Selim, advising him to return at once to Istanbul. He put it about that Süleyman was confined to his tent by an attack of gout, and issued daily orders in his name and congratulations on the victory. Then he took the embalmed body, sitting upright in a litter, all the way back to Istanbul where by that time Selim had arrived and Süleyman's death could be announced. If he really pulled it off, it was a masterpiece of diplomatic charade.

Around Süleyman's türbe runs a pretty colonnaded verandah, and the entrance is through a peristyle porch, once open but now glassed in to protect the magnificent twin panels of floral Iznik tiles. This is just a foretaste of things to come for the walls of the interior are almost entirely covered with tiles, including the pendentives which was the new idea. The dome is set with pieces of rock crystal which sparkle like stars in a terracotta firmament. It is, in fact, a false dome, separate from the outer one; the walls are also double, with a staircase between the two – not uncommon in Sinan's türbes. Süleyman's sarcophagus once dominated the interior in solitary state, but it has been joined by a host of others, including those of his favourite daughter, Mihrimah Sultan, and of Süleyman II and Ahmet II.

Just beyond Süleyman's türbe stands the **türbe of Haseki Hürrem**, the notorious Roxelana, who died in 1558, eight years before her husband. It is a much smaller and plainer affair, but it is decorated on the outside with some particularly beautiful tile panels with fruit trees in full blossom, foliate and floral designs, and a handsome inscription. There are also some lovely tiles inside.

At the back of the garden, projecting from the wall, is the **dar-ül kura**, a small square building consisting of a single room crowned by a dome, in which students learned to chant the Koran by heart. The entrance is on the other side of the cemetery wall.

Leaving the cemetery by the west gate, and going outside the precinct walls to where we first arrived at the complex, we will look at the various institutions associated with the mosque in a clockwise direction. The first building, on the corner of Süleymaniye Cad., is a little **mektep** where the children of the people who worked in various capacities within the mosque precinct received their primary education. It consists of a simple domed room, with an open domed area in front of it for use in the hot summers. All along the front of the medreses that face towards the mosque was a row of cobblers' shops and coffee houses, still known as Tiryaki Çarşısı, antidote, or opium market – tiryaki has both meanings, though the latter is more likely since the coffee houses seem to have done as brisk a trade in hashish, and doubtless opium too, as they did in tea or coffee.

Behind these shops are a pigeon pair of medreses, built in mirror image, the **evvel** (first) **and sani** (second) **medreses**. Their entrances are at the end of the narrow passage that divides them. Domed cells surround the courtyard – now a well-tended garden – with a dershane at the west end; and further west is a house for the tutor in charge of the 200 or so students in each medrese. At an early stage scientific subjects were taught here, but later it was dominated by theology and Islamic law, though mathmatics and astronomy were also taught. The Süleymaniye medreses (including those on the east of the precinct) were the most prestigious in the Empire, and greatly extended the scope of higher education in Istanbul, till then centred on Fatih Camii. Today these two buildings house the Süleymaniye Library, one of the richest collections of manuscripts in the city.

Beyond the medreses is the **tip medrese**, in its day the leading medical school in the empire, but now all that remains is a row of cells overlooking Tiryaki Çarşısı. The modern building that backs onto it is a maternity hospital. On the other side of Şifahan Sok, is the **darüşşifa**, a very large complex with 69 domes clustered around two courtyards, which was both a hospital for physical ailments and an asylum for the insane. It has been closed to the public for many years.

Next to the darüşşifa on the east, facing the mosque courtyard, is the **imaret**, another impressively large building with over 40 domes arranged in a double row around the courtyard with has a pretty marble fountain at its centre. The kitchens were huge, for the numbers of people who had to be cooked for – the poor of the district as well as students, teachers, patients, medical staff, clergy and travellers – ran into thousands. Used as a banqueting hall in the early 20th century, the imaret later became a museum. It now houses a restaurant, called Darüzziyafe, which serves Turkish cuisine in a beautiful 4-domed room, or in the courtyard in summer.

The **tabhane** next to the imaret is also an imposing building, the largest in Istanbul, whose guests, as was the custom, were entitled to three days' free food and lodging. A domed portico, supported on 16 columns, surrounds the courtyard which has an open pool at its centre, and behind them are closed cells for lodging and open eyvans for recreation.

A road runs diagonally across the corner of the mosque precinct east of the tabhane, and the triangular plot between the two roads has at its tip a **public fountain** built by Sinan – a pretty, octagonal building with a little dome and overhanging roof. Behind it, inside the walls, stands the open **türbe of Sinan**, set in what was once part of the architect's garden. He made his home here when he began work on the Süleymaniye in 1550, and remained till his death 38 years later. His house no longer exists and the site is built over, but the garden remains, filled with the graves of his family, amongst them the simple but lovely tomb that he constructed for himself in the last years of his long life. The grave is set inside an arcaded marble frame surmounted by a small dome. Inside, the tombstone is crowned in the customary manner with a great stone turban; but interestingly it is the turban of a Janissary, not of a master builder, for Sinan seems to have regarded his membership of the Janissary force as the greatest honour of his life.

Further along Mimar Sinan Cad., opposite the east side of the mosque and the cemetery, stands another mirror-image pair of buildings, the **salis** (third) **and rabi** (fourth) **medreses**, among the most beautiful and original of all Sinan's buildings of this type. Sadly they are not open to the public, but because of the slope on which they stand we can see something of them from the terrace above. It is on this side of the complex that we get an idea of the problems that faced Sinan with this steeply sloping site, and how he found solutions by the laborious building up of foundations and terraces. These buildings are in fact on several different levels, connected by flights of steps on either side of the dershanes which are by the road, and between the cells and the courtyards below. Below them is yet another, **mülazimler medresesi**, the novice students' medrese, a single long line of barrel-vaulted cells tucked into the slope beneath the double width of the higher buildings. The whole complex represents a highly original and attractive use of space.

Beyond the medreses, and slightly down the hill on the street that cuts diagonally across the southern end of the complex, stands the erstwhile **hamam**, surprisingly small for so large a complex, and only catering for men. Across the street, between the hamam and the garden of tombs, is the long line of the **dar-ül hadis**, where students learnt the traditions of the Prophet. Nowadays it is almost invariably closed; but those who do manage to penetrate the walls will find a design that is interesting and unusual. The main entrance, which is in the middle of the wall opposite the dar-ül kura, leads into a long narrow courtyard on one side of which 22 domed cells form a straight line, opening onto the courtyard, instead of the more conventional arrangement around a square. At the NE end stands the dershane, with an open loggia for summer. The dar-ül hadis overlooks a triangular space which was used as a wrestling ground, for wrestling was an activity of considerable importance and popularity.

RÜSTEM PAŞA CAMII

From the southern end of the Süleymaniye dar-ül hadis, we walk westwards along Ismetiye Cad. for about 200 m, and then turn left into Uzun Çarşı Cad., a long market street, which is precisely what its name indicates, an extended bustle of street-market vitality. This brings us, after a further 300 m or so, to Rüstem Paşa Camii which towers above the street on vaults occupied by shops whose revenues went to the upkeep of the mosque. Flights of steps, one at each end of the vaults, lead up to the terrace on which it stands – one of the finest of Sinan's smaller mosques.

Rüstem Paşa, the longest lasting of Süleyman's Grand Vezirs, was a Croatian by birth, brought into the Ottoman service by the devşirme, a man who combined financial genius ('an Aristotle in wisdom' Evliya Çelebi called him) with an incurable streak of avarice. According to the Imperial ambassador, de Busbecq, who knew him all too well, Rüstem 'neglected no source of revenue, however small, even scraping together money by selling the vegetables and roses and violets which grew in the Sultan's gardens; he also put up separately for sale the helmet, breastplate, and horse of every prisoner; and he managed everything else on the same principle. The result was that he amassed large sums of money and filled Soleiman's treasury.' This was an old and accepted custom, providing the Sultan with money for largesse; what made Rüstem Paşa unpopular was his imposition of a kind of VAT on the flowers.

Even before his appointment as Grand Vezir in 1544, Rüstem had married Süleyman's favourite daughter, Mihrimah Sultan; and throughout his time in office he worked hand-in-glove with Roxelana. He remained Grand Vezir for the rest of his life, apart from a two year gap from 1553, probably at his own request, when the Janissaries suspected him (rightly) of complicity in the murder of Prince Mustafa. As soon as the danger was past, Rüstem was reinstated. This unappealing man died in office in 1561, and this lovely mosque was built in his memory by his widow.

Rüstem Paşa Camii stands on a spacious platform, almost all of which is roofed by the double portico that fronts the mosque, the inner one surrounded by the outer on three sides. As there was no space for a şadırvan on the terrace, it was relegated to the bottom of one of the stairs – on the side nearest the Golden Horn – where it is still. The outside wall of the mosque is covered with tiles, but they are an inadequate advertisement for those inside since they have been restored in a muddled and injudicious manner, with little regard for continuity of design or period. But some panels are superb.

Inside, the first thing that strikes the eye is the lavish covering of almost every surface with tiles, in such a plethora of designs that it gives the impression of a pattern-book-in-the-round of this finest period of Iznik tilework. The use of Armenian bole should particularly be noted – a wonderful colour that is not quite red, nor yet tomato or flame, but has touches of all. It has never been adequately reproduced since this period in the late 16th and early 17th C. when it made its brilliant appearance in the work of the potters of Iznik. The profusion of tiles is almost bewilderingly extravagant – a curious irony for a mosque which commemorates a man with such a mean reputation. It seems that Sinan felt such profusion was excessive for he never indulged in all-over faience again.

The basic shape is rectangular, with aisles and galleries at the two sides, and the central square is converted into an octagon by the four semi-domes in the corners, and crowned by the circle of the dome. Some excellent restoration has been done in Rüstem Paşa Camii, and the painted patterns above the tiles and in the dome are attractive and simple, in harmony with Sinan's design. If it is allowed, it is worth going up into one of the galleries (that on the east is reached by a staircase on the terrace, that on the west by the inside staircase of the minaret), not only to see the tiles there, with their further range of patterns, but also for the different perspective it gives on the interior of the mosque.

11

Some Later Ottoman Mosques

The Ottoman dynasty had been blessed with a series of remarkably accomplished leaders who had increased the extent, the revenues and the power of the Ottoman Empire until, under the magnificent Süleyman, it dominated the world. They had also built up a highly complex system of government that depended, not just on the Sultan, but on a careful balance of power delegated to the ulema, the vezirs, the provincial governorates and the army. When these all cooperated under a strong Sultan the system worked well; and the succession of a strong Sultan had been made more certain by a method, however distasteful in its execution, that amounted to the survival of the fittest. Süleyman the Magnificent sowed the seeds of the decline of his Empire, not least in that he allowed his wife Roxelana to ensure the survival of probably the least fit of all his sons – Selim II.

It was Selim's chief kadın, the mother of his eldest son, the Venetian-born Nur Bânu, who when her son became Sultan Murat III, became the first of the powerful Valide Sultans who virtually controlled the Ottoman Empire until near the end of the 17th C., a period known as the kadınlar saltanatı, the sultanate of the women, Nur Bânu deflected any incipient interest in government on the part of her son by ensuring that his harem was constantly renewed with the most beautiful women to be found in the slave markets, and Murat obediently paid lavish and devoted attention to little else besides procreation and the creation of new buildings and works of art. Powerful as she was, Nur Bânu's position was gradually undermined by the mother of Murat's eldest son, Sâfiye Sultan. On Murat's death in 1595, Sâfiye reigned supreme, her son Mehmet III almost completely under her control; and the sale of offices which had begun under Murat III now became a widespread traffic. But Sâfiye's day died with her son in 1603, for her 13 year old grandson, Ahmet I, packed her off to Eski Saray along with his younger brother Mustafa. He was the first new Sultan since the Conquest who did not have his surviving brothers assassinated; from now on inheritance was to the eldest male member of the house of Osman, which added new complexities and possibilities for intrigue.

One of Ahmet I's kadıns Kösem, a Greek by birth, had very clear ambitions and she succeeded in captivating the Sultan by her beauty and intelligence, and in gaining more influence than his more senior wives. On Ahmet's early death from typhus in 1617, Kösem supported the succession of his imbecile brother Mustafa in order to hold on to power, but after only four months Mustafa was deposed in favour of Osman II, Ahmet's eldest son. Eclipsed in favour of Osman's mother, Kösem was banished to Eski Saray for four years until Osman had angered the Janissaries sufficiently for them to depose and murder him.

Once again Kösem returned to power in control of the lamentable Mustafa whose second Sultanate was worse than the first for it was a year longer. Finally in 1623 Mustafa was deposed for the second time and, as Ahmet I's next son, Murat IV, was under age, his mother, Kösem Sultan, became regent. Her influence became muted once the lion-like Murat came of age, who for a while halted the decline of the Ottoman empire, both with military victories and with reforms of the administration. But it was only temporary. On Murat's death in 1640, Kösem's other son, Mad Ibrahim, became Sultan; for eight years Kösem virtually ruled the Empire, while Ibrahim frolicked in his harem, and indulged his passion for furs and silks to such an extent that the already failing exchequer was all but run dry. The order and relative honesty that had been restored by Murat IV were replaced once again with flagrant bribery and corruption. In the end, the habit of deposition, which had already been established with Mustafa and Osman, was now revived and Ibrahim was replaced by his 6 year old son, Mehmet IV.

When Kösem tried to remain in power she encountered the powerful will of the new Valide Sultan Turhan Hatice who, after a period of bitter rivalry, had Kösem assassinated. Turhan Hatice was the last of the kadınlar saltanatı, but her power waned after the appointment in 1656 of the first of a remarkable dynasty of Grand Vezirs, the Albanian Mehmet Köprülü, succeeded five years later by his son Fadıl Ahmet. Two more members of the Köprülü family were appointed Grand Vezir in the remainder of the century. All four were renowned for their honesty and efficiency, but the odds against them were overwhelming.

It was during the long reign of Mehmet IV that the decline in Ottoman power became evident. Russia entered the international scene, and the Ottoman Empire was to lose vast territories to it in the century that followed. In 1683 the Ottomans failed in their second attempt to capture Vienna, but the worst of it was the virtual collapse of the army during their retreat. At the same time food shortages throughout Turkey were followed by famine and plague. Through all of it the Sultan rejoiced in his hunting and his harem. In 1687 he was deposed on the grounds that he was no longer fulfilling his duties as Sultan.

Mehmet IV was followed in quick succession by three nonentities –Süleyman II, Ahmet II and Mustafa II – during whose reigns the Empire lost great tracts of territory to the Austrian Empire, to Venice, Poland and Russia. It was the most visible indication of the decline of the Ottoman Empire. When Mustafa was deposed in 1703, his brother, Ahmet III, ushered in a time of cultural revival, culminating in the beautiful, but effete, Tulip Period. His people, suffering from inflation, famine and plague, staged occasional uprisings. He too was deposed.

It was not until the end of the 18th C. that any real reform was contemplated. Abdül Hamit I (1774–1789), hampered as he was by yet another war with Russia in which the Crimea was lost, attempted to introduce reforms in the existing system by eradicating corruption and introducing a more efficient administration. He also brought in foreign military advisers in an attempt to modernise the army and to halt the losses of war. His successor, Selim III, took this a step further by developing a new infantry force, the New Order, on European lines. But the Janissaries, fearing for the loss of their power that this would lead to, revolted and forced yet another deposition.

Mahmut II (1808–1839) was the first Sultan to make radical reforms, not merely improving the existing system but replacing parts of the system with new institutions based on European models. Owing his throne to the powerful, corrupt and unruly Janissaries, it took time to become master in his own house; but in 1826, having gradually appointed his own men to key positions in the administration, the religious hierarchy and the Janissary force itself, he moved with lethal efficiency to eradicate them. When the Janissaries rebelled against his reforms on 14 June, thousands of people rallied to support the Sultan, cornered the Janissaries in their barracks and set fire to them. On 16 June the Şeyh ül-Islam read the order of abolition of the Janissaries from the mimber of Sultan Ahmet mosque.

Many Europeans were brought to Istanbul to advise not only on the new army, but on every aspect of the administration and government. Mahmut himself adopted European dress, and replaced the turban with the fez. A secular educational system was introduced alongside the existing religious system in an attempt to educate and train administrators and technical experts for the modern world into which the Ottoman Empire had plunged. Old government institutions, like the old army before it, were swept away and replaced with specialist ministries on European lines. The most remarkable thing in all this was that Mahmut did not antagonise the religious authorities.

Under Mahmut II's sons, Abdül Mecit I and Abdül Aziz, reforms continued, known as Tanzimat-ı Hayriye, the beneficial reforms. But throughout this time (1839–1876) nationalist uprisings, which began under Mahmut II with the Serbian Revolt and the Greek War of Independence, followed each other with increasing frequency, finally winning full independence. They were supported by the Great Powers, with Turkey, now the Sick Man of Europe, incapable of holding an Empire together.

The relentless decline of the Empire, the attempts of Abdül Aziz in his later years to claw back the Sultanate's initiative in reform, and his resistance to a Constitution, resulted in his deposition in 1876. Later that year Turkey's first Constitution was promulgated with the agreement of the new Sultan, Abdül Hamit II, though only after many amendments which reserved certain powers to the Sultan. The new bi-cameral Parliament, with a Chamber of Deputies and a Chamber of Notables, was inaugurated by Abdül Hamit in March 1877 in a magnificent ceremony at Dolmabahçe Sarayı. Less than a year later he used the excuse of yet another war with Russia to dissolve Parliament –a right he had reserved in the Constitution. 'I made a mistake,' he declared, 'when I wished to imitate my father, Abdül Mecit, who sought to reform by persuasion and by liberal institutions. I shall follow in the footsteps of my grandfather, Sultan Mahmut. Like him I now understand that it is only by force that one can move people with whose protection God has entrusted me.'

Autocrat though he was, Abdül Hamit did continue with financial and other reforms, and with a strenuous programme of modernisation of railways, roads, steamship lines, posts and telegraphs, agriculture and forestry, mineral resources, industry, trade and commerce, medicine, the army and navy, justice and education, including the final establishment of a modern University in Istanbul. Paradoxically it was the vastly improved education that led many – who came to be known as the Young Turks – to look to the liberal ideals of Europe and to oppose their Sultan's autocracy. Uprisings broke out more and more frequently, exiles organised international resistance, and as opposition increased so the Sultan responded with increased repression. In 1908 the Young Turks finally forced Abdül Hamit to revive the Constitution after 31 years; but it was too late, and the following year he was deposed and sent into exile in Salonica. His brother Mehmet V Reşat who died in 1918, and his cousin Mehmet VI Vahideddin who was deposed four years later, brought the Ottoman Empire to a close. In 1923 Turkey was declared a republic.

SULTAN AHMET CAMII

The mosque of Sultan Ahmet I, known as the Blue Mosque from the predominating colour of its interior, stands majestically, dome above semi-domes above domes, to the south of the hippodrome, its harmonious and monumental proportions balancing the outline of Haghia Sophia on the other end of the public gardens. It is instantly identifiable from its six minarets, the only mosque in the city to be so abundantly endowed; the charge that it was sacrilege against Mecca to equal the number of the Holy City's minarets was drummed up by irate clergy. Entirely apocryphal is an amusing story that the Sultan asked his architect, Mehmet Ağa, for altın (gold) minarets, and Mehmet misheard and built altı (six) minarets instead. 'On the sacred nights,' wrote Evliya Çelebi, 'these six minarets are lighted up with 12,000 lamps, so that they resemble as many fiery cypresses.'

In 1609 Ahmet I was 19 years old, and had been Sultan for six years. Three years earlier he had had to make the Treaty of Szitva Torog in which for the first time the Ottoman Sultan recognised the Hapsburg Emperor as an equal monarch. This was bad enough; in addition, earlier that year there had been a scandal over the 16 year old Sultan's excessive attention to his harem. To placate Allah's clear displeasure, Ahmet resolved to build a great and glorious mosque – thus immediately incurring the displeasure of the ulema who were horrified at the expense at a time when the exchequer was at a low ebb.

The site itself posed a problem; once occupied by part of the Great Palace of the Byzantine Emperors, it now had two Ottoman palaces on it – one of them that of Sokollu Mehmet Paşa – which had to be purchased and demolished, both at great expense. But Ahmet was determined, and in August 1609, having gathered fine building

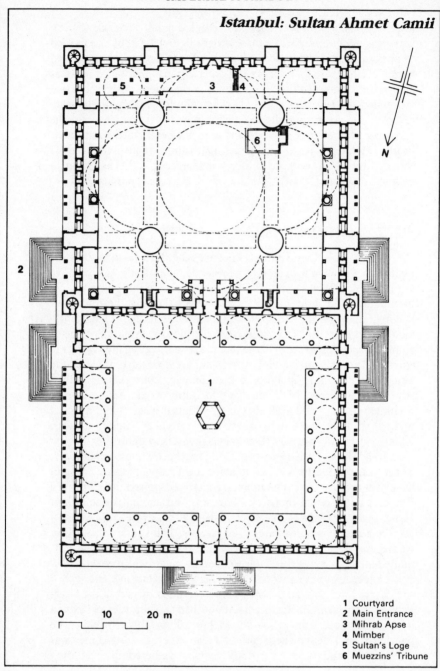

Istanbul: Sultan Ahmet Camii

N

1 Courtyard
2 Main Entrance
3 Mihrab Apse
4 Mimber
5 Sultan's Loge
6 Muezzins' Tribune

0   10   20 m

material from all over the Empire, he came in person to the site to dig the first turf. The opening ceremony was held in 1617, and a few months later Sultan Ahmet died of typhus, aged only 27. Despite the opposition of the ulema, his mosque quickly became the most popular in the city, and so it has remained.

The door used for entry into the mosque tends to vary with the season. In any case it is best, as usual, to look at the **courtyard** first, entering through the great ceremonial gate on the northern façade approached from the hippodrome, for in this way we get the full impact of the symmetry and interplay of the domes and semi-domes and minarets. It is a very tall gate, crowned by a small dome on a disproportionately high drum. There is a handsome inscription above the portal, executed by Evliya Çelebi's father; and inside, the canopy is of finely carved stalactite work. The courtyard is a spacious rectangle, and just off-centre is the hexagonal şadırvan – again ornamental rather than practical. The minarets at the north end of the court are the shortest pair, with two şerefes each, while the four at the corners of the **mosque** itself have three şerefes each. All the minarets are attractively fluted, and all the şerefes have finely carved stalactite corbels; they create a perfect frame for the harmoniously massed domes and semi-domes that rise between them.

The inside of the mosque immediately impresses with its bold interplay of light and strong colour within a vast space – marginally bigger than the court and more nearly square. As at Şehzade and Yeni Cami the plan is quatrefoil, the central dome flanked by four semi-domes. Three semi-domes have three exedras set into them, but the mihrab semi-dome has only two, and the mihrab niche is set into the flat wall. At 23½ m diameter the dome is still considerably smaller than that of Haghia Sophia. The four piers are colossal – basically circular, but they have been fluted all round above and below a flat band of inscription. Galleries run around three sides, borne on slender columns between the buttresses that form bays in those three walls. Every wall is filled with windows, as are the dome and semi-domes – there are 260 windows altogether. Originally they were glazed with Venetian glass, the gift of the Signoria of Venice, but today most are filled with less beautiful modern replacements.

The upper surfaces of the mosque are covered with painted decoration of the predominantly blue tone implied by the mosque's popular name. But it is the **tiles** that are the main glory – and very fine they are too, the last gasp from the Iznik kilns at their best. Unfortunately the loveliest are in the galleries which are not open to the public, but there are many panels at ground level, with designs of tulips, lilies, carnations and roses, and various trees. Ahmet I was obsessed with tiles, and wanted almost every surface covered with them, like an overgrown version of Rüstem Paşa Camii. Such a multiplicity of tiles is bewildering even in that small interior, and Sinan had never repeated the experiment. Here Ahmet seems to have worked on the principle that if something is good it is impossible to have too much of it, and over 50 designs vie for attention. To tile his mosque in this virtuoso manner, Ahmet prohibited production for other mosques or individuals so that everything could be concentrated on his own work. He put intolerable pressure on the Iznik potteries from which they never recovered.

Both the **mihrab** and the **mimber** are of richly carved marble, the latter heavily gilded; and the window shutters, doors and kürsü are of finely carved wood, with ivory, mother-of-pearl and tortoise shell inlay. The **sultan's loge** in the SE corner cannot be reached as the galleries are closed; but we can admire the carved marble latticework that surrounds it, the columns of rare marbles that support it; and also the gloriously painted ceiling beneath it, in a mixture of geometric and floral designs. 'In short,' wrote Evliya Çelebi, 'it was a most wonderful and costly mosque, and to describe it baffles the eloquence of any tongue.'

Of the institutions originally associated with the mosque, the hospital and tabhane no longer exist, and the imaret is incorporated into the garden of the Darüzziyafe restaurant near the SW end of the hippodrome. The **medrese** stands to the east of the mosque courtyard, and near it is the large, square **türbe** with its 3-domed porch, in which are buried not only Ahmet I, but also his favourite kadın, the notorious Kösem Sultan, who dominated the government of the Empire until her assassination in 1651. Also buried here are three of Ahmet's sons – Osman II (the first Sultan to be assassinated), Murat IV (the last Sultan to lead his army into battle), and Prince Beyazit (the last prince to be murdered on the accession of his brother, Murat IV), and an impressive number of these three sultans' sons and daughters. The **mektep** is also on this flank of the mosque precincts, raised above the surrounding wall.

At the SE corner of the mosque stands the royal pavilion, a handsome building, entered up ramps, which once gave access to the royal loge inside the mosque. Today it houses a **Carpet and Kilim Museum** (open Tuesday and Wednesday only), a fine collection gathered from ancient mosques around Anatolia, as well as from private sources, dating from every period back to the 14th C.

Stairs down from the royal pavilion take us to the terraced areas below Sultan Ahmet. Going down to the lowest level we find the **Arasta Çarşısı,** a long curving market street lined with shops on both sides, the majority selling carpets and ceramics. This was a vital part of the Sultan Ahmet complex, providing revenue for the upkeep of the mosque and its pious dependencies. This Ottoman market was built on top of part of the Great Palace of the Byzantine Emperors, and an opening in its southern side gives access to a garden of ancient columns and capitals at the entrance to the **Mosaics Museum** (open daily except Tuesday). In it are some of the vivid and finely executed mosaics, most in their original positions, which adorned the Great Palace, with pastoral, hunting and mythological scenes dating to the 6th C. or earlier.

Returning to the eastern end of Arasta Çarşısı, turn left and climb up Mimar Mehmet Ağa Cad. The first turning right brings us to the Cedid Mehmet Efendi Medresesi, restored by the Turkish Touring and Automobile Association under the inspiration of its previous Director, Çelik Gülersoy, and opened as the **Istanbul Handicrafts Centre.** As its new name implies, the erstwhile cells are now occupied by craftsmen in a variety of traditional media – marbling, illumination and miniature painting, cloth and porcelain painting and bookbinding – where visitors can watch the work and buy some of the artefacts. The medrese stands next door to the Yeşil Ev Hotel, an old wooden mansion also restored by the TTAA to its 19th C. splendour. Its shady garden is an ideal place for some refreshment after sightseeing.

YENI CAMI

Yeni Cami – or Yeni Valide Camii to give it its full name, the new mosque of the Valide Sultan – stands beside the Golden Horn at Eminönü, overlooking the colourful bustle of Galata Bridge and the ferry terminal. Its size (it is the fourth largest mosque in Istanbul), its low-lying position and its greyness tend to make it ponderously impressive rather than soaringly grand, and it is hard to respond to Lady Mary Wortley Montagu's declaration that it was the most beautiful structure she had ever seen – but it was only just over 50 years old when she saw it, its grandeur undimmed by decades of ferry-smoke. It is, in fact, the work of two Valide Sultans for it was begun in 1597 by Sâfiye Sultan, wife of Murat III and mother of Mehmet III, and completed in 1663 by Turhan Hatice Sultan, wife of mad Ibrahim and mother of Mehmet IV. Between these two dates lie half a century of inactivity.

177

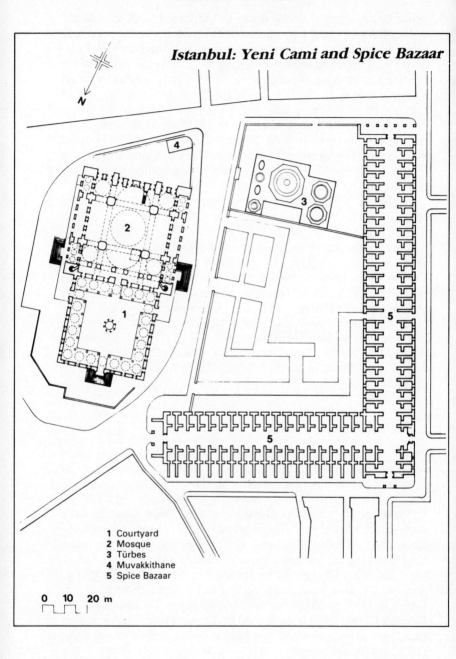

Istanbul: Yeni Cami and Spice Bazaar

1 Courtyard
2 Mosque
3 Türbes
4 Muvakkithane
5 Spice Bazaar

0 10 20 m

It was an awkward site for a large mosque, partly because the ground was unstable due to seepage of water from the Golden Horn, but also because it was a slum inhabited by an unorthodox Jewish sect called the Karai. Money to compensate the Karai for moving out was embezzled, and when that problem was resolved their synagogue had first to be demolished. The new mosque was designed by Davut Ağa, Sinan's successor as Architect of the Abode of Felicity, and was modelled very closely on Sinan's Şehzade Camii. When Davut Ağa was executed for his supposedly heretical beliefs in 1599, the work was taken over by his successor, Ahmet Ağa, who won the epithet Dalgıç, diver, from the depths to which he had to go to construct the foundations of this seaside mosque.

On Mehmet III's death in 1603, Sâfiye Sultan was relegated to Eski Saray and the new Sultan, Ahmet I, more concerned with building his own monumental Sultan Ahmet Camii, ordered the work here to stop. It was not until 1660, in Mehmet IV's reign, that the Valide Sultan of the day, Turhan Hatice, decided to continue the work, by which time it was not merely a partly-built shell, but a burnt-out partly-built shell. The new architect, Mustafa Ağa, inherited not only the site but also the original plans of Davut Ağa; but his first task was to build a pavilion from which Turhan Hatice Sultan could oversee the work in progress. It stands at the eastern corner of the mosque, approached by a long ramp, but it is not open to the public. It consists of a large hall, a salon, bedroom and lavatory on the first floor, and kitchens on the ground floor. When the mosque was completed, an opening was made to give direct access to the royal loge.

The grand ceremonial entrance to the mosque **courtyard** is in the north wall, at the top of an imposing flight of steps, and above the door is a handsome inscription – 'May health be yours! If you are worthy, enter for all eternity!' As this gate is now closed, we enter the square courtyard by either of the gates on the sides, close to the side entrances of the mosque itself. The elegant and finely carved şadırvan at the centre is a purely ornamental addition as ablutions have always been along the side wall facing the Golden Horn – an arrangement we have seen already in Sinan's imperial mosques. Before going inside, look up to the two **minarets**, which rise from the corners where mosque and courtyard meet, for the three şerefes have finely carved stalactite corbels; and between the minarets rise the domes and semi-domes, with four octagonal turrets around the central dome which are the external continuations of the great piers inside.

Inside, the dominant impression of the **mosque** is its vastness, the great central dome flanked, as at Şehzade, by four semi-domes, all supported by four polygonal piers joined by soaring arches. Galleries run around three sides, carried on slender marble columns, and the whole effect is enlivened by alternating large and small arches and the variation in their shapes. The columns are said to come from Alexandria Troas on the Aegean coast south of Troy – the supply in Istanbul had already been over-tapped, but there were still the ancient sites in Asia Minor. The upper two-thirds of the mosque is painted with an unexciting stencilled pattern, while the lower part, and also the great piers, are covered with tiles of blue and green designs on white, though without the quality and vitality of those in earlier mosques. The **mihrab** has a finely carved niche, though the stalactites are grossly picked out in gold; and the **mimber** and the **royal loge** are also worth noticing, the latter surrounded by a carved marble screen for the privacy of its royal occupants.

Leaving the mosque by the west door, we come out into a large garden, flanked on two sides by a handsome L-shaped building – the market associated with the complex and whose revenues went to the upkeep of the mosque and its pious foundations. But before getting immersed in the powerful atmosphere of the market, cast a glance at the **garden of tombs**, with Turhan Hatice's large, tiled, octagonal türbe at its centre. Her son Mehmet IV is also buried here, and also five later Sultans – Mustafa II, Ahmet III (the tulip Sultan), Mahmut I, Osman III and Murat V. Almost opposite, on the street corner near the mosque, is a small domed building that was once the **muvakkithane,** the room of the muvakkit or müneccim, a combination of astronomer and astrologer who worked out the times of sunrise and sunset for the calls to prayer, and also cast horoscopes for the Sultan and other notables. Of the hospital, mektep and hamam that were originally part of the Yeni Valide complex, nothing now remains.

The market is known in Turkish as Mısır Çarşı, the Egyptian Bazaar, reflecting its origins (endowed with customs-duties from Cairo); and in English as the **Spice Bazaar**, reflecting its original trade. From an entrance to the right of the tombs, in the centre of the west wing, we plunge into the bazaar within whose long arcades we see here and there some shops with open sacks of herbs and spices, dried fruits and pulses, still spilling out into the central passage. But the pungent aroma is much reduced now for no longer are herbs and spices the only trade here – there is a whole range of domestic goods as well – though the most fascinating shops are still those crammed with glass jars filled with colourful powders and potions, the ceilings festooned with dried roots and leaves, and cascades of sponges of all sizes and shapes from the south coast near Bodrum. There are herbal remedies for everything from kidney stones to haemorrhoids, including a paste of 41 spices mixed with honey advertised as 'Aphrodisiaque des Sultans'. There is also the fragrant and much prized attar of roses, a natural essence distilled by the Ottomans for centuries and still a flourishing industry supplied from the immeasurable rose-fields of Isparta.

The building of the Spice Bazaar was completed a few years earlier than the mosque itself. It consists of 86 vaulted rooms, each behind its arch on either side of the central passage. At the main entrances, at the ends of the L, there are further upstairs rooms – that on the end overlooking the Golden Horn occupied by Pandeli's Restaurant which is still a pleasant place for lunch, though it is always crowded.

Detour **Galata Bridge**

Between Yeni Cami and Galata Bridge is an area of throbbing vociferous human life, with the counterpoint of thundering traffic, fluttering pigeons, the cries of a hundred traders and the clatter of ferries as they arrive at and leave the terminal. Immediately in front of Yeni Cami stand hosts of street merchants, chanting the virtues of their own particular ware for the benefit of the thousands of people who pass by every day. The variety of small private enterprise is astounding – there are several men (or mere slips of boys) with aged bathroom scales, anxious to lure passers-by to weigh themselves for a modest fee; there are shoe-shine boys, purveyors of lottery tickets, pigeon feed, nylon washing lines, clothes pegs, biros, socks, plastic helicopters on sticks, invisible birdsong whistles, shirts – each impromptu stall selling only one type of article. Most sophisticated are the simitçis, with their glassed-in trolleys, within which their crisp, sesame-coated bread rings are piled high like so many edible Pisan towers.

On the waterfront several small boats line the quay, with fish being fried amidships as they rock with the waves, each portion tossed sizzling into a wedge of fresh crusty loaf to make a delectable sandwich for sale to passers-by.

The present Galata Bridge is the third to span the Golden Horn at this point. The first was a wooden one, built in 1845 by Bezmialem Valide Sultan, mother of Abdül Mecit I. This was replaced in 1912 by a ponderous piece of articulated floating iron which swayed with the movement of the water. Ugly it may have been, but it had great character, and for nearly eight decades much of the life and colour of the city gathered around and on it. But it became old and worn, and unable to cope with the huge increase in Istanbul's traffic; so it was given a new home further up the Golden Horn, between Hasköy and Balat, where it is subjected to less stress. It is simply called the Old Galata Bridge.

In 1994 the new bridge was completed – no beauty either, but certainly more practical with its four lanes of traffic going in each direction. In the centre are two bascule flaps which open upwards, rather like Tower Bridge, to allow ships to pass in and out of the harbour. What has not changed is the rows of hopeful fishermen who line the edge of the bridge, just as they did on the old one.

EYÜP SULTAN CAMII
Avoid visiting on Friday

Ferries no longer run as far as Eyüp, but local buses go there from all points along the Golden Horn. Alternatively, take a ferry from the northern (upstream) side of Galata Bridge to Hasköy where you can visit the excellent Rahmi M. Koç Industrial Museum near the jetty; and/or one of the loveliest late Ottoman royal pavilions, the only example from the 18th C. – Aynlıkavak Kasrı – about 600 m south of the jetty (see pages 190–92). To get to Eyüp from Hasköy take a bus or taxi; or a private boat from the jetty.

Eyüp Sultan Camii stands in a spacious paved square surrounded by gardens and trees, and with a large marble pool at its centre, the result of recent restoration. It also has a plethora of souvenir and food stalls to tempt its large numbers of mainly local visitors. It is the holiest shrine in Turkey because it is the supposed burial place of Eyüp Ensarî, one of the small group of Companions of the Prophet, and his standard-bearer. The glow of legend, rather than the clear light of fact, illumines the life of Eyüp Ensarî, but he is believed to have taken part in the first Arab siege of Constantinople in 674 to 678, in which he was killed and buried outside the walls. Later legends assume a more artificial glow, maintaining that the tomb was lost until miraculously re-discovered just before the Conquest of Constantinople in May 1453 – resolutely ignoring the fact that several Arabs who visited Constantinople in later Byzantine times referred to it.

According to Evliya Çelebi a week was spent searching for the tomb. 'At last Akshemsuddin [the Şeyh ül-Islam] exclaimed, 'Good news, my Prince, of Eyyub's tomb,' and thus saying he began to pray and then fell asleep. Some interpreted this sleep as a veil cast by shame over his ignorance of the tomb; but after some time he raised his head, his eyes became bloodshot, the sweat ran from his forehead, and he said to the Sultan, 'Eyyub's tomb is on the very spot where I spread the carpet for prayer.' Upon this, three of his attendants, together with the Sheikh and the Sultan, began to dig the ground, when at the depth of three yards they found a square stone of verd-antique on which was written in Cufic letters: 'This is the tomb of Eba Eyyub.' They lifted the stone and found below it the body of Eyyub wrapped in a saffron-coloured shroud, with a brazen play ball in his hand, fresh and well preserved.'

Whether or not the tomb was found by such a miracle, Mehmet the Conqueror built the first great shrine on this spot just five years after the Conquest. At a very early stage the tradition developed that each new Sultan should come to Eyüp to be girded with the sword of Osman, the founder of the Ottoman dynasty – the equivalent of coronation. It was a splendid but simple ceremony, the new Sultan arriving by boat, and at the tomb of Eyüp being met by the Chief Mufti and Chief Sword-Bearer, to be girded with the ancient sword by the Grand Master of the Mevlevi dervishes. The ceremony over, the Sultan would return to his palace on horseback, visiting en route the tombs of his ancestors.

By the late 18th C. the mosque was in ruins, probably toppled by the great earthquake of 1766 that destroyed Mehmet the Conqueror's other mosque in the city, Fatih Camii. In 1798 Selim III ordered it to be demolished, apart from a minaret built earlier that century by Ahmet III, and a new baroque mosque to be built in its place. It was completed in 1800.

The **outer courtyard** is a charming, irregularly shaped area, shaded by an ancient plane tree and swarming with pigeons, entered through generous baroque gateways. This leads into the **inner courtyard**, a garden with arcades on three sides, where another huge plane tree and a raised platform surrounded by railings mark the scene of the girding of the new Sultans, beside the tomb of the Prophet's standard-bearer. Inside, the **mosque** is filled with light, the lovely pale stone blending happily with the large quantity of white marble that was used, and the understated but jaunty gilded decoration on the mihrab and mimber. It is a grand fusion of the simple and the ornate. The basic design of the mosque is rectangular, with an octagon inscribed in the central square, crowned by a dome.

The most important feature of the mosque complex is, of course, the **türbe of Eyüp Ensarî**, the outside covered with panels of tiles of a variety of periods. Daily crowds of pilgrims file through the door which leads into the vestibule that precedes and partly surrounds the tomb itself. As I fumbled for my scarf in the bottom of a bag, a beaming elderly Turkish lady thrust her spare scarf into my hand, and took me by the arm to sit with her and her friends in animated conversation inside the vestibule – a far cry from the treatment meted out to the infidel in fiercer days. The octagonal türbe, adorned with some superb Iznik tiles, projects into the vestibule and a window allows a view of the elaborately decorated interior.

Detour 1   The tombs of Eyüp

Since Eyüp is a place of such holiness, it is an especially favoured place in which to be buried. As a result, there are some handsome türbes which may be seen within the immediate vicinity of the mosque, as well as an overwhelming number of tombstones. Several very interesting türbes can be seen in a 20 minute walk in a rough semi-circle around Eyüp Camii, in a clockwise direction.

Leaving Eyüp Sultan Camii's inner courtyard on the other side from the main square, and turning right, we see in front of us the **türbe and charitable foundation of Mihrişah Sultan**, built just a few years before Selim III rebuilt the mosque. The türbe is a splendid baroque structure, made of white marble with slender columns of verd-antique and red granite separating the 12 curved sides. Next to it stands the large **imaret**, with handsome porticoes on three sides of the courtyard. For over 200 years it has provided free food every day for poor people – and it still does. The numbers increase every year; in 1997 they had reached 900. It is paid for mainly by contributions from better off members of the community. On the other side of the imaret is an exuberantly ornate **sebil**, with a **çeşme** beside it, which used to provide drinking water for the local residents.

Continuing past the Mihrişah sebil towards the Golden Horn, we see the ornate **türbe of Husrev Paşa** to the right, and library on the left. In 1839, Mehmet Husrev Paşa forced the new and impressionable young Sultan, Abdül Mecit I, to appoint him as Grand Vezir in a vain attempt to halt the tide of reform. In the same year he built this türbe and library in the Empire style much in vogue at the time. In the following year he was ousted. He died in 1855.

Returning to Mihrişah's sebil and turning left, we see on our left, in a tree-filled garden, the large and ornate **türbe of Sultan Mehmet V Reşat**. Mehmet V succeeded his autocratic brother, Abdül Hamit II when the latter was deposed and exiled in 1909. Mehmet's survival as Sultan was due to his willingness to submit to the authority of parliament. He was the penultimate Ottoman Sultan and the last to die in his own capital (his heir, Mehmet VI Vahideddin, was deposed in 1922 and spent his last years in exile). Mehmet V died in 1918 and was buried in this heavy neo-classical türbe, surprisingly the only Ottoman Sultan ever to be buried in Eyüp.

At the next junction is a cluster of türbes, the most ornate, with its multi-coloured marbles and elaborate cresting, the **türbe of Ferhat Paşa**, briefly Grand Vezir under Murat III and Mehmet III; on both occasions he was sacked. He was executed in 1595.

The street on the right, in front of Ferhat Paşa's türbe, leads back to Eyüp Camii, passing between two classical türbes on either side of the street. On the right is the **türbe of Siyavuş Paşa** who died in 1601. It is decorated with some very fine Iznik tiles. Some people claim that it was built by Sinan (who died in 1588), having been originally commissioned by Siyavuş Paşa for some of his children who had died young, only later to be occupied by himself. It is certainly a handsome classical building, much in keeping with Sokollu Mehmet's türbe on the other side of the road which is certainly Sinan's work.

The **türbe and medrese of Sokollu Mehmet Paşa**, a work of Sinan, was commissioned by the great Grand Vezir around 1574. It was an awkward site, being long and narrow, resulting in a highly unusual design for this linked türbe and medrese. The first octagonal building beside the road is the türbe which is joined by a roofed colonnade of three open arches on each side to the dershane which is also octagonal. The doorways of the two buildings are the same except that the voussoirs of the respective arches are picked out in different colours. Both rooms are spacious and well-lit – the stained glass windows in the türbe are especially attractive, some of them original. At the other end, the dershane opens into the courtyard of the medrese, an attractive long narrow building now used as a children's clinic. The graveyard is crowded with the handsome tombstones of later members of Sokollu Mehmet Paşa's family, and at the end of it is a third octagonal building, the dar-ül kura, for the learning and chanting of the Koran by heart.

Detour 2   Zal Mahmut Paşa Camii

About 400 m south of Eyüp Camii, accessible from either of the two roads that run parallel to the Golden Horn, stands the most imposing mosque in Eyüp, built by Sinan for the contemptible man who administered the bowstring to Süleyman the Magnificent's heir, Prince Mustafa. Selim II, the ultimate beneficiary of his half-brother's murder, later married off one of his daughters to Zal Mahmut. The mosque was built between 1572 and 1580.

Zal Mahmut Paşa Camii is a towering structure with four rows of windows, built in alternate courses of stone and brick. A raised 5-bay portico, resting on six columns, precedes the **mosque** itself which is a vast rectangular space, surrounded on three sides by oppressively wide galleries. These are supported by two piers with four columns between them, and by four further columns on each of the sides between the piers and the **mihrab** wall. The square area thus formed is covered with a soaring dome. The mihrab is surrounded by some very lovely floral Iznik tiles; the mihrab canopy and the **mimber** are of finely carved marble.

There are **two medreses** associated with the mosque, both similarly built of brick and stone, and both of irregular design. One is on three sides of the courtyard, the other on lower ground to the NE, enclosing part of the garden. On the far side of the garden stands the very large and simply designed octagonal **türbe** in which are buried Zal Mahmut Paşa and his royal wife, Şah Sultan, who both died on the same night in September 1580.

Another Şah Sultan, half-sister of Selim III (1789–1807), has her ornate **baroque türbe** in a garden of tombstones on the other side of the wall next to Zal Mahmut Paşa's türbe. It is reached through a gate on the sea road. There is also a pretty mektep, built at the same time as the türbe as a pious foundation, with the classroom on the first floor supported on a handsome arcade.

Returning through the Zal Mahmut Paşa precinct, and going out onto the road on the other side, further from the Golden Horn, we see immediately opposite, **Silahi Mehmet Bey Camii**, a pretty little mosque dating from the time of Beyazit II (1481–1512). Its main claim to fame is the minaret with a highly unusual lantern with six windows that replaces the more usual şerefe.

LALELI CAMI

Laleli Cami, the tulip mosque, stands on a high terrace beside and above Ordu Cad, between Beyazit and Aksaray, the grandest baroque mosque in Istanbul. It was built by the then chief architect, Mehmet Tahir Ağa, in 1759–63 as the centrepiece of Mustafa III's imperial mosque complex. Built up on a spacious flagged terrace as it is, Mehmet Tahir cunningly transformed the base immediately under the mosque into a market area, its vaults supported by eight massive piers, and with a fountain at the centre. Steps lead up to the mosque which is build in alternate layers of brick and stone. The **courtyard** is a spacious rectangle with the minarets standing at either side – near the mosque but not attached to it as was more usual.

The **mosque** interior seems to be almost entirely covered by the central dome, for all but two of the eight columns on which it rests are integrated into the walls; but four exedras make the transition from octagon to square, and to east and west narrow side aisles extend the design outwards. A narthex at the entrance carries a gallery, making the overall shape rectangular, with a mihrab projecting at the south end. Windows at every level let in light to illuminate the wealth of coloured marbles that has been lavished on the interior of this mosque.

North-west of the mosque the **imaret** still stands on the terrace; and in the opposite corner, facing onto the street, is a very attractive **sebil** with bronze grilles between slender columns, covered by a canopy with a fluted edge. Beside it is the rather heavy **türbe of Mustafa III** who died in 1774; and here his son Selim III was also buried 33 years later, after his murder by the Janissaries, his brave attempts at reform having come to nothing.

12

LATE OTTOMAN PALACES
AND PAVILIONS

From their earliest days in Istanbul, the Ottoman Sultans established villas outside the city walls, beside the Golden Horn and, in particular, on both shores of the Bosphorus. Here they would come for recreation and enjoyment, to escape the pressures of government, for hunting or, during the heat of the summers, to enjoy the cooling breezes of the Bosphorus, and the luxuriant gardens and woodlands with which they surrounded their pavilions. These out-of-town palaces also provided useful alternative accommodation for the Sultan and his entourage when fire caused damage to Topkapı Sarayı, or when plague swept the city. Above all, it was their passion for gardens that the Ottoman Sultans loved to indulge, for they surrounded their palaces and pavilions with paradisical gardens, filled with trees and flowers of every kind, and murmuring with streams and fountains.

It was not only the Sultans who had their villas; favoured paşas would be given or sold a section of the Sultan's garden or woodland on which to build their own yalıs, or summer palaces, and soon all the wealthy families of Istanbul had followed suit. In winter they would live in their konak in town; in early spring the household would remove to one of the Princes' Islands or a resort on the Sea of Marmara; the summer would be spent in the yalı on the Bosphorus. By the early 19th C., when Julia Pardoe came here with her father, she marvelled at the multitude of these pavilions – 'Who shall number the kiosks! those gilt-latticed, many-formed, and graceful toys, which seem as though they had been rained from the sky during an hour of sunshine . . . anywhere, everywhere, you come upon them; and they are so neatly kept, so brightly gilt, and so gaily painted, that they look like gigantic flowers scattered over the landscape.'

The early palaces were built of wood, most with the oriental feature of first-floor rooms projecting over the ground floor, supported either on wooden consoles or slender columns. All the windows – especially those of the harem – were shuttered with elaborate wooden lattice-work jalousies, jealously guarding the inhabitants from the curious gaze of passers-by in their caiques.

Royal palaces and lesser houses alike were built in two main parts – the selamlık, where the male members of the family could receive guests, and the harem where the women presided and received women guests, and where the only men allowed to enter were those of the immediate family. In both harem and selamlık the main room on the ground floor was a large hall, often with a fountain in the centre, for the Turks have always loved the sight and sound of running water. A splendid staircase, often double, led up from the hall to the main reception room, or sofa, on the first floor. Into it opened the other rooms so that it formed the axis of the whole first floor layout.

Most of these early palaces were built at a variety of periods, restoration being undertaken by one Sultan after a period of neglect by his predecessor, an extra wing being tacked on as required; all of which added to the individual character of the building if not to its symmetry. This very irregularity delighted 18th and 19th C. travellers, and many commented on it. In 1717 Lady Mary Wortley Montagu wrote in a letter, ''Tis harder yet to describe a Turkish palace than any other, being built entirely irregular. There is nothing that can properly be called front or wings; and though such a confusion is, I think, pleasing to the sight, yet it would be very unintelligible in a letter.'

Turkish houses – even palaces – of this period had little in the way of free-standing furniture. Around the walls were low divans, spread with rugs or covered with silk or velvet brocade, and scattered with cushions. It was not until the 19th C., with its enthusiasm for European styles, that furniture became fashionable. Ceilings were usually decorated with a strip design in wood, or were richly carved and painted, and often had an elaborately carved centrepiece. Bedrooms were much the same, with a low divan rather than a free-standing bed; and cupboards for clothes and bed linen were built into the walls, often with beautifully carved, inlaid or painted doors. All the bedding was rolled up and put away out of sight during the day. The floors were covered with rush matting which would be spread with carpets, though the finest were hung on the walls as decoration. One of the few articles of moveable furniture was the mangal, an elaborate charcoal brazier made of copper or brass, which would stand in the middle of the room; these were less necessary in the Bosphorus palaces which were inhabited only in summer.

Mahmut II in the early 19th C., and his two sons who succeeded him, Abdül Mecit I and Abdül Aziz, began the rebuilding of royal pavilions not just in stone, but in a style that borrowed from the most extravagant and flamboyant European taste. In this they were served by a remarkable dynasty of Armenian architects who for three generations built mosques, barracks, factories, dams, aqueducts, fountains, and police stations – but particularly palaces – for these reforming and westernizing Sultans.

The first generation consisted of two brothers, Kirkor and Senekerim Balyan. Kirkor was the first Ottoman architect to study in Europe – at the Ecole des Beaux-Arts in Paris – and on his return he was appointed Chief Architect. His first major building for Mahmut II was the Nusretiye Camii, divine victory mosque, completed in 1826 soon after the Sultan's suppression of the Janissaries. Two years later Senekerim built the Beyazit fire tower, his only known building.

From then on almost every imperial building was the work of one or other member of the Balyan family. Working together as a family team, they were able to undertake several commissions simultaneously, and to complete quickly. Between them they succeeded in equalling – numerically and in acreage, if not in brilliance – Sinan's massive, and single-handed achievement. Kirkor's son Karabet was largely responsible for Dolmabahçe Sarayı, assisted by his son Nikoğos who, with his two brothers, Sarkis and Agop, had studied at St Barbe College in Paris under Henri Labrouste. It was these three who between them built the other palaces that still today adorn the shores of the Bosphorus.

AYNALIKAVAK KASRI

Open daily except Monday and Thursday. Ferries run from the south-west side of the new Galata Bridge to Hasköy; from there take a taxi south along Hasköy Cad., and the palace is just past the naval base, through a grand arch. The visit can be combined with seeing the Rahmi M. Koç Industrial Museum, very close to the Hasköy jetty.

Aynalıkavak Kasrı, the pavilion of the mirroring poplars, was apparently so called from the effect of the light on its multitude of windows, something quite new at the time, like the leaves of a poplar tree quivering in the breeze. The name acquired a double meaning in 1718, when the Venetians concluded the Peace of Passarovitz with the Turks in which they ceded the Morea and, as an extra expression of goodwill, sent Sultan Ahmet III some of the largest and finest of the mirrors for which Venice was famed, and this pavilion was the only one suitable to house the gift. 66 years later, on 9 January 1784, Sultan Abdül Hamit I signed another treaty, less favourable to Turkey, in this very building – the Treaty of Aynalıkavak, acknowledging the annexation of the Crimea by Catherine the Great of Russia.

According to Evliya Çelebi, the area was covered with a great vineyard belonging to the Byzantine Emperors. After the Conquest it became a favoured place of recreation of the Ottoman Sultans, in particular for practising their skill at archery, and after the imperial dockyard was established at Kasımpaşa, a handful of small kiosks were built, added to and embellished, and came to be known as Tershane Sarayı, dockyard palace.

Aynalıkavak Kasrı, set slightly back from the Golden Horn, is the only survivor of this palace, and it is thought that it was built by Ahmet III early in the 18th C.; it was repaired at the end of the century by Selim III who then abandoned it for the greater delights of his palace at Beşiktaş. Mahmut II in the early 19th C. made further restorations, undertaken by Kirkor Balyan, and it is in this form that we see it today. It is the only royal pavilion built in the traditional Ottoman style that survives outside Topkapı Sarayı; all the others were demolished, and replaced by buildings in the more fashionable and ostentatious Europeanized style associated with the Balyans.

The outside is delightfully irregular in shape and every wall is filled with windows – indeed where no real windows could be, unreal ones have been painted to maintain the effect. It is built on a slope with two floors on the Golden Horn side and one at the back, and is set in an attractive garden of lawns and fine trees. A porch on the side leads into an entrance hall which opens on the right into the salon – which still has the aspect of an Ottoman hall of audience – with recessed bays on three sides, lined with low, silk-covered divans. Around the walls runs a frieze with gold letters on a deep blue ground – poems of Selim III, added during his restoration. The room is virtually walled with windows on the three sides which overlook the gardens; and the windows are remarkable, with rectangular casements beneath others delicately ornamented with stained glass – all are double glazed!

The salon with its recessed sofas is the grandest room in the pavilion; but the bathroom, dining room and waiting room, and also the great hall and individual rooms at the Golden Horn end, all have their special decorative features and their understated charm. The lower floor houses an exhibition of Turkish musical instruments.

On the hills above Aynalıkavak Kasrı are the remains of the **Okmeydanı**, the place of the arrow, the imperial archery field which still has marble preserving for posterity the distance achieved by the Sultans' most remarkable shots. No Sultan, it seems was more intent on demonstrating his skill than Mahmut II. The etiquette was strict: first the Sultan would shoot his arrow, followed by the paşas and other invited dignitaries in their turn, all of whom doubtless took care not to exceed the Sultan's shot. And in order not to have to break off too long for prayers, a namazgâh, an alfresco mihrab niche, was erected on the Okmeydanı in the 17th C. by Sultan Murat IV.

Detour **Rahmi M. Koç Industrial Museum**

Across the road beside Hasköy jetty stands a fine 5-domed Ottoman naval foundry, restored as the home of an innovative industrial museum. It contains a remarkable collection of steam engines (road, rail and marine), both full size and models, including working models. All have been beautifully restored on the principle that 'a well-designed and well-engineered piece of machinery to a loving eye . . . gives lasting pleasure'. There are also displays showing the development of navigational instruments; electrical generators; telegraph; calculators; typewriters; telephones; TV; radio; cameras.

DOLMABAHÇE SARAYI

The palace is open daily except Monday and Thursday. Visitors are accepted as part of guided tours only, in groups of 30, with a choice of English, French, German, Arabic or Turkish-speaking guides. The selamlık, which includes all the main public reception rooms, may be seen alone; or an extra ticket can be purchased to include the harem.

It was at this point on the Bosphorus in the spring of 1453 that Mehmet II made his naval base for the siege of Constantinople, and some time after the Conquest the shore was transformed into a royal garden. Evliya Çelebi says that it was Mehmet's grandson, Selim the Grim, who first built a pavilion here, and a century later Ahmet I (1603–17) began the Herculean task of filling in the harbour, completed by his son Osman II in his brief reign. According to Evliya, 'By order of Sultan Osman II all ships of the fleet and all merchant ships at that time in the harbour of Constantinople, were obliged to load with stones, which were thrown into the sea before Dolmabahçe, so that a space of 400 yards was filled up with stones where the sea formed a bay, and the place was called Dolmabahçe, the filled-up garden.'

Pavilion was added to pavilion on this reclaimed land. In the early 19th C. it was an extensive structure, praised by Julia Pardoe for 'its walls of many tints, and its fantastic irregularity of outline.' Mahmut II had already made it his main residence, though a grander palace was being built by Kirkor Balyan within an arrow-shot of it at Beşiktaş.

In 1842 the young Abdül Mecit I commissioned Karabet Balyan and his son Nikoğos to replace the existing agglomeration of pavilions at Dolmabahçe with a new palace, which was to be both a royal residence and a place for official functions, grander and more sumptuous than any previous palace, in which he would be un-ashamed to receive European monarchs whose palaces – as he had seen in pictures – were beyond anything ever built in Turkey. Despite serious financial problems in the sinking Empire, he poured out money to provide the finest materials and workmanship as seemed suitable for the palace of a European sovereign. In 1853 the huge and ornate Dolmabahçe Sarayı was completed, a monument to extrava-gance and the most flamboyant 19th C. taste.

Abdül Mecit's brother and heir Abdül Aziz occupied the palace for the greatest length of time (1861–76); Abdül Hamit II (1876–1909) hated it and lived instead at Yıldız nearby. The Sultanate was abolished in 1922. After the Republic had been established, Atatürk used it as a presidential residence when he was in Istanbul, and it was here that he died on 10 November 1938.

The Selamlık

We enter the palace through a garden filled with flowers and trees, including magnolia trees of astonishing size. At the centre is a wonderfully dotty **fountain** with swans reposing in an outsize shell, water spurting out of their uplifted beaks, supported on the tails of three fantastical fish standing on their heads. The fountain has moved about a bit, having been previously in the harem garden at the other end of the palace, and before that, according to an old painting, at Yıldız Sarayı.

Inside, ornamentation runs riot, with chandeliers of Bohemian crystal – some of spectacular vulgarity – in every room, and furniture that might pass under the label of Abdül Mecit Quinze. The **crystal staircase**, curving like two pairs of snakes, has banisters supported by hundreds of crystal balusters, the glass dome above it rising from Corinthian columns of artificial marble. The stairs lead up to the huge **Salon of the Ambassadors** where almost everything is carved and gilded, or painted. Four fireplaces stand in the walls between the bays, each with painted Sevres porcelain surrounds, and a panel of faceted

Bohemian crystal above. Two **rooms for the ambassadors' inter-preters** open off the far end of the room, the walls hung with late 19th C. paintings. A **bathroom** near the salon has walls and fittings of alabaster, translucent with the sun on it. Also of alabaster, and more elaborately carved, is the **Sultan's bathroom** which may be seen later in the tour.

At the centre of the palace is the vast and ornate **Throne Room**, in which Nikoğos Balyan apparently sought to out-Versailles Versailles. It was intended for meetings and ceremonies of state for up to 2,500 people. Here, on 19 March 1877, Abdül Hamit II presided over the grand inaugural ceremony for the first Turkish bi-cameral parliament-ary system; but he dissolved it under a year later and reverted to autocratic rule. Borne on gilded Corinthian columns, the great central dome soars 36 m high, elaborately painted with trompe l'oeil windows, niches, drapes and carving. Also trompe l'oeil are the arches and colonnades in the galleries. From the centre of the dome hangs the vastest chandelier of them all, 4 tons of Bohemian crystal, with 750 light bulbs (not all working) every one converted from candles when the palace was electrified in 1912 by Sultan Mehmet V Reşat.

The Harem

Iron doors open into the harem, which occupies nearly two thirds of the building, leading first of all into a 150 m corridor with ornamental grilled windows through which the women could view unseen the ceremonies in the throne room below. The finest rooms in the harem include the **Valide Sultan's reception room** and **bedroom**; the **Mavi Salon** (blue salon), also with trompe l'oeil painted decoration, used as the ceremonial hall for the harem; **Atatürk's rooms**, including the relatively simply study where he worked, and his bedroom where every year on 10 November the national flag and bouquets of flowers are laid on the bed to commemorate his death there in 1938; the **Pembe Salon** (pink salon) for the recreation of the harem women – a room much favoured by Atatürk; Sultan **Abdül Aziz's bedroom** notable for the enormous size of the bed for this tall and very well-covered amateur wrestler; and the **school room** with book-rests on desks, a special chair for the crown prince, and all the furniture inlaid with mother-of-pearl. Along the front of the building one is constantly aware of the sea, its shimmering reflected light dappling the interior with ever-changing patterns. The sense of dark cloistering, so powerfully felt at Topkapı, is here less oppressive, and indeed the harem had become, while hardly liberated, a somewhat less confined institution.

The Aviary
Behind the palace is a charming and secluded garden with a miniature lake, a tiny pavilion, and both indoor and outdoor bird cages. The building which houses the indoor cages is rather like a miniature stable block – suitably grand accommodation for the Sultan's birds. It was made at the end of the 19th C. and filled with exotic and colourful birds. It has only recently been opened to the public after years of disuse, and a new collection of birds is being built up.

The Clock Tower
The elaborate 4-tier clock tower at the entrance to Dolmabahçe Sarayı was built by yet another member of the Balyan family called Bali. Until this time clocks had been the special preserve of the mosque, used to indicate the times of prayer. Now they were secularized, and clock towers were built in most major cities as a symbol of Europeanization and progress.

Dolmabahçe Camii
The waterfront mosque beside the palace was built by Nikoğos Balyan for the Valide Sultan Bezmialem, mother of Abdül Mecit I, and was completed in 1853 at the same time as the palace. Its only claim on our attention is for the unusual slenderness of its minarets, with şerefes that imitate Corinthian capitals.

IHLAMUR KASRI

Open daily except Monday and Thursday. This pair of pavilions is just over 1 km from the entrance to Dolmabahçe Sarayı at a junction of Nüzhetiye Cad, between the areas of Ihlamur and Teşvikiye.

Ihlamur Kasrı, the linden pavilion, is in fact two pavilions, set in what was once a linden grove, part of a royal park established by the pleasure-loving Ahmet III in the early 18th C. Just over a century later Abdül Mecit I built a kiosk here where he entertained special guests, including the French poet Lamartine. Later, between 1849 and 1855, he commissioned Nikoğos Balyan to replace it with the more grandiose pair of pavilions that we see today. Abdül Aziz used the park for wrestling matches, in which he was an enthusiastic participant, and also for cock and ram fights. The penultimate Ottoman Sultan, Mehmet V Reşat (1909–18) received foreign heads of state in the pavilions, including the Kings of Bulgaria and Serbia shortly before the outbreak of the Balkan Wars. During the 1950s and 1960s the pavilions were opened as museums: the smaller one as a Tanzımat

(Reform) Museum, the larger as an Historic Pavilions Museum. Both have recently been restored and re-opened to the public.

The pavilion immediately on the right of the entrance into the grounds, the **Maiyet Köşkü**, retinue kiosk, is the simpler of the two, used, as its name imples, for the Sultan's court retinue, and also, on occasion, for the women of the harem. It has now been converted into a very pleasant tea room.

At the back of the garden, with an ornamental pool in front of it, stands the **Merasim Köşkü**, the ceremonial kiosk, which boasts an extravagantly baroque exterior with flamboyant carved decoration and an elaborate double marble stairway leading up to the main entrance. Inside, walls are painted to imitate marble, ceilings have scenes painted on them, and moulding and gilding are lavished everywhere. Painted porcelain fire surrounds come from the kilns of Yıldız, ornate vases from Sèvres or Yıldız, crystal chandeliers from Bohemia, carpets from the imperial mills at Hereke; indeed all the furniture and furnishings display an eclectic and self-conscious variety of European styles.

YILDIZ SARAYI/THEATRE MUSEUM

Yıldız Sarayı stands on the hill above Beşiktaş. Going uphill along Barbaros Bulvarı, near the top a yellow sign points right.

The main palace of Yıldız is not open to the public. Some of its subsidiary buildings are used for international conferences and state functions while the palace itself is being restored. In October 1987 a Theatre Museum was opened in one of these buildings, and when visiting that we can glimpse the ornate exterior of another Balyan palace. It was originally built by Sarkis Balyan for Abdül Mecit I who installed in it a favourite odalisque, and further pavilions were added by Abdül Aziz. But it is mainly with Abdül Mecit's son, Abdül Hamit II, that the palace is associated for he never felt safe at Dolmabahçe and made his permanent residence here at Yıldız. He had come to the throne after the deposition and suicide of his uncle, Abdül Aziz, and the deposition after only three months of his elder brother, Murat V, on the grounds of insanity. He lived in constant fear, and only in the seclusion of Yıldız did he feel any kind of security. Rather than have a single palace building he inhabited a network of pavilions of varying sizes and grandeur, some that already existed here, others that he built himself – a refinement of the ancient Ottoman encampment, but made secure as a fortress. Most of them include a star motif in their decoration for Yıldız means star.

The **Theatre Museum** is a fascinating collection of photographs, costumes, a stage set, playbills (some in the old Arabic script of pre-1928) and other memorabilia of the Turkish theatre, now a flourishing and distinguished institution. It was the Armenians who first developed the theatre in Turkey in the 19th C., for it was not then considered a suitable occupation for Turks, especially Turkish women. Armenian women too were reluctant to take an active part to begin with, and many of the early female parts were played by men. This changed not long after the establishment of the Republic under the influence of Muhsin Ertuğrul whose stand was greatly encouraged by Atatürk. This museum is the first of its kind in Turkey.

YILDIZ PARK AND PAVILIONS

The park and pavilions are open daily. The gate is on the main road from Dolmabahçe Sarayı along the Bosphorus, between Beşiktaş and Ortaköy, on the left just beyond the gate to Çirağan Sarayı. Cars can be driven along much of the network of narrow roads, and can be parked in some areas by the roadside or in the car parks near the various pavilions that provide refreshments. It is a lovely place to walk among gardens and woods, streams and ponds.

During the reign of Abdül Aziz the women of the harem would, on occasion, be allowed an outing to Yıldız Park from the nearby Çirağan Sarayı, to walk in its woodlands. Abdül Hamit later transformed it, landscaping it and planting it with a variety of indigenous and exotic trees, as well as shrubs and flowers, and creating miniature lakes, waterfalls and bridges, and an aviary. Gardens and pavilions alike fell into disuse and disrepair in the 20th C., and it was only when the Turkish Touring and Automobile Association was made responsible for the park and smaller pavilions in 1979 that restoration was set in hand to create a delightful place to walk, and several cafés for refreshments. The **Malta Köşkü** (the most ornate) and **Çadır Köşkü**, both originally build by Abdül Aziz, have had their carved, painted and gilded decoration revived, and have been re-furnished in 19th C. style. Their ground floors and terraces dispense tea and cakes; so do two conservatories, one decorated in pink, the other in green. These are open all year round, while a number of open-air cafés, needless to say, are closed in winter.

YILDIZ ŞALE KÖŞKÜ

Open daily except Monday and Thursday. It can be reached by car or on foot at the top of Yıldız Park.

The Şale Köşkü – so called from its supposed likeness to a Swiss chalet – was built in two stages in the reign of Abdül Hamit. The first stage – when it was known as Merasim Köşkü, the ceremonial pavilion – was completed in 1889, in time to provide accommodation for the new young German Kaiser Wilhelm II and his wife, on their state visit to Istanbul. The second part of the building was completed nine years later when the Kaiser again visited the city. After the establishment of the Republic the palace was turned into a casino for a few years before reverting to its earlier role of guest house for visiting heads of state. The Shah of Persia, King Husein of Jordan, Emperor Haile Selassie and President de Gaulle have all stayed here.

Despite being called 'kiosk', Şale Köşkü is a considerable palace and, like all traditional Ottoman houses, it is divided into harem and selamlık. The rooms open to the public are all on the first floor. We enter through the main door of the harem and go up the fine staircase to a large reception hall whose doors are inlaid with mother-of-pearl. As in all 19th C. palaces in Istanbul, Bohemian crystal chandeliers abound, and the floors are covered with Hereke carpets. Beyond this hall are rooms that were specially fitted for the visit of the German Emperor and Empress, including a bathroom with a pretty flowered handbasin from the Yıldız porcelain factory. In another reception room some of the furniture was made by Abdül Hamit himself, an accomplished carpenter and furniture-maker – doubtless a therapeutic hobby in his life of tormented anxiety and intrigues.

Most spectacular of all is the vast reception room at the end of the building, its ceiling richly carved and gilded, its walls adorned with mirrors and painted panels, and its floor covered with a 7½ ton, 400 sq m single-piece carpet, specially made for the room in the royal carpet mills at Hereke. Three chandeliers and six free-standing candelabras light the room, which is still used for big international meetings and receptions. A magnificent marble staircase takes us to the ground floor again.

BEYLERBEYI SARAYI

Open daily except Monday and Thursday. This ornate palace and its various pavilions stand on the Asian shore of the Bosphorus immediately to the north of the first Bosphorus bridge. It can be reached by ferry to the Beylerbeyi jetty; or by bus, dolmuş or taxi from Üsküdar, or any of the ferry stops on that side of the Bosphorus. The tour can include the palace only, or the optional addition of some pretty pavilions in the gardens behind.

It is said that Constantine the Great erected a great cross in the grounds which now contain Beylerbeyi Sarayı, and that Justinian the Great built a waterside palace nearby of which nothing remains. In the late 16th C. the site belonged to one Mehmet Paşa, Murat III's beylerbeyi of Rumeli, who built a summer palace here, and after whom the area and the palace are named. Later it again became royal property, and in the early 19th C. Mahmut II built a considerable wooden palace here, described in glowing terms by Miss Pardoe as 'like a regal beauty contemplating her gorgeousness in the clear mirror of the Bosphorus . . . the prettiest and most fanciful of all the Imperial residences, and rendered doubly agreeable by its spacious gardens and overhanging groves.' When Mahmut's palace was destroyed by fire, the present Beylerbeyi Sarayı was built for Abdül Aziz by Sarkis Balyan and his brother Agop and completed in 1865, the most agreeable of the larger 19th C. palaces. It was built as a summer residence for the Sultan and his household, but was also used as a guest house for visiting royalty. For one of the first of these, the Empress Eugénie of France, Abdül Aziz had one room completely panelled in mother-of-pearl. The ex-Sultan Abdül Hamit spent the last six years of his life in luxurious imprisonment at Beylerbeyi, and here he died on 10 February 1918.

The palace is surrounded by extensive and delightful gardens, filled with trees and ponds and statues. On the waterfront opposite the entrance to the gardens stands a pretty octagonal kiosk, matched by its twin at the far end of the garden near the entrance to the palace. We go in at the entrance hall of the selamlık, where a splendid staircase grows upwards from single to double, and back to single again. The **waiting room** of the main reception hall is decorated with a variety of nautical motifs – ropes and knots, and ships painted on the ceiling – appropriate to its waterside position; and the theme is also discreetly taken up in the very large and ornate **reception hall** which stands between selamlık and harem. At the centre of the hall is a huge marble pool with carved intertwined dolphins supporting the central fountain. Three Bohemian crystal chandeliers hang from the elaborately painted and gilded ceiling, their lights brilliantly reflected in the pool beneath, while eight large candelabra stand around the room. A **virtuoso staircase** divides and curves and meets again as it rises to the floor above.

199

In the harem an attractive **dining room** overlooks the Bosphorus, with a smaller room off it in which to take tea or coffee, and beyond these are some **bedrooms**, including that in which Abdül Hamit died, his bed a big, heavily carved affair, decorated with painted scenes. Upstairs are more bedrooms and a very pretty tiled bathroom, and also the **Valide Sultan's salon** with its rich red hangings. Returning to the selamlık, the rooms again become more sumptuous. The **Sultan's study** has more nautical themes, and the ornate **Blue Salon**, immediately above the great reception hall, is gilded and hung with chandeliers, and its floors are covered with fine Hereke carpets. There are several more reception and waiting rooms, a prayer room complete with mihrab niche, and a dining room; throughout, crystal chandeliers, wood inlay and painted decoration abound. But for all its elaboration, Beylerbeyi has little of the deliberately overwhelming grandeur of Dolmabahçe Sarayı.

The gardens are terraced on steeply rising ground behind the palace, and in them are several small pavilions which are well worth a visit. **Mermer Köşkü**, the marble pavilion, stands beside a large boating pool. It was built as a hunting lodge, and may date from Mahmut II's complex. There is a small pool in the oval entrance hall, and fountains, with channels cut in the floor to take the water to the pool. A further room opens on each side of the hall, and all the walls are painted to look like marble. The ceilings are covered with fanciful paintings of birds and beasts of the chase in architectural settings. At the far end of the gardens, under the Bosphorus bridge, is **Ahır Köşkü**, the stable pavilion, quite the most beautiful stable block that one could hope to see, with a marble pool in a central bay between the summer and winter sections, so arranged for the comfort of the prize horses of the Sultan's stud. On a higher terrace at the other end of the garden stands **Sarı Köşk**, the yellow pavilion, also believed to be one of Mahmut II's structures, but restored for the use of Abdül Aziz's family. It is on two floors, the lower one providing grand accommodation for a very large conference table, while upstairs is a salon with elaborately painted walls and celings, and a smaller room on each side.

KÜÇÜKSU KASRI

Open daily except Monday and Thursday. Küçüksü Kasrı is on the Asian shore of the Bosphorus just south of Anadolu Hisarı and can be reached by ferry to the Küçüksu jetty, or by bus, dolmuş or taxi from other points along the Asian shore.

Next to the pavilion is a large open area, on either side of which the Küçüksu and Göksu rivers flow into the Bosphorus, known as the Sweet Waters of Asia. For centuries it was a favourite resort on summer high days and holidays for elaborate *déjeuners sur l'herbe* for the wealthy families of Istanbul, men and women sitting decorously apart. Julia Pardoe vividly describes 'the crimson-covered carriages – the white-veiled groups scattered over the fresh turf – the constant motion of the attendant slaves – the quaintly dressed venders of *mohalibè* and *sèkèl* (or sweetmeats) moving rapidly from point to point with their plateaux on their heads . . . – the *yahourt*-merchant, with his yoke upon his shoulders . . . – the vagrant exhibitors of dancing bears and grinning monkeys . . . – the never-failing water-carrier, with his large turban, his graceful jar of red earth, and his crystal goblet – the negroes of the higher harems, laden with carpets, chibouks, and refreshments for their mistresses – the fruit-venders . . . – the ringing rattle of the tambourine . . . all combine to complete a picture so perfect of its kind, that, were a European to be transported to Guiuk-Suy, without any intermediate preparation, he would believe himself to be under the spell of an Enchanter.' Today's picnic parties have less elegance, but evidently equal enjoyment.

Murat IV (1623–40) was the first to adopt this favoured spot, and a century later Mahmut I built a wooden pavilion which was used, with many repairs and restorations, for another century, through the reigns of Selim III and Mahmut II. The Revd. Robert Walsh, writing towards the end of Mahmut's reign, referred to this 'kiosk to which he retired in summer to practise archery or shooting with a rifle, and amuse himself with various sports, some very coarse, where buffoonery of a very indelicate kind form the principal part of the entertainment.' How did he know?

Adül Mecit I commissioned Nikoğos Balyan to replace the wooden pavilion with this rococo palace, completed in 1856. Its exterior is covered with exuberant carving; and from the waterfront it is approached by a very pretty double stairway which embraces a circular pool and fountain. Inside, from the round entrance hall a double staircase with an elaborate, gilded balustrade sweeps up in mirror-image curves to meet and continue together. Downstairs and up, the rooms are filled with carved and gilded decoration, crystal chandeliers and candelabra, fine mirrors, carpets, porcelain, marble fireplaces, furnishings and furniture. It is like a very rich dessert.

HIDIV KASRI

A pleasant excursion while on the Asian shore of the Bosphorus is to the art-nouveau summer palace of the last Khedive of Egypt, on the hill above Çubuklu. It is now a luxury hotel and is a delightful place for a passable (but not particularly inexpensive) meal. Çubuklu can be reached by ferry, or by bus or dolmuş along the Asian shore of the Bosphorus, and from there taxis can be found to take one up the hill to the hotel.

Set in the hills above the Bosphorus, with one of the most magnificent views to be had, and surrounded by rose-filled gardens and a large wooded park, the palace has been restored to its turn-of-the-century art-nouveau opulence. Abbas Hilmi Paşa, from 1892 to 1914 Khedive of Egypt, by then a semi-autonomous governorate within the Ottoman Empire, built this summer residence around 1900. In December 1914, when Britain declared Egypt's independence under British protection and the deposition of the Khedive, Abbas Hilmi was in Istanbul visiting Sultan Mehmet V Reşat – and there he stayed. He and his family continued to occupy this summer palace until the 1930s. In 1937 it was taken over by the Municipality of Istanbul, after which it gradually fell into greater and greater disrepair. In 1982 the ubiquitous Turkish Touring and Automobile Association restored it, and turned it into a very comfortable and beautiful hotel.

MASLAK KASRI

Open daily except Monday and Thursday. It can only be reached by taxi or private car. It is about 11 km from Dolmabahçe, on the main road from Levent to the Belgrade Forest. It is on the right hand side of the road near the Maslak Askeri Hastanesi (military hospital), and is helpfully indicated by yellow road signs.

This charming cluster of pavilions, set in a well-tended garden, was built in the time of Mahmut II, and used as a hunting lodge and place of recreation by Abdül Hamit both before and after he became Sultan. In fact it was in the wooden **Kasrı Hümanyûn**, the pavilion of the Sultan, that he first learned that his brother Murat V had been deposed on the grounds of insanity, and that he was now Sultan Abdül Hamit II. Suitably for the most austere of the last Ottoman Sultans, the pavilion is markedly less ornate than the others. The staircase is a more modest version of those in other palaces, starting single and continuing in twin curves to the light and airy salon above. Here and there in the pavilion we see not only Abdül Hamit's tuğra in flowing Arabic calligraphy, but also the more pedestrian-looking European letters AH, an indication of the increasing influence that Europe had gained both in culture and politics in 19th C. Turkey. Abdül Hamit himself spoke French.

Near this main pavilion stands **Mâbeyn-i Hümayûn**, the Sultan's private apartments. This leads into the **Limonluk**, or orangery, a magnificent glasshouse abounding in camelias, fern trees, bananas and a variety of hothouse plants, with a pool and grotto at the centre. A tiny octagonal kiosk, with overhanging roof and a surrounding balcony, also stands in the gardens, appropriately known as **Çadır Köşkü**, the tent pavilion.

THE BELGRADE FOREST

A few km further along the same road on which Maslak is situated is the Belgrade Forest, a delightful place to drive and walk and picnic. It is a very European forest, filled with chestnuts, oaks, beeches and a few conifers, interspersed with ancient dams and aqueducts. It is now a National Park, and a small charge is made at the entrance which is just the other side of a section of aqueduct (Bahçeköy Kemeri) and the village of Bahçeköy. Maps are provided on boards at the various parking places, indicating roads and walking routes.

The forest is named after the village that once stood at its centre, known as Petra to the Byzantines, but changed to Belgrade in 1521 when Süleyman the Magnificent, having conquered the city of Belgrade, forcibly transported many of its inhabitants to Istanbul. One group was established near the gate in the city walls that is still known as Belgrad Kapısı, and another was put here, for the express purpose of maintaining the reservoirs and aqueducts that brought water to the city. In 1898 the village was disbanded, apparently because the inhabitants, far from maintaining the waterworks, were damaging them instead.

Expatriate Europeans in Istanbul would spend some of the long hot summers in this Christian village, in the cool depths of the forest, among them Lady Mary Wortley Montagu, whose husband was English Ambassador from 1717 to 1718. Her enthusiasm for the place was expressed in letters to friends and relatives. To Alexander Pope she declared that it 'perfectly answers the description of the Elysian fields . . . in the middle of a wood consisting chiefly of fruit trees, watered by a vast number of fountains famous for the excellency of their water, and divided into many shady walks upon short grass, that seems to be artificial, but, I am assured, is the pure work of nature; within view of the Black Sea, whence we perpetually enjoy the refreshment of cool breezes, that make us insensible to the heat of the summer. The village is wholly inhabited by the richest among the Christians, who meet every night at a fountain forty paces from my house to sing and dance, the beauty and dress of the women exactly resembling the ideas of the ancient nymphs as they are given us by the representations of the poets and painters. To say the truth, I am sometimes very weary of this singing, and dancing, and sunshine, and wish for the smoke and impertinencies under which you toil.'

There are a few haunting remains of the **village of Belgrade**, though almost all has been reclaimed by the forest and only the outlines of buildings are still visible. The ruins are near one of the parking places, along a path behind the bekçi's cottage going back in almost the same direction as the road – but it may be best to ask the bekçi to show the way. The curved apse of a church, mentioned by Lady Mary in another letter, is the main distinguishable ruin; the rest are ivy-clad walls, old terracotta drainpipes, and a few underground vaults which the bekçi likes to think were wine cellars. But the fountain near her house still stands beside the road.

Dams and aqueducts were built here during Byzantine times, and were taken over by the Ottomans. Süleyman the Magnificent in particular took trouble to repair and build them anew, some the work of Sinan. Two of these, **Eğrikemer**, the crooked aqueduct, and **Uzunkemer**, the long aqueduct, are near the village of Kemerburgaz. Their names indicate their special feature: Eğrikemer (originally built in the late 12th C. but completely rebuilt by Sinan) includes an obtuse angle, and Uzunkemer is over 700 m long. The road to Kemerburgaz passes under another 12th C. aqueduct, the **Paşaderesi Kemeri**, also much restored. Largest of all the dams is the **Büyük Bend**, just south of the ruins of Belgrade village, originally built in early Byzantine times and frequently restored thereafter. In the 18th C. many of the old dams and aqueducts were repaired and new ones built, including the small **Karanlık Topuz Bendi**, built by Ahmet III in 1722, and the splendid marble **Mahmut I Bendi** ten years later. The **Bahçeköy** (or Mahmut I) **Kemeri**, the over 400 m-long aqueduct near the entrance to the park, was also built in 1732. The very handsome **Valide Bendi**, the dam of the Valide, was built in 1796 by Kirkor Balyan for Mihrişah Sultan, mother of Selim III.

13

GALATA AND PERA

When Byzas founded Byzantium in the 7th C. BC, some of his followers established themselves on the other side of the Golden Horn at the foot of a hillside covered with fig trees. They called it Sycae, the place of figs, and the name stuck for some 1500 years. In the 5th C. AD, when Theodosius II built his new walls, the city was divided into 14 regions, like Old Rome, with Sycae the 13th, corresponding to Trastevere. It had all things pertaining to life, comfort and safety in the late Roman world – baths, theatre, forum, harbour and defensive wall. In the late 6th C. a fortress was built by the water, and from it a boom ran across the water to a tower in Stamboul, cutting off access to the Golden Horn to unfriendly shipping.

The origin of the name of Galata, which gradually replaced Sycae from about the 9th C., is uncertain. Evliya Çelebi says that it came from 'gala, which in Greek is milk, because in the time of the Greek Emperors it was the abode of shepherds and their herds, and was celebrated for its dairies.' Of this there is no evidence; nor for the story that an early fortress here was named after the Galatians, a wild Celtic tribe who terrorised their way from western Europe to Asia Minor in the 3rd C. BC. The name Pera, by which the area was also known, is from the Greek word meaning beyond or across – for obvious reasons. The two names seem to have been interchangeable for the whole area, and it was only in more recent centuries that Galata came to refer to the lower area, and Pera to the top of the hill. The third name nowadays is Beyoğlu, lord's son, which some say refers to Alexius, son of the last Emperor of Trebizond, a convert to Islam to whom Mehmet the Conqueror granted land in this area. Others point to Luigi Gritti, son of the Doge of Venice and Venetian Bailo in the reign of Süleyman the

Magnificent who, like all Europeans, lived here. He too was known as 'Beyoğlu'.

Galata seems always to have been a place for foreigners. When Rabbi Benjamin of Tudela visited Constantinople in 1161 he wrote that 'no Jews dwell in the city; they are obliged to reside beyond an arm of the sea . . . Many of them are manufacturers of silk, many others are merchants, some being extremely rich . . . the quarter inhabited by the Jews is called Pera.'

But it was with the Genoese that the fortunes of Galata were truly established. The Comnene Emperors in the 12th C. had played off Genoa against Venice by allowing trade concessions first to one, then to the other. In 1267, shortly after the Latin occupation, Michael VIII Palaeologus offered the Genoese Republic free trade within the Empire and quarters in Galata. They were to be semi-independent, governed by their own Podestà who was appointed annually from Genoa. Here the Genoese remained, rapidly turning Galata into an ever more flourishing commercial town which, flying in the face of their agreement, they also fortified with a strong wall. As the Byzantine Empire decayed so the little Genoese colony became increasingly independent, and succeeded in creaming 87% of all customs dues.

During the Ottoman siege of 1453 the Genoese of Galata showed more neutrality than pleased the Byzantines who expected their help, and less than pleased Mehmet II; but after the Conquest their neutrality was reckoned to have been sufficient for the colony to escape the Sultan's wrath. The Genoese, he said, could keep their own houses, shops, vines, mills, warehouses and ships; existing churches could still be used but no new ones were to be built and no bells were to be rung. They could travel and trade freely throughout the Ottoman Empire but must submit to a Turkish governor and obey the Sultan's laws. All arms were to be handed over, and all walls were to be torn down. To show that he wished the area to remain a flourishing commercial centre, the Conqueror had a bedesten built near the waterfront, and it still exists.

In the centuries following the Conquest Galata's cosmopolitan and commercial flavour increased. Sephardic Jews, expelled from Spain in 1492 by Ferdinand and Isabella, came here; Moors also came from Spain, and Greeks and Armenians from Anatolia. Early in Süleyman the Magnificent's reign the French became allies of the Ottoman Empire; in 1535 they were granted wide trading privileges and, with a French ambassador to the Sulbime Porte, they too had their own enclave in Galata. In 1580, in Murat III's reign, much to France's chagrin, similar but separate privileges were granted to England, negotiated by the merchant William Harborne who was duly appointed first English ambassador.

Apart from bustling trade, it seems that in Evliya Çelebi's day Galata was awash with taverns. 'There are 200 taverns and wine houses,' he remonstrates, 'where these Infidels divert themselves with music and drinking . . . The taverns are celebrated for the wines from Ancona, Saragossa, Modania, Smyrna and Tenedos. When I passed through here, I saw many hundreds bareheaded and barefooted lying drunk in the street; some proclaimed their situation by proclaiming verse . . .

> My foot goes to the tavern, nowhere else,
> My hand grasps tight the cup and nothing else;
> Cut short your sermon, for no ears have I,
> But for the bottle's murmur, nothing else.'

As the centuries passed and more foreign countries entered into diplomatic relations with the Porte, so trade and diplomacy separated, with the merchants and bankers remaining in the lower areas near the waterfront, and the ambassadors and their suites withdrawing to the more salubrious heights of Pera where they established their embassies in mansions of considerable grandeur, enclosed and insulated in abundant gardens. Through the centre ran la Grande-Rue de Péra, in its heyday the height of elegance. As more Europeans began to visit Istanbul, especially after the completion of the Orient Express railway in 1889, horse-drawn carriages would bring them from Sirkeci Station to the embassies, or to the brand new Pera Palas Hotel.

Fires and neglect have obliterated much of the old Galata and Pera, but there are still reminders of its Genoese and Ottoman commercial past, and remnants of its diplomatic aspirations.

TOPHANE

We should begin our Galata/Pera exploration just outside the erstwhile walls of Galata at Tophane on the lower shore of the Bosphorus, between Kabataş and Karaköy. The area is named after the **cannon foundry** that stands above the main coast road. Its history goes back to the mid-15th C. when Mehmet the Conqueror established here the first Ottoman foundry in Istanbul. Under a century later Süleyman the Magnificent replaced it with a bigger and more modern foundry, designed to produce the more formidable artillery he required for his endless campaigns. The present structure dates to 1803, built during Selim III's unsuccessful attempt to reform the army. It is a handsome rectangular building in alternate courses of brick and stone, crowned with five domes. It spent some time as a military museum but has now been restored as an exhibition hall.

Opposite the foundry, on the other side of the road, is the wonderfully exuberant baroque **Tophane Çeşmesi**, a community fountain, built by Mahmut I in 1732. It is a square, domed structure with a widely overhanging roof, its marble sides richly carved with all manner of fruit and flowers.

NUSRETIYE CAMII

East of the Tophane fountain stands the first of the 19th C. waterfront mosques, begun in 1822 by Mahmut II. The architect was Kirkor Balyan, founding father of the remarkable family which dominated imperial architecture for the rest of the century. It was his first major commission, and it came when Mahmut II was in the final stages of his plans to eliminate the Janissaries. By the time the mosque was completed in 1826 the Janissaries were no more, and Mahmut rather pointedly called it Nusretiye Camii – the mosque of divine victory.

Kirkor Balyan, an Ottoman trained in Paris, a Christian building for a Muslim Sultan, produced an unsurprisingly eclectic design, with elements of Ottoman baroque rubbing shoulders with touches of the Empire style. Like the earlier baroque mosques, it is basically a square crowned by a lofty dome supported on great tympanum arches pierced with windows, and with bulbous pepper-pot turrets at each corner. The courtyard has been switched from the north to the east side, and is not surrounded with the usual porticoes. The north façade has instead been covered with an agglomeration of royal pavilions, as though attempting to combine a mosque and a palace in one space. On either side of the pavilions rise two exceptionally slender minarets. Inside, all is white marble, with swags and garlands in the Empire manner and a baroque mimber; and with much gilding and a lengthy inscription to set it all off.

KILIÇ ALI PAŞA CAMII

Returning to the Tophane fountain, we see on the other side of it a late mosque of Sinan, built in 1580 for the Grand Admiral Kılıç Ali Paşa. This ebullient character was Italian by origin, born in Calabria around

1500. He was captured by Algerian pirates in his youth and, on regaining his freedom after 14 years as a galley slave, he entered the Ottoman service in the only career he knew – buccaneering. His change of faith was marked by the Muslim name Uluç Ali which, according to one commentator, meant Ali the Apostate. So effective was he in his new life that he was made an admiral and Governor of Algiers. After the disastrous Battle of Lepanto in 1571 he was appointed Kaptan Paşa in recognition of his unique service in saving at least part of the Ottoman fleet. At the same time Selim II changed his name from Uluç to Kılıç – Ali the Sword. Two years after Lepanto he recaptured Tunis from Don John of Austria.

The Grand Admiral's time as a galley slave did not appear to give him a tender understanding of others in the same plight – when the English ambassador, William Harborne, had secured the release of three English galley slaves, he made a lifelong enemy of Kılıç Ali Paşa to whom the slaves belonged. What incensed the rich Admiral was the lack of compensation for them. He died in 1587, aged about 87, apparently in the arms of one of his concubines.

Kılıç Ali Paşa Camii was the only mosque that Sinan designed after the model of Aya Sofya, though the similarities are clearer from the inside than the outside. It was built appropriately close to the sea, its founder's life-long element, at a spot where there was once a bustling port. Inside the **courtyard** the mosque is fronted by a spacious double portico. Bronze grilles between the columns divide the two parts, and in the sofa of the outer portico, according to Evliya Çelebi, Kılıç Ali used to sit every Friday and distribute money to the poor. The portal does not have the traditional stalactite canopy above it, but a projecting triangular arrangement carved with a chevron design, into which are set two inscriptions, the upper an elaborately worked Koranic text, the lower giving the date of foundation.

The inside of the **mosque**, though clearly based on Aya Sofya, is much smaller and chunkier, without the soaring elegance of its model. As in Aya Sofya two semi-domes flank the central dome to north and south, and between the two pairs of circular piers on the east and west are two columns (as against four at Aya Sofya) which support the side galleries. The **mihrab** has a traditional stalactite niche which is well carved (as is the mimber), and the apse is adorned with some splendid Iznik tiles. There are tile panels also above the lower windows on the east and west sides under the galleries, and above these panels are colourful stained glass windows. The **preacher's chair** is worth looking at, handsomely inlaid with mother-of-pearl; and the ceiling under the **muezzins' tribune** still has its original painted decoration.

Behind the mosque, in a pretty garden of graves, stands Kılıç Ali Paşa's appealingly simple octagonal **türbe**, with its varying arrangement of windows in each façade. Beyond it, near the SW corner of the mosque, is the **medrese** which was part of the complex though may not have been built by Sinan, a square building now put to practical use as a clinic. In front of it is the **hamam**, designed as a single bath for men only, which has a large and handcome camekân, with two soğukluks opening off it instead of the normal one (though only one is used as such), both of which lead into the spacious marble-clad hexagonal hararet.

Between Kılıç Ali Paşa Camii and Galata Bridge is a labyrinth of narrow streets filling the rectangular space between Kemeraltı Cad. and the docks. It is a fascinating area, full of narrow, winding streets, the occasional building of surprising elegance, and a handful of unexpected, though not noticeably beautiful, Christian churches – Armenian, Greek Orthodox, Turkish Orthodox (a remarkable and very small group of Turkish-speaking Greeks who set themselves loose from the Greek Patriarchate after the Greco-Turkish War of 1919–22), and Russian. Most are 19th C. buildings, though founded soon after the Conquest when Mehmet the Conqueror and his successors encouraged the influx of people of all faiths to build up the population of Istanbul.

YERALTI CAMII

One of the strangest mosques in Istanbul, though not one of the most beautiful, stands near Galata Bridge, opposite the Karaköy ferry terminal. Its Turkish name means 'underground mosque', but this is evident only on its north side where steps lead down from the door. From the harbour side the entrance is on the level, leading straight into the large vaulted area which may once have been the cellars of the fortress built by the Emperor Tiberius II in the late 6th C. as part of the defences of Sycae. From here the chain ran across the Golden Horn to Stamboul. It is rather like a small squat underground cistern, supported on 54 short piers, now unaesthetically encased in wood. This curious place, filled with the gloom of so many centuries, is the scene of yet another miraculous revelation-by-dream of the tomb of a Muslim saint and martyr – or in this case two, Abu Sufya and Amiri Wahibi. They too were killed in the first Arab siege of Constantinople in 674–8, but their joint burial place was not dreamed of till 1640, whereupon Murat IV ordered them to be dug up and re-buried in grander tombs on the same site. A century later it was converted into a mosque. The tombs are under the vault in the NW corner.

On the other side of Karaköy Meydanı, running parallel with the Golden Horn, is Tershane Cad. dockyard street. Walking along it we should notice on the right the lower entrance to **Tünel**, Istanbul's pioneering underground railway system – all of a 1½ minute ride from the bottom to the top of the hill, or vice versa. It was built by the French in 1875, predating the first stage of the London Underground by 9 years and the Paris Métro by 23. Unlike them it never grew; but now new metro lines are now sprouting in other parts of the city.

KURŞUNLU HAN

Less than 200 m along Tershane Cad. from Karaköy, the narrow Kürekçiler Cad. leads to the left. Almost immediately on the right is the entrance to a dilapidated han, built by Sinan for Süleyman the Magnificent's Grand Vezir Rüstem Paşa in the mid-16th C. on the site of a Latin church dedicated to St Michael. It had to be fitted between existing buildings, which accounts for it being long and narrow, and it has a double staircase in the middle giving access to the upper floor. Both floors are surrounded by arcades, the lower arches rounded, the upper ogival. Several small businesses (mostly of the metal-cutting variety) operate from the rooms behind the arches. This seems to be a modification of its early use – kurşun means lead. Just inside the entrance, an upturned Corinthian capital serves as a stand for a communal tap. The building is also known as the Rüstem Paşa Hanı.

FATIH BEDESTENI

Returning to Tershane Cad. and turning left, we soon find on our left the main bedesten of the Galata area, built by Mehmet the Conqueror shortly after he had captured Constantinople. It is virtually square, covered by nine domes which are supported on four solid rectangular piers, and it is still a vital part of the commerce of Galata, filled with shops selling modern machinery.

AZAP KAPI CAMII

At the far end of Tershane Cad., along the last street on the left before Atatürk Bridge, tucked down by the water between the elevated approach road and the Golden Horn, stands another Sinan mosque, the second in the city that he built for the great Grand Vezir Sokollu Mehmet Paşa. If it lacks the distinction of the first, it is nevertheless a handsome building, completed in 1578, the year before Sokollu's assassination. By the early 20th C. it was lamentably dilapidated, and escaped demolition by a whisker when the Atatürk Bridge and its approach roads were build in 1942. Instead it was restored, its earlier dominance over the surrounding area lost to the overshadowing bridge.

The mosque stands on a high platform which once had shops in the arches of its base. Steps lead up at both ends of the north façade to the porch. Unusually, the minaret is detached, and stands near the NE corner, linked to the porch by a bridging passage. The mosque is rectangular and its dome, immediately in front of the mihrab apse risies from an octagon with alternating deep and shallow exedras. Galleries run around three sides. Both the mihrab and mimber are handsomely carved. The interior was originally decorated with panels of fine Iznik tiles, now replaced by less admirable 20th C. work from Kütahya.

Returning towards Tershane Cad. we should notice the enchanting baroque **Azap Kapı fountain**, built by Mahmut I's mother Saliha Sultan in 1732 as part of Mahmut's drive to improve the city's water supply. It consists of a projecting sebil and two flanking çeşmes, and is exuberantly decorated with carved floral and foliate motifs, and with elaborate grilles.

Back at Tershane Cad., we take the last road before the bridge on the other side of the street, Yolcuzade Sok., and turn first right into Yanık Kapı Sok., burnt gate road, its name taken from the **Genoese gateway** that bestrides it. It is the only surviving gate of the Genoese fortifications of medieval Galata, and has Genoa's coat of arms, the cross of St George, carved above it.

ARAP CAMII

To reach Arap Camii we continue along Yanık Kapı Sok., taking the second right into Abdüsselâh Sok. and then third left into Mahkeme Sok. Arap Camii is a tall, square and very handsome building whose belfry-turned-minaret is capped by a tall conical roof. Despite claims that it dates to 715, the present building was originally a Latin church built by the Dominicans in the early 14th C. and it still retains its simple rectangular shape with three apses, with no re-orientation. In the early 16th C. it was converted into a mosque for the use of a group of Moors who had been expelled from Catholic Spain, and it is after these that the mosque takes its name, the mosque of the Arabs.

Those who do not enjoy walking up steep hills can return to Tershane Cad., take the Tünel railway to the top of the hill, and walk down Galip Dede Cad. to the Galata Tower. The hardy should continue along the road on which Arap Camii stands and turn left after about 100 m into Perşembe Pazarı Sok., Thursday market road, climbing uphill. This street still has several charming **18th C. houses and hans** built in characteristic style in alternate layers of brick and stone. On the other side of Voyvoda Cad. (more commonly known as Bankalar, banks street, for reasons that are immediately apparent) steps lead up to Galata Kulesi Sok. which, as its name implies, goes to the Galata Tower.

GALATA TOWER

There are claims that this circular tower was built by the Emperor Justinian in the 6th C., but it is sheer romance, though an earlier tower may have been built here then. The present one was put up by the Genoese in 1348 as part of the defences of their colony, this – the Tower of Christ – being the apex of a triangle of walls with its base along the shore of the Golden Horn. Parts of the ruined walls can be seen just below the tower.

There is a restaurant at the top whose main attraction is its spectacular view of Istanbul by night. There is also a night club. In daytime (open daily) we can pay an entrance fee, take the lift to the 7th floor, and walk up two flights of stairs through the restaurant to the night club where a door opens onto the balcony which runs all round the outside of the tower. It is one of the finest vantage points in the city, with views up the Bosphorus, across to Usküdar and the hills of Asia, to Saray Point and along the Golden Horn, with Topkapı Sarayı, Aya Sofya, Sultan Ahmet Camii and all the other major mosques forming that magnificent skyline of domes and minarets.

TÜRBE OF GALIP DEDE/GALATA MEVLEVIHANESI

A short distance to the north of the Galata Tower is Galip Dede Cad., running on an east-west axis. Turning left up the hill, after 250 m or so we see on the right the gate to the Galata Mevlevihanesi. We enter first a courtyard surrounded by a burgeoning garden and a graveyard. At the entrance to the latter stands the **türbe of Galip Dede,** a 17th C. Mevlevi dervish, a mystic and poet, in his later years şeyh of the tekke beside this burial place.

At the back of the graveyard is the tombstone of an extraordinary maverick Frenchman. Claude-Alexandre, Comte de Bonneval, served with distinction in the French army until, in 1704, he felt he had been insulted and changed sides, winning a golden reputation in the Austrian army under Prince Eugene of Savoy. Then he quarrelled with his commander and again offered his services elsewhere. Rejected by several powers, he finally became a Muslim with the name of Kumbaracı (bombardier) Osman Ahmet, and was employed by Sultan Mahmut I to train the Ottoman army on European lines. Even here he fell in and out of favour several times; and he was casting about for some means of returning to France when he died in 1747.

The Mevlevi order, followers of the 13th C. mystic, poet and teacher, Mevlâna Celâleddin Rumi, are those popularly known as the Whirling Dervishes for they sought mystical communion with Allah through the sema, a ritual of music, chanting, prayers and a whirling dance. The Istanbul tekke, **Galata Mevlevihanesi,** (open daily except Monday) was founded during the reign of Beyazit II (1481–1512), and its first şeyh was a descendant of Mevlâna himself, Şeyh Muhammed Semai Sultan Divani. The present building dates to the end of the 18th C., rebuilt after a fire, and it was restored in the 19th C. and at the beginning of the 1970s. The semahane, the room where the dervishes whirled, is a magnificent octagonal hall, surrounded by galleries from which visitors could watch. All the dervish orders were abolished in 1925 and this tekke, like many others, has been turned into a museum. But the whirling dance continues, with regular performances here all year. The sema is also performed here on 17–20 December, the time when Mevlâna's death is commemorated in his home city of Konya.

ISTIKLÂL CADDESI

Galip Dede Cad. ends at Tünel Meydanı, the square on which stands the upper station of the Tünel underground railway. Istiklâl Cad., the once elegant Grande-Rue de Péra, leads off to the right with an air of cheerful bustle. It is now a pedestrian precinct with a tramway, along which colourful renovated trams trundle between Tünel and Taksim. Some old embassies and other buildings give a hint of Istiklâl's past glory; but many others were lost in one of several fires that ravaged the area, the two worst in 1831 and 1871. Since the establishment of the Republic in 1923 these have been reduced to Consulate-General status, and modern Embassies have been built in Ankara.

The first turning right is Sahkulu Bostanı Sok. At the T-junction we turn left, then almost immediately right into Serdarı Ekrem Sok., face to face with an imposing Anglican church – **Christ Church**, the Crimean Memorial – built in 1858–1 868 to commemorate the British soldiers who died in the Crimean War. It was designed by George Street, a leading exponent of the neo-Gothic style, who later designed the Royal Courts of Justice in London. The moving force in the church's establishment was Lord Stratford de Redcliffe, British ambassador for most of the time between 1825 and 1858, and a powerful influence on Sultan Mahmut II, and especially Abdül Mecit I. He laid the foundation stone in 1858. Within a century it was falling into disuse and was deconsecrated in 1976. In 1991 volunteers from the British Commonwealth community in Istanbul set about patching the roof, rewiring, reglazing, restoring the fine organ and equipping the church. It was reconsecrated for regular worship in 1993.

Returning to Istiklâl Cad. and turning right, we see on our right the **Swedish Embassy**, the oldest and loveliest of them all, dating to the late 17th C. Somehow it escaped the fires. Opposite it is an 18th C. building with a heavy columned façade – once the Russian Embassy.

The next road on the left, Asmalı Mescit Sok., leads to Meşrutiyet Cad., on the other side of which, to the right stands the most historic hotel in Istanbul, the **Pera Palas Oteli**. It was built in the 1890s by Georges Nagelmackers, the Belgian businessman who had just established the Orient Express railway between Paris and Constantinople; for many years it was the only place for visitors to stay. It is worth a visit, if only for a glimpse of the elaborate wrought-iron gates and the wooden cabin that is still used as a lift; and for a whiff of the old atmosphere of diplomatic (or other) intrigue behind the potted plants. Agatha Christie played her part in making the hotel famous; but more important to the Turks is the fact that Atatürk stayed here in the early days of the Republic, before he made Dolmabahçe Sarayı his Istanbul home. A suite of rooms on the first floor has been set aside as an Atatürk Museum.

Back on Istiklâl we see on the right, set back in a handsome garden, the **Russian Embassy**, an imposing 19th C. mansion built by the Swiss Fossati brothers on the orders of Czar Nicholas I for whom they had already done much work in Moscow. Having built this Embassy in 1837, the Fossatis changed master and remained in Istanbul for many years, working for Sultan Abdül Mecit I, in particular restoring

Aya Sofya. A little further on, on the same side of Istiklâl, a flight of steps takes us down to the lovely little Franciscan **church of St Mary Draperis**. The present building dates from 1789, but its history goes back to a few months before the Conquest when the Franciscans established a church on the other side of the Golden Horn. After the Conquest they had to move, first to Galata, and then in 1678 to this site.

The next street on the right starts off as Postacılar Sok. and then changes to Tomtom Kaptan Sok. On the left is the **Dutch Chapel**, an attractive early 18th C. building which nowadays houses the Union Church of Istanbul, a multi-national and non-denominational Protest-ant church whose services are in English. Further down the road, immediately on the left at the T-junction, is an entrance to the **chapel of St Louis of the French**, founded in the late 16th C. but, like the French Embassy to which it was attached, rebuilt after a fire in 1831. On the right of the T-junction is the old **Spanish Embassy** which no longer functions, even as a Consulate. A little further down the hill we come to a small square, on the right of which, surrounded by a pretty Italian garden stands the **Palazzo di Venezia**, once the Embassy and residence of the Venetian bailo, now the Italian Consulate-General. It dates to the late 17th C.; but the Venetians had been deeply involved in the city since Byzantine times, alternating trade and war with equal enthusiasm. On another side of the square is the 19th C. French Tribunal of Justice on the edge of the gardens of the Maison de France (see below).

Climbing back up the hill to Istiklâl Cad. and continuing northwards, we come next on our right to the very attractive **Dutch Embassy**, another of the Fossatis' buildings, completed in 1855. The original Embassy here dated to 1612. The next turning to the right leads to the **Maison de France**, an imposing structure built after the fire of 1831 as the French Embassy, and set in an extensive garden. François I's alliance with Süleyman the Magnificent in the early 16th C. – to the dismay of the rest of Europe – made France the first nation to establish diplomatic relations with the Ottoman Empire, with wide trading privileges included. Returning to Istiklâl and resuming our northwards direction, just over 100 m further on the right, through gates and across a courtyard, is the Franciscan **church of St Anthony of Padua**, a large red brick neo-Gothic church built in 1913 on the site of its early 18th C. predecessor.

Another 100 m or so brings us to Galatasaray Meydanı, which is not so much a square as a road junction. Set back on the right is a handsome building behind an imposing gateway – the renowned

Galatasaray Lisesi. Its origins go back to the end of the 15th C. when Beyazit II established here an off-shoot of the Palace School for the training of imperial pages. In 1868 the building was taken over for the first of a new type of secular secondary school, designed with the advice of the French Minister of Education, in which instruction was given in both Turkish and French in a much broader range of subjects than previously, and to a much higher level. It turned out many of Turkey's leading statesmen, businessmen and intellectuals. The present building dates to 1908, and it is still in use as a school.

Opposite Galatasaray Lisesi, just beyond the Post Office, is the entrance to the **Galatasaray Balık Pazarı**, or fish market, one of the most colourful and lively areas of old Pera, with cascades of fish, fruit and vegetables, and a great deal more besides, on stalls on both sides of the cobbled road. Delicious snacks of lamb, or mussels on a stick, dipped in batter and deep fried as you watch, can be bought from stalls and eaten as you go. The market street runs for some distance down the hill, with further streets opening off it. An opening to the right very soon after entering the fish market from Istiklâl is called **Çiçek Pasajı**, the passage of flowers, from its earlier use as a flower market. It later became one of the closest things in Istanbul to a British pub, but enlivened by very un-British itinerant musicians and food vendors, before becoming a rather ordinary restaurant area.

Beyond the Çiçek Pasajı the first turning to the left emerges opposite the main gate of the old **British Embassy**, a suitably imperial-looking Victorian pile built by Sir Charles Barry in 1845, during the time that his Houses of Parliament were being built in London. This too is surrounded by a considerable garden, very much in the English manner.

The rest of Istiklâl to Taksim Square is a travesty of its former self, mostly devoted to the rag trade, with confectioners, restaurants and a few lurid cinemas thrown in. Just before Taksim, on the left, stands the old **French Consulate** (they had both an Embassy and a Consulate), originally built in 1719 as a plague hospital.

TAKSIM SQUARE

On the very edge of Taksim Square is the water distribution centre, or **Taksim**, which gives the area its name. It is an attractive octagonal structure, built in 1732 by Sultan Mahmut I to improve the water supply tot he city. Water from the Belgrade Forest was channelled here for distribution to the various areas of Beyoğlu. Near the middle of the square is the **Monument of Independence**, a life-size group portraying Atatürk and other leaders of the Nationalist Movement who inaugurated the Turkish Republic in 1923. It is a work of the Italian sculptor Canonica, made in 1928. The eastern side of the square is occupied by a large plate-glass-fronted building called the Atatürk Kultur Sarayı (culture palace), but otherwise known as the **Opera House**. In it are staged a number of theatrical, operatic and ballet performances, especially during the international Istanbul Festival.

Looking back in the direction from which we have come, we can see the forbidding outline of the late-19th C. Greek Orthodox **church of Aya Triada** (Holy Trinity), set between Istiklâl and Sıraselviler Streets.

MILITARY MUSEUM

Open daily except Monday and Tuesday. The Mehter band concert is at 3 p.m.

The museum is about 1½ km north of Taksim Square: go along Cumhuriyet Cad., past the Hilton Hotel, turn right into Valikonağı Cad., and the entrance is a short distance along on the right. It houses a fascinating collection of military clothes, arms and equipment from various stages of Ottoman history.

From 3 to 4 pm the Mehter Band, rigged out in the uniforms and with the instruments of the old Ottoman military bands, parades up and down playing marches. When Mahmut II eliminated the Janissaries in 1826 and established his new army, he employed Giuseppe Donizetti, brother of the more famous composer Gaetano, to organise military bands on European lines. As there were no suitable tunes for the reformed army to march to, the Turkish Donizetti had to compose some, and they are still played today.

218

14

ÜSKÜDAR

Üsküdar is most quickly reached by the ferry from Kabataş which faces it on the European side of the Bosphorus. Other ferries from Eminönü also call there. Buses and dolmuşes run there from all points along the Asian side of the Bosphorus.

Üsküdar – as Scutari made famous by Florence Nighingale – was originally founded in the early 7th C. BC by Greeks from Megara, a few years before Byzantium was established on the opposite shore. Despite its promising name – Chrysopolis, the city of gold – it was for centuries subordinate to its greater neighbour Chalcedon (today's Kadıköy), scathingly referred to by the Delphic oracle as 'the land of the blind' for its founders' inability to see the superior merits of the site of Byzantium.

Both these Asian cities were, nevertheless, superbly sited on the edge of fertile territory reaching into northern Anatolia, in Greek the land of the rising of the sun. But the strong currents of the Bosphorus were not as favourable as they were to Byzantium for the landing of trading ships; and the shoals of fish, a major source of wealth in the ancient world, also tended to be carried towards Byzantium. Throughout the Hellenistic and Roman periods, Chrysopolis was overshadowed by Chalcedon, but it maintained its identity and increased in prosperity until it gradually outstripped Chalcedon in importance.

In AD 324 Constantine the Great, then Emperor of the West, defeated Licinius, Emperor of the East, in their final battle at Chrysopolis. When Constantinople became the new capital of the re-united Roman Empire, Chrysopolis and Chalcedon became suburbs of the city. Chrysopolis was important because all the major routes into Asia started there, and its position – in Asia, yet so close to Constantinople – made it a target for those aiming at the Byzantine capital. Early in the 8th C. a small band of Arabs reached Chrysopolis from the south and caused a great deal of damage, as well as panic in Constantinople, before withdrawing; and in 988 a rebellion that came close to unseating Basil II made its centre there, but the Emperor crossed the Bosphorus with an army of Russian allies and crushed the rebels. Equally, when Byzantine armies set out on expeditions into Asia Minor, it was at Chrysopolis that they mustered. From the 12th C. the town became known as Scutari from the Emperor's Scutarion palace. Neither this nor any other Byzantine building remains today.

In 1338 the Ottoman leader Orhan Gazi, having already captured Bursa, Nicaea (Iznik) and Nicomedia (Izmit), took Scutari and for the first time had a base within sight and sound of the Byzantine capital. Just over a century later, when Mehmet II captured Constantinople, Üsküdar reverted from being a frontier town to its old role of suburb, this time of the new Ottoman capital of Istanbul. Here in Üsküdar would gather every year the Sürre-i Hümayun, the Sacred Caravan of pilgrims who set out in a long and stately procession overland to the Holy Cities of Mecca and Medina, with a sacred white camel laden with gifts.

Soon after the Conquest the Sultans established an out-of-town palace at Üsküdar, rebuilt by succeeding generations. It no longer exists. Other members of the royal family also built palaces here, followed by wealthy paşas; and many of them added mosques, medreses and other pious foundations, turning Üsküdar into a seaside and rural town of immense elegance and charm.

Barracks and drill grounds were established on the outskirts of Üsküdar in the mid-18th C. by Mahmut I, and more were added by subsequent Sultans, making it one of the main military centres of Istanbul. In 1799 Selim III built wooden barracks just south of Üsküdar to house his New Order army, his brave attempt to replace the corrupt Janissary force. Nine years later he was deposed and then murdered by the Janissaries, and his barracks were reduced to ashes. When Mahmut II abolished the Janissaries in 1826, he commissioned Kirkor Balyan to build new barracks on the same site – called the Selimiye barracks after his unlucky predecessor – which were completed in 1828. Between 1842 and 1853 Abdül Mecit I had them enlarged to the imposing four-square structure that we see today, three storeys high and with a tower at each corner, dominating the shoreline between Üsküdar and Haydarpaşa. It was in these new barracks, converted into a British military hospital in 1854 for the Crimean War, that Florence Nighingale and her nurses tended the sick and wounded who had been shipped back from the Crimea. Her introduction of hitherto unheard-of standards of hygiene and care dramatically reduced the death-rate.

In 1873 the first stage of the Anatolian Railway was built, starting at Haydarpaşa just south of Üsküdar and running to Izmit on the Sea of Marmara – an up-dating of the more traditional modes of travel into Anatolia, but starting from more or less the same point. Then work stopped as the Ottoman Empire, the Sick Man of Europe, could not afford the costly business of railway building. Abdül Hamit II, seeking to improve the Ottoman economy at someone else's expense, found a more than willing bidder in the Deutsche Bank and the German Emperor Wilhelm II who saw great advantages for the German Empire. By 1892 the railway reached Ankara, and four years later Konya. On Wilhelm II's second state visit to Istanbul in 1898 the new station, built with German money, was inaugurated with much ceremony – the grandiose affair we see today to the south of the Selimiye barracks.

KIZ KULESI/LEANDER'S TOWER

Just offshore from Üsküdar stands a curious white building on a tiny rocky island, known to the Turks as Kız Kulesi, the maiden's tower. The name derives from a popular legend in which a princess was incarcerated here by her father. He was attempting to cheat fate, for a prophecy had foretold that she would die from a snake bite; but fate, in its usual spoilsport way, would not be mocked and a snake concealed in a basket of fresh figs ensured the fulfilment of the prophecy. Its popular English name confuses the location of Leander's legendary nightly swim to see his lover Hero, to end tragically in his drowning – a tale that is set in the Hellespont rather than the Bosphorus.

The first building that is known of here was erected in the 12th C. by Manuel I Comnenus and called the tower of Damalis. From it a chain reached to the tower of Mangana on the European shore below present-day Topkapı Sarayı, closing the entrance to the Bosphorus. The present building dates to the 18th C. Its position has made it a useful place to keep people in quarantine, to act as a lighthouse or customs control point, or for its current use by the Turkish Navy to monitor shipping.

MIHRIMAH SULTAN CAMII

The main square of Üsküdar by the ferry landing is appropriately known as Iskele Meydanı, jetty square; but before the advent of ferries it went under the more picturesque name of Doğancılar Meydanı, the square of the falconers. On our left, coming from the ferry, we should first cast a glance at the delightfully ornate **fountain of Ahmet III**, built by that tulip-loving Sultan and his Grand Vezir, Damat Ibrahim Paşa, in 1728.

Behind the fountain, raised on a high platform, is the harmonious outline of Mihrimah Sultan Camii, built by Sinan in 1547 for the favourite daughter of Süleyman the Magnificent and wife of the Grand Vezir Rüstem Paşa. The original complex consisted, apart from the mosque, of a medrese, an imaret and a mektep, but the imaret no longer exists. Steps lead up to the platform on which the mosque stands. It was an awkward site for Sinan to contend with, too narrow for a courtyard so it is preceded by a spacious double portico, in the middle of which an extra projection covers the handsome multi-faceted marble şadırvan. Inside, the **mosque** has an oddly irregular shape with three semi-domes around the dome instead of the more usual two or four; and it has little of the lightness, physical or visual, that we expect of Sinan. The mihrab and mimber are of fine work.

At the eastern end of the portico stands a clutch of **türbes** which do not include that of Mihrimah herself as she was buried in her father's türbe at the Süleymaniye. They do include, however, the türbe of Sinan Paşa, Grand Admiral and brother of Mihrimah's husband Rüstem Paşa, rather oddly placed here instead of at his own mosque complex at Beşiktaş, but presumably because that mosque was not finished when he died in 1554. Near them stands the **medrese**, an attractive square building now used as a clinic; while the **mektep** is on the steep slope behind the mosque, its handsomely arched and vaulted lower floor supporting a winter classroom and summer loggia. It is now a children's library.

YENI VALIDE CAMII

On the other side of Iskele Meydanı, set back from the square in a walled precinct shaded by plane, lime and chestnut trees, stands Yeni Valide Camii, the new mosque of the Queen Mother, built by Ahmet III in 1708–10 in honour of his mother, Gülnus Emetullah. Her handsome **türbe** can best be seen from Hakimiye Milliye Cad. It is a large octagon open to the elements and filled with rose bushes; it is decorated with arches-within-arches, stalactite capitals and elaborate grille windows in almost baroque ornateness. Similar in style are the erstwhile **sebil** which stands next to it, and the **şadırvan** in the mosque courtyard, both also octagonal. Above the entrance to the outer courtyard is the **mektep**, built in a mixture of stone and brick.

The **mosque**, by contrast, is basically classical in style, but in a somewhat tired, end-of-run manner, before the introduction of the baroque. The interior design is that of an octagon set in a square, crowned with a dome – rather like an overgrown Rüstem Paşa Camii, but decorated with inferior tiles whose only virtue is that there are not so many of them as in Rüstem's mosque. The painted decoration is worse. The mihrab and the mimber are finely carved, but someone with a passion for paint has picked out the lovely relief carving in gold on green.

ŞEMSI PAŞA CAMII

Returning to Iskele Meydanı, we can see Şemsi Paşa Camii standing on an island of grass between the entrance to the Bosphorus and the dual carriage road that runs around the coast. It is an enchanting little mosque, built by Sinan, set on the very edge of the water where there are always enthusiastic fishermen trying their luck.

Şemsi (solar) Ahmet Paşa became Grand Vezir shortly after the assassination of Sokollu Mehmet Paşa in 1579, a deed in which he may have had some part – he was certainly an opponent of Sokollu's policies. He was the first Grand Vezir since the Conquest who was not of foreign birth and brought into the palace service in youth by the devşirme; he was of Turkish and noble origin. Sinan built this mosque for him in 1580, the smallest of the Grand Vezirial complexes up to that time. He was sacked soon afterwards.

The **courtyard** is a charming, irregularly shaped garden, with the porticoes and cells of the L-shaped **medrese** on two sides, and the third side a window-filled wall looking directly onto the Bosphorus. The dershane is in the middle of the wing facing the mosque. The medrese arches are now glassed in and the building is used as a public library. The **mosque** occupies the fourth side of the courtyard, its short minaret rising above the dome, with fine stalactite carving under the şerefe, and **Şemsi Ahmet's türbe** beside it, a projection of the mosque itself, between it and the sea. Inside, the mosque is tiny and intimate, a square room crowned by a dome set on four semi-circular squinches. Şemsi Paşa's türbe is separated by a grille from the inside of the mosque.

RUM MEHMET PAŞA CAMII

Just beyond Şemsi Paşa Camii a road to the left leads uphill to one of the oldest mosques in the city, built in 1469 by Rum (Greek) Mehmet Paşa during the three years when he was Mehmet the Conqueror's Grand Vezir. Rum Mehmet Paşa was, as his name implies, a Byzantine by birth, but also by upbringing, a renegade who converted to Islam when he joined the Ottomans. Under the remarkable Grand Vezir Mahmut Paşa, appointed in 1453, Rum Mehmet rose to the rank of Second Vezir; but such was his ambition and ruthlessness that he spread rumours and lies to undermine the Sultan's confidence in Mahmut. In 1467, Mahmut was replaced by Rum Mehmet. He had nothing of the competence and loyalty of Mahmut and was himself replaced in 1470.

The mosque has something of the Bursa style in the double prayer hall inside and the two flanking tabhane rooms on each side. But it has also borrowed from Byzantine ideas, especially on the outside, with the shallow dome on its cylindrical drum, the undulating cornice lifting at intervals to include the windows set into the drum, and the square base below broken by tympanum arches which rise above it. Fronting the mosque is a portico of five domed bays – not original, though the columns are ancient and a mixed bag into the bargain. The interior is in two parts like the Bursa mosques, but the mihrab end is covered not by a dome but by a semi-dome, which looks very like an apse.

ATIK VALIDE CAMII

This magnificent mosque complex, one of Sinan's finest works, is rarely visited and rarely even mentioned in guide books, probably because it is about 1½ km from the Üsküdar jetty, on a hill above the town. But it is well worth a visit. Those taking a taxi should be warned that taxi drivers usually disclaim all knowledge of it, and will try to persuade you that what you really mean is Yeni Valide Camii. It is helpful to recite some names of streets en route – especially Toptaşı Cad. and Çavuşdere Cad. between which it stands – to avoid being wafted all round Üsküdar at your own expense.

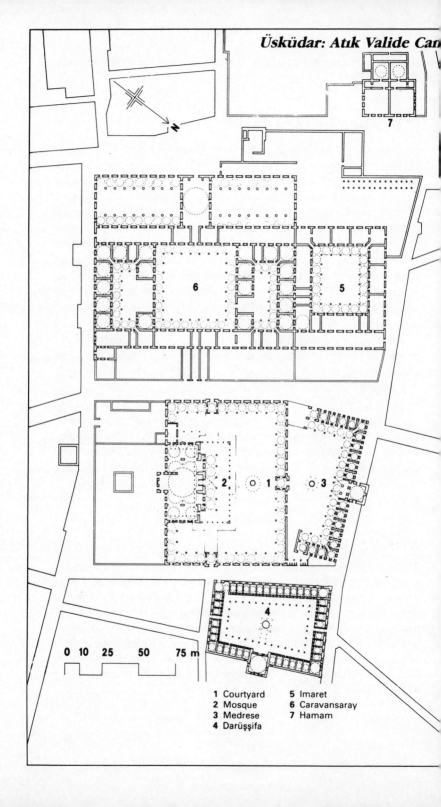

Üsküdar: Atık Valide Cam

0 10 25   50   75 m

1 Courtyard   5 Imaret
2 Mosque   6 Caravansaray
3 Medrese   7 Hamam
4 Darüşşifa

Valide Camii (as it was known until the completion of Yeni Valide Camii 127 years later) was built by the aging Sinan for the notorious Venetian-born Nur Bânu Sultan, mother of Murat III, the first of the powerful Valide Sultans who controlled the fortunes of the Ottoman Empire for almost a century. Construction probably began in 1577, and was completed in 1583, the year of Nur Bânu's death. She was, however, buried in Selim II's türbe at Aya Sofya. It was a very extensive complex including, besides the mosque, a medrese, mektep, dar-ül kura, dar-ul hadis, darüşşifa, imaret, caravansaray and a double hamam.

Unusually, the mosque is not so much preceded by a **courtyard** as enclosed within it, making the courtyard like an angular letter C with three fine gatehouses. It is a magnificent courtyard, surrounded by graceful arcades and a profusion of domes, shaded by two enormous and ancient plane trees, said to have been planted when the mosque was built. In front of the portico stands a handsome 16-sided şadırvan, each face slightly convex. Originally the mosque had a single 5-domed portico, but a second one was added in the following century when the mosque was enlarged. The windows in the inner portico are crowned with fine panels of inscriptive tiles, decorated with floral and foliate motifs, and both the capitals of the columns and the canopy over the main door are handsomely carved.

The interior of the **mosque** is wide and shallow, the extensions on either side, each under two domes, dating from the enlargement of the mosque in the 17th C. Sinan's mosque has a central dome covering a hexagon, with semi-domes over the four lateral sides and the projecting mihrab niche, and a flat arch above the entrance. Galleries run around three sides, supported on marble columns, with double the width on the west side thanks to the later extension. The ceilings under the galleries along the back still have some of their original lovely 16th C. painted decoration. The **royal loge** in the west gallery is screened by a wonderful, if incongruous, 18th C. baroque grille; but inside, only one panel remains of the architectural trompe l'oeil scenes that once adorned it. The mihrab apse is richly decorated with magnificent panels of Iznik tiles, including two rows of inscriptions and a design with trailing branches of blossom and vases of tulips. There are also inscriptive tiles over the windows. The marble **mihrab** niche and **mimber**, and also the wooden **preacher's chair**, are all elaborately carved and of fine work.

The gatehouse in the northern wall of the courtyard leads down stairs to a lower terrace on which stands the **medrese**, an attractive and irregularly shaped tree-filled courtyard surrounded on three sides by 18 domed cells fronted by porticoes. The dershane is in the middle of the north side, carried on arches which make a kind of bridge over the street below, whose existence necessitated the irregular shape. Each cell has a fireplace to keep the students warm in winter, a sign that this was a regular medrese and not a tekke for dervishes, for whom winter hypothermia was an accepted way of life.

To the east of the mosque and medrese stands the **darüşşifa**, a combined hospital and asylum, also irregularly shaped with 40 cells and arcades round a central courtyard, and a larger hall in the middle of the eastern side. It is now the boarding house for a local school.

West of the medrese stands the **imaret** which is joined to the large **caravansaray** on the south of it. Both are unrecognisable from the outside, being much built upon; but inside the two are integrated for the use of a school of considerable size, with domed classrooms and arcaded courtyards, that in the caravansaray filled with shady trees.

The **hamam** further west is in a rather degraded state, and is used for almost anything except baths.

ÇINILI CAMI

Turning left out of the Atîk Valide complex onto Çinili Cami Sok., brings us to Çavuşdere Cad. (at this point renamed Allame Cad.); we turn right and uphill until we see Çinili Cami on the right of the road.

Çinili Cami, the tiled mosque, is the charming foundation of the Valide Sultan who exerted the longest run of nefarious influence on the affairs of the Ottoman Empire. Kösem Sultan, the beautiful Greek girl who captivated Ahmet I, retained her influence in the two brief reigns of Ahmet's imbecile brother Mustafa, and was Valide Sultan in the reigns of her two sons, Murat IV and Mad Ibrahim. She was murdered in 1651 on the orders of her rival and successor, Turhan Hatice, when she tried to extend her influence into the reign of her grandson Mehmet IV. This mosque was built in 1640 when she was at the height of her power, at the beginning of Mad Ibrahim's reign.

It is a very agreeable building, set in a leafy and irregularly shaped courtyard, with a large şadırvan in one corner under an exuberant conical roof. The portico runs around three sides, and on the façade of the mosque are some of the tiles for which it is famed. Pretty as they are, they are noticeably less rich, both in design and colour, than the tiles of the best periods of Iznik's production, whose last gasp was in the great mosque of Kösem Sultan's husband – Sultan Ahmet Camii. Inside, the mosque has all the advantages of simplicity of design and smallness of scale, being a square crowned by a dome borne on plain pendentives, and this simplicity sets off to perfection the tiles that cover the interior. The mimber is finely carved, though the painting on it seems beyond the call of either duty or taste. SE of the mosque is the **medrese**, two rows of cells meeting at an acute angle with the dershane at the angle – a clever use of an awkward and steep site.

Detour 1 Cemetery of Karaca Ahmet

One of the most surprisingly enjoyable parts of Üsküdar, and a great favourite for walking in, is the vast and ancient cemetery of Karaca Ahmet. It is just under 1 km SW of Atık Valide Camii, and just over 1 km from Iskele Meydanı following Hakimiyeti Milliye Cad. which is renamed Gündöğümü Cad. about half-way.

Julia Pardoe in the 1830s wrote of the cemetery as though it were a scene in a Gothic novel – 'This extraordinary necropolis, perhaps the largest and most picturesque in the world, stretches its cold and silent shadows over hill and valley, covering upwards of three miles of country with the sable livery of death, and shutting out the sunlight from unnumbered graves.' This makes it sound a touch gloomier than it is, though its charm is certainly crepuscular, punctuated as far as the eye can see in every direction with the dark outlines of lofty cypresses, with ornately carved tombstones lurching at all angles at their feet. It is said that it was started in 1338 when Orhan's Ottomans captured Scutari from the Byzantines, and was named after one of the heroes who was killed in the battle. Needless to say, Karaca Ahmet's grave was revealed in a dream in later years, and also that of his horse, and both were rehoused in appropriately grander accommodation – a türbe (rebuilt in the 19th C.) for Karaca Ahmet and a less imposing domed monument for his horse.

The tombstones, in all their number and variety, tell stories of the men and women whose burial places they mark – if only we can interpret the symbols or read the Ottoman script. The varying styles of turbans on the men's tombstones indicate their rank and occupation, while those of women are carved with flowers, each bloom representing a child. One effect of the banning of turbans in 1828 was to make Turkish tombstones thereafter much duller.

Detour 2 Selimiye Barracks, Selimiye Camii and the Crimean War Cemetery

The **Selimiye barracks** (for the history see pages 220–1), since they are still used by the Turkish army, are not open to the public.

However, a small **museum** was opened some years ago by the Turkish Nurses Association in a room on the ground floor of the N tower in honour of Florence Nightingale. It was in this part of the barracks that Florence Nightingale lived during the Crimean War when it was a British hospital. It is mainly of interest to dedicated Nightingales, but the sheer size of the barracks at close quarters is impressive. The museum is open daily except Saturday and Sunday. The entrance is in the middle of the NE side of the building, and there are soldiers to show the way.

Also of interest is the handsome baroque **Selimiye Camii** beside the barracks, built by Selim III in 1804 when his wooden barracks, built with such hopes for his New Order army, were only five years old. Three years later the Janissaries deposed and murdered him. The mosque is set in an agreeable garden precinct, shaded by three venerable plane trees, its dome towering above the great window-filled tympanum arches, and with elaborate turrets at the corners. The interior is not quite as satisfactory as the exterior, but it is grand and well lit with its multiplicity of windows.

South of the barracks stands a large building, until recently Haydarpaşa Lisesi, but it now forms part of the University of the Marmara. West of it is the **Crimean War Cemetery**, which has no sign to identify it and is usually locked. But the bekçi will let you in to wander around the well-tended graves – of British soldiers who died of their wounds in Florence Nightingale's hospital; of several of her nurses who were also buried here; of British soldiers who died at Gallipoli and in World War II; and some British residents of Istanbul. There is a Victorian obelisk, and also a plaque in honour of Florence Nightingale, dedicated by Queen Elizabeth II on her state visit to Turkey in 1971.

Detour 3 **Büyük Çamlıca hill**

Büyük Çamlıca, the great place of the pines, the highest hill near Istanbul, is just over 4 km from the main square of Üsküdar. It is immediately distinguishable by the towering television mast near its summit which for many years, like the Beyazit tower, doubled as a nightly weather forecast station – a blue light for fine weather, green for rain and red for snow. It is a delightful place for a walk amongst the pine trees, for refreshments in the gardens and pavilions at the summit, and to enjoy one of the most spectacular views in the world. From Iskele Meydanı in Üsküdar buses run either right to the top of the hill, or to Kısıklı at its foot, from where it is a pleasant short walk to the top.

The top of Büyük Çamlıca has been transformed since 1980 by the restoration of its vegetation, and by the creation of a park filled with flower gardens and little marble kiosks, and two cafés in something like 18th C. style. The view from the top presents an astonishingly wide panorama, and with the influx of Europeans to Istanbul in the 19th C., it became a required view for painters to paint and writers to write about. Turning almost three-quarters of a circle, we see from the Sea of Marmara and the Princes' Islands across Stamboul, the Golden Horn, Pera, and almost the whole length of the Bosphorus to the Black Sea. At every time of day the vision changes, some parts clear as the sun shines full on them, others hazy with the sun behind them. On very clear days – a rare occurrence, and almost never in summer – it is possible to see the snow-capped Mount Olympus (Uludağ) rising to the south above the Sea of Marmara. Most breath-taking of all is the view at sunset, with the fabled skyline of the old city in sharp silhouette against the reddening sky.

15

THE BOSPHORUS

Say Istanbul and a seagull comes to mind
Half silver and half foam, half fish and half bird.
Say Istanbul and a fable comes to mind
The old wives' tale that we have all heard.
                                    Bedri Rahmi Eyuboğlu.

PRACTICALITIES

a) There are twice daily ferry tours of the Bosphorus which leave Galata Bridge from the Eminönü terminal opposite Yeni Cami. They run as far as Rumeli or Anadolu Kavağı, where they wait long enough for a leisurely meal in a fish restaurant before returning. The trip takes 1¾ hr each way, with a 2 hr wait at the far end. b) Alternatively, one can disembark at Rumeli Kavağı on the European shore and make one's way back by dolmuş, bus or taxi, or a combination of all three, stopping to explore various places en route. c) Many ferries or water dolmuşes (dolmuş mötörü) run between the European and Asian shores of the Bosphorus, enabling one to explore the Asian side as well, using the buses and dolmuşes that connect the villages on that side to Üsküdar and further south. d) Buses and dolmuşes run from Taksim Square to points on the European shore of the Bosphorus – often quicker than ferries. e) Those wishing to see the Upper Bosphorus should hire a motorised *sandal* from Büyükdere. f) On summer evenings several restaurant-boats provide a Bosphorus cruise with dinner, when the shore lights, the moon and stars are reflected in the waters, and provide more of an attraction than the merely passable food.

LEGEND AND HISTORY

It is inevitable that so beautiful and dramatic a stretch of water, unimaginably deep in places, and dividing the continents of Europe and Asia with its swift and varying currents, should be surrounded by legend. Its very name comes from the myth of Io, daughter of Inachus, first king of Argos, who was beloved of Zeus. To protect her from the jealousy of his wife Hera, Zeus transformed Io into a white heifer; but the canny Hera sent a gadfly to pursue her from land to land, in the course of which she swam this strait which has ever since been called the Bosphorus, the ford of the cow.

Then there is the legend of Jason and his Argonauts, who voyaged along the Bosphorus and into the Black Sea, to Colchis far to the east, to fetch the Golden Fleece. All the great heroes of the age accompanied Jason in the 50-oared Argo – Heracles (who dropped out early), Castor and Pollux, Orpheus, the seer Mopsus, Theseus, and many more. The voyage was fraught with perils – savage kings, harpies, clashing rocks and finally the fearsome dragon which day and night guarded the Golden Fleece. Even their return trip was difficult, for Jason was now accompanied by the uncomfortable Medea whose magic powers had helped him overcome the dragon, but who had a talent for attracting the wrath of gods and men. It is a fascinating tale, a parable of the questing spirit of the Greeks around 1000 BC, seeking new possibilities of colonisation and trade.

The Bosphorus is about 30 km in length, with a width varying from about 700 m to 3½ km. Its average depth is about 60 m but at certain points it is well over 100 m. The dominant current is from the Black Sea to the Sea of Marmara – in places up to 4 knots – but there are strong and erratic cross- and under-currents which make the Bosphorus more dangerous than the calm stretch of water it often appears to be.

Lady Mary Wortley Montagu wrote from Constantinople in 1717 that 'the pleasure of going in a barge to Chelsea is not comparable to that of rowing upon the canal of the sea here, where, for 20 miles together, down the Bosphorus, the most beautiful variety of prospects present themselves. The Asian side is covered with fruit trees, villages and the most delightful landscapes in nature; on the European side stands Constantinople situate on seven hills.' About a century later, when Byron in verse brought Don Juan here as a captive, it was not so much the landscape as the houses that caught his eye, for he wrote of

> The European with the Asian shore
> Sprinkled with palaces.

The Bosphorus must have been a magical sight then, long stretches fringed with palaces and yalıs leaning over the very edge of the water. The traditional colour for yalıs was terracotta, but pastel shades became popular from the 18th C., influenced by European taste. Behind them were wooded hills, and in front the waters of the Bosphorus, alive with the colourful traffic of caiques.

Of the hundreds of yalıs that lined the Bosphorus then, few remain; fire has claimed large numbers, and of those that survive many are in such a dilapidated state that they seem almost on the point of falling into the water. Preservation orders prohibit owners from demolishing their yalıs, but many cannot afford the enormous expense of maintaining them, let alone of restoring them to their former glory. Most problematic of all, Turkish inheritance laws are such that each family member inherits, but unequally, so many of the old houses are owned by anything up to 20 people, each of whom must agree before the house is sold, or any major alterations made. Inevitably, unanimous agreement is almost never reached and nothing is done. They are a unique part of Turkey's heritage, and the most endangered.

Both Lady Mary and Byron would have difficulty in recognising the Bosphorus today with its busy coast roads and new suspension bridges linking Europe and Asia, its rash of modern apartment blocks, hotels and cafés along the shores. Yet much is now changing for the better, for, officially at least, modern building on the water's edge has been prohibited, and some of the worst eye-sores have been replaced with waterfront parks.

Magic still surrounds this sinuous ribbon of deep water, but it is a changed magic; and if its rural character is sadly diminished it has not quite disappeared, for there are still fruit trees and villages and delightful landscapes to be seen. And in spring the whole Bosphorus catches fire with the blossom of the Judas trees along the hills.

THE EUROPEAN SHORE
BEŞIKTAŞ

Beşiktaş, otherwise known as Barbaros Hayrettin Paşa, stands on the water's edge just beyond Dolmabahçe Sarayı. In Byzantine times it was known as Diplokion, the Double Columns, from a pair of granite columns from Thebes which stood near the shore. Its present name means cradle stone, of doubtful origin, though one colourful tale

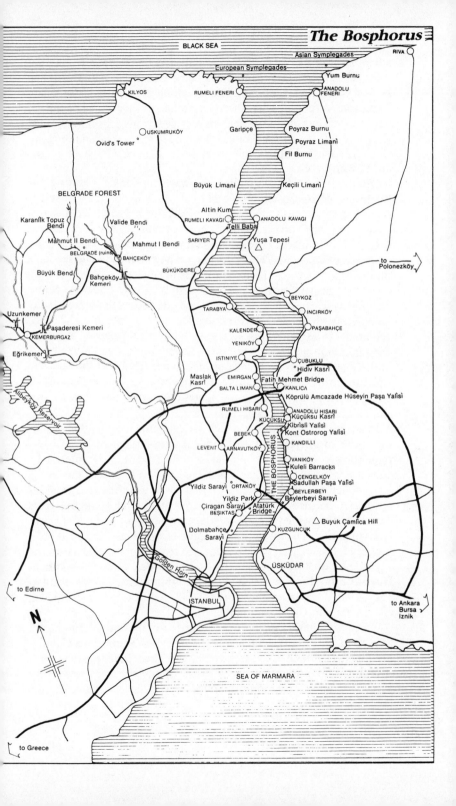

attributes it to a stone that was brought here – presumably by one of those relic-hungry early Empresses – on which, it was said, Christ had been washed after his birth. The Byzantine Emperors had a palace here, and so too did later Ottoman Sultans, in particular Selim III whose beautiful wooden palace was replaced by his cousin Mahmut II with a grandiose marble edifice. Not a trace remains of any of them. But a mosque and a türbe there – both by Sinan – and two museums, are all worth a visit.

250 m south of the ferry, along the waterfront, is the **Painting and Sculpture Museum** (Resim ve Heykel Müzesi; closed Tuesday and Wednesday), set in the faded glory of the north end of Dolmabahçe palace. In it are Turkish paintings and sculpture of the 19th-20th C.

The Deniz Müzesi, or **maritime museum,** is in two sections (open daily except Wednesday and Thursday). The entrance to one section is on the waterfront road between the Resim ve Heykel Müzesi and the ferry; in it is a stunning collection of mainly 19th C. imperial caiques, elaborately carved and decorated and gloriously appointed, some complete with models of oarsmen for greater realism. The galley required 144 oarsmen – enough to turn anyone to republican-ism! At the other end of the scale are three rowing boats – more like tubs – which Atatürk used for recreation. The other section of the museum, on the main road towards Dolmabahçe, includes a range of navigational instruments, ships' figureheads, arms, uniforms, models, paintings and memorabilia.

In a corner of the gardens which surround the ferry landing stands the **türbe of Hayrettin Paşa**, Süleyman the Magnificent's famous pirate-turned-Grand Admiral, the scourge of the Mediterranean, who almost single-handedly established Turkish sovereignty of the seas in the first half of the 16th C. Known to the west as Barbarossa from his red beard, he died on 4 July 1546, aged 80, having some five years earlier commissioned Sinan, only recently appointed imperial architect, to build this türbe within sight of the bay where his fleet mustered. It is an octagonal structure of great simplicity and harmony.

Opposite the türbe, in the centre of the gardens, stands a **statue of Hayrettin Paşa**, commissioned for the 4th centenary of his death in 1946, and it captures the spirit of this red-bearded, red-blooded adventurer and Grand Admiral.

On the other side of the main road is the mosque of another of Süleyman the Magnificent's Grand Admirals – **Sinan Paşa Camii** – built by his namesake, the architect Sinan. Sinan Paşa became Grand Admiral four years after Barbarossa's death, but was never very successful; probably his only qualification was the fact that he was the brother of the Grand Vezir Rüstem Paşa. The mosque was still being built when Sinan Paşa died in 1554, and it was completed two years later. It is one of Sinan's least successful mosques, based on the design of the Üç Şerefeli Cami in Edirne which had been built for Murat II over 100 years before, but it is smaller and altogether more cumbersome. The courtyard is small and narrow and has been insensitively restored with an overdose of metal-framed glass filling the arcades. The şadırvan looks somewhat like a sarcophagus. As at Üç Şerefeli, the dome is supported on six arches, with extensions to east and west, each covered with two domes. The great piers between the narthex and the main body of the mosque give a heavy appearance which the sombre decoration does nothing to relieve.

ÇIRAĞAN SARAYI

Çırağan Sarayı, the palace of illuminations, stands on the edge of the Bosphorus about 500 m from Beşiktaş jetty. It was yet another work of the prolific Balyan family, designed by Nikoğoṡ and built by Sarkis for Sultan Abdül Aziz, and completed in 1874. When Abdül Aziz was deposed on 30 May 1876 he was held for two days at Topkapı before being moved to Çırağan. On 4 June he was found dead in his bathroom, his wrists slashed with a pair of scissors he had requested to trim his beard –apparently suicide, but there were rumours of assassination. Three months later his nephew, Murat V, was deposed on the grounds of insanity, and he spent the remaining 29 years of his life, with his family, a prisoner in Çiragan Sarayı. Every month a suitably unfavourable report on his health was presented to his younger brother, Sultan Abdül Hamit II. After Murat's death in 1905 the palace lay empty until after the Young Turk Revolution in 1908 when it was converted for the use of the new Parliament. In January 1910 it was destroyed by fire – apparently caused by an electrical short circuit, but popular opinion was convinced that it was terrorists. It stood as a burnt-out shell for 78 years, but has now been restored as part of a new luxury hotel complex. Behind and beyond Çırağan, the trees of Yıldız Park occupy the slope.

ORTAKÖY

Ayios Phocas of the Byzantines, Ortaköy is today situated almost underneath the first bridge to cross the Bosphorus since Darius' 6th C. BC bridge of boats. The **Bosphorus Bridge** was opened in 1973 as part of the 50th anniversary celebrations of the founding of the Turkish Republic. At 1074 m it was the fourth longest suspension bridge in the world but, with the volume of bridge-building activity of the past few years, it has long since been relegated.

Ortaköy has an unexpected charm, with its pleasing jumble of old buildings and narrow streets. It has recently become a centre for artists and craftsmen who have their studios and galleries in the village. On Sundays there is a street market for paintings, craftwork, books and bric à brac. On the waterfront local fishermen bring in their catches, or sit mending their nets, overlooked by pleasant coffee houses and fish restaurants.

The most prominent monument in Ortaköy, set on a promontory like an outsize ship's figurehead, is the flamboyant **Büyük Mecidiye Camii**, built for Abdül Mecit I in 1855 by Nikoğos Balyan. A royal pavilion adjoins the front of the mosque, in the middle of which a double marble staircase sweeps up to the entrance, with slender minarets on either side. To say the mosque is a square surmounted by a dome is to do an injustice to its soaring, window-filled tympanum arches and the elaborate turrets at each corner. The interior is filled with marble or marble-effect, richly decorated with non-structural architectural forms and positively swinging with chandeliers.

On the main road stand an old synagogue and a modern church of St Phocas with handsome interior decor. Almost opposite this church is a down-at-heel 16th C. hamam, built by Sinan for Hüsrev Kethüda who served on the staff of the Grand Vezir Sokollu Mehmet Paşa.

ARNAVUTKÖY

On the other side of Atatürk Bridge is the village of Kuruçeşme, once the ugliest place on the Bosphorus, but the unsightly coal depots have been replaced by waterside parks. Here, it is said, Medea landed with Jason on the Argo's return trip from Colchis, and planted a laurel tree. The next village, Arnavutköy, the Albanian village, is one of the prettiest, with a profusion of old wooden houses; but its picturesque harbour has been sacrificed to a new coast road, built out into the Bosphorus, which was opened in 1988 Constantine the Great is believed to have built here a church dedicated to the Archangel Michael who had been appointed guardian angel of the Bosphorus. The church was repaired by Justinian. By the 15th C. it was in ruins and its stones were used by Mehmet II to build his nearby Rumeli Hisar. Just beyond Arnavutköy a headland called Akıntı Burnu, current cape, marks the deepest part of the Bosphorus (over 100 m) with a resulting current of 4 knots, known as Şeytan Akıntıısı, the devil's current.

BEBEK

Beyond Akıntı Burnu is the grand sweep of Bebek Bay, one of the beauty spots of the Bosphorus even now, despite its rash of modern apartment blocks. Chelae of the ancients, there was once a temple here dedicated to Artemis Dictynna, protectress of fishermen. Selim I established a summer pavilion in the early 16th C., and thereafter Bebek remained a favourite resort of Sultans and paşas. The palaces and kiosks have disappeared, and the only grand building remaining, standing just to the south of Bebek village, is the old **Egyptian Embassy**, build in the late 19th C. Near the jetty in the middle of the village is a tiny **mosque** built in 1912 in the neo-classical manner by Kemalettin Bey whose main claim to fame is that he was one of the last of the Ottoman architects. It is surrounded by a pretty, tree-filled park along the waterfront.

Boğaziçi Universitesi, the **University of the Bosphorus**, stands in the hills above and to the north of Bebek. It was an American foundation, established in 1863 with the vision of a missionary called Cyrus Hamlin and the money of a New York philanthropist called Christopher Robert, and named Robert College after the latter. It quickly became one of Turkey's most distinguished institutions of higher education. In 1971 it was converted into a Turkish university; instruction is still in both English and Turkish.

RUMELI HISARI

Open daily except Monday

The great fortress of Rumeli Hisarı, built by the new young Sultan Mehmet II in the spring and summer of 1452, stands a short distance north of Bebek, immediately opposite Anadolu Hisarı, the Anatolian fortress, built by Beyazit I Yıldırım about 60 years earlier. It was the first step in Mehmet's plan to capture the Byzantine capital, for with a fortress on either side of the Bosphorus, here at its narrowest at about 700 m, the Ottomans could sever Constantinople's communications with, and supplies from, the Black Sea, and could ferry reinforcements from Anatolia to Europe. 'Boğazkesen' the fortress was called – cut-throat or cutter of the strait – and it was completed in under four months. For someone as imbued as Mehmet with the stories of the heroes of the ancient world, it was especially significant that it was at this point in 512 BC that Darius had had a bridge of boats built, the inspiration of Mandrocles of Samos, and on it his 700,000-strong army had crossed into Europe and captured Byzantium as a prelude to his Scythian campaign.

During the winter Mehmet had sent out orders throughout his Empire for 1000 skilled masons and 2000 workmen to assemble here in the spring, and for lime, wood and building stone to be collected. Stone was brought was Anatolia, and ruined churches along the Bosphorus were used as quarries. Mehmet himself laid out the design, dictated by the lie of the land, and each of his three Vezirs – the Grand Vezir, Çandarlı Halil Paşa whom he did not trust, Zaganos Paşa and Saruca Paşa – was made responsible for building a tower, while the Sultan himself undertook the walls and bastions, thus introducing a healthy spirit of competition. As soon as it was completed a garrison of 400 Janissaries was stationed in it, and here they tried out the range of their new cannons by training them on any ships rash enough to try to pass. After a Venetian ship had been sunk and its captain impaled, enthusiasm to hazard the Ottoman blockade dwindled, and Constantinople was successfully cut off. After the Conquest the fortress found a new role as a prison, before gradually falling into disrepair.

In 1953, 500 years after the Conquest, Rumeli Hisarı was well restored, and the space inside laid out with lawns and paths. The cistern on which the mosque once stood – still marked by the stump of its minaret – was opened up and converted into an open-air theatre where plays and folk-dancing are performed during the summer, especially at the time of the Istanbul Festival.

BALTA LIMANI

The next village, Balta Limanı, Balta's harbour, is named after Mehmet the Conqueror's Grand Admiral and Governor of Gallipoli, Süleyman Baltaoğlu, a renegade Bulgarian who, at one stage in the siege of Constantinople, kept his fleet here. He was dismissed, dispossessed of titles and wealth, bastinadoed and then released, lucky to escape with his life, when he failed to prevent some Christian relief ships from entering the Golden Horn.

Balta Limanı is the site of the new Bosphorus bridge, Fatih Sultan Mehmet Köprüsü – **Mehmet the Conqueror bridge** – opened in 1988. At 1090 m, it just exceeds the length of its near neighbour, the

Bosphorus Bridge. It was necessitated by the unexpected volume of traffic on the first bridge, and the resulting congestion.

EMIRGAN

The village on the other side of the new bridge takes its name from the Persian Prince Emirgûne, ruler of Erivan, who cravenly surrendered his city to Sultan Murat IV in 1638. He was brought to Istanbul where his accomplishment in debauchery made him such a favourite with the Sultan that he was given not only ten purses of gold and a palace in the city, but another palace here by the Bosphorus. He decorated it in the Persian manner and filled it with Persian musicians to make him feel at home and to enliven his bacchanals. Not a trace of it remains. Emirgan is less scandalous today, a very popular place for people to come and drink tea in one of the open-air cafés in the pretty village square, shaded by ancient plane trees. Nearby stands a partly wooden baroque **mosque**, built in 1781–2 by Abdül Hamit I.

Above the village is **Emirgan Park**, once the gardens of the summer palace of a 19th C. Khedive of Egypt, Ismail Paşa. The various little pavilions have recently been charmingly restored, and serve refreshments in very agreeable surroundings. Emirgan Park is a pleasant place to walk, and is especially beautiful during the April Tulip Festival when its gardens are ablaze with every shape, size and colour of tulip.

ISTINYE

The deep bay of Istinye, the largest harbour of the Bosphorus and once its major shipyard, is now the preserve of boats for either fishing or pleasure. The name of the village is derived from one of its Byzantine names – either Leosthenius after its founder, a supposed follower of Byzas called Leosthenes; or Sosthenius after the temple of deliverance (sosthenia) which was erected here by Jason and his Argonauts in gratitude for their victory over Amycus, king of the savage Bebryces. Amycus used to force anyone who landed on his territory on the other side of the water to box with him, both wearing lethal gloves of hardened rawhide to add colour and excitement to the contest. Since he had the advantage of being the world boxing champion of the day, and a son of Poseidon into the bargain, Amycus invariably dispatched his opponents to the underworld. The Argonauts, having landed in Istinye bay to consider their position, were encouraged to proceed by a vision of a genius with the wings of an eagle, whereupon Polydeuces, or Pollux, twin brother of Castor and son of Leda and Zeus, accepted Amycus' challenge and killed him.

The zealous Constantine the Great converted the Argonauts' temple into a church, and the statue of the winged genius into the Archangel Michael, guardian of the channel. A century later Istinye reached the pinnacle of its Christian fame when it became the chosen residence of the stylite St Daniel. He ascended his pillar in 460 and was removed just over 33 years later when he died at the age of 84. Blazing summers and icy winters alike, Daniel prayed, mortified his flesh with fasting and exercise, and dispensed spiritual advice to the faithful. On one occasion the pillar was nearly toppled in a violent storm – it swayed perilously from side to side, St Daniel clinging limpet-like to his flimsy accommodation at the top, praying for dear life. Suddenly the storm ceased and the pillar came to rest. When Daniel died his hair reached his feet, his beard fell below his knees, and his fingernails were of an astonishing length.

YENIKÖY

Yeniköy – new village, a translation of its Byzantine name of Neapolis – has several modern (and very luxurious) villas and apartment blocks and a hotel on the waterfront. But the village itself is charming, and there are some pretty 19th C. wooden yalıs by the water. From beside the ferry stage in Yeniköy water dolmuşes – motor launches which operate on the same principle as their road-going namesakes – run frequently to and from Beykoz on the Asian shore of the Bosphorus. At the northern end of the village stands the first of what was once a string of handsome summer residences of the old embassies in Istanbul. Unlike several of them, this one, the **Austrian Embassy**, has not been burned to the ground. Beyond it is the hamlet of Kalender, named after the dervish order who once had a tekke here; and beyond that, just before Tarabya, is the summer residence of the **German Embassy**, surrounded by lovely gardens and a wooded park. The site was presented by Abdül Hamit II to Wilhelm I in 1880.

TARABYA

For centuries Tarabya, set on its beautiful bay, has been a favourite resort for Emperors, Sultans, ambassadors and others who could afford to escape the city during the summer. Today a rash of waterfront restaurants and a very big luxury hotel on the point, as well as a non-stop stream of traffic, have still not quite succeeded in ruining the place. In ancient times it was known as Pharmaceia, poisoning, for it was here, they say, that Medea, fleeing from her native Colchis with Jason, threw away the poison with which she had planned to kill him. A more cheerful generation, perhaps in the early 5th C. AD, changed the name to Therapia, healing, and so it is still called by the local Greeks, side by side with its Turkish form of Tarabya.

More **summer embassies** once lined the shore to the north of Tarabya: first the British, given by Abdül Mecit I in the time of Lord Stratford de Redcliffe between 1825 and 1858, burned down in 1911; then the French, given by Selim III in 1807 and burned down in 1923; and lastly the Italian, the only one to have been rebuilt (in 1906). All have lovely gardens climbing the hillside.

BÜYÜKDERE

The village of Büyükdere stands on the north shore of its grand and spacious bay. Great valley, its name means; Kalos Agros, or beautiful countryside, to the Byzantines – and to prove both, a broad and beautiful valley strikes off westwards from the head of the bay, its tree-lined road leading to the Belgrade Forest. Büyükdere, like Bebek and Tarabya, has some excellent fish restaurants.

To the north of the village a row of houses overlooks the new road along the Bosphorus, one of them a handsome late 19th C. yalı which now contains an ethnographic museum of considerable interest, the **Sadberk Hanım Müzesi**. Sadberk Hanım was the wife of Vehbi Koç, a leading Turkish industrialist; with a sharp eye for quality, she collected old silver, porcelain, jewellery, furniture and embroidery. After her death her family took up her idea of finding a house to exhibit them, and this museum was opened in 1980. It also includes a wonderful collection of 18th and 19th C. clothes, and three set-piece rooms with appropriately dressed models – one showing a 19th C. coffee ceremony, another a maternity room, and the third a circumcision room with a smiling boy in the elaborately decorated bed.

In 1988 the museum extended into the adjoining yalı, to house the remarkable collection of antiquities of Hüseyin Kocabaş which the Koç family had acquired. These impeccable objects are from every period from late Neolithic to Byzantine, and are superbly displayed. Both parts of the museum are open daily except Wednesday.

SARIYER

Sarıyer, yellow place, is a charming village, the fishing capital of the Bosphorus, with a busy harbour, a lively and colourful fish market, and several excellent waterside fish restaurants. For those on land, the buses continue to Rumeli Kavağı or to Kilyos, a resort on the Black Sea. For Telli Baba's shrine and Altın Kum beach further along the Bosphorus, you need to take a taxi.

Detour Ovid's Tower *and* Kilyos beach

From Sarıyer you can find a taxi to take you the 12 km or so to Uskumruköy (mackerel village), from which Ovid's tower is only a short walk. It is a small detour off the road to Kilyos, another 3 km on. The view along the Bosphorus, in both directions, as you climb into the hills from Sarıyer is spectacular.

Ovid's tower is a curious monument, mentioned in Murray's Handbook for Constantinople of 1893, but ignored by most other guidebooks. It is a rectangular tower with a projection on one side, and was evidently used as a watch tower. According to the Handbook it was 'the old Pharos, from which torches were held up at night, whose light, placed in a straight line with those at the mouth of the Bosphorus, saved the ships navigating the Black Sea from being wrecked on the Cyanean rocks or the Thracian coast.' It adds that the barbarous locals lit rogue beacons to lure ships onto the rocks where they would then rob them.

The name is even more curious – in 8 AD, at the age of 50, Ovid was banished from Rome by the Emperor Augustus, ostensibly for offending public morality with his brilliant, witty but explicit love poems that were all the rage in the city. But a reason of more personal animosity is suspected, perhaps connected with the life and loves of the Emperor's granddaughter Julia, known to Ovid but kept secret from Augustus. His place of exile was Tomi on the Black Sea coast near the mouth of the Danube, as uncivilised a place as could be conceived of for the exile of this most sophisticated of men. Despite repeated plaintive petitions to Augustus, and to his heir Tiberius, Ovid's exile was never revoked, and he died in Tomi ten years later. At the most Ovid might have glimpsed this spot as his boat passed by.

Kilyos is the most popular beach resort for Istanbullus, being within such easy reach of the city, and it is often crowded in summer – but the sandy beach extends as far as you may wish to walk, and further. Approaching the village, there are on the left three imposing ruined towers, called suterazisi (lit.,water balance). These were a less

244

costly alternative to an aqueduct, using a system of natural build-up of pressure and siphoning to bring water to the village from the Belgrade Forest. The 14th C. Genoese castle is inaccessible as it is in a military area.

TELLI BABA SHRINE

About half-way between Sarıyer and Rumeli Kavağı, set on the very edge of the water, is the türbe of Telli Baba, a holy man whose türbe is one of the most popular shrines in the area, for Telli Baba is thought to be especially helpful to women who wish for a husband. The suppliant leaves a strand of tinsel on the holy man's tomb, taking a second strand away with her. When the wish is granted she returns to give thanks and to leave the second strand of tinsel on the tomb.

RUMELI KAVAĞI

The last ferry stop on the European shore of the Bosphorus is Rumeli Kavağı, Rumelian (European) poplar, a delightful little village with the ruins of a medieval castle and several fish restaurants, some of which have a spectacular view over the wild and rocky scenery of the last stretch of the Bosphorus to the Black Sea, and looking across to the more substantial castle on the Asian shore above Anadolu Kavağı. In its heyday a wall connected each castle to the quay, from which a mole projected into the channel on each side. Here the Byzantines collected tolls and customs dues from passing ships. In times of danger they could cut off all shipping with a chain linking the moles – a formidable continuous line of defence from hilltop to hilltop.

The remains of the castle, **Imros Kalesi**, are on top of the hill above the village, originally built by Manuel I Comnenus in the latter part of the 12th C. to guard his customs point. Yoros Kalesi on the Asian shore was built about 100 years later. In the 14th C. both were taken by the Genoese who took over the tolls and customs dues, severely damaging the already ailing Byzantine economy. Mehmet II captured them in 1452, giving him, with Rumeli and Anadolu Hisarı further down the Bosphorus, two points at which he could stop pro-Byzantine ships. The batteries below the castles are late 18th C. additions, built and added to by French engineers in the service of Abdül Hamit I and Selim III, both of whom were involved in wars with Russia.

In ancient times there was in this area a Serapeion, or temple of Serapis; and here Jason, on his return from Colchis, having made sacrifices to the 12 great gods at the Hieron on the opposite shore, erected an altar to the goddess Cybele.

A short distance beyond Rumeli Kavağı the road leads to the beach of **Altın Kum**, golden sand, which can be reached either by road or by boat. It has a narrow sandy beach, changing rooms, and a restaurant well shaded by a clump of trees.

THE UPPER BOSPHORUS

The character of the remaining length of the Bosphorus to the Black Sea changes dramatically, with wild cliffs rising from the water, interspersed with sandy beaches, and most of it untouched by human habitation. It is a numinous stretch of water, alive with the legend of Jason and the Argonauts; in this stretch of water were concentrated several of the perils that beset them. The best way to see it is by boat.

The Bosphorus opens out beyond the narrows between the two castles, on the Asian side forming a great curve known as **Keçili Liman** the bay of goats – presumably the only creatures to feel at home in those rugged cliffs that surround it. The curve ends with the rocky promontory of **Fil Burnu**, elephant cape, followed by the bay of **Poyraz Limanı** with its magnificent beach, named after the wild and gusty NE wind whose Turkish name comes from the Greek Boreas, characterised as a god. The bay is sheltered from its namesake wind by **Poyraz Burnu**, one of the few places where there is a village; there is also an 18th C. fortress built by Baron François de Tott, a Hungarian turned Frenchman who spoke Turkish like a Turk and was employed by Mustafa III to advise on military reforms, including the building of new defences.

Immediately opposite Poyraz Burnu on the European shore is the aptly named promontory of **Garipçe**, meaning somewhat strange; and it is indeed a weirdly shaped crag. It has a fortress on it that is the twin of that on Poyraz Burnu, also the work of Baron de Tott. Its ancient name was Gypopolis, the city of vultures, here identified with the fearful Harpies who afflicted the local king, Phineus, whose first wife was a daughter of Boreas. Phineus had received the prophetic gift from Apollo, but when he foretold unerringly to men the sacred will of Zeus, the father of the gods was angry; Phineus was blinded, and the Harpies were sent to remove or befoul any food that was set before him. By the time Jason arrived Phineus was no more than skin and bones, and he offered to give the Argonauts valuable advice for their voyage if only they would rid him of the Harpies. This was done by

Zetes and Calais, winged sons of Boreas, who took pity on their brother-in-law. True to his promise, Phineus advised the Argonauts on their route to Colchis, and in particular how to tackle the Symplegades, the fearsome 'clashing rocks'.

The **Symplegades**, also known as the Cyanean (bluish) Rocks, were, according to the legend, two rocky islands at the entrance to the Bosphorus which clashed together with great force, crushing any ship which attempted to pass between them. Phineus' advice was that the Argonauts should release a dove to fly between the rocks; its fate would indicate the fate of the Argo. This they did, and as the dove survived, with only the loss of some tail feathers, so did the Argo suffer some relatively small damage to its stern. Thereafter the clashing rocks became fixed.

There is an excellent candidate for the European half of the Symplegades just offshore from the lighthouse of **Rumeli Feneri**. More or less flat on the top, it towers to the same height as the cliff behind (about 20 m) and extends to almost 200 m of craggy, fissured length. It is known as Oreke Taşı, midwife's stool rock. On the top are the remains of an ancient altar known as the Pillar of Pompey – doubly misleading since it is neither a pillar nor has it any likely connection with Pompey; and the pillar that once was there has long since disappeared. The best candidate for the Asian half of the Symplegades is a jagged rock that rises from the sea in front of **Yum Burnu**, the promontory on the edge of the Black Sea, beyond the Anatolian lighthouse. This is the Ancyraean Cape of the ancients – anchor point, named after the stone anchor that Jason took from here.

THE ASIAN SHORE

ANADOLU KAVAĞI

North of Anadolu Kavağı, more or less where the castle now stands, there was in ancient times a temple of Zeus Ourios, Zeus of the fair wind, and also a Hieron with shrines dedicated to the 12 gods. The temple and shrines were said to have been founded by Phrixus en route to Colchis on the flying ram with the golden fleece – the beginning of the whole Argonautic saga. Jason, on his return trip from Colchis, having retrieved the golden fleece, made sacrifices here and dedicated altars.

The castle, **Yoros Kalesi** (see page 245 for history), misleadingly called the 'Genoese castle', is well worth the climb up the hill, if only for the breath-taking view that it gives to the Black Sea. Anadolu Kavağı is still small – a cluster of houses, a few restaurants by the Bosphorus, tea-houses shaded by great plane trees, fishermen mending nets; just a pretty fishing village with a calm, unhurried attitude to life; but it is fast becoming more popular, particularly since it is no longer a military area.

South of Anadolu Kavağı rises **Yuşa Tepesi**, Joshua's hill, named after a holy man of old called Yuşa Dede whose mosque is on the summit. But the hill is also called Giant's Mountain, for by the mosque is an enormous filled-in hole, about 18 m long by 1 m wide, which legend associates with Yuşa Dede. In ancient times it was known as the Bed of Hercules; and was also identified as the grave of the pugilistic King Amycus (see pages 241–242). Yuşa Tepesi is a place where many Muslims like to visit, and to worship at the shrine, particularly on Fridays and during Ramazan.

BEYKOZ

Beykoz, the lord's walnut, was the reputed home of King Amycus, and here, on the spot where he fell in battle with Polydeuces, was planted a bay tree, *daphne maiomene* (frenzied), which caused madness in any who decked themselves with its branches. It is one of the larger villages on the Asian shore of the Bosphorus and, despite industrial growth around its edges, the centre is still very appealing, with lovely old houses, good restaurants and a shady main square with what was once a splendid **18th C. fountain** in it. It is a large 4-square structure with columns and arcades forming a kind of domed loggia, covered by a pitched roof. It was built in 1746 by Işak Ağa, Mahmut I's Inspector of Customs, but it has recently been restored in a way that makes one realise how lovely it must have been before.

Two km north of Beykoz is the area known as **Hünkâr Iskelesi**, the imperial landing-stage, so named because in the wooded valley nearby Mehmet the Conqueror built a royal pavilion, rebuilt by Süleyman the Magnificent, and the Sultans landed here when they visited it. It was here in October 1833 that the Treaty of Hünkâr Iskelesi was signed between Russia and the Ottoman Empire, the Turks acknowledging Russia's earlier gains in war and agreeing to prohibit the warships of other European powers from passing through the Dardanelles in time of war. This treaty so disturbed France and Britain that they determined to support the Ottomans in order to counter the growing Russian influence. 20 years later Britain and Turkey allied against the

Russians in the Crimean War; and their fleets assembled in Beykoz Bay. The little palace here was built after the Treaty – one of the many works of the remarkable Balyan family. It is now a hospital.

Detour 1 Riva beach *and* Şile

Buses run between Beykoz and the Black Sea resort of **Riva**. It has an excellent beach and a small 14th C. Genoese castle and, except at weekends, it is less crowded than Kilyos on the European shore. There is also a road from Beykoz to **Şile**, a charming seaside village with a beautiful beach, pleasant accommodation and restaurants. It is somewhat further from Istanbul, and consequently less crowded.

Detour 2 Polonezköy

This delightful village is about 25 km from Beykoz; it can only be reached by taxi or car. There are roads from Beykoz, Paşabahçe or Çubuklu, all going through green agricultural valleys between hills thickly wooded with oak, beech, chestnut and pine.

Polonezköy, the Polish village, was founded in 1842 by refugees from Poland who called it Adampol after the exiled Polish leader Prince Adam Czartoryski. In 1853 Prince Adam organised a Polish contingent to fight with Turkey and Britain in the Crimean War, and they served with such distinction that Abdül Mecit I granted them this area of land in perpetuity. Today many of the younger generation have left; but there are still some Polish families who farm the land. What started as a sideline – providing gargantuan Polish meals (home-produced pork was a speciality, especially for foreigners), simple accommodation and peaceful rural seclusion to visitors from Istanbul – became so popular that the village now appears to consist mainly of restaurants, pensions and hotels. It has become a favoured weekend resort for Istanbullus, and there are many good walks in the area. The simple church, built in 1914, and the cemetery up the hill from it, are peaceful and lovely places.

PAŞABAHÇE

South of Incirköyü, fig village, stands the larger village of Paşabahçe, the Paşa's garden, named after Hezarpare Ahmet Paşa, the last Grand Vezir of Mad Ibrahim, and his son-in-law. It was Ahmet Paşa's wild enthusiasm for bribes and furs that led to his own and his Sultan's downfall in 1648. The epithet 'Hezarpare', 1000 pieces, is a posthumous reference to his execution and mutilation. Of his gardens and palace here not a trace remains, and the main monuments in Paşabahçe today are an **18th C. mosque** built by Mustafa III which is not really worth a visit, and the renowned **Paşabahçe Glass Factory** which is. (Appointments for visits by individuals or small groups can be made by phoning (216) 413–1810; and an English-speaking guide can be arranged). The factory was established here only in 1933, but the glassmaking tradition goes back to the 19th C. when it was based at Beykoz and Çubuklu, on either side of Paşabahçe. There is a shop beside the factory, as well as several in Istanbul.

KANLICA

The tiny village of Çubuklu between Paşabahçe and Kanlıca is today mainly notable for its petroleum tanks, but also for access to Hidiv Kasrı (see page 202). A little further south is Kanlıca, famed for its yoghurt. It has a shady and agreeable main square beside the ferry landing and behind it, set back from the water, is the **Iskender Paşa Camii**, a very simple square structure which – surprisingly – was built by Sinan. It was commissioned by Iskender Paşa, a vezir of Süleyman the Magnificent, and was built in 1559–60. It has been considerably altered, including the replacement of its original wooden dome with the present flat tiled roof, and the addition of its wooden porch.

Just south of the new bridge is a dilapidated little wooden structure literally hanging over the edge of the water – all that remains of the once grand **Köprülü Amcazade Hüseyin Paşa Yalısı**, the oldest yalı to survive – if only in part – on the Bosphorus. It was built in 1698 by Hüseyin Paşa, the fourth Grand Vezir from the remarkable Köprülü family who had temporarily halted the decline of the Ottoman Empire. However, the year after this yalı was built the Treaty of Karlowitz was signed here, in which Turkey acknowledged the loss of much territory to the Austrian Empire, Venice, Poland and Russia.

What remains today is a once-beautiful one-roomed kiosk, rapidly falling into ruin. Every interior surface was covered in painted decoration of the highest quality; now the paint is peeling and the dome has had to be propped up to prevent it from falling in. Early this century the Société des Amis de Stamboul did some restoration work and published a magnificent book about the room, with a preface by Pierre Loti. A few years ago the Turkish Touring and Automobile Club was given permission to renew the wooden props that held the front of the room above the water, and to replace the broken windows.

Since then nothing has been done. Yet it is a unique monument of great historic and artistic interest, and it would well repay careful restoration.

ANADOLU HISARI

Anadolu Hisarı is an exceptionally picturesque village, with its late **14th C. castle** – once known as Güzelce, the beautiful one – and the gentle Göksu, or sky-blue stream, idling its way between old houses to join the Bosphorus. Anadolu Hisarı, the Anatolian fortress, was built in the early 1390s by Beyazit I to control Beyzantine access to the Black Sea. For the rest of the decade he subjected Constantinople to repeated sieges before he was himself defeated and captured by the Mongol Timur the Lame in 1402. In 1452 Mehmet II restored and enlarged the fortress while building Rumeli Hisarı. It is small and homely compared with its younger neighbour; and instead of having a mosque for the garrison to worship in, there was, and still is, an open-air namazgâh.

KÜÇÜKSU

For the Sweet Waters of Asia and the Küçüksu Kasrı, please see pages 200–1.

To the south of Küçüksu stands the long, white-painted outline of the largest of the 18th C. yalıs, the **Kıbrıslı Yalısı**, built around 1760 and added to at various dates since. It was redecorated in European style in the mid-19th C. by the present owners' ancestor, Kıbrıslı Mehmet Emin Paşa, who became Grand Vezir three times in the reigns of Abdül Mecit I and Abdül Aziz. He was known as Kıbrıslı, the Cypriot, to distinguish him from two other Mehmet Emins, both Grand Vezirs on several occasions during the same reigns, and the yalı was named accordingly.

In the mid 1970s I met Leila Hanım, the eldest great-grand-daughter of Kıbrıslı Mehmet Emin Paşa, and she told me how in her childhood the division between harem and selamlık was strictly maintained, the harem ruled by her deeply traditional grandmother. So devout was she that her salon was almost like a mosque, with prayers at regular intervals every day; and during Ramazan the chanting of the Koran could be heard unceasingly throughout the day. Yet alongside this the selamlık had modernized, the garden parties and cocktail parties were held, to which the more liberated women of the harem were free to go. It must have presented an extraordinary contrast between two concepts of life existing side by side within the same house.

The French writer Pierre Loti visited the house once when Leila Hanım was a young girl, but she was too shy to look at him, keeping her eyes fixed to the ground – which enabled her to see that the great man wore rather high heels to mask his shortness. And when the Empress Eugénie was entertained here on her visit to Istanbul in the mid-19th C. it is said that Mehmet Emin Paşa presented her with a diamond concealed in the petals of a rose – the cause of much excited gossip.

Just beyond the Kıbrıslı Yalısı stands another smaller yalı, built around 1790, possibly by an Italian architect, and painted in the traditional terracotta colour. It is known as the **Kont Ostrorog Yalısı** after the French-Polish Count Ostrorog, a legal adviser of the Sultan's, who acquired it in the 19th C. and whose family still own and live in it. The house retains the oriental arrangement of rooms grouped around the central hall on the ground floor, and around the sofa on the first floor, the two connected by a magnificent double staircase. On both floors these rooms stretch from the back to the front of the house, very much in the Venetian idiom. Its exterior is exceptionally lovely, the waterfront façades filled with windows. Pierre Loti stayed here on one of his visits to the city, and the bed and writing table that he used are still in the yalı.

KULELI BARRACKS

Past another 'devil's current' around the promontory at Kandilli, and the gentler waters of Vanıköy, the next notable building is the Kuleli Barracks, now a college for training naval officers. The original barracks here were erected by the ill-fated Selim III in about 1800, shortly after he had built the Selimiye barracks near Üsküdar in his attempt to reform the Janissaries. The Kuleli barracks, as well as the Selimiye, were used as a military hospital during the Crimean War, both under the supervision of Florence Nightingale. Almost immediately after the war Abdül Mecit I had the old building rebuilt and enlarged to its present form, and it was completed in 1860.

The site has a long and colourful history. At an early stage yet another church dedicated to the Archangel Michael stood here; and in the 6th C. the Empress Theodora, herself a prostitute-made-good, founded here a home with the express purpose of forcibly reforming those of her erstwhile colleagues who had not had the same chance in life as she had. Sad to say, according to Procopius who was scarcely a fan of Theodora's, many of the unwilling converts threw themselves off the parapets at night, preferring death by drowning to a life of enforced virtue.

A tale of doubtful authenticity accounts for the name Kuleli, towered. Selim the Grim, it is said, in a fit of rage ordered his chief executioner to strangle his son, Prince Süleyman. Pretending he had done the deed, the executioner instead hid Süleyman in a tower here. Three years later, when Selim returned victorious from Egypt, he lamented the lack of an heir to succeed him (he had already executed three other sons); then, on hearing the truth, rejoiced that Süleyman was alive. When he became Sultan, Süleyman made a garden at the place of the tower.

South of Kuleli is Çengelköy, hook village, so called according to Evliya Çelebi, from a cache of Byzantine anchors found here shortly after the Conquest. Just south of the village stands the lovely early 19th C. **Sadullah Paşa Yalısı**, painted terracotta, which has been beautifully restored after years of neglect. Sadullah Paşa, a poet himself and a translator of other poets, including Lamartine, held the post of chief Scribe to Sultan Murat V in his three month reign, and then Abdül Hamit II sent him to Berlin as Ottoman ambassador. Later he was exiled. His descendants lived in the yalı until recently. Next is the village and palace of Beylerbeyi (for which see pages 198–200). Beyond lies Kuzguncuk, and then an unlovely stretch of shore before Üsküdar, the last ferry stop on the Asian shore.

16

IZNIK

Iznik, one of the most delightful and sleepy of Turkish towns, sits comfortably in a burgeoning valley on the shore of a large lake ringed by mountains. Daily life is unhurried, farming and fishing being the main occupations, and it has not been much developed as a tourist resort. Consequently the accommodation is simple, though normally clean, and the view over the lake goes a long way to mitigate the vagaries of the plumbing. Iznik makes a very enjoyable one day or overnight stay.

From Istanbul there is a regular and excellent bus service. By car, the best route from Istanbul is to drive to Kartal on the Asian shore of the Sea of Marmara, and take the car ferry to Yalova (about ½ hr); the alternative is to drive around the gulf and through industrial Izmit. From Yalova, drive due south to Orhangazi (about 20 km), then east for about 40 km along the northern shore of the lake, Iznik Gölü. It also makes an easy day trip from Bursa, where there are hotels of higher rating. The loveliest and most unspoilt route from Bursa is via the small road along the tree-clad southern shore of the lake (1½ hr).

History

At roughly the same time as Greek colonists from Megara established themselves at Chalcedon and Byzantium, Bithynians from Thrace migrated across the Bosphorus and settled in this beautiful and well-watered area of NW Asia Minor which became known by their name – Bithynia. Its mountains dropped into fertile plains which yielded rich harvests of grain and fruit. Almost certainly they had a settlement where Iznik now stands; but towards the end of the 4th C. BC, in the confused period that followed the death of Alexander the Great in 323, a city was founded here by Antigonus Monophthalmos, the one-eyed, one of Alexander's generals who had made himself king over Asia Minor. He gave the city his own name, Antigoneia. In 301 another of the generals, Lysimachus, defeated and killed Antigonus and took over western and central Asia Minor. He enlarged and fortified Antigoneia and, in memory of his late wife, gave it her name – Nicaea. The shape of the city which Antigonus and Lysimachus established remains, with two main streets crossing each other at right angles, leading to four gates in the great encircling wall.

Being inland, Nicaea depended on its routes to the sea for trade. The main outlet was Cius (present-day Gemlik), about 50 km to the west; but it was also linked to the north with the port of Nicomedia (present-day Izmit), founded some 40 years after Nicaea by Nicomedes I, second king of Bithynia, who transferred his capital there from Nicaea. Nicaea's most important product was scarlet cloth, dyed with kermes gall, a profitable item of trade then and throughout the Roman period. Thanks to this, and to the fertility of the land around it, Nicaea flourished.

The kingdom of Bithynia was founded as Lysimachus' power declined; Zipoetes, a local dynast, defeated him in battle and became king, and over the next 100 years or so Bithynia grew from an insignificant principality into a considerable state. It remained independent, though harrassed by Pergamum and Rome, until 74 BC when the last of the Bithynian kings, the degenerate Nicomedes IV, in emulation of Attalus III of Pergamum some 60 years before, bequeathed his kingdom to Rome.

Roman republican rule in the province of Bithynia was no more enlightened than it was elsewhere in Asia Minor. Money-lenders and tax-gatherers extorted money from the local population, and the first governor, Marcus Cotta, was later tried in Rome for his misdeeds and stripped of his position and his senatorial rank. Under the Emperors the situation improved and prosperity returned, witnessed by an enormous amount of building that was put in hand in all the cities, and certainly in Nicaea.

Nicaea and the other Bithynian cities were apparently so hopeless at organising their finances that when the Emperor Trajan appointed Pliny the Younger as governor, his first task was 'to inspect the accounts of the various towns, for they were evidently in confusion.' Financial irresponsibility, was Pliny's judgment. But it was a temporary aberration and Nicaea continued to prosper through the centuries.

There is a tradition that Bithynia was evangelised by St Andrew, brother of St Peter. A few years later the region just missed a visit by St Paul who attempted to come here with his companions from neighbouring Mysia, 'but the Spirit of Jesus did not allow them.' It was 300 years later that Nicaea came to prominence in the Christian world, for two of the great councils of the early church met here, both of considerable significance.

In 325, Constantine the Great summoned the bishops of the Roman Empire to attend the First Ecumenical Council in the imperial palace at Nicaea, he himself giving the opening address on 20 May and hosting a magnificent banquet at its conclusion on 25 July. In the intervening two months the Council deliberated on the teaching of Arius, an elder of the Alexandrian church, that Christ was not of the same nature as God the Father, but of similar but subordinate nature. The Council condemned this as heretical, and issued a statement of doctrine on the matter, later developed into the Nicene Creed.

The Seventh Ecumenical Council was summoned in 787 by the Empress Irene during a lull in the Iconoclast controversy. It was held in the church of Haghia Sophia, whose ruins still exist, between 24 September and 13 October. Its final conclusion was that icons deserved reverence (*proskynesis*) but not adoration (*latreia*) which was reserved for God alone, and that on this basis the use of icons in Christian worship should be reinstated. As the result of an inept translation of the two significant words, the statement issued by the Council scandalised the church in the west, for it appeared to advocate that Christians should worship icons in the same manner as they worshipped God himself. So bitter was the resulting division, that this Council was the last to be recognised by both branches of the church; from then on the Roman Catholic church and the Eastern Orthodox church went their separate ways. In the east, the ruling of the Seventh Ecumenical Council lasted only until 813 when the ban on icons was reimposed, to be finally revoked in 843.

In the years that followed the defeat of the Byzantines at Manzikert in 1071, the victorious Selçuks advanced westwards. In 1081 they captured Nicaea and established there the capital of their new Sultanate of Rum, under first Süleyman and then his son Kılıç Arslan. It was the second brief occasion that the city was the capital of a kingdom. But in 1097 the Byzantine Emperor, Alexius I Comnenus, with the help of the army of the First Crusade, won Nicaea back from the Selçuks, and thereafter the city and its territory remained in Byzantine hands for 234 years. The Selçuks established a new capital at Iconium – Konya.

In 1204 Nicaea once again became a capital city. After the capture of

Constantinople by the Fourth Crusade, Theodore Lascaris, a son-in-law of Alexius III Angelus, gained control of a large area of western Asia Minor and established the Byzantine Empire of Nicaea with himself as its first Emperor. Under pressure from the Latins in Constantinople, and from the Selçuks to the south, the little Empire had no easy road to survival; but not only did it survive, it succeeded in taking almost all the Latin possessions, first in Asia and then in Europe, and by 1250 had confined the Latins to a small area around Constantinople.

Meanwhile, Nicaea had become the centre of a cultural revival that started under the Lascarids and grew in brilliance under the Palaeologus dynasty after the restoration of the Byzantine Empire to Constantinople in 1261. Because of the need for careful housekeeping, little was built in Nicaea during the 57 years that it was the Byzantine capital; and less survives, for much was destroyed in 1922 in the final stages of the Greco-Turkish War.

After 1261 Nicaea reverted to its role of prosperous provincial town, though it became overshadowed by its still more prosperous near neighbour Prusa, or Brusa as it was commonly called. 70 years later, on 2 March 1331, the Ottoman leader Orhan Gazi, son of Osman, having already captured Brusa in 1326, took Nicaea after a long siege. From now on the city was known as Iznik, a Turkification of its Greek name. Ibn Battuta, a delightful Arab traveller from North Africa, who visited Iznik very soon after the Ottoman capture, found it 'in ruins and uninhabited except for a few men in the Sultan's service.' That sorry picture soon changed, for a flurry of building activity followed, with several mosques, medresses, hamams, tombs and a public soup kitchen being put up before the end of the century, and many houses. Orhan even made his capital at Iznik for a short time, and it was said to be the favourite town of his remarkable Byzantine-born wife, Nilüfer Hatun. New architectural ideas were tried out here, though some buildings were decorated in a style which looked back to the Selçuks.

Like most cities of Asia Minor, Isnik was sacked by a raiding party of Timur the Lame's troops in 1402, but when the Mongois withdrew shortly afterwards, prosperity quickly returned. It was from this period, for about 300 years, that Iznik became famous for its exceptionally beautiful ceramic work, in particular the tiles that still adorn so many of the mosques and other Ottoman buildings of this period. Prior to this the potteries here had produced what is known as Miletus ware, relatively simple work with designs in blue, turquoise and purple on a base of red clay. Suddenly in the 15th C. it was replaced by pottery of astonishing sophistication with a white base and

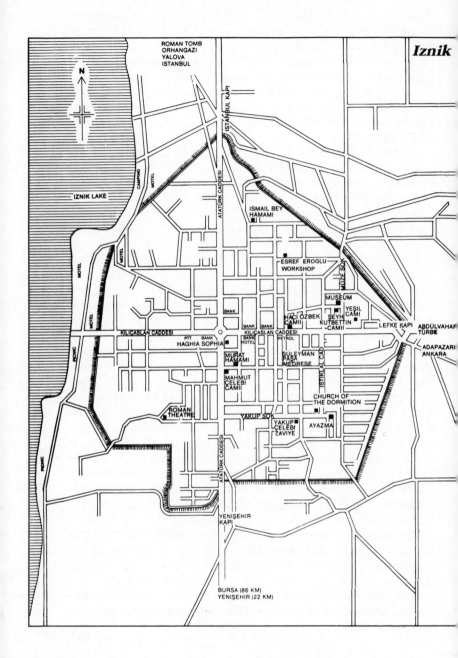

Iznik

ROMAN TOMB
ORHANGAZI
YALOVA
ISTANBUL

İSTANBUL KAPI

IZNIK LAKE

CAMPING

MOTEL

ATATÜRK CADDESI

ISMAIL BEY
HAMAMI

ESREF EROGLU
WORKSHOP

MÜZE SOK

MOTEL

MUSEUM

MOTEL

HACI ÖZBEK
CAMII

BANK

SEYH
KUTBETTIN
-CAMII

YEŞIL
CAMII

LEFKE KAPI

ABDÜLVAHAP
TÜRBE

PICNIC

KILIÇASLAN CADDESI

BANK

BANK

KILIÇASLAN CADDESI

PTT BANK
HAGHIA SOPHIA

BANK
HOTEL

PETROL

ADAPAZARI
ANKARA

MOTEL

MURAT
HAMAMI

SULEYMAN
PAŞA
MEDRESE

ISTIKLAL CAD

MAHMUT
ÇELEBI
CAMII

CHURCH OF
THE DORMITION

ROMAN
THEATRE

YAKUP SOK

PICNIC

YAKUP
ÇELEBI
ZAVIYE

AYAZMA

ATATÜRK CADDESI

YENIŞEHIR
KAPI

BURSA (86 KM)
YENIŞEHIR (22 KM)

faience glaze that looked very like porcelain. That the change was so sudden indicates a completely new beginning under outside influence.

The Iznik potteries continued into the 18th C. – a French traveller wrote that work was still going on in 1736 – but they were already in decline, and by the middle of the century nothing at all was left. The potters moved to Kütahya where they never achieved the excellence of design and production that had existed in Iznik in its golden age. After the demise of its potteries, Iznik began a slow decline, suddenly accelerated by the Greco-Turkish fighting in 1922, into the pretty but dilapidated backwater that it is today.

THE CITY WALLS

The walls of Nicaea were originally built by Lysimachus around 300 BC, but of these not a trace remains. Various rebuildings, repairs and additions were undertaken during the Roman and early Byzantine periods, and the walls were frequently put to the test, though with varying results. The Goths besieged Nicaea in the mid-3rd C. AD, broke through the walls and plundered the city. In 717 and 725 the Arabs attacked, but this time the walls withstood the onslaught. It was a near run thing though, and in 726 Leo III had the walls rebuilt. The Selçuks in 1081, and the reclaiming Byzantines and Crusaders in 1097, both broke through the city's defences; and at the beginning of the 13th C. Theodore I Lascaris, the first Byzantine Emperor of Nicaea, had the walls repaired once again. They fell to Orhan Gazi in 1331, and to the Mongols in 1402. The double walls that we see today, both of them reinforced by strong towers, are thus mostly Byzantine, but repaired and partly rebuilt by the Ottomans.

Coming from Istanbul, we enter the town through a gap in the walls beside **Istanbul Kapısı**, best preserved of the Nicaean gates. There are three parts, two forming openings in the inner and outer walls, and the third a triumphal arch built between them in honour of a visit by the peripatetic Emperor Hadrian in AD 123. The outer gate is flanked by two great round towers, and there are carved reliefs – on one side horsemen fighting, on the other two relief statues, now badly chipped. The triumphal arch shows how much the level of the ground has risen, for the statue niches are far too low. This arch also has round Byzantine towers on either side, made of brick. The innermost gate, built with huge stones, has slots for a portcullis and sockets for a swing gate. Two carved theatrical masks gaze tragically from the top.

From Bursa, the road comes in through **Yenişehir Kapısı**, also a triple gate but not so well preserved as the Istanbul Gate, largely because it was at this point that both the Selçuks and later the Ottomans broke into the city. A fragment of inscription affirms that the Roman gate was built by the Emperor Claudius II in AD 268; but most of the surrounding structures are Byzantine.

THE ROMAN THEATRE

Not far from Yenişehir Kapısı is the oldest surviving monument of Nicaea – the Roman theatre. 'Surviving' is scarcely the right word, for it is well nigh extinct. Parts of the cavea and stage building have been excavated, revealing some finely carved marble for what was clearly designed as a very grand theatre. It was under construction in Pliny the Younger's governorship of Bythinia in AD 111–12; but Pliny felt obliged to write to the Emperor Trajan about it, for an enormous amount of money had already been expended when the building started to sink and great cracks appeared. It seems that the Nicaeans had launched themselves with more enthusiasm than sense into this costly project, and had failed to have the site properly surveyed – 'misapplication of public funds,' Pliny wearily called it.

THE CHURCH OF HAGHIA SOPHIA (key from the Museum)

From the theatre we make our way back to Atatürk Cad., the main north/south axis of the town, and turn left to the central roundabout where Atatürk Cad. is crossed by Kılıçarslan Cad., the west/east axis. Here, at the heart of the city, was the gymnasium, also badly planned according to Pliny, and far too big for their needs. Today nothing is left of this second Nicaean folly; but just on the intersection stand the ruins of the church of Haghia Sophia, the principal place of worship in Byzantine Nicaea. Excavations in the mid-1930s revealed that the original church was built in the 6th C. in the reign of Justinian. It was in that church that the seven sessions of the Seventh Ecumenical Council were held in September/October 787. 350 bishops and many monks met here under the presidency of the Patriarch Tarasius, their deliberations frequently inflamed as some of the wilder Iconodules tried to condemn not only Iconoclasm in general, but individual Iconoclasts in particular, whether or not they had abjured their heresy. With much difficulty and the exercise of great diplomacy, moderation in the end prevailed.

In 1065 Haghia Sophia was destroyed in an earthquake, and a new church was built in its place, essentially the basilica that we see today. It was the cathedral of the Byzantine Empire of Nicaea in the 13th C., and in it the Emperors were crowned.

When Orhan Gazi captured Iznik, Haghia Sophia was converted into the main mosque of the city – Ulu Cami, the Great Mosque. Orhan also built a medrese attached to it, the first in the Ottoman empire. Timur's Mongols caused much damage to it in 1402, as also to much else in the city; and in the middle of the following century the mosque was gutted by fire. Süleyman the Magnificent commissioned Sinan to restore it, and the interior was decorated with some of the tiles for which Iznik was famed. As the city declined in the later Ottoman period, so neglect and decay reduced the mosque to a pitiable state; and in 1922 its last viable remnants were destroyed.

Today the stump of the minaret provides a nesting place for storks. Inside, the level of the second church is well over 1 m higher than the earlier one. A glasshouse protects what is left of the once fine mosaic floor of the nave; while in the wall of the north aisle in a low arch are the remains of a Deesis fresco of Christ with the Virgin and John the Baptist. The apse, part of the earlier church, has a synthronon with semi-circular rows of steps around the back for the clergy to sit on – similar to that at Haghia Eirene in Istanbul. On both sides of the apse steps lead up and then down into little domed rooms with the remains of painted decoration around the windows; the room on the south also contains a sarcophagus which, until recently, was glassed over to protect the ancient bones that lay inside it.

HACI ÖZBEK CAMII

From Haghia Sophia, we turn right into Kılıçarslan Cad. which takes us towards the main Islamic monuments of the town. About half-way along on the left stands the oldest mosque in Iznik, the tiny Hacı Özbek Camii, built in 1333 just over two years after the Ottoman capture of the city, and quite dreadfully restored in 1960. Particularly gross is the hideous new porch, tacked on to compensate for the loss of the original portico which was demolished when the road was widened. Closing our eyes to such infelicities, this little building represents an Ottoman mosque reduced to its barest essentials, a square prayer chamber crowned by a dome on a raised polygonal drum. The roof tiles are interesting – made of terracotta, they are specially moulded to fit the curve of the dome. Inside, the dome rests on a cornice with a dart design, deeply incised into the corners. The mihrab is plain, modern and ugly, and the original clarity of the interior space has been cluttered by a gallery.

SÜLEYMAN PAŞA MEDRESESI

A short detour south of Hacı Özbek Camii along Mehmet Gündem Sok. brings us to the oldest surviving Ottoman medrese in Turkey. The Süleyman Paşa Medresesi, immediately distinguishable with its agreeable cluster of terracotta tiled domes, was restored some years ago and is once again in use for the purpose for which it was originally designed – as a Koran school – and it is usually open. It was built by Süleyman, eldest son of Orhan Gazi, a few years after the capture of Iznik, and it was one of the first purpose-built Ottoman medreses – previously monasteries had been converted. It therefore represents the embryo from which future medreses developed. The courtyard, originally with a pool in it, is surrounded on three sides by domed porticoes, behind which are enclosed cells, also domed. Each cell has a round window in the outside wall – a highly unusual feature. The dershane is just off-centre, and projects into the street behind.

YEŞIL CAMI

Returning to Kılıçarslan Cad., we turn right and continue to Müze Sok. where we turn left. Almost immediately on our right is one of the jewels of Iznik – Yeşil Cami, the green mosque, named for the rich turquoise green tiles that once adorned its Selçuk-style minaret. The tiles in situ today are later and vastly inferior work from Kütahya. The entrance is on the far side, reached by turning right off Müze Sok. and crossing an attractively laid-out garden of trees and roses. The mosque was built between 1378 and 1391 by Çandarlı Kara Halil Paşa, Chief Judge of Iznik under Orhan Gazi, Grand Vezir to Murat I, and the first of a long line of hereditary Grand Vezirs. The architect is recorded as Hacı bin Musa – the earliest Ottoman mosque with a named architect.

The deep portico is entered through an unusual and elaborate false door in the central arch, and crowning it is a small fluted dome, set high on an octagonal drum with a deeply cut diamond design. Inside the mosque is a kind of narthex, the central bay also having a little dome over it. Two massive granite columns with stalactite capitals support the large central arch and the two smaller side arches that lead into the main body of the mosque – a square surmounted by a large dome which rests on the deeply incised dart design cornice on the inside of the drum. The marble mihrab is finely carved.

NILÜFER HATUN IMARETI/ARCHAEOLOGICAL MUSEUM

The Museum was opened in 1960 in another of Iznik's loveliest buildings, the Nilüfer Hatun Imareti. It was built in 1388 by Murat I, son of Orhan Gazi, in memory of his mother, Nilüfer Hatun was one of the most remarkable women in Ottoman history, born into a noble Byzantine family, her father being lord of the nearby province of Yarhisar. There is a tale (not mentioned in any Byzantine source) that she had been betrothed to the Byzantine lord of Bekoma (now Bilecik), but that in 1299 Osman Gazi abducted her for his eldest son Orhan. As wife of a nomadic Turkoman leader, her new life must have been in striking contrast to the old; but such was her flexibility and intelligence that she now played a significant role in the nascent Ottoman state, not infrequently being left in charge of the government when Orhan was away on one of his many military campaigns. On the death of their eldest son, Süleyman, Nilüfer's next son, Murat, became heir to the Ottoman throne, and Sultan on Orhan's death in 1360. Although Orhan had other wives – including a Byzantine princess from 1346 – Nilüfer Hatun was the only one of real significance, and when she died she was buried beside him.

This building was designed not only as an imaret, but as a zaviye for members of the Ahi sect, known as the Brotherhood of Virtue or Young Brotherhood. These young artisans and merchants lived in their own homes, but used the zaviye as a kind of club for their religious community and a place for meetings and instruction. With their own earnings they gave hospitality at the zaviye to travellers, especially itinerant dervishes. They also had a considerable political role, greater in some regions than in others, but at the least they seem to have acted as a local watchdog committee, to curb injustice and maintain the rule of the Sultan. Throughout his travels in Anatolia Ibn Battuta stayed with the Ahis and 'nowhere in the world,' he wrote, 'will you find young men so eager to welcome strangers, so prompt to serve food and to satisfy the wants of others.'

Ibn Battuta was 50 years too early to stay in this zaviye. It is entered through a spacious 5-bay portico, much used in the hot summers, and inside it is T-shaped, a design repeated in the later Bursa mosques. We first enter a light and airy square room crowned by a great dome resting on a striking dart-design cornice, which leads to two further domed rooms to left and right. Ahead, forming the foot of the T, is a raised area divided in two by a great arch, on either side of which is a little dome; the first with bold and elaborate stalactite plasterwork in the surrounding vault, while the second rests on an octagonal drum with a simple design of darts and rectangles. In all the rooms of the zaviye are displayed antiquities, mainly from the Iznik area, from the Early Bronze Age, through the Greek and Roman periods, to 16th and 17th C. Iznik tiles.

YERALTI MEZAR/FRESCOED UNDERGROUND TOMB

The Museum holds the keys to a fascinating frescoed tomb 6 km out of Iznik, known as Yeraltı Mezar, the underground tomb. It is Roman in style, but may be early Byzantine in date. If you are lucky, one of the museum staff may come with you – in your car or by taxi. But do not count on it as the museum is chronically under-staffed.

The single barrel-vaulted chamber is cut into the rock with three open graves around the sides. All available surfaces are plastered and vividly painted with birds of various kinds, bowls of fruit, and geometrical designs with patterns of leaves and flowers inside. On the far wall is a handsome pair of peacocks in side view, between which used to be a vase of flowers – but the local villagers got wind of the idea that there was gold beneath the vase so they chipped away more and more of the plaster in their fruitless search. It is because of this that the tomb is kept locked. The doorway consists of four blocks of stone, the two uprights resting on the base stone and supporting the lintel. There are holes in the top and bottom stones, into which would have fitted equivalent projections on the stone door so that it could swing open and shut.

ISMAIL BEY HAMAMI

On the way back to the Museum turn left just inside the Istanbul Gate and stop for a moment at the almost completely broken down Ismail Bey Hamamı, a sad little Ottoman bath house of uncertain date, though no later than 16th C. Two domes survive, and it is the insides of these that are worth looking at; one in particular is splendidly whorled, with flutes swirling out like a Catherine-wheel, pierced by scores of hamam lights. Beneath is an elaborate and deep cornice. In all four shells of rooms there are battered remains of superb decorative plasterwork which must have made this hamam, in its heyday, a delightful place to get clean in.

The remaining monuments of Iznik can be sacrificed without undue loss for they are either in ruins or grossly restored; but for the indefatigable they are as follows:

A mosque in ruinous condition stands immediately beside the Museum – **Şeyh Kutbettin Camii**, dating to 1492. Only the Şeyh's türbe has been restored. Ancient columns and other pieces of carved marble lie strewn in the ruins, and the once lovely brick and tile minaret is topless and tile-less.

The last of the three surviving city gates, **Lefke Kapısı**, is a short walk from the Museum. Like the others a triple gate, it includes a triumphal arch built, as was the one at the Istanbul Gate, in honour of Hadrian's visit in AD 123. An inscription states that it was put up by the proconsul of the day, Plancius Varus. There are some relief carvings in the outer gate, of Romans conquering Germans.

Returning towards the centre of town along Kılıçarslan Cad., turn left into Istiklâl Cad. After the third intersection you will see on your right the ruins of the **Church of the Dormition** (Koimesis) of the Virgin. Built in the late 7th or early 8th C., it remained a Christian church until 1922 when it was destroyed in the Greco-Turkish War. In it were several superb mosaics, in particular a Virgin and Child in the conch of the apse, executed after the final restoration of icons in 843. Today this church – the burial place of Theodore I Lascaris in the 13th C. – consists of a few melancholy walls just above ground level.

A few metres away, and today almost hidden by filth, some steps lead down to a dreary little fountain house, all that remains of an **ayazma**, or sacred spring.

Heading west down Yakup Sok., after the first intersection **Yakup Çelebi Zaviyesi** stands on the left. Like the Zaviye of Nilüfer Hatun, it was built at the end of the 14th C. as an Ahi hospice, and it too is T-shaped. The founder, Yakup Çelebi, was the younger of Murat I's two surviving sons, but his brother had him assassinated after Murat's death in 1389 to ensure his own peaceful accession as Sultan Beyazit I – the first example of a practice that now became habitual in the Ottoman royal family. The building has suffered from being converted into a mosque, and from insensitive restoration. Yakup Çelebi's türbe, a domed open structure, stands just to the west of the mosque.

Continuing west along Yakup Sok., turn right into Atatürk Cad.

and, shortly before the ruins of Haghia Sophia, **Mahmut Çelebi Camii** stands on the right, its entrance on Millet Cad. It was built in 1442 by Mahmut Çelebi, brother-in-law of Murat II; but it has been horribly restored. The 3-domed portico, whose two centre columns are of ancient verd-antique, has been glazed, the marble door-frame disfigured by its modern metal equivalent. Inside, the square prayer hall is harmoniously crowned by a dome set on a deep dart-design cornice; but the whole effect is marred by Koranic inscriptions in white on brown which have been painted wildly all over the upper half of the walls.

On the other side of Millet Cad., and a little further east, stands **Murat II Hamamı**, an attractive 15th C. bath house built in the time of Murat II, which provides separate bathing times for men and women throughout the day. It has two large domes pierced by glass lights, and inside all is marble and steam.

Next to the hamam excavations by Istanbul University have revealed the remains of some kilns and clay preparation tanks, believed to be part of the renowned **Iznik potteries**. Judging by the huge volume of ceramic production in Iznik's heyday, this can only be a fraction of the industrial area in operation in the 16th-17th C.

No visit to Iznik is complete without a visit to the **tomb of Abdülvahap** set on a hill to the east of the town. It is reached by driving through the arches of Lefke Kapısı and continuing for about 3 km, with the tomb in its cluster of trees always visible. The tomb is of no architectural interest; the virtue of the place lies in the magnificent view over the walled city of Iznik, and also in the legend of Abdülvahap. This redoubtable character came to Iznik to give a precious talisman to Battal Gazi, the commander of one of the Arab armies which raided Byzantine Asia Minor in the 8th C. Unfortunately Abdülvahap was killed by the Christians of the city before fulfilling his commission, so he tucked his head under his arm and continued up the hill to this place where, having delivered the talisman, he was duly buried.

It is also very pleasant to lunch in one of the restaurants beside the lake, watching tiny boys netting tinier fish at the water's edge, and looking out over the hazy blue of the ancient Ascania Lake to the surrounding hills.

Postscript. In the heart of Iznik a modern craftsman has re-invented the art of tile-making, with designs and colours that faithfully reflect those of the 16th C. Iznik work. **Eşref Eroğlu Workshop** is a short walk from the Yeşil Cami and the Museum, and is well worth a visit.

17

BURSA

One of the most beautifully sited of Turkish towns, Bursa spreads itself along the foothills of Mount Olympus (one of several so named in the Greek world), and looks across the abundant valley of the Nilüfer Çayi to the hills north of it and to the Sea of Marmara. On a clear day (a rare occurrence now, with industrial development) you can even see Istanbul.

Bursa can be reached in four hours by bus or car from Istanbul: by road to Kartal and then taking the car-ferry to Yalova (see page 254, as for Iznik). For foot passengers the journey can be quicker as there is a fast sea-bus between Kabataş and Yalova several times every day; or once a day between Kabataş and Mudanya. From both Yalova and Mudanya frequent buses and dolmuşes run to Bursa. From Iznik the road on the southern shore of the lake takes about 1½ hours.

Spring is the best season here, late April or early May, for then every tree is a different shade of green – poplars, olives, planes, pines, figs – and when the Judas trees are in bloom there is the occasional brilliant splash of pink to set off the pervading whiteness of the apple blossom. Then, if it is not lost in cloud, you catch your first glimpse of Mount Olympus – Uludağ, the Great Mountain, to the Turks – soaring majestically above the earth, with its eternal snow.

In the early 1970s Bursa was a small town with a population of less than 200,000. Today, with its ever increasing car assembly plants, its soft drinks factories, and other industries, the city and its surrounding area has over 2 million inhabitants. Despite this, Bursa remains an exceptionally agreeable place.

The town is built on a roughly east/west axis, with Uludağ to the south and the Nilüfer valley to the north. Many hotels have their own thermal baths, filled with steaming water from one of the multitude of hot springs.

Bursa has two culinary specialities which are worth trying. One is 'kestane', a delicious confection of chestnuts in syrup; the other is 'Iskender (Alexander) kebab', also known as 'Bursa kebab' – slices of döner kebab on a base of unleavened pide bread and covered with tomato sauce. The restaurant where it was invented, Kebabçı Iskenderoğlu (son of Alexander), still stands on Atatürk Cad. in the heart of town. An unpretentious but clean fast-food joint, it (and any number of other kebabçıs) provides an excellent meal for those prepared to trade sophistication for local colour.

History

In early times Prusa, set on its little acropolis, was of secondary importance in Bithynia, overshadowed by those rivals for supremacy, Nicomedia and Nicaea. It was also later, reputedly established by Prusias I, fourth king of Bithynia, who named it after himself. It must have been built after 202 BC, when Prusias was given this region by his brother-in-law Philip V of Macedon, and before 183 when Prusias died. A story, quoted by Pliny the Elder, associates Hannibal with its foundation, doubtless because the Carthaginian leader visited the court of Prusias I around 190, but it is quite likely that Prusa had already been established by then.

Prusa's main port was Myrleia, just over 30 km away on the Gulf of Cius, another gift of Philip V, and renamed by Prusias in honour of his wife Apameia. Although not especially important at this time, Prusa was significant enough to be given certain rights of local government under the later Bithynian kings; but in 74 BC, along with the rest of the kingdom, it was bequeathed to Rome and became part of the Roman Province of Asia.

Prusa was the first Bithynian city whose finances were investigated by Pliny the Younger in 111 AD, and he wrote to the Emperor Trajan that he was 'finding the inspection increasingly necessary the more I look into the accounts; large sums of money are detained in the hands of private individuals for various reasons, and further sums are paid out for quite illegal purposes.' Pliny also received a request from the citizens of Prusa that their old and dilapidated public bath should be rebuilt, and he assured Trajan that the money would be available in part from 'the sums I have begun to call in from private individuals.' He added that the scheme was 'worthy of the town's prestige and the splendour of your reign.' It was for its baths, and especially the hot mineral springs which supplied them, that Prusa was renowned. Then as now it was an important centre for medical treatment, to its considerable enrichment.

Another source of renown and wealth came in the 6th C. when the silkworm made its first appearance in the Byzantine Empire, and the city, then known as Brusa, became a world centre for silk production and the manufacture of silk cloth. Under the Ottomans this expanded into a major international industry for making luxury fabrics such as velvet and brocade, with over 1000 weaving establishments by the early 16th C. The city is still known for its silk, reduced in quality though it is; but also, at a more pedestrian level, for the manufacture of excellent towels.

Brusa remained in Byzantine hands until 1075 when it was captured by the Selçuk Turks for their Sultanate of Rum, but it reverted to the Byzantines soon after; and from 1204 to 1261 it was part of the Empire of Nicaea. Its secondary status was brought to an end in 1326 when the forces of the aging Osman Gazi, led by his son Orhan, captured the city after years of siege, and made it the main capital of the rising Ottoman state. Osman did not live to see his new capital, but his body was later brought here by Orhan to be buried in the citadel.

The Ottomans treated the conquered city with clemency. The Byzantine commander was allowed to go to Constantinople, but his chief adviser chose to stay with the Ottomans; the bishop was permitted to continue his spiritual care of the Christians who remained in Bursa, though they were evicted from the castle and resettled below. Orhan built his palace within the castle walls, near a Byzantine church which he converted into a mosque.

The capture of Bursa was a turning point in Ottoman history. Although Osman Gazi had had other bases, he and his followers were essentially a nomadic group. Now the Ottomans became a settled people with territorial borders and a state organisation centred on Bursa which became Orhan's main residence. Its claim to be the first Ottoman capital derives from the fact that here, in 1327, Orhan minted the first Ottoman coin, the silver akça. He also set about beautifying his new capital, breaking out of the Byzantine walls around the citadel and expanding along the hillside. So successful was he that when Ibn Battuta visited Bursa in 1332, he commented with enthusiasm on its fine bazaars and broad streets. 100 years later, when the Spaniard Pero Tafur came, he found the city 'greater and better than any in Turkey . . . and since the Turks have owned it they have much improved the place . . . I believe that in the whole of Turkey today there is no other place so large, nor so well peopled, nor so rich.'

Bursa retained a special, semi-sacred place in the hearts of the Ottomans, and in particular of the Sultans. Even after their main

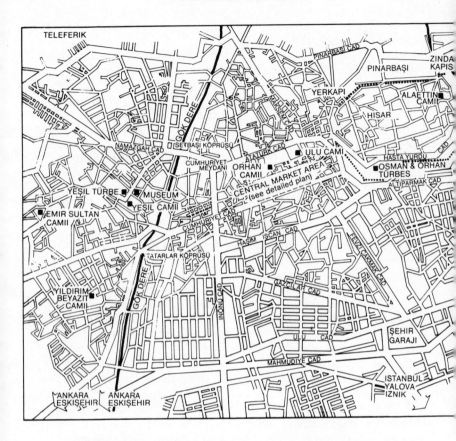

capital had been transferred to Edirne in the 1360s, the Sultans continued to be buried here until after the conquest of Constantinople in 1453; and they endowed it with some of the finest of early Ottoman mosques, türbes, medreses and imarets. Despite earthquakes, in particular a very violent one in 1855, many of these buildings still stand, making of Bursa one of the architectural and decorative treasure houses of Turkey.

The monuments

It is best to start at the far west of Bursa, and to work eastwards through the ancient citadel with its narrow streets and old houses, to the mosques and markets at the centre, and finally to the supreme glory of Yeşil Cami, the green mosque.

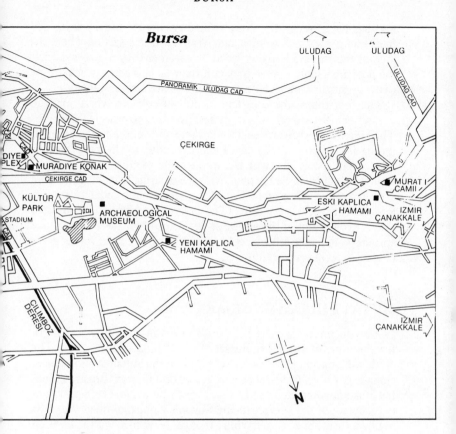

ESKI KAPLICA HAMAMI

At the western end of Çekirge Cad., on the right hand side of the road, a beautiful cluster of recently restored domes, announces the Eski Kaplıca Hamamı, the oldest baths in Bursa. It is said that earlier baths on this site were built by Justinian and Theodora, and that may well be so for the present building incorporates columns and capitals that could well be Justinianic, or even earlier. The hamam that we see today was built by Murat I, son of Orhan, in the late 14th C.

Evilya Çelebi, that delightful writer and traveller of the 17th C., informs us, clearly from personal experience, that after a bath here 'the flesh feels as soft as an ear lap and all uncleanliness is boiled out as it were from the body.' He adds that 'to drink the water is a good remedy for palpitation and throbbing of the heart.' Those wishing to try the effect for themselves can have a private room, bath, scrub and massage for a modest fee. Non-bathing visitors are usually welcomed free – both men and women may visit the men's section where the incumbents are modestly wrapped, but women may not always enter the pool area. Only women may visit the women's baths which, in any case, are smaller, more recent, and of less architectural interest.

The first room, the camekân, is full of cubicles where men lie around being dried off, or simply resting after the ordeal of the bath. Then into the fairly warm soğukluk where all-over marble and human inertia are the order of the day. Finally we enter the hararet, the bath room itself, spectacular with Byzantine columns crowned with ornate capitals which encircle the pool, with steam rising from its waters like a scene from a Wagner opera. Men swim around lethargically, or lounge about the edge chatting. The water is a testing 45°C in the pool – but it comes out of the spring at 90°. Curiously, there are also icy springs on the same hillside, cold enough, so the Turkish saying goes, to crack open a watermelon.

MURAT I HÜDAVENDIGÂR CAMII

Just up the hill to the west of Eski Kaplıca stands another of the very few buildings of Murat I in Bursa, Murat I Hüdavendigâr Camii. His epithet, Hüdavendigâr, modestly claims for the Sultan the function of God the Creator – its literal meaning. The building was begun in 1366, but was not completed for 19 years which points to a certain lack of urgency about the project in the Sultan's campaign-filled life. It is highly unusual in design, having a mosque combined with a zaviye on the ground floor, and a medrese on the floor above; thus boldly uniting under one roof both mystical and orthodox elements of Islam. It was said that the workmen included Christians; in fact, Evliya Çelebi declared that the mosque was 'built in a peculiar style because the architect was a Frank.' Whether or not that is so, the building is remarkably similar to the early 14th C. church of Haghia Sophia in Ohrid in Dalmatia. The design of the two storeys, built in alternate layers of brick and stone, is well integrated on the exterior, especially in the main façade. Here the five arches of the portico of the mosque are matched by five more arches above, each of which contains two small arches within it, springing in the centre from a Byzantine column and capital.

Entering the lower floor from the portico, we come first to the rooms associated with the **zaviye**, while the prayer hall of the mosque is at the far end. The first room is a small hall, on either side of which a doorway leads to a staircase to the upper floor. Beyond both stairs a further doorway leads into a room, one in each corner of the building, probably used as zaviye store-rooms. Beyond the first hall is another, even smaller, with openings right and left leading to handsomely proportioned rooms. This second hall, covered by a later and unfortunate wooden gallery, opens into the central **courtyard** which rises through both storeys and is covered by a great dome. The marble fountain is another unfortunate addition. On either side is a large vaulted eyvan, and beyond these is a further corner room. From the courtyard four steps lead up to the barrel-vaulted **mosque prayer hall**, which also rises through the upper floor.

The overall plan of the **medrese** (which is not usually possible to visit, though you may be allowed onto the balcony) is the same as that of the lower floor, but with the domed courtyard and the mosque area excluded. A U-shaped corridor runs around this area and gives access to the vaulted cells. The dershane is immediately over the entrance hall, and it opens onto the long balcony above the portico. A curious feature is the narrow passage on each side of the area occupied by the prayer hall below, leading to a little domed room immediately above the mihrab. What this room was used for, and by whom, is a puzzle.

On the other side of the road, and set in a colourful garden, stands the **türbe of Murat I** – a square building, crowned by a dome, which has been much restored, not to say rebuilt, both in 1741 and after the big earthquake in 1855. Inside, the lofty dome is supported by eight handsome columns; but the restorations have done nothing for the decor. Murat I was assassinated on 27 August 1389 at Kossova in Serbia, on the eve of a great victory over a combined Balkan army led by Lazar, prince of Serbia. In his father's place Prince Beyazit led the Ottoman forces into the final victorious battle, and shortly afterwards he had Murat's body brought back to Bursa for burial here in this garden beside his mosque, with a wide view over the great open valley.

YENI KAPLICA HAMAMI

Returning towards town, hamam enthusiasts can divert down a sharp turning to the left opposite the Çelik Palas Hotel to see the Yeni Kaplıca Hamamı. It is a very large thermal establishment, with accommodation attached for those seeking a cure, and it was built in the middle of the 16th C. by Rüstem Paşa, Süleyman the Magnificent's energetic but unlovable Grand Vezir. Evliya Çelebi says that Süleyman had been cured of gout after a visit to the small baths that then occupied this site, so he ordered Rüstem to rebuild it, which he did in a manner more appropriate to its status as healer of the royal foot. It may have been designed by Sinan. The most striking feature are the Damascus-ware Iznik tiles on the walls of the hararet – but centuries of steam from the pool have sadly damaged them. There are also patches of lovely mosaic pavement. To reinforce the levelling effect of a bath house, a Turkish verse was inscribed on its walls –

> In life on your apparel lay no stress
> As every body must his body here undress.

Evliya adds that the Yeni Kaplıca did not have such a good reputation as the Eski Kaplıca, 'yet it is a pleasant place, where lovers delight with their beloved, especially in the long winter nights; when these baths are lighted with candles, are a thousand tricks played by the bathers, some diving, some swimming, some wrestling in the water, some swelling their aprons into sails, others spouting water from their mouths, some lying dead flat on the water, others joining hands and imitating the cries of boatmen, "Tira Mola", drive the water round like a whirlpool, which forces all those who are in the water to follow the quick rotation of it.' Such energetic goings-on in water of 45°C!

KÜLTÜR PARKI AND ARCHAEOLOGICAL MUSEUM

Just beyond the Yeni Kaplıca is the Kültür Parkı, a public park full of trees and grass – a popular and pleasant place to take a stroll, to row on the lake or have a casual meal, or to enjoy the wilder delights of the Luna Park. The only noticeable culture to justify the park's name is to be found in the Archaeological Museum (open daily except Monday). It has an interesting collection of mainly local finds dating from the Bronze Age, the Hittites and Phrygians, through the Hellenistic, Roman and Byzantine periods.

MURADIYE COMPLEX

Opposite the park entrance to the Archaeological Museum we turn right off Çekirge Cad., and follow signs to Muradiye. This is one of the great mosque complexes of Bursa, especially renowned for its magnificent garden of imperial tombs.

Murat II, father of Mehmet the Conqueror, built his mosque, and the associated medrese and imaret, between 1424 and 1426, the last imperial complex to be built in Bursa. The **mosque** is fronted by a 5-domed portico which includes two ancient granite columns. The central dome is elaborately moulded, and the main door is of wood and is finely carved with a geometrical design which encloses flowers and leaves in relief. The mosque is T-shaped, like most of the earlier imperial mosques in Bursa, with a domed court at the axis of the T; on either side of this is a square eyvan covered by a dome, originally designed as a tabhane. The prayer hall is raised above the courtyard and is also crowned by a great dome, nearly as wide as that over the court, but not so high. All the domes rest on bold cornices, that of the court unusually deep, and the pendentives too have large and striking designs. Early tiles from Iznik, in deep blue, turquoise, green and white, adorn the walls of the prayer hall in bold geometric designs, surrounded by a patterned border. A small band of particularly lovely tiles, polychrome and moulded, is on each side of the arch dividing the court from the prayer hall.

Murat II's imaret has all but disappeared; but the **medrese**, a handsomely proportioned square building around a central court has, since 1951, been put to practical use as a TB clinic. Visitors are tolerated for a glimpse into the courtyard, now an abundant garden with a fountain at the centre. The decorative brickwork on the façade of the dershane, and some original tiles inside, are worth noticing.

Beside the mosque is one of the loveliest of gardens, shaded by venerable plane trees interspersed with cypresses like giant spearheads, and filled with flowers and murmuring fountains. The sense of peace that these create blends well with the gentle melancholy of the dozen magnificent türbes of various members of the Ottoman royal family, built in alternate layers of rose-pink brick and white stone. The largest is the **türbe of Murat II** himself which he completed in 1437, well in advance of his death in February 1451. The canopy over the entrance is a baroque addition and, lovely as it is, it is somewhat out of keeping with the original simplicity of the building, and indeed with the austerity of the man himself. He was the first and last Ottoman Sultan voluntarily to retire, but he was recalled from his chosen life of contemplation and mysticism, to return to that of imperial action, after only two years.

The interior of his türbe is simple and monumental, his grave beneath an open dome supported by four piers, with four marble columns between them. Richard Knolles, who wrote his *Turkish History* in the early 17th C., was impressed by the simplicity of this 'Chappel without a roof, his Grave nothing differing from the manner of the common Turks; which (they say) he commanded to be done in his last Will, that the Mercy and Blessing of God (as he termed it) might come unto him by the shining of the Sun and Moon and falling of the Rain and Dew of Heaven upon his Grave.' The columns, and the capitals at both top and bottom (all of them different), are recycled Byzantine building material, and the transition from square base to circular dome is made via an octagonal drum. In a side room are the tombs of Murat's two elder sons who died before him and for whom he seems to have had more affection than he did for his eventual heir, the future Mehmet the Conqueror, for whom he cared little. Another of his sons is also buried here, and a daughter.

Murat II was the last Ottoman Sultan to be buried in Bursa; Mehmet II and all his successors preferred the new capital of Constantinople. But in the 100 years or so that followed the building of Murat's türbe here, it was joined by those of various Ottoman princes, wives and favourites. Many of them tell a sorry tale of the mutilation and assassination of brothers who caused – or might cause – problems for the smooth accession of the new Sultan. One of the finest is the **türbe of Cem Sultan**, named after him because of his fame, though he was not the first to be buried here. This son of Mehmet the Conqueror had disputed the throne with his elder brother Beyazit II, and sought help in Europe. He died in 1495. Beside his sarcophagus is that of Mehmet's favourite son, Mustafa, who had died in 1474; and the two other sarcophagi are said to be those of two sons of Beyazit II. They share a splendid hexagonal türbe, decorated with tiles of turquoise and dark blue.

The türbes Ahmet and Mahmut, sons of Beyazit II, are both octagonal and adorned with similar dark blue and turquoise tiles. Mahmut was executed in 1506 for rebelling against his father, and his three sons joined him six years later, executed by their uncle Selim I, the Grim, to dispose of possible rivals. Ahmet, Beyazit's eldest son, died in 1513, also a victim of Selim's purge of the royal house, and he is buried with another murdered brother, Şehinşah. Also octagonal, and decorated with some of the loveliest mid-16th C. Iznik tiles, is the **türbe of Prince Mustafa**, the highly-regarded heir of Süleyman the Magnificent. He was strangled in 1553 as a result of the intrigues of Süleyman's wife, Roxelana, who wanted the route to the throne cleared for one of her own sons, the eventual Sultan Selim II.

Behind the mosque is a conventional graveyard, filled with tombstones of varying dates and grandeur. On the far side of it are two more türbes, the larger, the **Hatuniye**, having been built for Mehmet the Conqueror's mother, Hüma Hatun in 1449. Her real name is unknown, but her father was Abdullah, a common name for a convert. Hüma – bird of paradise – was a posthumous appellation.

MURADIYE KONAK *and* HÜSNÜ ZÜBER EVI

On the square in front of the Muradiye mosque stands an attractive 17th C. wood-frame house, now a museum (theoretically open daily except Monday, but frequently closed due to staff shortages). It is known as **Muradiye Konak** mainly from its location, though it is said, with more imagination than evidence, that Murat II lived in an earlier house on this site. It is well worth a visit for the view it gives of 17th to early 19th C. Ottoman life, and for its lovely painted decoration on the doors, cupboards and ceilings.

Returning towards the Muradiye and turning right, we follow signs up a narrow winding hill to the **Hüsnü Züber Evi** (open daily except Monday), a small 19th C. Ottoman house whose restoration has been done with delightful restraint. First a guesthouse, then the Russian Consulate, it became a private house in 1887. In 1988 Mr Hüsnü Züber restored it and later opened it as a museum for its architectural and decorative interest. The wooden ceilings and painted alcoves are especially worth noticing. The ground floor has a display of Hüsnü Züber's own craft of 'pyrogravure' – burnt designs on wood.

TÜRBES OF OSMAN GAZI AND ORHAN GAZI

Our next visit is to the shady garden just inside the ancient citadel which contains the türbes of Osman Gazi and Orhan Gazi – 19th C. reconstructions after the earthquake of 1855. Osman Gazi, who had set his heart on capturing Bursa and had besieged it for many years, lived just long enough to hear the news that his son had at last captured the city. Later Orhan brought his father's body to Bursa for re-burial in a converted Byzantine chapel on this site. It was roofed with lead which shone so brightly that it was called Gümüşlü Türbe, the silvery tomb.

Orhan's tomb, side by side with that of his father in the original church complex, still retains some of the Byzantine mosaic floor. In the garden between the tombs the names of Osman Gazi and Orhan Gazi have been picked out in miniature box hedges; but the best feature is the view over the town and valley below.

HISAR

If you have the time, it is worth walking up the hill from the tombs and taking the first turning on the left to wander among the narrow winding streets of the citadel, known as Hisar – the castle. Many of its old wooden houses have crumbled and been replaced with unaesthetic concrete boxes; but others have been restored, or rebuilt in the old style, and several delightful corners remain. Orhan cleared Hisar of its existing Byzantine inhabitants, and built himself a wooden palace which was maintained and used by the Ottoman Sultans until the 17th C. Not a trace of it remains. Many other houses were built within the old walls – Bertrandon de la Broquière, writing in 1432, speaks of 1000, which must have made it fairly crowded.

On the far side of the citadel a gap in the walls in an area known as **Pınarbaşı**, spring-head, marks the point at which Orhan's troops breached the walls and made their first entry into Bursa on 6 April 1326. From here we can walk along a road immediately outside the ancient walls. After about 500 m we reach **Zindan Kapısı**, the prison gate, where we re-enter the citadel.

ALAÊTTIN CAMII

About 200 m inside the gate, following the left-hand road which curves round to the right, we come to the earliest purpose-built mosque of Bursa. Alaêttin Camii was built in 1335 by Alaêttin Bey, brother and vezir of Orhan Gazi, in the days before distrust and death came between a new Sultan and his brothers. It is a tiny and simple mosque consisting, like the Hacı Özbek Camii in Iznik, of a square surmounted by a dome; but here the portico has been rebuilt in the same style, so we can get a better idea of the original mosque. The portico of four Byzantine columns and capitals supports a single barrel vault with an odd little dome in the centre. Inside, the main dome rests on a handsome deep cornice of large and irregular triangles.

ORHAN GAZI CAMII

Returning to the tombs of Osman and Orhan, we now leave the citadel and drop down into the commercial centre of Bursa where, in 1339, Orhan Gazi built the first of the imperial complexes of Bursa. There was a mosque, medrese and imaret; also two hamams and a han whose revenues supported the religious foundations. The medrese and imaret have gone; and the Orhan Gazi Camii that we see today is the result of two rebuildings, though both on the same plan as the original. The first mosque was burnt down by the emir of Karaman and his marauding troops and rebuilt in 1417, to be ruined for a second time in the earthquake of 1855. It has been further restored at least twice since then.

Orhan's mosque was intended also as a zaviye for the Ahis and dervishes. A deep 5-bayed portico leads into what looks like a narthex, with a narrow room at each end. A central doorway opened into the court at the axis of this T-shaped building (the first in Bursa), which is covered by a dome on a triangle-design cornice. On either side are domed eyvans, raised above the level of the court, which were used by the Ahis and dervishes for accommodation and teaching. The prayer hall, divided from the court by a pointed arch, is raised higher still, and its great dome rests on four squinches with an elaborate triangle design.

THE CENTRAL MARKET AREA

From the Orhan Gazi Camii we can visit some of the hans of the various trades that operated in Bursa during the Ottoman period. In the 17th C. Evliya Çelebi tells us there were 180 hans; today there are vastly fewer, earthquakes, fires and sheer age having taken their toll. The most recent devastation was a fire in 1955, since when rebuilding and restoration of mixed sensitivity has put the area back into business. Here, in the heart of the commercial quarter, we can see a handful of fine hans of varying dates and states of repair, as well as the bedesten and a hamam. The confusing nature of the streets and covered areas around them makes it difficult and tiring to see them all; if time and energy evaporate, it is probably best to concentrate on Koza Hanı, the centre of the silk trade, and the Bedesten, two of the finest of early Ottoman commercial buildings, and well restored.

Just outside the NW corner of the Orhan Gazi courtyard, a passage leads into the irregularly shaped inner courtyard of **Koza Hanı**, the silk cocoon han, where we go through an arch into the main 2-storey courtyard, the handsomest in Bursa. It is not hard to imagine the caravans of camels and donkeys making their way into this spacious courtyard, their owners shouting instructions in a Babel of languages, the universally understood call to prayer ringing out from the little mescit in the centre, and then the bustle as the animals were loaded with bales of silk cloth and set off again on their long journeys.

The han was built in 1490 by Beyazit II, son of Mehmet the Conqueror, and the joint architects are named as Ali ibn Aptullah and Yakup Şah ibn Sultan Şah – both involved in the building of Beyazit II's mosque in Istanbul. The cobbled courtyard is almost square, with

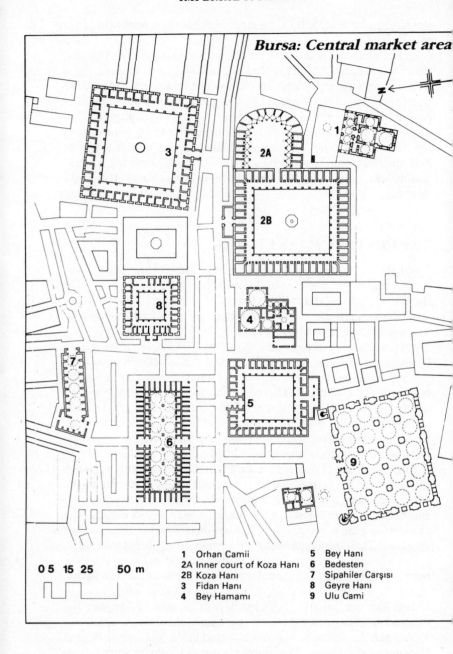

Bursa: Central market area

1 Orhan Camii
2A Inner court of Koza Hanı
2B Koza Hanı
3 Fidan Hanı
4 Bey Hamamı
5 Bey Hanı
6 Bedesten
7 Sipahiler Carşısı
8 Geyre Hanı
9 Ulu Cami

0 5 15 25   50 m

rounded lower arches and pointed upper ones, and is shaded by plane and lime trees. The little domed octagonal mescit, built above the open arches of the central şadırvan, is one of the most attractive features of the han, especially the octagonal column at the centre of the şadırvan, with its handsome stalactite capital, from which the vaulting fans out.

On both storeys an open passage runs round the courtyard behind the arches, and behind this are enclosed rooms, on the upper floor roofed by rows of domes. The passage on the ground floor has been incorporated into the shops. The han is still used by the silk trade, though in incarnations that would scarcely be recognised by their predecessors. One thing they might recognise is the annual silk market, held here in June and July, when every day silk cocoons by the thousand are bought and sold.

By the time this han was built, Bursa was already established as a major international centre for the manufacture of, and trade in, silk; and it continued to grow, especially from the mid-16th C. when silk worm breeding began in Bursa. Traders came from Iran, Egypt and Europe to purchase the luxury brocades and velvets that were produced only here, and also lighter silks such as taffeta. Yet for all this export, the principal market remained the Ottoman court – which stood Bursa in good stead in the 18th C. when the French and Italians started to produce their own high quality silk cloth, seriously reducing Bursa's exports. The introduction of steam power into the workshops here in 1837 meant that Bursa could continue to compete in the manufacture of silk cloth, while still remaining a major producer of raw silk.

Leaving Koza Hanı by the main gateway and turning right, **Fidan Hanı** is a few metres on the left. It is also known as Mahmut Paşa Hanı after the man who built it, the most remarkable of Mehmet the Conqueror's Grand Vezirs. It is much the same size and plan as the somewhat later Koza Hanı, but has not been so well restored and is now occupied by offices and shops. The court, once filled with saplings (fidan) which grew into venerable shade-giving trees, has now become a car park round the central şadırvan-cum-mescit. Only one old tree survives, but there are several younger ones.

On the other side of Koza Hanı, just inside the covered market, the first passage on the left, named Eski Aynak Çarşi, leads into all that remains of **Bey Hamamı**. If you keep your eyes down, there is nothing to be seen except shops full of antiques and souvenirs – but look up and you will see first the largest of the old domes, and further on two more domed areas, pierced with tiny round windows. This was one of the hamams associated with Orhan Camii and built in 1339 – the first known baths complex in the Ottoman Empire.

Beside this erstwhile hamam stands **Bey Hanı**, also known as **Emir Hanı**, another part of Orhan's mosque complex, designed to provide revenue for his mosque and its religious foundations. It too was damaged by earthquakes, and has been restored without undue insensitivity to provide shops and offices. It is much smaller than the other two hans, and it still has trees in the courtyard and a fountain. One of Ulu Cami's minarets overlooks the courtyard where men sit around talking business, or chatting, while shoe cleaners wander round in pursuit of business.

Almost opposite the main entrance to Bey Hanı, a passage leads down steps to the **Bedesten**, or **Kuyumcular Çarşısı**, goldsmiths' market, the heart of commercial Bursa. From the time that it was built by Beyazit I in the late 14th C., it has been both a safe-deposit and a trading area for jewellers and dealers in other precious merchandise, including the costly brocades, for it was the only area that could be securely locked. Inside are two rows of seven domed bays, supported on six piers which run down the middle and are joined to each other, and to the side walls, by rounded arches. There are four entrances, the two main ones being those on the long sides to north and south. Down each of these long sides is a row of small lock-up rooms, in front of which shops are set up and business is transacted. All around the outside of the bedesten is a second row of shops.

Leaving by the north gate, we go straight ahead and then veer right to find **Sipahiler Çarşısı**, the market of the cavalrymen, built in the early 15th C. by Mehmet I, a dingily atmospheric place which has so far escaped the restorers. We enter a high vaulted hall with a dome set just off centre; to the right and set askew to the hall, is the main part of the market, a long building with four domed bays, each bay being divided in two at the sides. It is today used as a warehouse for modern furniture of spectacular ugliness.

Almost opposite the east end of the bedesten is the entrance to the last remaining han in the area, **Geyve Hanı**, also known as Ivaz Paşa Hanı after Hacı Ivaz ibn Ahi Beyazit who built it, who was also responsible for building Yeşil Cami for Mehmet I. It is a small square han, with five arches on each side, and it is much cluttered by its shops and workshops.

ULU CAMI

Taking the passage immediately east of Bey Hanı, we climb the steps to Bursa's magnificent Friday mosque, Ulu Cami, the Great Mosque, built in 1396 to 1399 by Beyazit I. Early in life Beyazit was nicknamed Yıldırım, Lightning or Thunderbolt, from the rapidity with which he moved his armies to crush his enemies – until he was himself defeated and captured by the Mongol Timur the Lame. The son of Murat I and a Byzantine woman, he was the first Ottoman to murder a brother to ensure his own peaceful accession when his father died in 1389. Beyazit spent much of his short reign at war; and it was his victory on 24 September 1396 over a Crusader army at Nicopolis on the Danube that provided the wealth of booty which financed the building of this mosque, the biggest and grandest that had been built up to that time.

Ulu Cami is built in a lovely pale honey-coloured limestone, quarried from Uludağ, in a large rectangle whose exterior façades are relieved by arches and windows. The main portal may have been damaged when Timur sacked the city in 1402, and rebuilt by him, but local wisdom hotly denies the charge. The vast interior space of 3165 sq m is covered by 20 domes, with 12 piers in three rows of four. It was said that Beyazit had impetuously vowed to build 20 mosques with his newly won booty, but the diplomatic compromise of 20 independent domes was suggested by his more realistic adviser Emir Sultan, later to become his son-in-law.

Inside, facing the main portal, is a huge **şadırvan** with a central fountain – a stylish 19th C. replacement. Originally the dome above was an open oculus, allowing rain and snow to fall into the pool, 'wherein', says Evliya Çelebi, 'fish are swimming and whence the Muslim community take the water necessary for their ablutions.' Today the fish have gone and the dome has been almost entirely glazed to cater for the less hardy worshippers of today; but the ablutions, the murmuring of the water and the susurration of the faithful, doubtless remain as they ever were.

The perspectives inside the mosque are magnificent, with pier after pier and arch after arch receding into the distance in every direction. The decor is heavily out of keeping with the building itself, the large painted Koranic inscriptions, daubed by a 19th C. hand over most of the available space on the piers, being artistically almost as distracting as the Italianate decorations above them. And someone has had a very heavy hand with the gold paint on what is otherwise a handsome **mihrab**. Mercifully untouched, and the *chef d'oeuvre* of the mosque, is the magnificent **mimber** which Evliya Çelebi rightly declared 'must absolutely be seen, for it is so wonderful that it cannot easily be described, and has no equal anywhere except at Sinope.' It is made of walnut and carved – differently on both sides – in an intricate geometric design of multi-pointed stars radiating in all directions, the spaces filled with finely carved wood of different shapes or bulbous bosses. Most astonishing of all is that not a single nail nor drop of glue was used in its making.

YILDIRIM BEYAZIT CAMII

From Beyazit I's Ulu Camii we go to the east of town to see his earlier Yıldırım Beyazit Camii. From Atatürk Cad. turn left into İnönü Cad. at Cumhuriyet Meydanı; after about ½ km turn right onto Cumhuriyet Cad. which crosses Tatarlar Köprüsü (Tatar Bridge), after which keep in a north-easterly direction through a network of streets which lead up the hill to Yıldırım Beyazit Camii.

Beyazit I began work on his mosque and its associated foundations within a year or so of becoming Sultan in 1389. It was completed in 1395, the third of Bursa's imperial complexes after those of Orhan and Murat I. The mosque has had the usual restorations and repairs necessitated by earthquakes and age, but remains the same basic shape as the original which, like its predecessors, was designed as both mosque and zaviye. In Beyazit's day the site was deep in the country, and it still has an air of seclusion, surrounded by trees on its little hill overlooking the town.

The feature that immediately impresses on the exterior is the noble **portico** of five domed bays, each lofty arch framing the windows behind, and the mihrab niches with their glorious stalactite canopies, all of which repay closer inspection. From the portico we step into a small hall with even smaller rooms on either side and a larger room in each corner. The domed court at the heart of the building has not only the standard raised eyvan on each side, but a further room reached by doors on either side of the arch which divides the court from the prayer hall. These two far rooms have spectacular plasterwork shelf recesses which cover the south wall on either side of a tall fireplace, though the majority of it is modern replacement. These rooms were originally designed as tabhanes for offering hospitality to travelling dervishes, and the shelves would then have held a variety of objects such as Korans and bookrests, water jugs, lamps, turbans and jars of highly prized attar of roses.

The **prayer hall**, like the eyvans, is raised above the level of the court

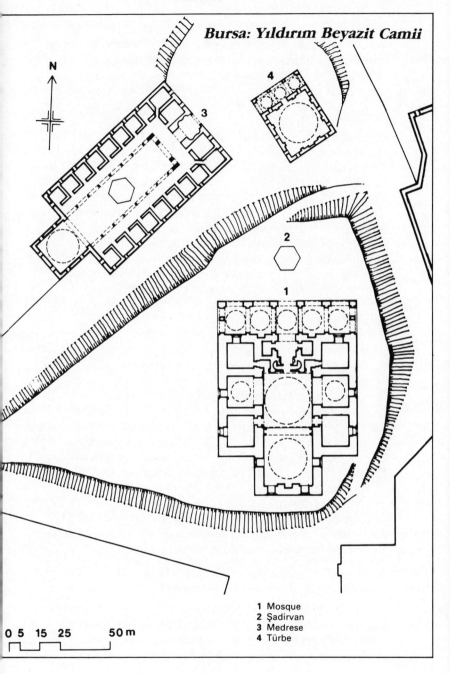

Bursa: Yıldırım Beyazit Camii

N

4

3

2

1

1 Mosque
2 Şadirvan
3 Medrese
4 Türbe

0 5 15 25   50 m

285

whose size it nearly matches. The two areas are divided by a magnificent arch, the first example of what became known as the 'Bursa arch', which was used in several later mosques, is particular Yeşil Cami. Its distinguishing feature is a flat section at the top, slightly recessed above the rest. It springs from consoles half-way up the side piers, carved with an elaborate stalactite design rising from the niche below. The mihrab has a fine stalactite canopy, but is over-enthusiastically gilded, and surrounded with heavily painted geometrical designs, Koranic inscriptions, flowers, and swagged curtains. The walls are decorated with inscriptions, contained within medallions and other shapes, including that of a fish. Above them all soars the dome, on a deeply incised dart design cornice; this and the floor-level windows, together with some smaller ones higher up, give the prayer hall a light and airy grandeur.

From beside the hexagonal şadırvan in front of the portico, we can look down onto the **medrese**, an unusually long rectangular building, clearly dictated by the slope of the hill, with a domed dershane at its western end, and two smaller domes over the entrance at the eastern end, the inner one with an elaborate stalactite design inside it. The building is now a clinic.

Beyazit's türbe still stands in its original form, below the mosque and east of the medrese, though it has been rebuilt and restored often. The thunderbolt Sultan was captured by Timur at the Battle of Ankara on 28 July 1402. Richard Knolles, in his *Turkish History*, tells us that Beyazit refused to be submissive to Timur and spoke his mind without regard to the consequences. 'And what wouldst thou have done to me (said Tamerlane) had it been my fortune to have fallen into thy Hands, as thou art now in mine? I would (said Bajazet) have inclosed thee in a Cage of Iron, and so in triumph have carried thee up and down my Kingdom. Even so (said Tamerlane) shalt thou be served.'

Whether or not Beyazit beat his brains out against the bars of his iron cage, as Marlowe dramatised the scene in *Tamburlaine*, his captivity came to an end with his death in Akşehir on 8 March 1403. In the words of Marlowe, he was mourned by his favourite wife, a Serbian princess, who shared his captivity –

> O Bajazeth, my husband and my lord!
> O Bajazeth! O Turk! O Emperor!

Beyazit's body was given by Timur to his son Musa to take to Bursa for burial. Such was the confusion, and the antipathy between Musa and his brothers during the next ten years of civil war, that it was not until 1406 that a türbe was built by his eldest son, Süleyman. When

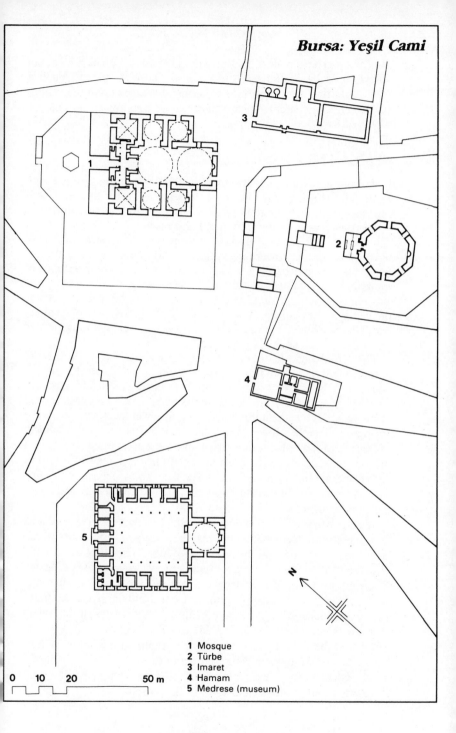

Bursa: Yeşil Cami

0   10   20   50 m

1 Mosque
2 Türbe
3 Imaret
4 Hamam
5 Medrese (museum)

287

the Karaman hordes attacked Bursa in 1417, the türbe was ruined, but was restored by Mehmet I, the victor in the civil war. Through a 3-bayed portico, with Byzantine columns on either side of the central bay, we enter the simple square chamber surmounted by a dome. mounted by a dome.

YEŞIL CAMI

Returning towards the centre of town, just before the bridge a sign points left to Emir Sultan. The road also leads to Yeşil Cami, the Green Mosque, the crowning glory of early Ottoman architecture in Bursa, the masterpiece of Sultan Mehmet I and his architect, Hacı Ivaz ibn Ahi Beyazit, Prefect of Bursa. Its position is superb, set on a prominence amidst towering cypresses, and commanding a magnificent view over the valley, with Beyazit's mosque, the precursor of Mehmet's own, on its little hill in the near distance.

Mehmet began his mosque complex soon after he had emerged as the victor in the civil war, reuniting the divided territories of Anatolia and Thrace. When he died suddenly in May 1421, his mosque was unfinished – and so it has remained.

The unfinished area is immediately apparent as we approach the entrance, for it is a mosque without a portico. Where the portico would have been are two raised platforms on either side of the portal; and between the two open loggias of the upper level of the façade, and immediately above the mihrab niches of the lower level, we can see the springing of arches that never were. The mihrab niches are finely carved; and on either side are windows surrounded by carved inscriptions and arabesques. In the centre is the magnificent portal, with elaborate niches cut into the sides, the whole crowned with a fine stalactite canopy. The beauty of the façade is enhanced by the lovely pale gold stone of which it is built.

We enter first a long narrow lobby which looks very like a narthex (complete with Byzantine columns and capitals), and from which stairs on either side lead up to the **royal loge**. The stairs are usually closed and the loge must be viewed from inside the mosque below. The tiles with which it is decorated are of exceptional beauty, the work, according to an inscription, of one Muhammed al-Majnun, variously translated as 'mad' or 'eccentric'. Another inscription refers to Nakkaş (decorator or artist) Ali ibn Ilyas Ali who, it appears, supervised the decoration of the interior. Captured by Timur, he had been taken to Samarkand where the art of faience was already highly developed. After his release and return to Bursa, what he had learned there was given glorious expression in this mosque.

From the entrance lobby we pass through a small crepuscular hall covered with dark green tiles in which are set medallions with arabesque designs in blue, white, black and deep purple. Emerging into the central court, it is impossible not to be dazzled by the brilliance of the decoration, so much in contrast with other mosques in Bursa. Never before had the Ottomans used tiles in this way to adorn the interior of their mosques; it set a precedent that was to be developed in the next century when the potteries of Iznik were producing their finest work, though in a style very different from those here. The Selçuks had used tiles with spectacular effect, but they too were quite different in type and design from these here in Yeşil Cami.

These polychrome tiles were made by the *cuerda seca* technique in which the colours were separated by a fine thread which burnt to nothing during the firing. The colours include a wonderful yellow as well as white, a wonderful sage green which is easy to miss, and a deep purplish blue, together with a restrained use of gold, painted on after the tiles had been fired. The designs, a happy blend of the formal and the unconfined, include arabesques, palmettes, peonies and rosettes, together with leaves and intertwining stems. There are also some moulded tiles which, especially in the mihrab, create a 3-D design.

In the centre of the court under the dome is a great **şadırvan** with a splendid marble fountain in the middle. It was originally used for ablutions, and shoes were deposited in the papuçluk recesses beside the steps leading to the prayer hall. Today ablutions take place outside and the court has become an integral part of the mosque. On either side of it are the two tiled eyvans; and on either side of the door through which we entered are two smaller recesses which face the mihrab and are even more richly tiled than the eyvans, especially on the ceiling where the central medallion is both filled and surrounded by intricate arabesques, flowers and leaves. Beyond the two eyvans are two further domed rooms, originally used as tabhanes, with fireplaces surrounded by plasterwork shelves, and also some tile decoration. The domes are elaborately fluted and supported on magnificent stalactite squinches, those in the right hand room with traces of old painted designs – as are the domes above the eyvans.

Beneath the 'Bursa' arch that divides the two main areas of the mosque, four steps lead up to the prayer hall whose culminating glory, the **mihrab**, is enhanced by the plainness of the tiles on the side walls. The great polychrome tile-surround reaches almost to the top of the wall in which it is set, and is decorated with bands of geometric design, and of inscription, which serve to emphasise the controlled exuberance of the predominating patterns of flowers, leaves and arabesques, executed in turquoise, deep blue and white, with delicate touches of gold. At its heart is the mihrab niche with its superb stalactite canopy of moulded tiles. It is, as Evliya Çelebi maintained, beautiful beyond all conception.

YEŞIL TÜRBE

Mehmet's Yeşil Türbe, set on an eminence beside the mosque, was completed after Mehmet's death by the same Hacı Ivaz who built the mosque. The outside is adorned with turquoise tiles, inferior replacements from Kütahya of the originals destroyed in the 1855 earthquake. The wooden doors are magnificently carved, and just inside is a lovely fluted arch covered in polychrome tiles. The tilework inside, especially that of the mihrab, is as glorious as that in the mosque; and the Sultan's tomb, raised on a tiled platform and decorated with all the designs and delicate colours that the craftsmen were capable of, with a flowing inscription in yellow superimposed, is a work of superb virtuosity. It was intended to stand alone on its plinth in imperial isolation, but the space was too valuable not to be used, and various sons and daughters, and also a nanny, have joined Mehmet I.

MUSEUM OF TURKISH AND ISLAMIC ARTS

The old imaret, now greatly altered, is just south of the mosque. The fine **medrese**, now the Museum of Turkish and Islamic Arts, stands 100 m or so back towards town on the right, and is well worth a visit. The building is almost square, with cells around three sides of the tree-filled courtyard, the domed dershane occupying the fourth side. The exhibits are well displayed, and include a fascinating range of furniture, pottery, clothes and embroidery, carpets and kilims, arms, jewellery, glass, dervish impedimenta, early decorated Korans, and domestic utensils.

EMIR SULTAN CAMII

A pleasant coda to any tour of Bursa is a visit to Emir Sultan Camii, just up the hill from Yeşil Cami. It is not so much the mosque that is worth seeing, but the superb view over the plain. In front is Yıldırım Beyazit's mosque on its hilltop, and from the graveyard on the west are Mehmet I's Yeşil Cami and türbe, especially lovely when, at certain times of year, they are silhouetted against the setting sun.

The original mosque here was built between 1366 and 1429 by Şeyh Bokhara Şemsettin Mehmet Emir, he who persuaded Yıldırım Beyazit to build the 20 domes of Ulu Cami instead of 20 mosques. Emir Sultan was a dervish from Bokhara, revered both for practical wisdom and saintliness, and was one of Beyazit's most trusted advisers. In 1401, the year before the disastrous Battle of Ankara, Emir Sultan married Beyazit's daughter Hundi Hatun. 20 years later, on the sudden death of Beyazit's son Mehmet I, the 17 year old Murat II ascended the Ottoman throne, and Emir Sultan provided crucial support to withstand two rebellions – by a supposed uncle and a brother, both called Mustafa.

The first mosque fell in an earthquake in the late 18th C., and in 1804 Selim III ordered it to be rebuilt. The old stones were used, but the original form was jettisoned in favour of the more fashionable baroque style. Even today the renown of this saintly dervish brings many pilgrims here to pray at his tomb, like the mosque a reconstruction, built in 1868 by Abdül Aziz.

MOUNT OLYMPUS/ULUDAĞ

According to Strabo, Mt Olympus had in ancient times 'places so well fortified by nature that they can support bands of robbers.' It is not hard to imagine marauding bands hiding in the towering fastnesses of this subsidiary abode of the ancient gods and, like the gods themselves, descending on the dwellers of the fruitful lowlands in a fit of boredom, envy or rage. Even so, according to Homer, did the gods descend on nearby Troy of the Lofty Gates, and on the Greeks encamped in the ringing plains beside their beaked ships. They must have been a hardy lot, gods and robbers alike, for in winter the cold on Mt Olympus is perishing, and even in summer the snow never quite melts from the peaks.

In Byzantine times the mountain was demythologised, monks replacing robbers as the principal human occupants, withdrawing from the world and its seductive warmth for a life of hypothermic contemplation and prayer. When the Ottomans took over in the 14th C., dervishes moved into the abandoned monasteries on the renamed Uludağ, the Great Mountain, and Islamic mysticism replaced its Christian counterpart.

Today the monasteries have disappeared in favour of a cluster of

Swiss-style chalet hotels with steeply pitched roofs, for all the world like an Alpine resort, complete with skiing in winter. In summer there are mountain walks and views to enjoy; and some of the hotels and restaurants and thermal baths stay open all year.

The best way to get there is by the cable car, or teleferik, which operates frequent trips throughout the year, and throughout the day, from its terminal just outside the centre of town; dolmuşes and taxis run from the head of the teleferik to the village. The whole trip takes about 45 minutes. By car or taxi the journey takes just over one hour.

Driving up, it is fascinating to watch deciduous trees – mainly beech, oak and hazel – gradually give way to conifers, in particular black pine. In late April multitudes of grape hyacinths and tiny bright blue crocuses were growing wild in areas clear of snow. Higher up the snow patches grew bigger, finally blanketing the earth, and the cascading streams turned to ice. After the lulling warmth of the valley, the cool clear mountain air was like an energizing tonic.

18

EDIRNE

Edirne, embraced in a curve of the Tunca river where it meets the Arda and Maritsa, and surrounded by green water-meadows and feathery willow trees, stands at the head of the east Thracian plain. The second city of European Turkey, it is 6 km from the Greek border and 18 km from the Bulgarian. It was the Ottoman's main capital for almost a century before the Conquest of Constantinople in 1453, and remained a favourite spot of many Sultans thereafter. It is about 3 hrs drive from Istanbul either by car or bus, and can be seen in a very full day or a gentler 2-day trip. The new highway, usually busy with long-distance traffic from Europe, passes through some rolling steppe-like landscape, in summer bright with sunflowers.

It is well worth making a brief stop en route at Lüleburgaz, where Sinan built one of his loveliest mosque complexes for the great Grand Vezir, Sokollu Mehmet Paşa.

History

Ancient Thrace was a vast territory stretching from the Danube in the north to the Sea of Marmara and the Aegean in the south, and from the borders of Macedonia on the River Strymon in the west to the Black Sea. Homer called it 'rich-soiled Thrace, the mother of sheep', and referred to the inhabitants as 'horse-breeding Thracians', indications of their mainly agricultural and warlike preoccupations. It was an immensely wealthy region, but the Thracians consisted of numerous tribes who, while they all spoke the same language, were incapable of speaking with one voice.

According to the 5th C. BC Herodotus, the Thracian tribes had some very odd ways. The Getae believed they never died but simply passed on to a new life with the god Salmoxis, and every five years they would choose one of their number by lot to take a message to the god. The fortunate winner would be thrown up and impaled on waiting javelins as he fell. The Trausi reversed the normal expression of grief and joy at a birth or death on the principle that life was full of suffering and sorrow. In a third tribe, where polygamy was the fashion, on a man's death his wives would compete fiercely to be judged the most beloved of their late husband, for the privilege of being killed and buried with him. All tribes ran a brisk export trade in their own children; they were content for their daughters to consort with whoever they pleased, but kept an eagle eye on the virtue of their wives. Primarily, Herodotus says, the Thracians were warriors, their most reputable sources of income being war and plunder.

In those early days the settlement on the site of Edirne was called Uscudama. In the 4th C. BC Philip of Macedon, dreaming of leading a Greek army against the Persian Empire, saw as his first task the reduction of Thrace to enable his armies to march to the Hellespont. This accomplished, many cities were renamed, Uscudama receiving the Greek name of Oresteia. The Thracians were too independent to remain under foreign rule for long; when Alexander died in 323, his general Lysimachus, who had inherited Thrace, first had to reconquer it. Two years after Lysimachus' death in 281 the Galatians came and conquered, ruling for about 60 years before the Thracians succeeded in throwing them out.

The Romans kept the province more or less in submission, establishing new cities and administrative districts to which powers of local government were delegated. One of these new cities was established in the 2nd C. AD by the Emperor Hadrian on the site of Oresteia, and named after himself, Hadrianopolis. When Constantinople became the capital of the Roman Empire in 330, Hadrianopolis grew in importance, for its position on the Via Egnatia meant that it benefitted from the great increase in trade along the major routes to the new capital. It soon overtook the old Thracian capital, Philippopolis, in prosperity and size, and became established as the leading city of Thrace.

Hadrianopolis, or Adrianople, remained a border city, the first prize on any northern invader's route to Constantinople. Already in 323 it had seen a victory by Constantine, Emperor of the West, over Licinius, Emperor of the East. 55 years later the Emperor Valens was defeated and killed here by an army of Goths; it was besieged by the Avars in 586, captured by the Bulgars in 914, besieged twice by the Pechenegs in 1049 and 1078, and was the scene of the Battle of

Adrianople in 1205 when the Latin Emperor Baldwin I was captured by the Bulgars who, like the Byzantines, wanted neither Latin religion or Latin rule.

It was the Byzantines themselves, restored since 1261 to Constantinople, who opened the door for the Ottomans to enter Thrace. John Cantacuzenus, aiming at the Byzantine throne, was helped first by Umur Bey, ruler of the Aydınoğlu Turks, and then by the Ottoman leader, Orhan Gazi. In 1346 Orhan led an Ottoman force into Thrace and defeated the Emperor John V Palaeologus, enabling Cantacuzenus to become co-emperor as John VI. Orhan was rewarded with the new Emperor's daughter Theodora in marriage. Six years later the Ottomans gained their first possession in Europe, the fortress of Tzympe in the Dardanelles, and they used it as a base from which to raid and to annexe more Thracian territory. Suddenly the people of Constantinople recognised the Ottoman threat, and some European states even began to talk of a new Crusade to liberate Constantinople. But no action was taken and over the next few years the Ottomans took Çorlu, Lüleburgaz, Malkara and Tekirdağ, as well as other centres along the main lines of communication between Constantinople and the Balkans.

By the early 1360s the scene was set for the new Ottoman Sultan, Murat I, to close in on Adrianople. In 1361 his father had defeated a Byzantine force at Sazlı Dere, SE of the city, and soon afterwards Adrianople surrendered, on condition that its Byzantine inhabitants might live there without constraints. With Adrianople (now Turkicised to Edirne) as their main military base, the Ottomans continued to expand their European territory at the expense of the crumbling Byzantine Empire.

It was in Edirne that Mehmet II planned the conquest of Constantinople, built up his troops and tested his cannons. Even after his victory he did not immediately move his capital to Istanbul but continued to hold court in Edirne for several years. Many later Sultans spent a proportion of each year at Edirne. A particular attraction was the excellence of the hunting. In the mid-16th C. the Imperial ambassador, de Busbecq, wrote about 'a large area of flooded country . . . where the rivers converge, abounding in wild ducks, geese, herons, sea eagles, cranes, hawks and other birds.' It was largely for the sport of capturing these that the Sultan, Süleyman the Magnificent, was 'in the habit of repairing almost every year to Adrianople when winter comes on, and not returning to Constantinople until the frogs begin to be a nuisance with their croaking.' Frogs or no frogs, other Sultans stayed in Adrianople in the summer.

The city's decline began in the 18th C. as the Ottoman Empire itself began its long decline. In Edirne this was accelerated by a disastrous fire in 1745 and an earthquake six years later. In 1829, in one of the Russo-Ottoman wars, Russian troops occupied the city for some time and many of the Muslim inhabitants left. 50 years later the Russians again occupied Edirne and were responsible for widespread damage. In 1913, during the Balkan Wars, Edirne was occupied for four months by the Bulgarians who subjected it to a reign of terror. After World War I, when the Ottoman Empire was in its final stages of disintegration, the whole of eastern Thrace was given by the Allies to Greece, and in 1920 Edirne was occupied yet again, this time by the Greeks. The resistance mounted by Mustafa Kemal, later known as Atatürk, finally resulted in the Treaty of Lausanne in 1923 which included the restoration of Edirne and eastern Thrace to Turkey. Despite these nightmares of the past, Edirne has regained much of its old confidence and prosperity; and it has retained not only some magnificent reminders of the days when the Ottomans were beginning their bid for the mastery of the world, but also the supreme masterpiece of the supreme Ottoman architect – Sinan.

BÜYÜKÇEKMECE BRIDGE

The new highway to Edirne now by-passes Büyükçekmece, so a detour is needed to see its very handsome bridge, one of Sinan's masterpieces. It was built in 1563 on the urgent orders of Süleyman the Magnificent who had nearly drowned in a sudden flood while out hunting in the marshy estuary. It is not a single unit, but a series of 4 hump-back bridges, one after the other, with a total of 28 unequal arches whose piers had to be placed where the ground was firmest.

LÜLEBURGAZ
SOKOLLU MEHMET PAŞA MOSQUE COMPLEX

Diverting from the main Istanbul-Edirne road into the centre of Lüleburgaz, yellow road signs indicate Sokollu Mehmet Paşa külliyesi, one of the most harmonious of Sinan's complexes, built in a lovely pale gold local limestone. The mosque and medrese, together with a dar-ül kura, were built as a combined unit in 1549 for Sokollu Mehmet Paşa, who had in that year been appointed beylerbeyi of Rumeli, an extensive province that included Thrace, Macedonia, Bulgaria, Serbia and Albania.

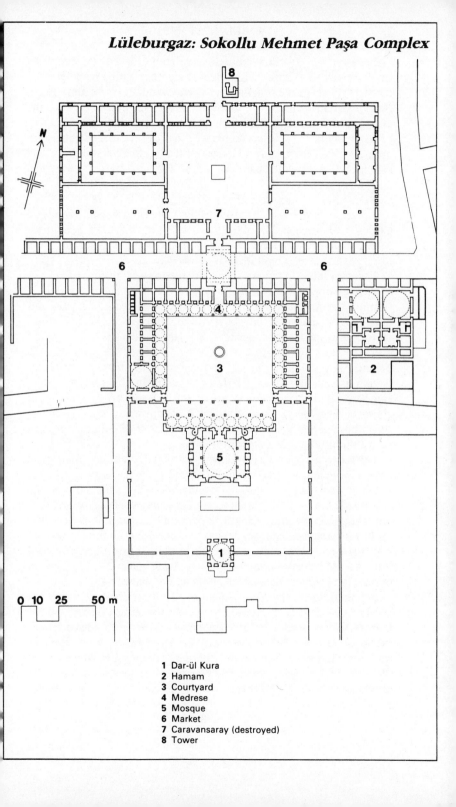

Lüleburgaz: Sokollu Mehmet Paşa Complex

N

8

7

6

6

4

3

2

5

1

0 10 25 50 m

1 Dar-ül Kura
2 Hamam
3 Courtyard
4 Medrese
5 Mosque
6 Market
7 Caravansaray (destroyed)
8 Tower

20 years later Sokollu commissioned Sinan to add to the complex a caravansaray of exceptional grandeur, together with a hamam and a market. By this time Sokollu had been Grand Vezir for four years, Süleyman had been dead for three, and Sinan was already building the great Selimiye mosque in Edirne for Selim II, presumably stopping off occasionally in Lüleburgaz on his way to or from Edirne to check on progress. The canvansaray no longer exists; but there is still the ageing hamam where the merchants would go for washing and barbering, and to have their clothes laundered. But only the mosque, medrese and dar-ül kura, and most of the market, are still in use.

A car park is at the southern end of the walled and tree-filled mosque garden; and in the middle of the south wall is the dar-ül kura, a simple square structure with an octagonal drum and dome. It is now used as a library, and is frequently locked.

The entrance to the mosque and medrese is just opposite the decaying hamam. The entrance arch leads into a rectangular vestibule running the full depth of the narrow back courtyard, the cells and portico of the **medrese**, and above it is an attractive domed gatehouse. Its twin is immediately opposite it. The large courtyard is surrounded on three sides by the domed portico of the medrese with its cells behind. The dershane is, unusually, beside the western entrance, distinguishable by its much larger dome. In the middle of the courtyard is the şadırvan, its fountain enclosed by 12 arches and columns, and the whole covered by an exuberantly wide and wavy roof whose outer edge is supported by a further 12 columns. It is an 18th C. addition, and a delightful one.

The **mosque** is fronted by a double portico, its columns a mixture of grey marble and granite, with one of red granite. As the portico is much wider than the mosque to maintain the symmetry of the courtyard, the back wall at either end contains windows which look onto the garden behind. The entrance portal has a handsome stalactite canopy, and stalactite niches cut into the sides. Inside, the central area is a square surmounted by a dome, and on either side four arches lead into the side areas, above which are wide galleries. The overall impression is one of agreeable simplicity and harmony.

In the middle of the row of medrese cells opposite the mosque is a third way in and out of the courtyard, and this leads directly into the **market**, a long arcaded street whose shops on the south side back onto the medrese cells. Where the dershane is normally to be found in traditional medreses, there is instead a large domed area which covers the width of the market street, and which used to open straight into the caravansaray. Today all that is left of the caravansaray is a square tower with a dome on top; it was never part of the caravansaray but stood outside its north entrance. Now it stands alone.

EDIRNE

The domes and minarets of Selimiye Camii, Sinan's soaring master-piece, are visible long before we reach Edirne, silhouetted against the sky across the flat Thracian plain. The road from Istanbul brings us into the main square, surrounded by three of its great mosques – the Selimiye, Eski Cami and Üç Şerefeli Cami. The roads are spacious and tree-lined, the buildings low because of a local law to allow the mosques to be seen. The whole feel of Edirne is gentle and rural.

ESKI CAMI

Resisting the temptation to go straight to the Selimiye, we should rather start with the oldest of the three, Eski Cami, the Old Mosque, standing 4-square behind its ponderous portico, a smaller, but more developed, version of Yıldırım Beyazit's Ulu Cami in Bursa. Begun in 1403 by Beyazit's eldest son Süleyman only three years after the Bursa Ulu Cami had been completed, and soon after Beyazit himself had died a prisoner of Timur, it was completed in 1414 by his youngest son, Mehmet I, the victor of the 10 year struggle for the Ottoman throne. The architect is named in an inscription as Ala al-Din of Konya. It was the Ulu Cami of Edirne, the great Friday mosque, until the bigger and grander Üç Şerefeli Cami was built some 40 years later, usurping the role and necessitating the change in name to Eski Cami.

A row of taps run across the front of the 5-bayed portico for worshippers to perform their ablutions. It is an unaesthetic solution to the problem created when the şadırvan was removed from the interior of the mosque. The portico is, in any case, a somewhat later addition; and on its back wall, on either side of the entrance portal, are dramatic Arabic inscriptions of the names of Allah and Muhammed.

Inside, nine spacious domes, arranged in a perfect square, spring from four central piers and the side walls. The first dome, just inside the entrance, with its oculus, used to be above the original şadırvan; it and the two in front of it, have octagonal bases, each with a different design of cornice. All the others rise from hexagons and plain pendentives. On the walls are more large inscriptions, together with some decorated tuğras (monograms) of a handful of Sultans, the size and blackness of the calligraphy giving an air of heavy solemnity

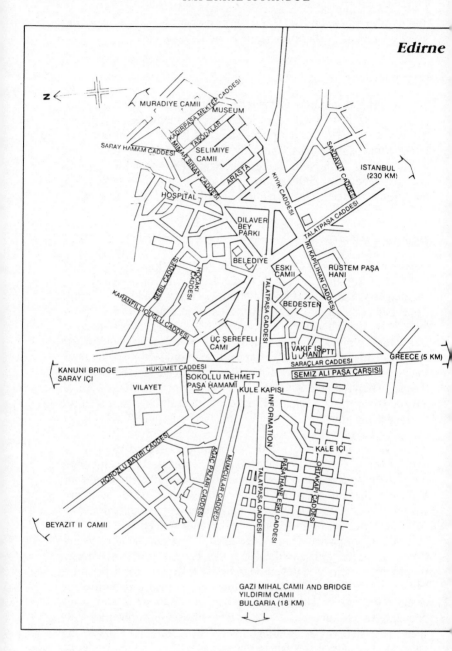

Edirne

oddly at variance with the fanciful decoration in the two baroque domes.

BEDESTEN

To the west of Eski Cami stands the handsome Edirne Bedesten, built by Mehmet I to provide revenue for his newly dedicated mosque. It is closely modelled on the Bursa Bedesten with its two rows of seven domes supported on six piers, an entrance in the middle of each side, and a row of shops in the arches around the outside. So precious were the goods here that Evliya Çelebi tells us that in his time it was guarded at night by 60 Janissaries; Lady Mary Wortley Montagu, who stayed in Edirne in April 1717 and was an enthusiastic sightseer, described it as 'glittering everywhere with gold, rich embroidery and jewels, it makes a very agreeable show.' Today it is less spectacular.

RÜSTEM PAŞA HANI

On the other side of the Bedesten stands the handsome Rüstem Paşa Hanı built by Sinan for Süleyman the Magnificent's scheming Grand Vezir and son-in-law a year or two before he died in 1561. According to the Imperial Ambassador, de Busbecq, who worked for years in Constantinople to arrange a peace treaty between the Emperor and Sultan Süleyman the Magnificent, 'Roostem was always gloomy and brutal, and wished his words to be looked upon as orders . . . the Sultan strongly suspected him of taking bribes.' He was certainly immensely rich, but he did spend some of his vast wealth on worthwhile building projects.

The han is built in alternate courses of brick and stone, with some cheerful little shops operating in the arches of the outer walls, and with small domes over the cells and porticoes that surround the two courtyards inside. The building was restored some years ago, and it is now a tourist hotel.

SEMIZ ALI PAŞA ÇARŞISI

Turning westwards onto Çilingirler Cad. we come to Saraçlar Cad., on the other side of which, behind shops, stands a spectacularly long, narrow covered market built by Sinan for Rüstem Paşa's successor as Grand Vezir. Ali Paşa came from a Christian family in Herzegovina and was carried off at an early age in the devşirme to be educated in the Palace School in Istanbul. He became successively Ağa of the Janissaries, beylerbeyi of Rumeli, and Governor of Egypt. When Rüstem Paşa died in 1561 Ali became Grand Vezir and remained in the job until his death in 1565.

A particularly agreeable picture of him is painted by de Busbecq who found him 'of a mild and calm disposition, polite, highly intelligent; he has a mind which can deal with the most difficult problems . . . he is tall of stature, and his face has a serious expression which is full of charm . . . He is anxious to obtain by courtesy and fairness – in fact, by treating me as a friend – the objects which Roostem sought to gain by bullying and intimidation and threats.' Small wonder that it was with Ali that de Busbecq finally negotiated the peace treaty. Two features which de Busbecq does not mention, but for which Semiz Ali Pasa was renowned, were his spectacular corpulence (semiz = fat) and his wit. He would hardly recognise the down-market merchandise in his market today, a far cry from the 'rich goods' that Lady Mary Wortley Montagu saw in 1717. But the bustle and backchat are doubtless much as they always were.

KALE IÇI

On the other side of Semiz Ali Paşa's market is an area known as Kale Içi (inside the castle), the heart of ancient and Byzantine Adrianople and, until earlier this century, the home of Edirne's Greek and Jewish population. It is laid out on a grid plan in the triangle bounded by the Tunca river, Saraçlar Cad. and Talat Paşa Cad. Parts of the Byzantine walls can be seen near the river at the far west end. It is a pleasant area to stroll in, still with several of its old wooden houses. At the SE end of Cumhuriyet Cad. is the shell of a once fine synagogue, built in 1906, for which restoration is rumoured.

KULE KAPISI

From the end of Semiz Ali Paşa Çarşısı that abuts on Talat Paşa Cad. (the broad avenue that leads to the Bulgarian border), we can see on the other side of the avenue and a short distance down a side street a solid and squat Byzantine tower. It tapers slightly at the top, and on it is set a smaller octagonal tower. Kule Kapısı, tower gate, is all that is left of the main gate of the citadel of Byzantine Adrianople. The original defences were built by Hadrian, and in 1123 were rebuilt, together with this tower, by John II Comnenus in his attempt to keep out the Pechenegs. Until its restoration for touristic purposes, it was used for another kind of defence by the municipal fire brigade.

ÜÇ ŞEREFELİ CAMI

Beside Cumhuriyet Meydanı rises the distinctive outline of Üç Šerefeli Cami, its four minarets of varying heights and decorated with different designs. The tallest has three balconies (üç şerefe), said to have been the first such in Islam, and certainly a sufficient novelty to give the mosque its name. At 67 m it remained the tallest minaret in the Ottoman Empire for over 100 years until Sinan capped it at the Selimiye. Each balcony of each minaret is reached by its own spiral staircase, up which the müezzins of old would make their separate ways to harmonize the call to prayer. Today, by way of anticlimax, a loud-speaker system is operated by a single müezzin at ground level.

Üç Şerefeli Cami was built between 1438 and 1447 by Murat II, son of Mehmet I and father of Mehmet the Conqueror, to replace his father's foundation as the great Friday mosque of Edirne. At the time it was the grandest and most ambitious mosque anywhere in the Ottoman Empire, exceeding in scale, and originality of design, anything that had been built in Bursa or elsewhere.

Unlike the Bursa mosques the **courtyard** is outside, and it is this that we enter first, a large rectangular space surrounded by porticoes with alternating red and white stones in the voussoirs of the arches. The six great marble columns in front of the mosque support five large arches, while around the other three sides the arches are smaller and closer, carried on suitably smaller columns, all but one of verd-antique. The şadırvan in the centre is an attractive and unadorned low pool with 24 facets, and open to the sky. The main entrance to the mosque has a handsomely carved stalactite canopy.

Inside, the **mosque** consists of a long narrow rectangular space, whose small windows cast a peaceful and shadowy light, much in keeping with the mystical spirit of Murat II. As we enter we come immediately under the great shallow dome which covers the whole of the central area. 24 m in diameter, it was by far the largest dome yet attempted by the Ottomans, and at the time it seemed a miracle of apparently unsupported space.

Unusually, the dome covers a hexagon formed by four piers set in the walls and two great free-standing piers. A diamond-pattern cornice runs around the top of the arches, with two corbels in each angle, and above it the dome is pierced by small windows. Beyond each pier are two smaller domes, covering areas originally for the use of dervishes. The lovely limestone of the walls sets off the unusually restrained painted decoration; and the plain mihrab and mimber add to the simple beauty of this grand and spacious mosque.

SOKOLLU MEHMET PAŞA HAMAMI

On the other side of Hükümet Cad. from Üç Şerefeli Cami stands a hamam built by Sinan for Sokollu Mehmet Paşa in 1579. It is in two parts, one for men, the other for women. It is considerably less grand than it used to be because all the tiles have been lost, but it is still a handsome and harmoniously proportioned building, with some beautiful decorative plasterwork.

SELIMIYE CAMII

Having so far resisted the pull of Selimiye Camii, we should now give in and make our way across the gardens that climb the little eminence on which it stands. It rises from its hilltop with majestic symmetry, each level seeming to suggest the one above, its semi-domes and arched windows and the little turrets around the drum – all emphasising the crowning curve of the dome. At the four corners stand the identical fluted minarets, slenderest of sentinels, each soaring to 70 m and each punctuated with three finely decorated balconies.

The only incongruity of this elegant and harmonious mosque is that it should have been created for Selim II, the obese and alcoholic son and heir of Süleyman the Magnificent. It was begun in 1569, three years after Selim became Sultan, and was completed in 1575, a year after his death. In commissioning the by now elderly Sinan to build it, he provided that supreme artist with the chance to create what he himself regarded as his finest work.

Running along the entire west side of the complex, and providing one of the entrances up to the walled terrace that surrounds the mosque, is a T-shaped covered market – the **Kavaflar Arasta** or cobblers' market. It was built by Sinan's pupil and successor as chief architect, Davut Ağa, about ten years after the completion of the mosque, and was intended to generate income for it by providing 126 shops for cobblers – evidently a trade for which there was much call in Edirne. It also included a mektep near the centre of the market, and its

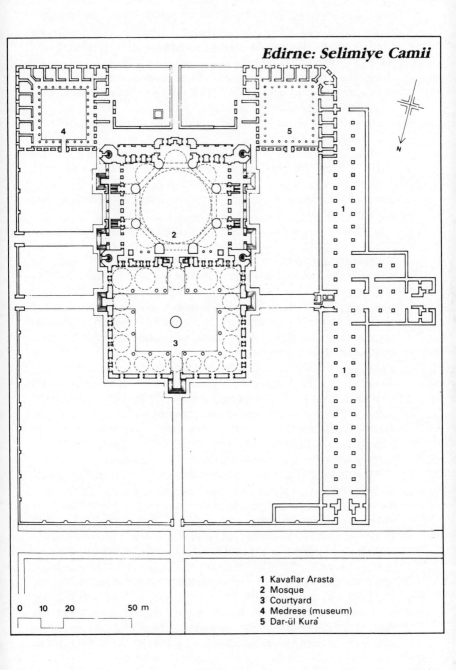

Edirne: Selimiye Camii

N

1 Kavaflar Arasta
2 Mosque
3 Courtyard
4 Medrese (museum)
5 Dar-ül Kura

0   10   20   50 m

fine loggia remains. Today there is not a cobbler to be seen, nor even many shoe shops, the arcades occupied instead by retailers of every kind of useful household article, sweets, souvenirs, clothes and jewellery. The junction of the T is covered by a dome on a 16-sided drum which is decorated with elaborate pierced stone carving between miniature columns and arches. Behind this domed area a wide staircase leads up to the mosque precinct above.

Opposite the top of the stairs is one of the three entrances to the courtyard, and to the right of it is one of the main doorways into the mosque itself. Unlike the Üç Şerefeli Cami, where the courtyard seems a necessary prelude to the mosque itself, here one of its functions has been usurped by subsidiary taps outside other doors, where worshippers can perform their ablutions and go directly into the **mosque**.

Inside, all is space and light, that soaring dome covering a larger area than seems possible, springing from eight piers which, though huge, are set around the edge of a vast central space in a way that gives no sense of heaviness. For the first time the dome surpassed that of Aya Sofya in width. That it was Sinan's express intention to do so is made clear in a passage in the *Tezkeret-ül-Bünyan*, notes which he dictated about his work: 'Those that pass for architects among the Christians say that they have defeated the Moslems because no dome has been built in the Islamic world that can rival the dome of Aya Sofya. It greatly grieved my heart that they should say that to build so large a dome was so difficult a task. I determined to erect such a mosque, and with the help of God, in the reign of Sultan Selim Khan, I made the dome of this mosque six cubits (nearly 3 m) wider and four cubits (nearly 2 m) deeper than that of Aya Sofya.' He is guilty of wild hyperbole over the width – it is just over ¼ m wider; but at seven days journey from Istanbul, the Sultan may have been taken in.

Four semi-circular exedras reach into the corners of the central square; and aisles on the east and west sides, with galleries above them, extend the overall ground plan to a rectangle. The mihrab apse in the middle of the south wall, crowned by a semi-dome, seems somewhat apart from, though integrated with, the main body of the mosque. The **mihrab** is of Marmara marble, almost plain apart from its stalactite canopy, and its very simplicity highlights the lovely floral tiles from the very best period of Iznik's production that adorn the lower parts of the apse walls, with a deep frieze of tiles with Koranic inscriptions running across the top of them. Indeed, throughout the mosque the soft honey-colour of the sandstone of which it is built sets off to perfection the restrained areas of radiant tile decoration. These include the marble **mimber,** carved with astonishing delicacy in elaborate geometrical designs. The conical cap also has fine tiles.

Beneath the dome stands a low wooden **tribune,** painted inside and out with designs of flowers and leaves. It rests on 12 marble columns linked by jaunty foliate arches. The column at the NW corner is more like a sawn-off pier, and within it are the stairs by which the chanters reached their elevated position. The pier also contains recesses for jugs to be filled with water from the drinking fountain beneath the tribune.

In the SW corner of the mosque the gallery extends outwards to form the **imperial loge,** supported on verd-antique columns linked by four slightly pointed arches in whose spandrels are more fine floral Iznik tiles. The loge itself, usually closed to the public, is also adorned with fine Iznik tiles, with interweaving flowers, stems and leaves, trees in blossom waving in the breeze with tulips growing at their feet, crowned with a frieze of flowing Koranic inscriptions. But some of the original tiles were taken by the Russians in 1878 In the south wall is the mihrab niche, but it contains a surprise, for at its centre is a pair of superb inlaid doors which open to reveal a window with a view of houses and trees and the sky above.

Emerging into the **courtyard** it is hard not to be struck by its blend of grandeur and warmth, the sweep of its arcades emphasised by the alternate red and white of the voussoirs. Three great rounded arches on tall columns stand in front of the mosque, with two little ogee arches tucked in on either side of the central span. The columns are in such a variety of marble, grey and red granite, and verd-antique that they give the impression of being a job lot taken over from crumbled Byzantine buildings; but the capitals have fine 16th C. stalactite carving, and echo the elaborate design above the portal. In the centre of the courtyard stands a lovely low 16-sided şadırvan pool, open to the sky, with delicate pierced carving around the top.

Unlike the Süleymaniye and other imperial mosque complexes in Istanbul, the Selimiye has few associated foundations. We have seen the Kavaflar Arasta, and there remain two others, one in each of the southern corners of the precinct. In the SW is the **dar-ül kura** for the readers of the Koran, and in the SE the **medrese;** both have cells on two adjacent sides of a square courtyard. Between them is a cemetery, dotted with cypress trees. The medrese now houses a **Museum of Turkish and Islamic Arts.** In another building behind it there is an **Archaeological and Ethnographical Museum.** Both are open daily except Monday.

The other monuments of Edirne are outside the centre of town, and are most easily reached by car or taxi unless you have plenty of time and an enthusiasm for walking. Both the Muradiye and Beyazit II Camii should not on any account be missed.

MURADIYE CAMII (only open immediately after prayer times)

It takes about 10 mins to walk to Muradiye Camii from the Selimiye, along Mimar Sinan Cad., which first goes uphill, then dips before climbing another small hill on the right, on top of which stands this enchanting mosque. So intimate is it that you would hardly suspect that it was built by the same Sultan who built the grand Üç Şerefeli here, or the Muradiye complex in Bursa. Yet this too is a work of Murat II, built just a few years before he started on the Üç Şerefeli; but it looks back to old models rather an experimenting with new.

Muradiye Camii was built in 1435 as a dervish zaviye. Murat was profoundly influenced by the dervishes and their mysticism, and on this occasion he had dreamed that Mevlâna Celâleddin Rûmı, the 13th C. founder of the Mevlevi order, came and asked him to build a hospice in Edirne. Murat chose this secluded hilltop, with a wide view over what was then open countryside; today it includes the outskirts of Edirne where the town meets the fields, some of them green with vegetables, others gold with corn, and all fringed with the dark green of the trees by the river.

In this peaceful spot Murat built a zaviye modelled on those T-shaped imperial mosques in Bursa that were both mosque and zaviye. Steps lead up to the prayer hall which has eyvans on either side of the first domed area. Murat had his zaviye decorated with exceptional early 15th C. tiles, some hexagonal with blue and white flower patterns showing a distinct Chinese influence, others with colours and designs similar to those in the Yeşil Cami in Bursa – blue, green, yellow, purplish blue, turquoise and white. The **mihrab** is an exuberant composition, with moulded tiles forming a stalactite canopy, framed by arabesques and surrounded by geometrical designs and Koranic inscriptions. The upper areas still show the remains of painted decoration – when everything was new and glowing the interior of the zaviye must have been magnificent indeed.

Later in Murat's reign it was converted into a mosque, and a tekke was built beside it to house the dervishes. In 1751, it was badly damaged in an earthquake, and extensively repaired, though to its original plan.

SARAY IÇI

Back at the main square, we turn right for a short distance along Talat Paşa Cad., then right again beside Üç Şerefeli Cami. Those with time only to see Beyazit II Camii should turn left where the yellow sign indicates, and the road leads over the Tunca river to the mosque complex. Alternatively keep straight ahead, and this road comes soon to **Kanûni Süleyman Köprüsü**, the bridge of Süleyman the Magnificent (known to the Turks as kanûni, the lawgiver), built for that Sultan by Sinan in 1554.

This handsome bridge crosses the Tunca and brings us to **Saray Içi**, 'inside the palace', the island where Murat II began, and Mehmet II and his successors continued, the famous Edirne Sarayı. It was blown up by the Turks when the Russians occupied their city for the second time in 1878, because it contained all their munitions. Now only a few of the great trees remain, planted by Mehmet, but there are no reminders of the resplendent palaces and pavilions that stood among them. Here, in the spring of 1457, splendid 2-month-long celebrations were held in honour of the circumcision of Mehmet's two sons, Beyazit and Mustafa. There were readings from the Koran, theological discussions, poetry recitations, story telling, horse races, archery contests, the distribution by the Sultan of money and fine clothes, and magnificent presentations to the Sultan from his loyal subjects. Only the ruins of a few later buildings still stand.

Today the island is famous for the Kırkpınar Wrestling Matches, held here every year in June/July. It is one of the great events in the Turkish calendar, with all the atmosphere and trappings of a huge carnival – a time when Edirne is to be headed for, or avoided at all costs, according to taste. The contest is said to date from the mid-14th C. when the Süleyman, son of Orhan Gazi, had won the first Ottoman foothold in Thrace and his heroes needed an active occupation to while away the time between battles with the Byzantines.

On the other side of the island **Fatih Sultan Köprüsü**, the much restored bridge of the Conqueror, takes us onto the other bank of the Tunca. As its name suggests, the bridge was built by Mehmet the Conqueror at the time when he was extending the palace that his father had started.

BEYAZIT II CAMII

Taking the first road (or footpath) to the left on the other side of the river, we soon see Beyazit II Camii and its attendant foundations, built

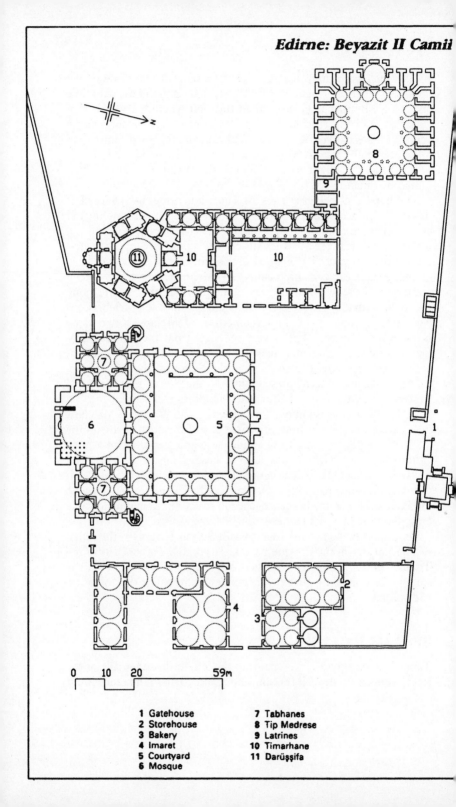

Edirne: Beyazit II Camii

0   10   20   59m

1 Gatehouse   7 Tabhanes
2 Storehouse   8 Tip Medrese
3 Bakery   9 Latrines
4 Imaret   10 Timarhane
5 Courtyard   11 Darüşşifa
6 Mosque

on the river bank behind substantial dykes. It is an exceptionally handsome and extensive complex, crowned by over 100 domes, and set in an irregularly shaped walled precinct large enough to accommodate the camels and impedimenta of the caravans that stopped here. It was built 1484–8, probably by an architect called Hayrettin who worked on several buildings for Beyazit II. It includes a mosque, tip medrese, hospital, asylum, tabhanes, imaret, storehouse and a bakery – an astonishingly wide-ranging establishment for social and religious welfare in a harmonious and tightly planned architectural unit.

The gatehouse opens into the precinct opposite the entrance to the mosque courtyard. On the far left are two smaller buildings, the first with 12 small domes, 8 in front covering a large **storehouse** for food, behind which is the **bakery** with two large ovens beside it. The second, larger, building is the **imaret** which has 11 domes arranged around a courtyard which opens onto the road outside the precinct. Two long refectories, each covered with three domes, border the courtyard on the south and west sides, while under the remaining five domes to the north is the kitchen, and the vestibule that leads to it.

The mosque **courtyard** is rectangular with columns of ancient verd-antique in front of the mosque, and the voussoirs of the linking arches in alternating bands of grey and white. All but three of the other columns are of grey marble, the rogue ones being granite, a red and two grey, and on these three sides the voussoirs are picked out strikingly in red and white. All the columns are crowned with handsome stalactite capitals. The insides of the domes behind these arches are worth looking at; four in the portico have the original plasterwork that transforms them into whorls and shells. In the centre of the courtyard is a low şadırvan pool that clearly once had a canopy, for the bases of the eight columns on which it rested are still visible. Well-heads stood in the two northern corners, but only one remains.

Passing through the finely carved marble portal, we enter the **mosque**, a simple square whose dome soars in a single dramatic sweep from pendentives which spring from deep in the corners to form four great arches. Sadly the bold simplicity of the design has been cluttered by some wildly rococo painting on every available surface. The most interesting feature is the **imperial loge** to the left of the mihrab which is supported on a forest of small columns (most of them recycled from some more ancient building), each connected to those around it by elegant arches.

On either side of the mosque stand two identical **tabhanes**, each under a cluster of nine domes, the interiors arranged in a cross shape, with four eyvans opening off a central square court, and with an enclosed room at each corner.

At the NW end of the precinct stands the **tip medrese**, its domed cells arranged around three sides of the square central courtyard, and the dershane with its larger dome in the middle of the west side. The domed portico, however, runs round all four sides. Commodious latrines are in the SE corner, linking the medrese with the hospital. It has been restored by the University of Thrace, as too has the hospital complex adjacent to it.

A doorway in the wall on the right as we come out of the medrese leads into the first part of the hospital, the **timarhane**, or asylum, which surrounds a garden. In the NE corner stand three rooms which housed the hospital kitchens, while down the entire west side runs a portico of 11 arches, behind which are seven cells; the first contains the latrines (now modernised) that once connected with the medrese.

At the far end is a handsome domed gatehouse which leads, on the left-hand side, to a 2-domed room in which the University of Thrace has made an interesting little **Museum of Health**. But the main function of the gatehouse is to lead from the garden to the heart of the hospital complex, through a courtyard at the other side of which is the magnificent hexagonal hall of the **darüşşifa**, the hospital proper, entered through another splendid portal. It is a double hexagon, the central court with its central şadırvan and lofty dome opening into six domed eyvans; and in each corner a further square room is reached through the eyvans. Above the arches of the central court runs a fine stalactite cornice, cascading down into squinches at the angles, and from it rises the dome, pierced by 12 windows around its base, and with a little cupola on top. Under this dome, according to Evliya Çelebi, ten singers and instrumentalists would come three times a week to play music for the hospital patients to provide 'a cure for the sick, a medicine for the afflicted, spiritual nourishment for the mad, and a remedy for melancholy.' 'Melancholy' was the euphemism for mental derangement caused by the widespread use of very large quantities of hashish – up to 100 gm (¼ lb) daily.

That the hospital catered for physical as well as mental illnesses is indicated by the generous provisions made for staffing it. Beyazit's original vakfiye stipulated a head doctor, two assistants, two ophthalmic specialists, two surgeons, a dentist, four nursing attendants, a pharmacist, two cooks, a clerk, steward, major-domo, cleaner and washer of corpses. The hospital continued to function until 1916.

YILDIRIM CAMII

The oldest mosque in Edirne, now in a sad state of disrepair, is fairly close to Beyazit II Camii as the crow flies, being a little further downstream on the same side of the Tunca river. Turn left out of the Beyazit complex, and left down its west side, then right onto the footpath along the embankment, or the un-metalled road beside it. At the main road, by a bridge over the Tunca, turn right. If coming from the town centre, Talat Paşa Cad. leads direct to this bridge. 200 m after the bridge, turn right over a narrow 16th C. bridge and a short distance the other side of it stands an old mosque variously known as Yıldırım Camii (after Beyazit I) or Küpheli Cami, the mosque with earrings. The latter name has two possible sources: one from two marble hoops that used to be inside the mosque near the mihrab, the other from the theory that Yıldırim Beyazit had the mosque built for his daughter Küpheli Hatun. However, it has now been convincingly argued by Professor Aptullah Kuran that Yıldırım Beyazit had nothing at all to do with the mosque and that it was built by his father, Murat I, some time after he captured Edirne in 1361. It was built on the ruins of a Byzantine church, the lower courses of which are still distinguishable, and was intended as a combined mosque and zaviye with eyvans opening off the central court. In front of the mosque is an şadırvan pool and a Byzantine column.

MIHAL GAZI CAMII AND BRIDGE

Returning towards town, just before you reach the bridge, on the right hand side of the road stands Mihal Gazi Camii, built in 1421 by a Byzantine nobleman, one of many who converted to Islam and joined the Ottomans. So enthusiastic was he in his new religion, and in the wars in which he fought, that he was awarded the title Gazi – Warrior of the Faith. The bridge beside his mosque was originally a 13th C. Byzantine structure, but it is called Mihal Gazi Köprüsü by proximity to the mosque, and has almost become Ottoman after centuries of repairs.

Postscript. 10 km out of Edirne, just off the main road to the Greek border, is the **Karaağaç railway station**. This grand building was constructed in the late 19th C. for the new Orient Express railway from Paris to Constantinople, and was closed in 1974. A short section of track remains, complete with a very stationary steam locomotive. The building is being used by the University of Thrace.

APPENDIX A

THE ARCHAEOLOGICAL MUSEUM
(Open daily except Monday)

The first collection of antiquities found in the Ottoman Empire was begun in 1846 by the then Minister of War, Fethi Ahmet Paşa, a brother-in-law of Sultan Abdül Mecit I. They were stored in the church of Haghia Eirene, but by 1874 space there had become restricted, and the antiquities were moved to the nearby Çinili Köşk. But the real founder of the museum was the director who was appointed in 1881. Hamdi Bey was an artist and the son of an earlier Grand Vezir, Ibrahim Edhem Paşa, a combination which gave him a foothold in the camps of both art and power. One of his first acts was to prohibit the further export of antiquities from the Empire. In 1887 he excavated the royal necropolis at Sidon and discovered the group of sarcophagi, including the Alexander Sarcophagus, that are the chief glory of the museum.

It was these sarcophagi – too big for the Çinili Köşk – that necessitated the construction of the present building, the main body of which was opened to the public in 1896. The north wing was added in 1902, and the south in 1908. A new extension, immediately behind the original building, was opened in 1991 to celebrate the 100th anniversary of the foundation of the museum. The entire interior has been completely redesigned and all the objects are superbly displayed. It is one of the finest museums in the world.

This outline lists only items of outstanding interest, starting at the far end of the old building, on the left of the main entrance, and working back to the other end of the building in Room 20; then going to the new extension, starting from the ground floor and working up.

Rooms 1 – 7 – currently closed. When re-opened, the main object of interest is the splendid, lavishly carved, 2nd-3rd C. AD **Sidamara sarcophagus**. There are also some stelae and mosaics.

Rooms 8 & 9 – The Royal Necropolis of Sidon.

Room 8 contains the late 4th C. BC **Alexander Sarcophagus**, not that of Alexander himself, but named for the magnificent high relief sculptures on its sides, with two figures of Alexander, one in battle, the other at the hunt. In the same room is the **mourners' sarcophagus**, *c.*350 BC, also beautifully carved, and 3 smaller sarcophagi.

Room 9 contains more sarcophagi from the royal necropolis at Sidon, including the *c.*500 BC **Tabnit sarcophagus**, and the **mummy** of the Sidonian King Tabnit; also two fine carved sarcophagi – the *c.*400 BC **Lycian sarcophagus** and the 5th C. BC s**atrap sarcophagus**. There are also some 5th-4th C. BC **anthropoid sarcophagi**, similar to Egyptian mummy cases, and several objects found in the Sidon tombs.

Rooms 10 – 12. These rooms now contain shops, an entrance to the new wing, and the main entrance to the museum. In the entrance stands a colossal 6th C. BC **statue of Bes**, the Cypriot Hercules, minus his customary fountain and manhood.

Room 13 – Sculpture of the Archaic Period, 7th-6th C. BC
This room contains some fine statues and reliefs, especially a superb smiling **head of Kronos**, lions, bulls and seated figures from the **sacred way from Miletus to Didyma** and votive steles and a **statue of Cybele**.

Room 14 – Anatolia under the Persians, 546–333 BC
These funerary stelae, statues and reliefs show the new style introduced by the Persians. They include a **statue of a lion from the Mausoleum of Halicarnassus**, other **statues from Sardis** and **reliefs from Xanthus**.

Room 15 – Attic Grave Stelae and Reliefs, 6th-5th C. BC
Originals, and Roman copies of earlier Athenian sculptures and reliefs, including a **statue of Athena** and several **reliefs** depicting scenes from classical mythology.

Room 16 – Sculpture of the Hellenistic Period, 330–30 BC
There are **3 heads of Alexander the Great**, one a copy *c.*300 BC of Lysippus' original; a mid-3rd C. BC **statue of Alexander** from Magnesia-on-the-Maeander with the inscription 'Maenas the sculptor' on it.

Room 17 – Examples from the Sculpture of Magnesia-on-the-Maeander and Tralles; Hellenistic to Roman periods
These sites were excavated between 1890 and 1902; the sculpture includes a wonderful 3rd C. BC **athlete**, and a **caryatid**, both from Tralles.

Room 18 – Roman Portrait Art
This room exhibits statues and busts of Emperors, including a fine **head of Arcadius**.

Room 19 – Three Marble Cities of Roman Anatolia
Aphrodisias, Ephesus and Miletus were major centres of marble carving in the Roman period. This room, dedicated to the memory of the archaeologist Kenan Erim, who excavated Aphrodisias, shows some of the fine carving that came from their workshops.

Room 20 – Sculptural Art in the Roman Period, end 1st C. BC to 4th C. AD
Statues and reliefs of gods and mythological characters and scenes.

THE NEW EXTENSION
The ground floor includes a children's museum and a reconstruction of the façade of the Doric temple of Athena at Assos.

The first floor contains an imaginative display showing **Istanbul through the Ages**, from the Lower Palaeolithic period (400,000 years ago), through the Chalcolithic, Neolithic and Iron Ages, and into Hellenistic, Roman, Byzantine and Ottoman times. Within each period, objects are grouped by subject and area and show the relevant tools, carvings, paintings and jewellery, as well as photographs and reconstructions. Here we can see the things that were removed for safe-keeping from sites – such as the frescoes of St Francis from the church of the Kyriotissa (Kalenderhane Camii) and the rich carvings from the church of St Polyeuctos. There are also sections on the Bosphorus, the Ottoman Conquest of 1453, Genoese Galata, and the Golden Horn.

The second floor contains further displays portraying different periods of **Anatolian history and civilisation** from earliest times. There are also some fascinating and beautifully arranged subject/area displays of Troy, the Hittites and the Phrygians.

the Turkish Naval Academy, where once stood the Byzantine Church of the Panaghia Kamariotissa, the chapel of one of the two former monasteries.

Proti, near. The least developed of the four big islands, it still has lovely wild areas and coast; but the population – once predominantly Armenian – has increased greatly since the mid-1980s, and restaurants have opened. Virtually nothing remains of the island's two Byzantine monasteries.

APPENDIX B

THE MUSEUM OF THE ANCIENT ORIENT

This houses a superb collection of antiquities from some of the earliest civilizations in the Middle East – areas where the Ottoman writ once ran. The building dates to 1883 when it housed the School of Fine Arts; in 1917 this was moved to a new site and the building was converted into a museum to house the influx of items brought here for safe keeping during World War I.

The youngest items are from pre-Islamic **south Arabia** and **Nabataea**, 4th C. BC–6th C. AD. Of astonishing antiquity, some from the 4th to the end of the 1st millenia BC, are **Sumerian**, **Akkadian** and **Assyrian** objects; **Egyptian** (*c.*3200–300 BC); **Hatti** (*c.*3000–1700); **Hittite** (*c.*1700–1200 BC); **neo-Hittite** (*c.*1200–700 BC); **Babylonian** (*c.*2000–6th C. BC); **Urartu** (early 1st mill. BC).

APPENDIX C

THE PRINCES' ISLANDS

There are nine islands in this little archipelago off the Asian shore of the Sea of Marmara, and ferries, run to the four largest from either Sirkeci or Kabataş jetties. Many Istanbullus live on one of the islands for the summer, commuting to work in Istanbul by ferry. It is a delightful excursion for visitors to the city to do a reverse commute and spend a day, or part of a day, on one of the islands, for here all motorized vehicles are banned, and the peace is broken only by the muffled clip-clop of the horses (shod with rubber to prevent slipping on the hills), as they pull antiquated phaetons occupied by residents and visitors alike. In Byzantine times the islands were wild and remote, perfect settings for the numerous monasteries that were established there for withdrawal from the Byzantine complexities of life in the capital. They were also used for the banishment of inconvenient empresses or co-emperors. There the monasteries remained throughout the Ottoman period, with small but increasing numbers of Armenians and Greeks living there too.

Büyükada, Principo to the Byzantines, is the largest, most populated, and most popular island, and one of the most beautiful. The town has grown in recent years and now sports chic boutiques and restaurants, but it still has great charm. The phaeton drivers in the main square offer a short tour (küçüktur) or a long one (büyüktur) of the island, the latter doing the full circuit along the shore road. Lovely old wooden houses, as well as modern villas, line the road and the shore, gradually thinning out until at the far end of the island there is no human habitation at all, just the sounds of the sea, the breeze in the pine trees and the horses hooves on the road. At the top of both hills are monasteries, that on the far end the very attractive Monastery of St George, of Byzantine origin but with a modern building.:s Greek name of

Heybeliada, Byzantine Halki, is the next largest island. There are also restaurants in the town, and the phaeton drivers also offer short and long tours, both considerably shorter than those in Büyükada, but just as agreeable. The building that dominates the town, beside the landing stage, is the Turkish Naval Academy, where once stood the Byzantine Church of the Panaghia Kamariotissa, the chapel of one of the two former monasteries.

Burgaz was known as Antigone in Byzantine times, and is still called that by the Greeks who live there. It is considerably less developed than the two larger islands, but the town is charming and has a few restaurants. There are a couple of modern Greek churches, built on the sites of Byzantine churches.

Kınalı is the nearest to Istanbul which accounts for its Greek name of Proti, near. The least developed of the four big islands, it still has lovely wild areas and coast; but the population – once predominantly Armenian – has increased greatly since the mid-1980s, and restaurants have opened. Virtually nothing remains of the island's two Byzantine monasteries.

The remaining 5 islands, Kaşık (spoon), Sedef, Yassı, Sivri and Tavşan, are tiny, the last 2 uninhabited; only Sedef has occasional ferries in summer.

THE TURKISH LANGUAGE

SPELLING AND PRONUNCIATION

Modern Turkish spelling has been used throughout this guide. Most letters
have a similar sound to their English equivalents, but each is pronounced in
one way only; others are similar to French or German, and there are some
letters that are unique to Turkish. The following guide may be helpful:

a	as in c*a*rt
c	as *j* in *j*acket
ç	as *ch* in *ch*ance
e	as in b*e*t
g	always hard as in *g*et
ğ	unsounded, but lengthens preceding vowel; e.g. Ağa is pronounced A-a
ı	similar to the *a* in *a*bout
i	as in b*i*t
j	as in French; or as *s* in plea*s*ure
ö	as in German; or as *ur* in h*ur*t
ş	*sh* as in *s*ugar
ü	as in German; or as *u* in t*u*be

Stress tends to fall fairly evenly, or slightly more on the last syllable; never on
the penultimate syllable as in English.

A BASIC PRIMER

0	*sıfır*
½	*yarım*
1½	*bir buçuk*
1	*bir*
2	*iki*

3	*üç*
4	*dört*
5	*beş*
6	*altı*
7	*yedi*
8	*sekiz*
9	*dokuz*
10	*on*
11	*on bir*
12	*on iki* – etc.
20	*yirmi*
21	*yirmi bir* – etc.
30	*otuz*
40	*kırk*
50	*elli*
60	*altmış*
70	*yetmiş*
80	*seksen*
90	*doksan*
100	*yüz*
101	*yüz bir* – etc.
200	*iki yüz* – etc.
1000	*bin*
1001	*bin bir* – etc.
2000	*iki bin* – etc.
1 million	*bir milyon*
Sunday	*Pazar*
Monday	*Pazartesi*
Tuesday	*Salı*
Wednesday	*Çarşamba*
Thursday	*Perşembe*
Friday	*Cuma*
Saturday	*Cumartesi*
January	*Ocak*
February	*Şubat*
March	*Mart*
April	*Nisan*
May	*Mayis*
June	*Haziran*
July	*Temmuz*
August	*Ağustos*
September	*Eylül*
October	*Ekim*
November	*Kasım*
December	*Aralık*
minute	*dakika*
hour, time	*saat*

day	*gün*
week	*hafta*
month	*ay*
year	*sene, yıl*
today	*bugün*
yesterday	*dün*
tomorrow	*yarın*
morning	*sabah*
noon	*öğle*
afternoon	*öğleden sonra*
evening	*akşam*
night	*gece*
hello	*merhaba*
welcome	*hoş geldiniz* (reply: *hoş bulduk*)
thank you	*teşekkür ederim or merci*
please	*lütfen*
good morning or good day	*günaydın*
good evening	*iyi akşamlar*
good night	*iyi geceler*
yes	*evet*
no	*hayır*
there is	*var*
there isn't	*yok*
tea	*çay*
coffee	*kahve*
good	*iyi*
nice, beautiful	*güzel*
very	*çok*
very nice	*çok güzel*
bad	*fena*
I	*ben*
you (sing.)	*sen*
you (plur.)	*siz*
we	*biz*
he, she, it	*o*
they	*onlar*
how are you?	*nasılsın* (sing.)/*nasılsınız* (plur.)
I am well	*iyiyim*
where?	*nerede?*
here	*burada*
there (near)	*şurada*
there (far)	*orada*
when?	*nezaman?*
now	*şimdi*
a little later	*biraz sonra*
later	*sonra*
why?	*niçin?*
what?	*ne?*

320

how?	*nasıl?*
how many?	*kaç?*
how much?	*ne kadar?*
money	*para*
change	*bozuk para*
expensive	*pahalı*
cheap	*ucuz*
where are you from?	*nerelisiniz?*
I am English/American	*Ingilizim/Amerikalıyım*
what is your name?	*isminiz nedir?*
hot	*sıcak*
cold	*soğuk*
small	*küçük*
big	*büyük*
tired	*yorgun*
sick	*hasta*
right	*sağ*
left	*sol*
straight ahead	*doğru*
car	*oto*
petrol	*benzin*
taxi	*taksi*
shared taxi	*dolmuş*
bus	*otobüs*
ticket	*bilet*
restaurant	*lokanta*
food	*yemek*
plate	*tabak*
knife	*bıçak*
fork	*çatal*
spoon	*kaşık*
glass	*bardak*
cup	*fincan*
bottle	*şişe*
water	*su*
mineral water	*maden suyu*
wine	*şarap*
milk	*süt*
bread	*ekmek*
salt	*tuz*
pepper	*biber*

GLOSSARY

ARASTA	Covered market associated with a mosque
BEDESTEN	Lockable domed building at the heart of a market area where the most precious goods were sold and stored
BEKÇI	Custodian of a building or site
BEND	Dam
CAMEKÂN	Disrobing room of a hamam
CAMI (CAMII)	A mosque where the Friday sermon is preached, in addition to the weekday prayers
ÇARŞI	Market
ÇEŞME	Drinking fountain
DAR-ÜL HADIS	College where the traditions of Islam were taught
DAR-ÜL KURA	House for readers of the Koran
DARÜŞŞIFA	Hospital, sometimes combined with a timarhane
DERSHANE	Lecture hall of a medrese
DIVAN	Council of State and Justice
EXEDRA	Semi-circular recess
EYVAN	Vaulted or domed bay, open at one side
HAMAM	Bath house, often attached to a mosque
HAN	Inn, or large building associated with a trade
HARARET	Hot room of a hamam (lit. fever/heat)
HAREM	Women's apartments in a home; the female members of a man's household
HOCA IMAM }	Muslim priest/teacher

322

IMARET	Soup kitchen for the poor, students, travellers etc.
KADI	District judge
KADIASKER/KAZASKER	Chief military judge
KAPLICA	Bathing establishment supplied by a hot spring
KILIM	Flatweave carpet woven on a loom
KÖŞK	Pavilion
KONAK	Large house, usually built of wood
KÜLLIYE	Educational and charitable complex attached to a mosque
MEDRESE	Islamic theological school
MEKTEP	Koran school for small boys, primary school
MESCIT	Small mosque with no mimber where there are daily prayer times but no Friday sermon
MEYDAN	Square, open space
MIHRAB	Decorated niche indicating the direction of Mecca, and therefore of prayer
MIMAR	Architect
MIMBER	High, hooded pulpit from which the noon Friday sermon is preached
MÜEZZIN	Man who gives the call to prayer
MUVAKKITHANE	Room used by timekeeper/astronomer/astrologer
NAMAZGÂH	Open-air mosque with mihrab only
ODA	Room
PENDENTIVE	Curved triangular surface which makes the transition between an angle and a curve to support a dome
PIR	Head of a dervish convent
SARAY	Palace
SEBIL	Public fountain where cups of water were issued by an attendant
SELAMLIK	Men's apartments in a home
SEMAHANE	Hall in a dervish convent used for ritual dances
SICAKLIK	Hot room of a hamam
SOĞUKLUK	Cool room of a hamam
SU TERAZISI	Tower for siphoning water
ŞADIRVAN	Fountain for ritual ablutions before prayer
ŞEREFE	Balcony of a minaret from which the call to prayer was made
ŞEYH	Head of a religious order
SOFFIT	Surface on the under side of an arch

TABHANE	Hospice attached to a mosque complex, usually for travelling dervishes, where 3 days free board and lodging was provided
TAKSIM	Water distribution point
TEKKE	Dervish convent
TIMARHANE	Asylum for the insane
TUĞRA	Sultan's monogram, or seal
TÜRBE	Tomb or Mausoleum
ULEMA	Doctors of Islamic law; religious leaders of the Empire
VAKFIYE	Deed of endowment
VEZIR	Cabinet Minister
YALI	Mansion, usually of wood, on the Bosphorus
ZAVIYE	Hospice of the Ahi sect, the Brotherhood of Virtue

CHRONOLOGY

BYZANTINE EMPERORS

Constantine I, the Great	324–337
Constantius	337–361
Julian the Apostate	361–363
Jovian	363–364
Valens	364–378
Theodosius I, the Great	378–395
Arcadius	395–408
Theodosius II	408–450
Marcian	450–457
Leo I	457–474
Leo II	474
Zeno	474–475
Basiliscus	475–476
Zeno (again)	476–491
Anastasius I	491–518
Justin I	518–527
Justinian I, the Great	527–565
Justin II	565–578
Tiberius I Constantine	578–582
Maurice	582–602
Phocas	602–610
Heraclius	610–641
Constantine III and Heraclonas	641
Heraclonas	641
Constans II	641–668
Constantine IV	668–685
Justinian II	685–695
Leontius	695–698
Tiberius II	698–705

Justinian II (again)	705–711
Philippicus Bardanes	711–713
Anastasius II	713–715
Theodosius III	715–717
Leo III	717–741
Constantine V Copronymus	741–775
Leo IV	775–780
Constantine VI	780–797
Eirene	797–802
Nicephorus I	802–811
Stauracius	811
Michael I Rangabe	811–813
Leo V	813–820
Michael II	820–829
Theophilus	829–842
Michael III	842–867
Basil I, the Macedonian	867–886
Leo VI, the Wise	886–912
Alexander	912–913
Constantine VII Porphyrogenitus	913–959
Romanus I Lecapenus (co-emperor)	920–944
Romanus II	959–963
Nicephorus II Phocas	963–969
John I Tzimisces	969–976
Basil II	976–1025
Constantine VIII	1025–1028
Romanus III Argyrus	1028–1034
Michael IV, the Paphlagonian	1034–1041
Michael V Calaphates	1041–1042
Zoë and Theodora	1042
Constantine IX Monomachus	1042–1055
Theodora (again)	1055–1056
Michael VI	1056–1057
Isaac I Comnenus	1057–1059
Constantine X Ducas	1059–1067
Romanus IV Diogenes	1067–1071
Michael VII Ducas	1071–1078
Nicephorus III Botaniates	1078–1081
Alexius I Comnenus	1081–1118
John II Comnenus	1118–1143
Manuel I Comnenus	1143–1180
Alexius II Comnenus	1180–1183
Andronicus I Comnenus	1183–1185
Isaac II Angelus	1185–1195
Alexius III Angelus	1195–1203
Isaac II (again) and Alexius IV Angelus	1203–1204
Alexius V Murzuphlus	1204
Theodore I Lascaris*	1204–1222

John III Ducas Vatatzes*	1222–1254
Theodore II Lascaris*	1254–1258
John IV Lascaris*	1258–1261
Michael VIII Palaeologus	1261–1282
Andronicus II Palaeologus	1282–1328
Andronicus III Palaeologus	1328–1341
John V Palaeologus	1341–1391
John VI Cantacuzenus (co-emperor)	1347–1354
Andronicus IV Palaeologus (co-emperor)	1376–1379
John VII Palaeologus (co-emperor)	1390
Manuel II Palaeologus	1391–1425
John VIII Palaeologus	1425–1448
Constantine XI Dragases	1449–1453

* denotes ruler of Nicaean Empire

LATIN EMPERORS OF CONSTANTINOPLE

Baldwin I of Flanders	1204–1205
Henry of Flanders	1206–1216
Peter of Courtenay	1217
Yolande	1217–1219
Robert of Courtenay	1221–1228
Baldwin II	1228–1261

OTTOMAN SULTANS

Osman Gazi (not Sultan)	1280–1326
Orhan Gazi	1326–1362
Murat I Hüdavendigâr	1362–1389
Beyazit I Yıldırım	1389–1402
Civil war	1402–1413
Mehmet I	1413–1421
Murat II	1421–1451
Mehmet II, the Conqueror	1451–1481
Beyazit II, the Pious†	1481–1512
Selim I Yavuz (the Grim)	1512–1520
Süleyman I, the Magnificent	1520–1566
Selim II, the Sot	1566–1574
Murat III	1574–1595
Mehmet III	1595–1603
Ahmet I	1603–1617
Mustafa I†	1617–1618
Osman II†‡	1618–1622
Mustafa I (again)†‡	1622–1623
Murat IV	1623–1640
Ibrahim, the Mad†‡	1640–1648

Mehmet IV†	1648–1687
Süleyman II	1687–1691
Ahmet II	1691–1695
Mustafa II†	1695–1703
Ahmet III†	1703–1730
Mahmut I	1730–1754
Osman III	1754–1757
Mustafa III	1757–1774
Abdül Hamit I	1774–1789
Selim III†‡	1789–1807
Mustafa IV†‡	1807–1808
Mahmut II, the Reformer	1808–1839
Abdül Mecit I	1839–1861
Abdül Aziz†	1861–1876
Murat V†	1876
Abdül Hamit II†	1876–1909
Mehmet V Reşat	1909–1918
Mehmet VI Vahideddin†	1918–1922
Abdül Mecit II (Caliph only)†	1922–1924

† denotes deposed ‡ denotes murdered

BIBLIOGRAPHY

Alderson, A. D., *The Structure of the Ottoman Dynasty* (Oxford, 1956)
Apollonius of Rhodes, *The Voyage of Argo* (trans. by E. V. Rieu, Harmondsworth 1971)
Aslanapa, Oktay, *Turkish Art and Architecture* (London, 1971)
Babinger, Franz, *Mehmet the Conqueror and his Time* (trans. from the German by Ralph Manheim, Princeton, 1978)
Busbecq, O. G. de, *The Turkish Letters of Ogier Ghislin de Busbecq* (trans. by E. S. Forster, Oxford, 1927)
Browning, Robert, *The Byzantine Empire* (London, 1980)
Byron, Lord, *Don Juan* (London, 1863)
Cahen, Claude, *Pre-Ottoman Turkey* (New York, 1968)
Clary, Robert de, *The Conquest of Constantinople* (trans. by E. H. McNeal, New York, 1936)
Clavijo, R. G. de, *Embassy to Tamerlane 1403–06* (trans. by Guy le Strange, London, 1928)
Comnena, Anna, *The Alexiad* (trans. from the Greek by E. R. A. Sewter, London, 1969)
Craven, Lady Elizabeth, *A Journey through the Crimea to Constantinople* (London, 1789)
Encyclopaedia of Islam (London/Leiden, 1960 on)
Evliya Efendi (Evliya Çelebi), *Narrative of Travels in Europe, Asia and Africa in the 17th century* (trans. by J. von Hammer-Purgstall, 3 vols., London, 1834, 1846 & 1850)
Freely, John, *Istanbul* (Blue Guide), 2nd ed. (London, 1987); *Stamboul Sketches* (Istanbul, 1974)
Gilles, Pierre (Petrus Gyllius), *The Antiquities of Constantinople* (trans. by John Ball, London, 1729)
Goodwin, Godfrey, *A History of Ottoman Architecture* (London, 1971)
Hammer-Purgstall, J. von, *Histoire de l'Empire Ottoman* (trans. from the German by J.-J. Hellert, 18 vols., Paris, 1835–43)
Harrell, Betsy, *Mini-Tours near Istanbul*, 2 vols. (Istanbul, 1975 and 1978)
Hearsey, J. E. N., *The City of Constantine 324–1453* (London, 1963)

Herodotus, *The Histories* (trans. by Aubrey de Sélincourt, Harmondsworth, 1954)

Hotham, David, *The Turks* (London, 1972)

Ibn Battuta, *Travels in Asia and Africa 1325–54* (trans. and sel. by H. A. R. Gibb, p/b edn., London, 1983)

Inalcık, Halil, *The Ottoman Empire: The Classical Age 1300–1600* (London, 1973)

Joinville and Villehardouin, *Chronicles of the Crusades* (trans. by M. R. B. Shaw, London, 1963)

Jones, A. H. M., *Cities of the Eastern Roman Provinces* (Oxford, 1971)

Kinross, Lord, *The Ottoman Centuries* (London, 1977); *Atatürk: The Rebirth of a Nation* (London, 1964)

Knolles, Richard, *Turkish History*, 3 vols.. (London, 1687–1700)

Kritovoulos, M., *The History of Mehmet the Conqueror* (trans. by C. T. Riggs, Princeton, 1954)

Lancaster, Osbert, *Sailing to Byzantium* (London, 1969)

Levey, Michael, *The World of Ottoman Art* (London, 1975)

Lewis, Raphaela, *Everyday Life in Ottoman Turkey* (London, 1971)

Loti, Pierre, *Constantinople* (trans. by Marjorie Lawrie, London, 1927)

Magie, David, *Roman Rule in Asia Minor, to the end of the 3rd century after Christ*, 2 vols. (Princeton, 1950)

Marlowe, Christopher, *Tambourlaine* (London)

Mathew, Gervase, *Byzantine Aesthetics* (London, 1963)

Melling, Anton Ignaz, *Voyage Pittoresque de Constantinople et des Rives du Bosphore*, 2 vols. (Paris, 1819)

Millingen, A. van, *Byzantine Churches in Constantinople* (London, 1912); *Byzantine Constantinople: the walls of the city and adjoining historical sites* (London, 1899)

Murray's Handbook for Travellers in Constantinople, Brusa and the Troad (London, 1893)

Ostrogorsky, George, *History of the Byzantine State* (trans. by Joan Hussey, 2nd edn., Oxford, 1968)

Pardoe, Julia, *The City of the Sultan and the Domestic Manners of the Turks in 1836* (illus. by W. Bartlett, London, 1837)

Penguin Book of Turkish Verse (ed. Nermin Menemencioğlu with Fahir Iz, Harmondsworth, 1978)

Penzer, N. M., *The Harem* (London, 1936)

Pitton de Tournefort, Joseph, *Relation d'un Voyage au Levant* (Amsterdam, 1718)

Pococke, Richard, *Description of the East, and some other countries*, 2 vols. (London, 1743–5)

Procopius, *On Buildings*; *The History of the Wars* (both in Loeb Classical Library series); *The Secret History* (trans. by G. A. Williamson, London, 1966)

Psellus, Michael, *Fourteen Byzantine Emperors* (trans. E. R. A. Sewter, London, 1966)

Roe, Thomas, *Negotiations in his Embassy to the Ottoman Porte from 1621 to 1628* (London, 1740)

Runciman, Steven, *Byzantine Civilization* (London, 1933); *The Fall of*

Constantinople 1453 (Cambridge, 1965); *A History of the Crusades*, 3 vols. (Harmondsworth, 1965)

Rycault, Sir Paul, *The History of the Present State of the Ottoman Empire 1623–1677* (London, 1680)

Sanderson, John, *The Travels of John Sanderson in the Levant, 1584–1602* (ed. Foster, London, 1931)

Shaw, Stanford, *History of the Ottoman Empire and Modern Turkey*, 2 vols. (Cambridge, 1976–77)

Sumner-Boyd, Hilary, & Freely, John, *Strolling through Istanbul*, 2nd edn. (Istanbul, 1974)

Tafur, Pero, *Travels and Adventures 1435–39* (trans. by Malcolm Letts, London, 1926)

Talbot Rice, David, *The Byzantines* (London, 1962)

Talbot Rice, Tamara, *The Seljuks* (London, 1961)

Tudela, Rabbi Benjamin of, 'The Oriental Travels of Benjamin of Tudela 1160–73', in Komroff, Manuel (ed.): *Contemporaries of Marco Polo* (New York, 1928)

Vasiliev, A. A., *History of the Byzantine Empire*, 2 vols., 2nd edn. (London, 1952)

Walsh, R., *Constantinople and the Scenery of the Seven Churches of Asia Minor* (illus. by T. Allom, 2 series, London, 1838)

White, Charles, *Three Years in Constantinople, or Domestic Manners of the Turks in 1844* (London, 1846)

Wortley Montagu, Lady Mary, *Selected Letters of Lady Mary Wortley Montagu* (ed. by Robert Halsband, Harmondsworth, 1986)

Xenophon, *The Persian Expedition* (trans. by Rex Warner, Harmondsworth, 1949)

RECENT PUBLICATIONS

Freely, John, *Istanbul, The Imperial City*, (London, 1996)

Freely, John, & Burrell, A.R., *Sinan, Architect of Süleyman the Magnificent & the Ottoman Golden Age*; photographs by Ara Güler, (London, 1992)

Goodwin, Godfrey, *A History of Ottoman Architecture*, new edn. (London, 1992) *Sinan: Ottoman Architecture & its Values Today*, (London, 1993); *The Janissaries*, (London, 1994); *A Guide to Edirne*, (Istanbul, 1995)

Güler, Ara, *A Photographic Sketch on Lost Istanbul*, b/w, (Istanbul, 1994); *Vanished Colours*, colour images of Istanbul 1950–94, (Istanbul, 1995)

Hellier, Chris, *Splendours of the Bosphorus*, (London, 1993)

Kelly, Laurence, *Istanbul: A Travellers' Companion*, (London, 1987)

Kuban, Doğan, *Istanbul: an Urban History*, (Istanbul 1996)

Kuran, Abdullah, *Sinan*, photographs by Ara Güler, (Washington, 1987)

Mansel, Philip, *Constantinople: City of the World's Desire, 1453–1924* (London, 1995)

Norwich, John Julius, *Byzantium: The Early Centuries*, (London, 1988); *Byzantium: The Apogee*, (London, 1991); *Byzantium: The Decline & Fall*, (London, 1996)

Pope, Nicole and Hugh, *Turkey Unveiled*, (London, 1997)
Zücher, Erik, *Turkey: A Modern History*, (London, 1997)

INDEX

Names of places and monuments are printed in **bold**; names of individual people in *italics*; everything else in ordinary type. Greek, Roman and Turkish names are listed under the first name; European names under the surname.

Unless otherwise indicated, monuments are in Istanbul. Monuments in Iznik, Bursa and Edirne are listed under the name of the city.

333

INDEX